"Care for th[e] welfare state found in thi[s]

362.61 ARM
Armstrong, Pat
The privatization
nursing homes edited by Pat Armstrong and Hugh Armstrong.

niversity, Canada

"This is a very impressive collection of contributions and insights from international experts in the study of Long Term Care. It brings valuable insights and frameworks to help deepen the understanding of how the LTC sectors have developed in each country and what challenges remain."

– **Brooke Hollister**, *Associate Professor at the Institute for Health and Aging, University of California San Francisco, USA and Center for Care Research, University of Agder, Norway*

"These are dangerous times. Government leaders and their sponsors are turning away from their citizens and toward private corporations. It is refreshing to read a collection of research papers that work against the tide of this New Managerialism. The international character of the book stands as one of its highlights. The authors, while examining a variety of locations, have arrived at remarkably compatible conclusions."

– **Tim Diamond**, *California State University, Los Angeles, USA*

The Privatization of Care

Nursing homes are where some of the most vulnerable live and work. In too many homes, the conditions of work make it difficult to make care as good as it can be. For the last eight years an international team from Germany, Sweden, Norway, the UK, the US, and Canada have been searching for promising practices that treat residents, families and staff with dignity and respect in ways that can also bring joy. While there were ideas worth sharing from this research, there was much more evidence of a disturbing trend toward privatization.

Privatization is the process of moving away not only from public delivery and public payment for health services but also from a commitment to shared responsibility, democratic decision-making, and the idea that the public sector operates according to a logic of service to all.

This book documents moves toward privatization in the six countries and their consequences for families, staff, residents, and, eventually, us all. None of the countries has escaped pressure from powerful forces in and outside government pushing for privatization in all its forms. However, the wide variations in the extent and nature of privatization indicate privatization is not inevitable and this research shows there are alternatives.

Pat Armstrong is Distinguished Research Professor of Sociology at York University, Canada, and Fellow of the Royal Society of Canada. Dr. Armstrong is the author, co-author, editor, and co-editor of over 30 books as well as numerous articles and book chapters focusing on the fields of social policy; women studies; work; and the health and social services. She is Principal Investigator on the project that is the basis for this book.

Hugh Armstrong is a Professor Emeritus of Social Work, Political Economy, and Sociology at Carleton University, Ottawa, Canada, and a co-investigator on the Reimagining Long-Term Residential Care project.

Aging and Society
Edited by Carroll L. Estes and Assistant Editor Nicholas DiCarlo

This pioneering series of books creatively synthesizes and advances key, intersectional topics in gerontology and aging studies. Drawing from changing and emerging issues in gerontology, influential scholars combine research into human development and the life course; the roles of power, policy, and partisanship; race and ethnicity; inequality; gender and sexuality; and cultural studies to create a multi-dimensional and essential picture of modern aging.

Aging A – Z:
Concepts toward Emancipatory Gerontology (2019)
Carroll L. Estes with Nicholas DiCarlo

The Privatization of Care:
The Case of Nursing Homes (2020)
Edited by Pat Armstrong and Hugh Armstrong

<u>Forthcoming:</u>

Age and the Research of Sociological Imagination:
Power, Ideology, and Life Course (2020)
Dale Dannefer

For more information about this series, please visit:
https://www.routledge.com/Aging-and-Society/book-series/AGINGSOC

The Privatization of Care

The Case of Nursing Homes

Edited by
Pat Armstrong and Hugh Armstrong

Routledge
Taylor & Francis Group
NEW YORK AND LONDON

First published 2020
by Routledge
52 Vanderbilt Avenue, New York, NY 10017

and by Routledge
2 Park Square, Milton Park, Abingdon, Oxon, OX14 4RN

Routledge is an imprint of the Taylor & Francis Group, an informa business

© 2020 Taylor & Francis

The right of Pat Armstrong and Hugh Armstrong to be identified as the authors of the editorial material, and of the authors for their individual chapters, has been asserted in accordance with sections 77 and 78 of the Copyright, Designs and Patents Act 1988.

All rights reserved. No part of this book may be reprinted or reproduced or utilized in any form or by any electronic, mechanical, or other means, now known or hereafter invented, including photocopying and recording, or in any information storage or retrieval system, without permission in writing from the publishers.

Trademark notice: Product or corporate names may be trademarks or registered trademarks, and are used only for identification and explanation without intent to infringe.

Library of Congress Cataloging-in-Publication Data
A catalog record for this title has been requested

ISBN: 978-1-138-34601-7 (hbk)
ISBN: 978-1-138-34602-4 (pbk)
ISBN: 978-0-429-32366-9 (ebk)

Typeset in Bembo by
Servis Filmsetting Ltd, Stockport, Cheshire

Printed in the United Kingdom
by Henry Ling Limited

Contents

List of Figures x
List of Tables xi
Acknowledgments xii
Contributors xiii

An Introduction to the Team and to Teamwork 1
PAT ARMSTRONG

PART I
Privatization in Six Countries 15

1 Privatizing Care: Setting the Stage 17
PAT ARMSTRONG AND HUGH ARMSTRONG

2 The Growth of the For-Profit Nursing Home Sector in
Norway and Sweden: Driving Forces and Resistance 38
GUDMUND ÅGOTNES, FRODE F. JACOBSEN,
AND MARTA SZEBEHELY

3 Privatization of Nursing Homes in the United Kingdom
and the United States 51
CHARLENE HARRINGTON, ALLYSON M. POLLOCK, AND SHAILEN SUTARIA

4 The Marketization and Commodification of Long-Term
Care in Germany: Effects on Work and Relationship-
Based Care in Nursing Homes 68
BEATRICE MÜLLER

5 Privatization of Long-Term Residential Care
  in Canada: The Case of Three Provinces   87
  PAT ARMSTRONG, HUGH ARMSTRONG, MARTHA MACDONALD,
  AND MALCOLM DOUPE

6 Labor Restructuring and Nursing Home Privatization in
  British Columbia, Canada   102
  ANDREW LONGHURST, SAGE PONDER, AND MARGARET
  MCGREGOR

PART 2
Key Issues   123

7 Public Funds, Private Data: A Canadian
  Example   125
  TAMARA DALY

8 Accountable For-Profits in Nursing Home Services?   141
  FRODE F. JACOBSEN AND GUDMUND ÅGOTNES

9 Marketing Long-Term Care: Website Analysis
  of For-Profit Corporations in Sweden and
  Canada   156
  RUTH LOWNDES, JACQUELINE CHOINIERE,
  AND SARA ERLANDSSON

10 Nurse Staffing in Nursing Homes in Industrialized
   Countries   177
   CHARLENE HARRINGTON AND FRODE F. JACOBSEN

11 Devalued Later Life: Older Residents' Experiences of
   Risk in a Market System of Residential and Nursing
   Homes   196
   LIZ LLOYD

12 Shifting Responsibilities for Care: The Experiences of
    Staff and Families in Long-Term Residential Care   209
    RACHEL BARKEN AND PAT ARMSTRONG

13 **Promoting Public Care**   224
    PAT ARMSTRONG

    Index   237

Figures

6.1	Government spending by sub-sector in British Columbia, 1979–2015	105
7.1	The Ontario cost and quality data trail	132
7.2	Public LTC data available to Ontarians	134
7.3	US Nursing home compared	135
8.1	Norlandia care ownership structure, 2014	149

Tables

4.1 Forms of Marketization in Germany   77
6.1 Publicly Funded Long-Term Residential Care Facilities
     Covered by Industry-Wide Master Collective Agreement,
     British Columbia, 2016   116

Acknowledgments

Although the chapters have the names of individual authors, this book is in many ways the product of our entire team. We wish to acknowledge collective contributions of these other members by listing their names below.

In addition, we would like to thank Wendy Winters, the person who has kept the large and often unwieldy team project together, and who has made multiple valuable contributions to this publication. We would also like to thank Jane Springer for her thoughtful and careful initial editing of the manuscript. At Routledge, Dean Birkenkamp has been effectively responsive and wonderfully supportive, as has Carol Estes. We have Charlene Harrington to thank for initiating this connection.

Finally, none of this would be possible without financial support from the Social Sciences and Humanities Research Council of Canada and the European Research Area in Ageing 2 (in Canada from the Canadian Institutes of Health Research). Of course, none of these organizations can in any way be held responsible for the content.

Co-investigators

Annmarie Adams, McGill University; Donna Baines, University of Sydney; Susan Braedley, Carleton University; Sally Chivers, Trent University; Jacqueline Choiniere, York University; Megan Davies, York University; Monika Goldmann, Technische Universität Dortmund; Monique Lanoix, St. Paul University; Joel Lexchin, York University; Kathryn McPherson, York University; James Struthers, Trent University; Hildegard Theobald, University of Vechta; Pauline Vaillancourt Rosenau, University of Texas.

Contributors

Gudmund Ågotnes holds a PhD in Social Anthropology from the University of Bergen, Norway, and is an Associate Professor in the Department of Social Work at the Western Norway University of Applied Sciences. Through an empirical focus on the health and care sector, and nursing homes in particular, Ågotnes' research has covered themes such as the logic of practice within the health sector, organizational features of care work, multiculturalism, and variation in services and practice.

Hugh Armstrong is a Professor Emeritus of Social Work, Political Economy, and Sociology at Carleton University, Ottawa, Canada, and a co-investigator on the Reimagining Long-Term Residential Care project.

Pat Armstrong is a Distinguished Research Professor of Sociology at York University and a Fellow of the Royal Society. She held a Canadian Health Services Research Foundation (CHSRF)/Canadian Institutes of Health Research (CIHR) Chair in Health Services and Nursing Research, and has published on a wide variety of issues related to long-term care, health care policy, and women's health. Written with Suzanne Day, her most recent book is *Wash, Wear and Care: Clothing and Laundry in Long-Term Residential Care* (Montreal: McGill-Queen's University Press, 2017).

Rachel Barken is a Social Sciences and Humanities Research Council (SSHRC) postdoctoral fellow in the Department of Sociology at York University, Toronto. Her research interests include aging, formal and informal care arrangements, the social and political aspects of home and long-term care, and gender. Her recent publications appear in *Ageing & Society*, *Qualitative Health Research*, and *Canadian Journal on Aging*.

Jacqueline Choiniere is an Associate Professor with the School of Nursing, Faculty of Health, at York University in Toronto, Ontario. Dr. Choiniere's primary areas of research are health policy, women's work and health, health-care reform, and accountability and political economy.

Tamara Daly is an Associate Professor with the School of Health Policy and Management, Faculty of Health and with the Faculty of Graduate Studies programs in Critical Disability Studies, Women's Studies and Health Policy and Equity at York University in Toronto, Ontario. She held a CIHR Chair in Gender, Work, and Health. Her research focuses on health care work, aging and long-term care policy, and gender and health policy.

Malcolm Doupe is an Associate Professor in the Department of Community Health Sciences with the Faculty of Medicine at the University of Manitoba in Winnipeg, Manitoba. Dr. Doupe is also a Senior Research Scientist at the Manitoba Centre for Health Policy. He conducts research on issues related to care continuity for older adults, factors that affect quality care and functional status in nursing homes, risk factors of home care and nursing home uses, and health service utilization.

Sara Erlandsson is a Researcher at Stockholm University and holds a PhD in Social Work. Her research focus is on social policy, and care, support, and service for older persons and persons with a disability.

Charlene Harrington PhD, RN is a Professor Emeritus of Sociology and Nursing at the University of California, San Francisco. Elected to the American Academy of Nursing and the National Academy of Medicine, she has conducted extensive research and written many articles on long-term care, testified before the US Congress, and lectured widely in the US and internationally.

Liz Lloyd is Professor of Social Gerontology at the School for Policy Studies, University of Bristol, England. Her research, teaching, and publications focus on older people's changing experiences of caring relationships. She is committed to developing feminist perspectives within gerontology, informed by the ethics of care. Liz has taken a lead role on the UK work in the Reimagining Long-Term Residential Care project.

Frode F. Jacobsen is a Professor at Western Norway University of Applied Sciences, a Professor II at VID Specialized University, Norway, and Research Director at the Center for Care Research at the Western Norway University of Applied Sciences. His research interests are health and health-seeking behavior in a social and cultural context, comparative health services systems, and health and care services for older people. His most recent publication is "Active Ageing," *International Practice Development Journal (IPDJ)*, 2017.

Andrew Longhurst is a Research Associate with the Canadian Centre for Policy Alternatives (CCPA–BC) in Vancouver, British Columbia and a Researcher and Policy Analyst with the Health Sciences Association of BC. His research interests include health and social policy, labor market change, and public-sector innovation. His publication *Privatization and Declining*

Access to BC Seniors' Care (2017, CCPA–BC) examined the implications of seniors' care restructuring on access and equity. Andrew holds an MA in Human Geography from Simon Fraser University.

Ruth Lowndes is a Research Associate at York University, engaged full time on the project, Reimagining Long-Term Residential Care: An International Study of Promising Practices. She is a co-applicant on a related international project, Changing Places: Unpaid Work in Public Spaces, which uses team-based rapid ethnography within a feminist perspective to examine how the paid and unpaid work involved in care changes with a person's transition into long-term residential care. She is registered with the College of Nurses of Ontario and is a Certified Diabetes Educator.

Martha MacDonald is a Professor of Economics with the Department of Economics at the Sobey School of Business at St. Mary's University in Halifax, Nova Scotia. Dr. MacDonald is also involved with the Women's Studies and Atlantic Canada Studies programs. Her areas of specialization include economic restructuring, gender and the economy, social security policy and restructuring in rural Atlantic Canada.

Margaret McGregor MD, MHSc is a Clinical Associate Professor with the University of British Columbia Department of Family Practice and a Research Associate with the UBC Centre for Health Services Policy Research and the Vancouver Coastal Health Research Institute's Centre for Clinical Epidemiology and Evaluation. She is a family physician at the Mid-Main Community Health Centre in Vancouver, where as part of her practice, she provides care to patients in long-term residential care. She has completed a number of research projects in the area of nursing home health services delivery.

Beatrice Müller is a Political Scientist and holds a PhD in Social Work/ Education Science. She is a Postdoctoral Researcher at the University of Vechta, Germany. Her work is on feminist-Marxist theory, ethics of care, marketization, and working conditions in long-term care.

Allyson M. Pollock BSc, MSc, MBChB, FFPH, FRCGP, FRCP(Ed) trained in medicine and public health. She is Professor of Public Health and Director of the Institute of Health and Society at Newcastle University, England.

(Caroline) Sage Ponder is a Sessional Lecturer in Urban and Economic Geography and Political Economy at the University of British Columbia, Vancouver, British Columbia, Canada.

Shailen Sutaria BMedSci, MBBS, MSc is a Public Health Doctor and Researcher at Queen Mary University of London. He is a member of the Faculty of Public Health and works clinically at the Royal London Hospital.

Marta Szebehely is a Professor of Social Work at Stockholm University and has been studying the consequences of changing public policies in Nordic eldercare services for more than three decades. She leads the research program, Individualised Care and Universal Welfare: Dilemmas in an Era of Marketisation, involving more than 20 Nordic and Anglo-Saxon scholars. With Gabrielle Meagher, she edited the research report, *Marketisation in Nordic Eldercare* (Stockholm University, 2013).

An Introduction to the Team and to Teamwork

Pat Armstrong

For ten years, an international team of 26 academics, some 60 students, and several post-doctoral fellows along with some research associates have been working together to reimagine long-term residential care. We have been searching for promising practices that treat residents, families, and staff with dignity and respect in ways that can bring joy and not just safety. Although we have been looking for good ideas worth sharing, we also uncovered some worrisome practices. Growing out of our collective work, this book documents the increasing privatization of long-term residential care and identifies negative impacts as well as some possible alternatives.

Long-Term Residential Care

Long-term residential care facilities, or what are most commonly called nursing homes in North America, have not received a great deal of research attention. Yet, as the World Health Organization (WHO, 2002: 5) puts it, "A society that treats its most vulnerable members with compassion is a more just and caring society for all." Those who live and work in nursing homes are often among the most vulnerable. Long-term residential care is a barometer of values and practices; a signal of economic, cultural and social perspectives. It thus raises issues that go well beyond specific services and practices: issues such as fundamental human and social rights; the role of the state; responsibilities of individuals, families, and governments; work organization and skills; and approaches to care.

The overwhelming majority of those who live in long-term care facilities are older women, many of them with few economic resources and now without partners. Few residents can make the kinds of contributions that are most valued in our market-based culture, but most have done so in the past and may well contribute in new ways, if given the opportunity. The overwhelming majority of those who provide the care are also women and, in high-income countries, a significant proportion is from immigrant and/or racialized communities. How we treat this vulnerable resident population and those who provide their care is a critical indicator of our approach to equity and social justice, as well as to care and responsibility.

Although long-term residential care has not received a great deal of research attention, it is getting considerable attention from those interested in profit-making as well as from those opposed to government services. The growing number of older people has been defined as both a crisis for health care and as an opportunity for investment. This aging of the population has coincided with the rise of neoliberal approaches to government that emphasize competitions and market strategies that shift more responsibility to corporations, communities, families, and individuals, raising the question of what this development means for those who live and work in long-term residential care. It is that question we address in this book.

Our Team

Our project titled "Reimagining Long-Term Residential Care: An International Study of Promising Practices" is focused on six countries: Norway, Sweden, Germany, the United Kingdom, the United States, and Canada. We focused on these six countries because they fit neatly into Gøsta Esping-Andersen's (1990) welfare regime typology, offering a basis for comparison in approaches to care, to government involvement, and to responsibility for care. In his terms, Canada, the US, and UK can be defined as liberal, while Germany provides an example of what he calls the corporatist-conservative approach, compared to the social democratic traditions in Norway and Sweden.

Our choice of investigators, collaborators, partners, and research sites was made with an eye towards fostering creative exchanges. The members of our team come from different and, at times, conflicting disciplinary perspectives. The team includes faculty members trained in sociology, economics, political science, literary studies, history, medicine, anthropology, nursing, social work, architecture, health policy, epidemiology, gerontology, and philosophy. Our five post-doctoral fellows also come from a range of disciplines and countries. We brought researchers long familiar with the field and with qualitative methods together with those new to a focus on long-term residential care and to qualitative approaches but with a history of quantitative and equity work, a strategy designed to bring fresh eyes to the project while ensuring expertise.

Our partners were also selected to bring together often conflicting interests. There are five unions involved, each representing somewhat different components of the labor force. In addition, we included as partners two employer organizations from the non-profit sector and a seniors' organization that gives voice to community concerns. A clinical associate of a gerontology research center joined us as a collaborator.

The tensions involved in bringing together such a diverse group helped ensure a vibrant and exciting process, encouraged committed participation, and enabled the sorts of original thinking and intellectual breakthroughs that are so urgently needed in long-term residential care. Our work has been organized to ensure continual teamwork to build on these tensions and this diverse knowledge; work that crosses disciplines, jurisdictional, and interest lines.

Our Conceptual Framework

Feminist political economy, broadly defined, provides a background framework for our research. Like theory in general, this approach guides us in where to look, how to look, and what to do with what we find. It is neither true nor false but rather more or less useful in understanding the forces and processes at work (Armstrong & Armstrong, 1990). For political economists, politics, economics, discourses, and ideas are integrally related and operate on multiple levels from the intimate to the global. As Estes makes clear, "it is a systematic view predicated on the assumption that old age can be understood only in the context of social conditions and issues of the larger social order" (2001: 1). These interconnected parts are shaped but not determined by the dominant means of providing for food, clothing, shelter, jobs and joy, as well as for the next generation. In our countries, the search for profit profoundly influences how we live, work, talk, reproduce, and play. This implies a primary focus on selling more and paying less, especially when it comes to the labor that is a major cost for employers. According to Braverman (1974), it also implies efforts to control labor and reduce the recognized skilled proportion of the work. At the same time, people make their own history although under inherited, historically specific conditions.

Feminist political economists insist that social reproduction on a daily and intergenerational basis is central to the analysis, making the gendered construction of social relations and the interconnections between paid and unpaid labor critical to our understanding of how things work. They emphasize the multiple bases of inequities in power and resources, pointing to an intersectional approach, and to forces in addition to the search for profit (Armstrong & Connelly, 1992; Armstrong & Armstrong, 1978; Estes, 2001; Luxton & Braedley, 2010: Laslett, & Brenner, 1989). Feminists draw particular attention to the gendered construction of skills and their value, especially in relation to paid and unpaid care work.

Drawing on this theory, our conceptual approach began with certain assumptions in addition to the recognition that context, gender and other social locations such as class and race as well as the search for profit, matter. For us, the conditions of work are the conditions of care, both paid and unpaid work require skills, and care is a relationship that requires not only managerial but also structural and cultural support (McLean, 2007). Like Estes (2001: 11), we emphasize social rights linked to notions of interdependence and solidarity. It is important to note that we assume conflict and tensions, some of which cannot be eliminated but do need to be addressed. And we assume that managers, staff, residents, and families are active in shaping both care relations and the context for care. At the same time, we understand they do so within unequal relations of power. Because we assume that context, history, and both social location and social relations matter, we also assume that there is seldom one right way or "best practice." There are, nevertheless, good ideas worth sharing as well as worth struggling for, and poor ones worth resisting.

All research, as E. P. Thompson (1978) put it, is a dialogue between theory and evidence. Like David Harvey (2006: 79), we understand theory "as an evolving structure of argument sensitive to encounters with the complex ways in which social processes are materially embedded in the web of life." Our conceptual approach has developed through this kind of dialogue, enriched by the exchanges among investigators, collaborators, and partners, all bringing diverse perspectives and coming from diverse locations.

Our theoretical approach is both interdisciplinary and multi-scalar, drawing on a range of perspectives to capture the complexity of issues and social relations at various levels of theory and practice. We have extended the line of inquiry established by Burawoy et al. (1991, 2011), which strives to make visible the impact of global political and economic forces on the local, as well as of the local on other scales. Given the increasing pressure of global corporations and private equity firms to transform elder care into a site for capital accumulation, combined with the growth in the older population, it is crucial to understand how global forces are shaping the terrain of long-term care. By "grounding globalization," as Burawoy terms it, we have struggled to make significant theoretical and practical contributions, demonstrating how international, national, and jurisdictional decisions influence on-the-ground practices. At the same time, our exploration of promising practices allows us to reflect back on models of care, work organization, accountability, financing and ownership, contributing to theory building in the process.

To do this, we have created spaces for new theory as well as for new empirical data.

The Structure of Our Work

Based on our earlier work, our theory, and the literature, we structured our research around four interrelated themes.

The first of these themes, **approaches to care**, has involved an examination of policy regimes, national programs, organizations and institutional applications in long-term care. It has also included "an assessment of the cultural values that underlie existing systems" and an exploration of ethical issues related to the "ongoing efforts to fashion a coherent and appealing general theory of justice," to use the words of the WHO (2002: xi). The context for care is set at the global, national, regional, and local levels, all shaped by notions of rights and responsibilities as well as by specific models of care and the role of medicine within them (Bakker, 2003: Kittay, Jennings, & Wasunna, 2005; McLean, 2007). Different approaches to care and models of care (medical, social, market) reflect and guide the contexts in which services are structured and shape the practices, locations, built spaces, and discourses of care as well as the social relations between those people who provide and those who need care (Adams & Chivers, 2016). From our perspective, care is a relationship and approaches to care are assessed in terms of how they promote care relations that support residents, staff, families, and managers.

Approaches to care reflect not only ideas about what constitutes necessary, appropriate, effective, and efficient care but also ideas about gender, individual, and family responsibility, citizenship, dependency, and the sense of self (Williams, 2001; Fraser & Gordon, 1994). "Tradition, deeply embedded notions of woman's social worth and the value of her work, and the distribution of power within a society all explain, in part, why caregiving tasks have fallen disproportionately on women" (WHO, 2002: viii). Models of care represent how such ideas are operationalized and embedded at multiple levels of policy and practice. While some scholarship has explored different models of care (Béland et al., 2006; McLean, 2007; Struthers, 2008), these models have not often been located within larger national and global contexts that shape their approaches to care, as we attempted to do in this project.

As we illustrate in the May 2016 special issue of the *Journal of Canadian Studies*, the approaches to care theme has also involved identifying key institutional, fiscal, and cultural structures that have informed the history of policy-making in this field. The stigmas of poverty and dependency associated with pre-war institutions for the aged continue to act as powerful deterrents to the acceptance of new models and structures of caring for the frail elderly. "We have to concede that, with some few exceptions, residential/nursing provision is still seen as the option of last resort" (Peace, Kellaher, & Willcocks, 1997: 10). Hospitals have also shaped the highly medicalized approach to long-term care in many of the jurisdictions informing our study. Concern that the chronically ill older population was "blocking" access to expensive, insured hospital beds influenced much decision-making around the design and programming of long-term care facilities (Struthers, 1998; 2003; Armstrong et al., 2009). Care options for the aged have also been shaped by gendered assumptions that "naturalize" care for older people as the responsibility of women within families. In most of the jurisdictions in our project, the history of decision-making in both the home and residential care sectors has been deeply inscribed by policy-makers' fears and biases regarding actions that might undermine the "normal" obligations of family members, mostly women, to provide unpaid care (Keating et al., 1994; Struthers, 2003), reinforced by current neoliberal approaches.

The second of our four themes focuses on **work organization**. Research, including that by members of our team (Armstrong et al., 2008; Armstrong et al., 2009), has shown that care work is highly gendered and increasingly racialized. The predominantly female workforce is expected to provide care under any conditions, including conditions of significant violence and exploitation (Armstrong et al., 2009; Baines, 2006; Lanoix, 2009). Working conditions such as violence and poor pay exist within particular contexts, sets of relations and models of workplace organization (Aiken et al., 2002). High rates of illness and injury among health care workers have been associated with "work overload, pressure at work, lack of participation in decision-making, poor social support, unsupportive leadership, lack of communication or feedback, staff shortages or unpredictable staffing, scheduling or long work hours and conflict between work and family demands" (Yassi & Hancock, 2005: 32). Care quality and employer costs suffer as a result.

How work is organized and staffed has significant consequences not only for workers but also for residents and employers. For example, international research has shown that the substitution of materials for labor leads to higher rates of morbidity and mortality (Cawley, Grabowski, & Hirth, 2006) and has demonstrated a strong link between workload and staff turnover, with cost implications for employers (Castle, 2006), while Canadian research suggests a relationship between violence towards workers and low levels of both autonomy and staffing (Armstrong et al., 2009). The research by members of our team, and especially by Charlene Harrington and others (2001; 2004), has been critical in demonstrating how important staffing and the distribution of work is to the quality of care. At the same time, we are just starting to explore how physical environments shape the organization of work, facilitating or hindering caring labor (Armstrong & Braedley, 2016).

Because we assume that the conditions of work are the conditions of care and that putting residents first means creating the conditions that allow staff, families, volunteers, and managers to provide quality care, we also assume that care involves the entire range of people who do paid and unpaid work in the nursing home. Unpaid work is not only done by relatives and volunteers but by those otherwise paid to do the job. Research by Baines (2004a, 2004b) has shown that women are more likely than men to put in unpaid overtime in order to compensate for the care deficits, just as women are more likely than men to provide unpaid care to family and friends who live in nursing homes (Grant et al., 2004). In care work, we include all those involved in the home. We have explored what Dorothy Smith (1990) calls the relations of ruling and Braverman (1974) calls mechanisms of control, as well as the conditions under which staff are encouraged to develop and use the skills they need (Armstrong, 2013).

The third of our four themes is **accountability and governance**. Especially with significant and growing amounts of funding invested in long-term residential care, accountability has become a major issue. Accountability is particularly important where public funds and vulnerable populations are involved (Choiniere, 2007). However, the tendency is to rely on quantitative measures that count what can be counted, leaving out important indicators of quality (Armstrong, Armstrong, & Coburn, 2001). Audits and inspections tend to focus on workers' activity as well as on other aspects of internal organization, while leaving structural factors such as staffing levels and ownership alone (Banerjee & Armstrong, 2015; Choiniere et al., 2016). This orientation promotes standardization, rather than standards, with an emphasis on measurable outcomes and performance-based indicators intended to hold providers accountable. A manifestation of this accountability approach is the nursing home resident assessment instrument, a universally adopted, computerized outcome measurement technology developed in the US (Armstrong, Daly & Choiniere, 2016). Yet research suggests that there are critical problems with the oversight, enforcement, and evaluation of standardized assessment tools (Harrington & Carrillo, 1999; Harrington et al., 2004). When accountability is narrowly conceived and practiced, and not understood in broader contexts, its measures "are often impoverished and abstracted from the processes involved in care delivery and the environment in which they occur" (Coughlan & Ward, 2007: 48). The voices of residents and providers are often silenced and their perspectives on quality largely ignored. Instead, complicated, elaborate measures are frequently imposed, taking up valuable care time without producing visible, positive results (Armstrong et al., 2009; Choiniere et al., 2016). As the OECD (2005) points out, little attention has been paid to developing effective, appropriate means of assessing and ensuring quality for long-term care residents and providers.

Quality is, of course, a complex concept, embracing features that range from the maintenance of health status and the prevention of injury, abuse, and violence to the establishment of rewarding social relations and a sense of accomplishment and joy. The central concern of the approaches to care theme – quality – was addressed in the accountability theme in terms of the impact of organizational and governance structures on democratic accountability. Training and certification mechanisms are understood to be significant aspects of accountability, and related to staffing levels, ongoing education opportunities and staff empowerment (Armstrong & Daly, 2017). At the same time, we take seriously the feminist critiques of the gendered ways skills are recognized, assessed, certified, and rewarded (Armstrong, 2013).

Our fourth theme is **financing and ownership**. This theme is obviously central to the subject of this book. At a time when the demand on government health and social care spending is increasing, it is important to examine the relationship between financing, ownership, and quality of care, taking into account the displacement of costs when poor long-term care is provided. There are also important questions about who pays for care, on what basis, and with what impacts. Funding dimensions include intergovernmental relationships which structure the financing, delivery, and control over residential care, as well as the design of the payment structure and physical space. The rest of this book illustrates how we addressed these questions.

Membership in each theme was interdisciplinary and international. Half of the theme members switched to another theme as we entered the second half of our project to further ensure cross-fertilization. Theme members met regularly through electronic means and face-to-face at our annual team meetings. Our annual meetings were focused on developing and sharing our collective work, as well as on exploring the ways the various themes overlapped. Although we separated the themes for organizational purposes, we brought them together analytically through our conceptual approach and practically in our team meetings.

Our Methods

Our research methods reflect our conceptual and organizational framework. They take two basic forms; namely, analytical mapping and rapid, site-switching team ethnography.

By analytical mapping, we mean analysis of data that creates a portrait of what is happening with aspects of long-term care. The intent is to produce a better understanding of developments in long-term care and how as well as why these differ across the jurisdictions in our project. These analyses are based on a variety of sources and data collection, reflecting our interdisciplinary approach. For example, some of this analytical mapping relies on quantitative data such as that produced by inspections (e.g., Choiniere et al., 2016) or government statistical organizations and corporate reports (e.g., Harrington et al., 2017). Some rely on historical documents (e.g., Davies, 2016) while others study architectural plans (e.g., Adams & Chivers, 2016) or media coverage (Lloyd et al., 2014). Our analysis of privatization draws heavily on these analytical maps, most of which were produced by members of the team working together.

Our second method is rapid, site-switching, team ethnography. We began with a team workshop led by an experienced ethnographer who took us through the main principles of ethnographic work and through our own proposed approach. We also organized a year-long seminar in which we discussed existing ethnographic research on nursing homes. We studied books such as Tim Diamond's (1992) *Making Grey Gold*, Daniel Jay Baum's *Warehouses for Death* (1997), Townsend's *The Last Refuge* (1962) and *The Last Refuge Revisited* (Johnson, Rolph & Smith, 2010). Two members of our team, Donna Baines (Baines & Cunningham, 2011) and Marta Szebehely, had previous experience with rapid ethnography and they shared their knowledge with the rest of us.

We began our ethnographic studies by consulting key informants in unions, in government policy, and in community organizations to ask what nursing homes they would recommend where we could find promising practices and why they would go there. On this basis, we approached nursing homes to ask if they would be willing to have a team of 12 to 14 researchers study their home. In addition to permission to study the home and to seeking ethics approval, we asked for a range of background documents, pre-site visit interviews and some ideas about whom to interview. In each jurisdiction we studied one home over a week and another for a full day. In the study that took place over a week, we began observing and interviewing at 7 a.m. and continuing until after midnight. We worked in pairs, in shifts, and in two different units. In the full-day study, the entire team that was involved in the larger study went to another site in the same jurisdiction, observing and interviewing over the day. The teams in both kinds of study were international and interdisciplinary, another way we introduced our "fresh eyes" approach. Each team was different and by the end of the project almost all of the faculty members involved had participated in at least one site visit. Students were also full members of the team on these site visits. In all cases, there was continual consultation and reflection among team members both as a result the formal organization and of serendipitous encounters. With over 550 interviews, hundreds of pages of fieldnotes and stacks of documents, we have been able to work together to capture the rich complexity of long-term residential care and to identify ideas worth sharing. A detailed description of this method can be found in *Creative Teamwork: Developing Rapid, Site-Switching Ethnography* (Armstrong & Lowndes, 2018). Like the analytical maps, these ethnographies provide a grounding for the various chapters in this book.

This Book

This book is a collective effort, built on our shared research and analysis. Although individual chapters have specific authors, the entire team has been involved in the collection and analysis of the data that are the basis for this book. Chapter 1 sets the stage.

Because we understand that context matters, we begin by analyzing privatization in specific jurisdictions in Chapters 2 through 6. The first of these chapters focuses on the two social democratic countries in our project, Sweden and Norway. Taking a comparative perspective allows the authors to explore differences between two countries that are often assumed to be similar in their approaches to care and to offer possible explanations for differences in their forms of privatization. The following chapter compares the UK and the US, countries that have gone farther towards privatization than others in our project even though they began from quite different approaches to care. In addition to documenting privatization, the authors set out some of the consequences for access to quality care. Both the unique and shared aspects of privatization in Germany are the subject of Chapter 4. With their traditional corporatist approach to social services, Germany differs in some important ways from the other five countries and thus helps reveal the differences history as well as culture can play. The final chapters in this section focus on Canada. Nursing homes in Canada are under provincial/territorial jurisdiction and each jurisdiction has taken a somewhat different approach to marketization. Chapter 5 explores developments in three of the four Canadian provinces in our study: Ontario, Nova Scotia, and Manitoba. It illustrates how even within the same country, privatization may take different forms and proceed at different rates. The other chapter on Canada in this section of specific jurisdictions explores the specific case of British Columbia, the fourth province in our study. Drawing on a literature review, descriptive statistics, historical interventions, and media analysis, it provides a detailed analysis of how privatization developed and has been resisted. Together these five chapters demonstrate both the significant variation in forms of privatization and the contradictory developments, suggesting that there are alternatives to a steady march towards privatization.

The rest of the book examines key issues that cross jurisdictions, drawing on both our analytical maps and our ethnographic data. The first of these, Chapter 7, explores the assumptions behind what and how data are collected, access to and analysis of the data, how people are trained to use the data and how those data are presented. This form of privatization is often invisible at the same time as it has profound implications for funding, ownership, and democratic control as well as for the organization of work and the quality of care. This chapter leads directly to Chapter 8 on accountability, given that accountability is increasingly understood as counting. Based primarily on the Norway experience, this chapter sets out strategies intended to ensure for-profit homes are accountable to the community at various levels before going on to assesses their effectiveness.

While governments are busy trying to ensure some form of accountability in the face of the privatization of ownership, for-profit companies are busy trying to sell their services. Based on an analysis of public websites, Chapter 9 illustrates the similarities and differences between the websites for not-for-profit and for-profit, corporate homes. Meanwhile, a growing body of research indicates that there are often significant differences in the quality of care and the quality of work between those homes seeking a profit and those that do not. This is especially the case when it comes to the evidence on staffing. A significant body of research demonstrates that staffing levels are related to the quality of care. The next chapter brings together that research with the research on ownership, showing how the increasing privatization of nursing homes contributes to a reduction in staffing levels and thus to lowering the quality of care.

The final two chapters in this section focus on what happens within nursing homes. Chapter 11 explores how privatization influences more than staffing levels and decision-making. It also shapes approaches to care and can lead to the devaluing of later life, as this chapter explains with specific reference to the UK. And it also influences who does what work. When people move into a nursing home, it is often assumed that families and friends will no longer have to do care work, that workers will be paid to provide care and residents can relax as they would at home. Chapter 12 documents how privatization often means more, rather than less care work for families, and more unpaid work for those otherwise paid for the job. At the same time as residents may be required to take more responsibility for payment, they may face more limits on providing for their own personal care.

While all these chapters focus primarily on the trend towards privatization and the negative consequences for the quality of work and care, the concluding chapter identifies some promising practices for ensuing older adults' right to appropriate, accessible, quality care, and for creating decent conditions of work. With contributions from all the authors in the book, Chapter 13 provides examples of strategies related to regulations, legal challenges, union actions, community organizing, and reclaiming public ownership; strategies designed to support the right to care.

References

Adams, A., & Chivers, S. (2016). There's no place like home: Designing for long-term residential care in Canada. *Journal of Canadian Studies, 50*(2), 273–298.

Aiken, L. H., Clarke, S. P., Sloane, D. M., Sochalski, J., & Silber, J. H. (2002). Hospital nurse staffing and patient mortality, nurse burnout, and job dissatisfaction. *JAMA, 288*(16), 1987–1993.

Armstrong, H., Daly, T.J. & Choiniere, J.A. (2016). Policies and Practices: The Case of RAI-MDS in Canadian Long-Term Care Homes. *Journal of Canadian Studies, 50*(2), 348–367.

Armstrong, P. (2013). Puzzling skills: Feminist political economy approaches. *Canadian Review of Sociology/Revue canadienne de sociologie, 50*(3), 256–283.

Armstrong, P. & Armstrong, H. (1978) *The double ghetto: Canadian women and their segregated work.* Toronto: McClelland and Stewart.

Armstrong, P. & Armstrong, H. (1990) *Theorizing women's work.* Toronto: Garamond Press.

Armstrong, P., Armstrong, H., & Coburn, D. (2001). *Unhealthy times: Political economy perspectives on health and care.* Toronto, ON: Oxford University Press.

Armstrong, P. & Braedley, S. (2016). *Physical environments for long-term care: Ideas worth sharing.* Ottawa, ON: Canadian Centre for Policy Alternatives.

Armstrong, P., Banerjee, A., Szebehely, M., Armstrong, H., Daly, T, & Lafrance, S. (2009). *They deserve better: The long-term care experience in Canada and Scandinavia.* Ottawa, ON: Canadian Centre for Policy Alternatives.

Armstrong, P. & Connelly, P. (Eds.) (1992) *Feminism in action: Studies in political economy* Toronto: Canadian Scholars Press, 1992

Armstrong, P., & Daly, T. (2017). Complexities, tensions, and promising practices. In K. Christensen & D. Pilling (Eds.), *The Routledge handbook of social care work around the world* (pp. 289–300). New York, NY: Routledge.

Armstrong, P., Armstrong, H., & Scott-Dixon, K. (2008). *Critical to care: The invisible women in health services.* Toronto, ON: University of Toronto Press.

Armstrong, P., & Lowndes, R. (Eds.). (2018). *Creative teamwork: Developing rapid, site-switching ethnography.* New York, NY: Oxford University Press.

Baines, D. (2004a). Caring for nothing: Work organization and unwaged labour in social services. *Work, employment and society, 18*(2), 267–295.

Baines, D. (2004b). Losing the eyes in the back of our heads: Social service skills, lean caring, and violence. *Journal of Sociology & Social Welfare, 31*(3), 31–50.

Baines, D. (2006). Staying with people who slap us around: Gender, juggling responsibilities and violence in paid (and unpaid) care work. *Gender, Work & Organization, 13*(2), 129–151.

Baines, D., & Cunningham, I. (2011). Using comparative perspective rapid ethnography in international case studies: Strengths and challenges. *Qualitative Social Work, 12*(1), 73–88.

Bakker, I. (2003) Neo-liberal governance and the reprivatization of social reproduction: Social provisioning and shifting gender orders. In I. Bakker & S. Gill (Eds.) *Power, Production and Social Reproduction* (pp. 66–82) London and New York: Macmillan-Palgrave.

Banerjee, A., & Armstrong, P. (2015). Centring care: explaining regulatory tensions in residential care for older persons. *Studies in Political Economy, 95*(1), 7–28.

Baum, D. J. (1997) *Warehouses for Death: The nursing home industry*. Don Mills, ON: Burns and MacEachern, 1977

Béland, F., Bergman, H., Lebel, P., Dallaire, L., Fletcher, J., Tousignant, P., & Contandriopoulos, A. P. (2006). Integrated services for frail elders (SIPA): A trial of a model for Canada. *Canadian Journal on Aging/La revue canadienne du vieillissement, 25*(1), 25–42.

Braverman, H. (1974). *Labor and monopoly capital*. New York, NY: Monthly Review Press.

Burawoy, M. (1991). Introduction: Researching for the global. In M. Burawoy, J. A. Blum, S. George, Z. Gille, & M. Thayer (Eds.), *Global ethnography: Forces, connections and imaginations in a postmodern world* (pp. 217–290). Berkeley, CA: University of California Press.

Burawoy, M., Blum, J. A., George, S., Gille, Z., & Thayer, M. (2011) *Global ethnography: Forces, connections, and imaginations in a postmodern world*. Berkeley, CA: University of California Press.

Castle, N. G. (2006). Organizational commitment and turnover of nursing home administrators. *Health Care Management Review, 31*(2), 156–165.

Cawley, J., Grabowski, D. C., & Hirth, R. A. (2006). Factor substitution in nursing homes. *Journal of Health Economics, 25*(2), 234–247.

Choiniere, J. A. (2007). *Accounting for care: The costs of managerial transformations in nurses' practices*. Toronto, ON: York University.

Choiniere, J. A., Doupe, M., Goldmann, M., Harrington, C., Jacobsen, F. F., Lloyd, L., & Szebehely, M. (2016). Mapping nursing home inspections and audits in six countries. *Ageing International, 41*(1), 40–61.

Coughlan R., & Ward, L. (2007). Experiences of recently relocated residents of a long-term care facility in Ontario: Assessing quality qualitatively. *International Journal of Nursing Studies*, Jan; *44*(1), 47–57.

Davies, M. J. (2016). A humanist in the house of old: Moyra Jones and early dementia care in Canada. *Journal of Canadian Studies, 50*(2), 446–481.

Diamond, T. (1992) *Making grey gold. Narratives of nursing home care*. Chicago: University of Chicago Press.

Esping-Andersen, G. (1990). *The three worlds of welfare capitalism*. Hoboken, NJ: John Wiley & Sons.

Estes, C. (2001) 'Political economy of aging: A theoretical framework'. In C. Estes and Associates. *Social policy and aging* (pp.1–22). London: Sage.

Fraser, N., & Gordon, L. (1994). A genealogy of dependency: Tracing a keyword of the US welfare state. *Signs: Journal of Women in Culture and Society, 19*(2), 309–336.

Grant, K. R., Amaratunga, C., Armstrong, P., Boscoe, M., Pederson, A., & Willson, K. (Eds.). (2004). *Caring for/caring about: Women, home care, and unpaid caregiving*. Toronto, ON: Garamond.

Harrington, C., & Carrillo, H. (1999). The regulation and enforcement of federal nursing home standards, 1991–1997. *Medical Care Research and Review*, *56*(4), 471–494.

Harrington, C., Jacobsen, F. F., Panos, J., Pollock, A., Sutaria, S., & Szebehely, M. (2017). Marketization in long-term care: A cross-country comparison of large for-profit nursing home chains. *Health Services Insights*, *10*, doi:10.1177/1178632917710533.

Harrington, C., Mullan, J. T., & Carrillo, H. (2004). State nursing home enforcement systems. *Journal of Health Politics, Policy and Law*, *29*(1), 43–74.

Harrington, C., Woolhandler, S., Mullan, J., Carrillo, H., & Himmelstein, D. U. (2001). Does investor ownership of nursing homes compromise the quality of care? *American Journal of Public Health*, *91*(9), 1452–1455.

Harvey, D. (2006). *Spaces of global capitalism: Towards a theory of uneven geographical development*. London, UK: Verso.

Johnson, J., Rolph, S. & Smith, R. R. (2010) *Residential care transformed: Revisiting the last refuge*. Basingstoke: Palgrave Macmillan.

Keating, N., Kerr, K., Warren, S., Grace, M., & Wertenberger, D. (1994). Who's the family in family caregiving? *Canadian Journal on Aging/La revue canadienne du vieillissement*, *13*(2), 268–287.

Kittay, E. F., Jennings, B., & Wasunna, A. A. (2005). Dependency, difference and the global ethic of longterm care. *Journal of Political Philosophy*, *13*(4), 443–469.

Lanoix, M. (2009). Shades of gray: From caring to uncaring labor. *International Journal of Feminist Approaches to Bioethics*, *2*(2), 31–50.

Laslett, B. & Brenner, J. (1989) Gender and social reproduction: Historical perspectives. *Annual Review of Sociology*, 15(1), 381–404

Lloyd, L., Banerjee, A., Harrington, C., F. Jacobsen, F., & Szebehely, M. (2014). It is a scandal! Comparing the causes and consequences of nursing home media scandals in five countries. *International Journal of Sociology and Social Policy*, *34*(1/2), 2–18.

Luxton, M. & Braedley, S. (Eds.) (2010) *Neoliberalism and everyday life*. Montreal-Kingston: McGill-Queens University Press.

McLean, A. (2007) *The person in dementia: A study of nursing home care in the United States*. Peterborough, ON: Broadview Press

Organization for Economic Cooperation and Development (OECD). (2005). *Long-term care for older people*. Paris: OECD.

Peace, S., Kellaher, L., & Willcocks, D. (1997). *Re-evaluating residential care*. Buckingham, UK: Open University Press.

Smith, D. E. (1990). *Texts, facts and femininity: Exploring the relations of ruling*. New York, NY: Routledge.

Struthers, J. (1998). "A nice homelike atmosphere": State alternatives to family care for the aged in post World War II Ontario. In L. Chambers & E.-A. Montigny (Eds.), *Family matters: Papers in post-Confederation Canadian family history* (pp. 335–354). Toronto, ON: Canadian Scholars Press.

Struthers, J. (2003). No place like home: Gender, family, and the politics of home care in post-World War II Ontario. *Canadian Bulletin of Medical History*, *20*(2), 387–417.

Struthers, J. (2008). Comfort, security, dignity: Home care for Canada's aging veterans, 1977–2004. In E. Heaman, A. Li, & S. McKellar (Eds.), *Essays in honour of Michael Bliss: Figuring the social* (pp. 315–480). Toronto, ON: University of Toronto Press.

Thompson, E. P. (1978). *The poverty of theory and other essays*. London, UK: Merlin Press.

Townsend, O. (1962) *The last refuge: A survey of residential institutions and homes for the aged in England and Wales*. London: Routledge and Kegan Paul.

Williams, F. (2001). In and beyond New Labour: Towards a new political ethics of care. *Critical Social Policy, 21*(4), 467–493.

World Health Organization (WHO). (2002). *Ethical choices in long-term care: What does justice require?* Geneva: WHO.

Yassi, A., & Hancock, T. (2005). Patient safety – worker safety: Building a culture of safety to improve healthcare worker and patient well-being. *Healthcare Quarterly 8*, 32–38.

Part I

Privatization in Six Countries

Chapter 1

Privatizing Care
Setting the Stage

Pat Armstrong and Hugh Armstrong

The development of public care has been uneven, varied, contradictory, and as Wahl (2011) makes clear about the welfare state in general, always a result of compromises. By public care, we mean not only public delivery and public payment for health services but also a commitment to shared responsibility, democratic decision-making, and the idea that the public sector operates according to a logic of service to all. Privatization is the process of moving away from any or all of these. This chapter provides the framework for the chapters that follow, applying our feminist political economy approach. It presents an analysis of developments, rather than simply providing the kinds of descriptions more common in gerontology (Estes, 1979). Like Estes, Biggs and Phillipson (2003: 20), we explore the parts capitalism, states, ideas and struggles over power play in marginalization and domination.

What came to be known as the welfare state is the result of multiple forces that were particularly evident in the period following the Second World War. The Great Depression that preceded it demonstrated that unemployment and poverty were not primarily the result of individual failures, raising serious questions about the benefits of capitalism and unregulated markets. In response, governments introduced programs such as the New Deal in the US; programs that were specifically designed to limit capitalism and markets. And the war saw the expansion of state investment, of government services such as health care, and the regulation of markets. For the six countries in our study, the economic boom that followed the war contributed to the strength of unions and to their efforts both to expand protections for individuals and to limit capitalism. There was an expectation of and demand for a better world from various communities after the sacrifices of war, as well as a sense of shared responsibility and risk. At the same time, there was a fear of rebellion both from the many women who had taken up jobs during the war and from the military personnel who were returning (Armstrong, 1997). As the Canadian economist Yalnizyan (1994: 31) put it, "the shiver of universal risk had swept over everyone, and people started demanding protections by pooling the risks across society." This was combined with a fear of communism, a system that seemed to promise greater equality and services for all.

For many, there was a positive notion of shared responsibility and collective rights. Access to health and care was declared a human right in a statement signed by all but a handful of countries.[1] Although there was considerable variation among countries, reflecting the power relations and ideas within them, the welfare state expanded everywhere. The Scandinavian countries provided the most comprehensive protections and market interventions (Ginsburg & Rosenthal, 2006), based on a positive social commitment. But even in the US, where the welfare state was the least developed, at the war's end 35.4% of non-agricultural workers belonged to unions (Mayer, 2004: 12) and by the mid-1960s, there was a form of universal health care for the older population. Although welfare states have been critiqued for failing to create equity and for limiting effectively the negative consequences of markets (see, e.g., Sainsbury, 1999), they undoubtedly contributed to better access to health and care for many.

The expansion of public health care was particularly important for women, and helped reduce inequalities across the population. Women are the majority of those who use the health care system, in part because they have the babies and because they tend to live longer than men. They are also the majority of those who provide paid and unpaid care. In nursing homes in all six countries in our project, four out of five employees and residents are women (OECD, 2017: Table 11.20). Moreover, it is within health care that employed women are most likely to have union protection (Laxer, 2015). As a result, women found some of their best jobs in health services at the same time as these services helped reduce their unpaid care workload.

By the 1970s, though, the economy was no longer booming. Manufacturing jobs especially were disappearing in high-income countries as technology replaced workers at home and as corporations searched for cheaper sources of labor in low-income countries. Profits failed to grow at previous levels. Running out of new places to invest, corporations looked to government-owned services. These services were particularly attractive because many of them guaranteed payment and, in some case, even customers. Canadian public health care, for example, was described in trade talks as an unopened oyster, ripe for takeover by for-profit concerns (Peterson, 1997). These same corporations pressured government to reduce taxes and to remove regulations on employers or at least those regulations that restricted profit-making, claiming that this would attract investment and create jobs. Governments then argued that they did not have the money to support the social programs of the welfare state, although neoliberals also argued that the government should not be providing such services in any case.

The increasingly predominant economic theory maintained that governments should steer and not row the ship of state, to use Osborne and Gaebler's (1992) metaphor for what has come to be called New Public Management. Rather than provide services, government should ensure that services are provided and do so through supporting competition and markets. "According to economic theory, competitive markets generally result in the most efficient allocation of resources, where resources consist of individuals with different skills, capital goods (e.g., computers, machinery, and buildings), and natural resources" (Mayer, 2004: 4). Restrictions on commerce and on labor – especially through unions – were to be removed in order to allow markets to determine practices, which would permit benefits to trickle down to the deserving. At the same time as there was a call for governments to reduce and get out of the way of markets, they were also called to intervene in order to improve competition, or at least profits.

This was not the only contradiction in this neoliberal approach. Governments were attacked as bureaucratic and unresponsive. The antidote was the application of for-profit managerial strategies to any government services that remained. People were to be treated as customers with money to spend rather than as citizens with rights. Staffing was to be reduced to a minimum and security as well as benefits reduced as a way of limiting red tape while ensuring efficiency and discipline. At the same time, the performance measures integral to ensure a focus on outcomes meant increased requirements for monitoring through audits (Power, 2003). In other words, the result was more bureaucracy, albeit of a somewhat different kind. Moreover, although cutting costs was emphasized, there was no shortage of calls to spend money in order to attract and support the corporate sector, as we shall see when we discuss public-private partnerships later in this chapter. In addition, there was a continuing expectation that governments would use tax dollars to purchase services that they no longer provided, based on the assumption that separating purchaser and provider meant more choice as well as lower cost.

Part of the call to reduce government was to make corporations, communities, individuals, and families more responsible for health and care. Increasingly termed "responsibilization," applied to corporations it was framed as social responsibility reinforced by competition for customers and by transparency via performance indicators. Bercovitz (1998: 322) summarizes this approach applied to families and to individuals as "a 'pull yourself up by the bootstraps' alternative to state intervention." Those who work in health services were increasingly held responsible not only for the care they provided but for their own health and safety (Gray, 2009).

Today the evidence of growing inequality is contributing to the skepticism about neoliberal strategies even among some former supporters. The Organization for Economic Cooperation and Development (OECD, 2011), for example, points to regulatory reforms along with tax and benefit regulations as factors producing growing inequality and suggests these strategies should be revisited. Although the OECD (2011: 19) has identified population aging as a factor exacerbating inequality, it has also used this aging as a justification for introducing and intensifying neo-liberal strategies throughout high-income countries. The common argument is that governments cannot meet the demand for care and that the innovation and efficiency needed to meet the growing demand is best achieved through market competition and private funds (Prada, 2011).

This chapter outlines the major forms of privatization that are evident in long-term residential care. Drawing on research conducted by our team, as well as on other sources, it provides the background for the more detailed explorations that follow. It is framed by a feminist political economy approach. From this perspective, economic, cultural, and political forces combine to structure activities on multiple scales. Although shaped by the search for profit and the unequal relations of power, collective and individual actions influence local as well as national and global developments in historically specific, geographically variable, and often contradictory ways. Class is not the only relation of inequality and of struggles over power. Indeed, classes themselves are divided. Gender, race, and other social relations are understood as central and unequal, conditioned by and reacting to forces at multiple levels at the same time as they shape them. By emphasizing social reproduction and intersectional oppressions, feminist political economy draws attention to the entire range of paid and unpaid work in the public and private sectors of the formal economy, in the community, and in the household, as well as to divisions within these sectors (Armstrong & Armstrong, 2005). It asks the classic political economy questions: Who benefits?

The Privatization of Nursing Home Ownership and Care Delivery

Home Ownership

The most obvious form of privatization is the move to the private ownership and delivery of nursing home care. The private delivery of nursing home care is not new. What is new is the nature of the private ownership. For decades, many homes have been owned by non-profit organizations such as churches. It was not uncommon, especially in Canada, the US, and the UK, for individuals or families to own and operate small nursing homes that made a small, if any profit. Beginning in the 1970s, however, national and international chains that owned or managed two or more homes started to move in. Some governments, guided by a neoliberal philosophy, supported this development by introducing a competitive bidding process, by dropping public services and failing to establish new ones to meet new needs, and by simultaneously introducing regulations that were difficult for small enterprises and non-profit organizations to meet, and removing others that might interfere with profit-making. Later chapters on specific jurisdictions elaborate on these changes. These chapters also illustrate the variation in and complexity of for-profit ownership within and across countries.

Members of our team (Harrington et al., 2017) recently documented, to the extent possible from the available data, the trends in five of the six countries involved in our project. Their analysis of the data for 2014 clearly demonstrates the massive expansion of chains as well as the complex nature of the ownership. According to this research (Harrington et al. 2017, Table 1), by 2014 the UK had the highest proportion of for-profit ownership (86.3%), followed by the US (69.8%). The lower proportion (37.4%) of for-profit ownership in Canada is still much higher than found in the Scandinavian countries. The apparent for-profit decline in Canada may be a matter of classification. According to Statistics Canada, the for-profit proportion stood at 46.7% in 2012 (calculated from Statistics Canada, 2012, Table 1.1), virtually unchanged from 2005. In all countries, chains have taken over many smaller for-profits, thus reducing the overall number of homes. The growth of for-profit ownership is pronounced in the provinces of Ontario, where it began in the 1970s, and of British Columbia (BC), where it is a more recent development. These provinces together account for over half the Canadian population (Statistics Canada, 2018). In BC, for example, between 2001 and 2016, the number of beds in for-profit homes increased by 2,621, while those in non-profit homes declined by 2,082 (Longhurst, 2017: Table 3).

These data also demonstrate that for-profit ownership is not the only way to provide nursing home care in these times. Norway and Sweden, with their history of stronger, more expansive welfare states and of state ownership, have by far the lowest rates of for-profit ownership. As the chapter on Norway and Sweden explains, even these countries have not escaped neoliberal strategies. However, the expansion of for-profit ownership has been limited by popular support for public care and, in the case of Norway especially, by successful public opposition based on evidence.

For-profit ownership is not a single category. It still includes the dwindling number of single homes owned by an individual or family. But most exist within chains. Those that own two or more may be chains that are publicly traded on the stock exchange or in over-the-counter markets where only shareholders have the right to certain kinds of information. Publicly traded companies may be owned by a corporation or a trust. Even though they are publicly traded, however, they may have complex corporate structures that make it difficult to follow the money. The private companies that are owned by individuals, managers, or a group of investors are even more difficult to monitor. To further complicate matters, chains are frequently involved in real estate investment trusts (REITS), reflecting their efforts to separate the operation of a home from the real estate and buildings involved. In addition to hiding crucial financial information, this separation means it is possible to profit from selling the land on which the home is based while still profiting by relocating the beds to areas where real estate is less expensive. When, for example, a Chinese corporation with unclear ownership bought a group of retirement homes primarily in BC, the financial pages of a national newspaper made it clear that "What makes it even more attractive is that it also owns holdings of unused or partly developed land that would allow a major expansion of facilities in the future" (Chase, 2016). This suggests that it is the real estate and not the services that are the investment attraction. Another twist on the ownership category is the public–private partnership, which itself can take multiple forms from joint capital to a division of responsibility. In the Canadian province of New Brunswick, the government entered a public–private partnership to build nursing homes after requesting exemption from its own legislation in order "to lease nursing home beds without going through a tendering process" (Auditor General, 2009: 118).

Contracting Services

For-profit ownership is further complicated by the contracting out of services within non-profit and government-owned homes. One form of contracting out involves hiring individuals. Instead of hiring their own therapists and other professionals, homes contract for individuals to provide these services through private agencies. Similarly, homes fill gaps in their nursing and other staff by using temporary help agencies. This form of contracting out may be based on the argument that the home does not need these individuals full time and thus paying by the day or by service is a more efficient way of hiring. Another growing form of contracting involves handing over entire services to a private agency. Cleaning, dietary, laundry, and security services are increasingly contracted out, often to international corporations that provide services to a wide range of industries outside health care. This kind of contracting is based on the argument that these are ancillary services rather than health care services, and that they are more efficiently and more effectively undertaken by corporations with experience in these activities because they can achieve economies of scale (Armstrong, Armstrong, & Scott-Dixon, 2008; Armstrong & Day, 2017).

While this form of contracting brings the private sector into specific areas within a care home, the contracting out of management services to for-profit corporations changes the way the entire home is operated. This is one of the fastest growing contracted services in recent years (Day, 2014). For example, the largest corporation operating in the province of Ontario's nursing home sector manages more homes than it operates. Extendicare (2017) promises to "help you provide care and services to those who depend on you, while maintaining a close eye on your bottom line." It is a promise based on the notion that market principles apply.

The Problems with Private Ownership and Delivery

The problems with the private ownership and delivery of nursing home care have been documented by our team, among others. There is little evidence for the claim that for-profit provision lowers cost and improves quality while increasing choice, reducing bureaucracy, and increasing transparency (McGregor & Ronald, 2011). Indeed, the opposite is more often the case.

One reason for the failure to deliver on the promise is that the major operating cost in long-term care is staffing and in order to make a significant profit, staffing costs must be lowered. As Chapter 3 by Charlene Harrington, Allyson Pollock and Shailen Sutaria indicates, there are clear patterns of lower staffing in for-profit homes and of lower staffing contributing to lower quality care. The strategies in relation to staffing are not only about fewer staff but also about a different mix of staff, with more staff having fewer formal qualifications. Those with fewer credentials are paid less on this basis. Here, too, there is evidence that staffing mix has an impact on the quality of care, demonstrating the importance of a mix that includes staff with more formal qualifications. For-profit strategies also encourage more precarity, hiring more casual and part-time staff and failing to replace staff absent for leaves or other reasons. Precarity makes it more difficult to have continuity in care and to develop care as a relationship.

Impact on Quality

The tendency for quality to be lower in for-profit care has also been documented in relation to a variety of other factors. For example, hospitalizations tend to be higher from for-profit chains (Tanuseputro et al., 2015), and hospitalizations suggest problems with the care received in the home and may put residents at risk (Ågotnes et al., 2016). Verified complaints are also higher (McGregor et al., 2011). That the non-profit Baycrest home in Toronto has a wait time estimated as 1,034 days compared to the 38 days needed to gain admission to the for-profit Leisureworld Caregiving Centre, even though Baycrest has more beds, suggests that the public knows about the differences in quality care (Toronto Central CCAC, 2017). Leisureworld (now the Sienna chain) may be near the bottom of reputational rankings in Ontario, and Baycrest near the top, but overall in 2010, 67% of the first choices for nursing home admission were to non-profit and public homes, although they accounted for only 46% of all homes in the province (Buchanan, 2011, slide 7).

Impact on Costs

For-profit ownership status does not, however, lower the costs incurred by government. A team analysis (Harrington et al., 2016: 33) from four jurisdictions in our project (California, England, Norway and Ontario) indicates that both revenues and expenditures went up in all jurisdictions, indicating that there was no evidence of cost-saving through privatization. This is not surprising, given that some of the revenue in the homes was allocated to profits rather than to care. The "two countries with higher levels of for-profit and chain ownership spent less on direct care, and direct care declined as a proportion of revenues in both California and England," although even in those corporations that spent more on care there was significant profit. Meanwhile, much of the payment came from government coffers.

Impact on Accountability

At the same time, there was little evidence of the promised transparency. Indeed, "none of the countries had strong financial accountability for public dollars on administration and profits" (Harrington et al., 2016: 34). As another study by members of our team indicates, the complex ownership structures contributed to the efforts to reduce taxes, litigation actions, and regulatory oversight (Harrington et al., 2011). Moreover, the hiring of for-profit managers blurs the lines between non-profit and for-profit, making it harder to track the differences in quality and costs. We could find little research documenting the impact of for-profit management on non-profit homes, and as Tamara Daly makes clear in Chapter 7, the big data available are not much help in doing further research (see also Daly, 2015). No key informant for our project recommended a home with such an arrangement, perhaps because such homes do not provide examples of promising practices. In a linked project,[2] however, we did encounter a for-profit management service in a non-profit home. A lower level manager employed by the home reported that worker injuries went up as a result of cost-cutting strategies and that there was a revolt against managers' efforts to cut food costs, suggesting that the quality of work and care declined. But much more research is required in order to assess the claims for improvement under for-profit management in a non-profit home. Another home we studied brought their contracted food service back in house in response to widespread complaints about the quality.

As for the promise of less bureaucracy and more responsiveness, there is evidence that the reverse is the case with the expansion of for-profit ownership and delivery. Our study of media scandals (Lloyd et al., 2014) found they grew in tandem with the rise in for-profit ownership and financing while the government response was more and more detailed regulations of processes within the nursing home. Our comparison of nursing home inspections and audits in the six countries in our project (Choiniere et al., 2016: 56) "suggests that jurisdictions with the highest level of for-profit ownership also have the most standardized, complex and deterrence-based regulatory systems, and stronger regulatory enforcement." In other words, bureaucracy increased while flexibility and choice declined. These regulations did not, however, address larger structural factors such as ownership and staffing or reporting, all of which would make financing and ownership structures transparent in ways that would allow democratic oversight. An expanded notion of accountability is also required, as Frode Jacobsen and Gudmund Ågotnes explain in Chapter 8.

Impact on Staff

The contracting out of non-management services can create additional problems. Contracting individuals through agencies disrupts continuity in care and makes it difficult to establish the relationships that are particularly important for those with dementia. Contingent staff are also more expensive than permanent employees because the agency takes a profit by charging more than the cost of wages. This kind of hiring can also mean more work for the permanent staff and is thus less efficient, as the following interview with two care workers from a Canadian home illustrates:

> Sometimes during the days when we change their clothes, you know, and then some other clothes is mixed [up]. That's the big problem for us too. We're getting the clothes. "Oh this is not for her. This is for the other." I don't know why that is happening because we sorted out already ... Because there's names on the wall and there's names on the clothes. So why is her clothes down the hall and three doors down? Well that's people that's part time and they are casual and they get it mixed up.

Contracting out what are often called ancillary services creates other problems. It is based on the false assumption that food, laundry, and cleaning are not integral and critical aspects of care (Armstrong, Armstrong, & Scott-Dixon, 2008). It creates divisions among those who work in the home and makes it difficult to construct care as a relationship. Accountability is problematic, given that there is more than one employer within the home. In a Canadian home we studied that contracted out food services, food trays were delivered on carts that arrived and left at specified times, limiting the choices of residents and staff. Staff had to begin wheeling in residents long before the food arrived, leaving them, in one case, to sit watching a food show on television as they waited. There were no tempting food smells because food was cooked far from the residents and the full, pre-filled plates turned some residents off eating at all. A sign on the wall warned residents, staff, and families not to talk to the dietary workers employed by the contracting firm, providing a clear message about the separation of these workers from care and from other staff.

Although these contracted corporations may provide some savings as a result of economies of scale and of technologies not available within the home, they too rely primarily on staff. Thus the main way they save money and make a profit is by paying staff less, by providing fewer benefits, and by reducing job security. In the process, union protections and gains for women such as pay equity are often lost (Cohen & Cohen, 2004). A cleaner in Canada employed by an international corporation explained to us that she had worked at the airport but that contract had been lost and she was out of work. When the government moved to privatize housekeeping in nursing homes, her company got the contract and she had a job again. Asked about training for working in health care or for older people, she said they were only told that "if we go to the room and we find something we always have to surrender that" because otherwise the cleaners will be accused of theft. According to her, "there is only one housekeeping [staff member] in one floor with the three wings ... in the three wings there is like about over 30 rooms." She reported that her manager said it was "way too big for one person cleaning." The cleaner added that "the company is like that. That's all the budget that's there." She went on to say, "But anyway, there's no reason of complaining now because this company is going."

The turnover in companies and in staff disrupts relationships among staff as well as with residents, families, and managers, which is one reason why contracting out work in nursing homes is associated with an increase in deficiency citations (Bourbonniere et al., 2006). Moreover, once the service has been contracted out, it is hard to return it in-house even if the research demonstrates that this would be the appropriate strategy. When, for example, a home closes the kitchen and gets rid of the equipment because the food services are contracted out, the cost of building a new kitchen in-house can be prohibitively expensive. And it is not just the service corporation that may disappear. Privatized homes may close because they want to move elsewhere in order to make a profit from the land, because they are not realizing a profit or because they go bankrupt. Southern Cross, a large UK chain, went bankrupt in 2011, leaving the government scrambling to provide the service. In 2017, the government faced a new rescue with another major chain at risk (Drury, 2017).

This decline in the quality and the conditions of care work has a gendered impact, given that women account for more than four out of five workers and residents in long-term care. In all of the countries we studied, immigrants and/or those from racialized groups make up a growing number of those providing care and of those defined as employed in ancillary services, so these forms of privatization have a particular impact on people from these populations.

Building nursing homes with government promising to pay the bulk of the bills and with high occupancy virtually guaranteed means there is little of the competition and risk assumed to make the market produce quality care. There is even less risk in taking over the management of a non-profit home. At the same time, however, the managerial strategies imported from the private sector shape practices in all the nursing homes, often creating a race to the bottom in terms of work intensity and pay. This can mean a primary orientation to tasks rather than to care and to cost savings through work intensification, lower pay, fewer benefits, and less job security. The focus can become just enough care by just enough people with just enough education and just enough pay, to borrow terms from the industrial sector. The focus on control and standardization can mean less autonomy and choice for residents, families, staff, and even local managers (Choiniere et al., 2016). An inquiry resulting from a nurse confessing to killing care home residents in the Canadian province of Ontario were told by a lawyer representing the residents' councils that the for-profit homes that employed her "fell short when it came to training staff, understanding their reporting obligations, thinking under pressure" and dealing with this nurse's workplace problem (Boyle. 2018: A2).

Privatization by Stealth

The less obvious form of privatization is that which results from a failure to respond to the need for public health care services and to supply appropriate care within care homes. As Macarov (2003: 71) explains, privatization

> is sometimes attained not by outright sales but by deliberately allowing services to run down, by erecting barriers to access, by withholding information and by making receiving benefits so difficult and demeaning that the public has little alternative but to turn to the private sector.

We would add that it also includes cost shifting and work shifting, as well as the shifting of responsibility onto individuals, their families and, to a lesser extent, facilities. It is very difficult to track this kind of privatization because so many factors are involved, making it especially difficult to compare across jurisdictions.

Inadequate Supply

Lack of spaces in publicly subsidized homes pushes people into alternatives where they are responsible for the entire cost. According to the OECD (2017, Table 11.23), both Sweden and Canada have made significant reductions in the number of beds available in long-term residential care. By 2015, Canada had 51.3 beds per 1,000 people aged 65 and over, compared to 65.3 in Sweden (OECD, 2017, Table 11.22). Comparing these numbers is complicated by several factors, however. For example, Swedish women over age 65 are healthier than Canadians (OECD, 2017: 202), suggesting they are less likely to need care in a nursing home. Sweden supplies more home care (OECD, 2017: 206) and spends more than Canada on the long-term care (OECD, 2017: Table 11.24), suggesting that there are more public alternatives to nursing home care in Sweden and that the quality within those homes is higher. Moreover, the extent to which alternative residential care is available for younger people is not taken into account. In other words, the differences between Canada and Sweden in terms of access to quality public care are even greater than the data suggest, and the reliance on private care is thus also greater. Comparisons with the US are even more difficult to make, given the complex mix of public support from Medicare, Medicaid, and the Veterans' Health Administration, as well as the financing from private insurance plans. The long waiting lists for care in the Canadian city of Toronto, though, provide an important indication of inadequate supply.

Shifting Payment

With relatively few spaces available in publicly supported nursing homes, those with increased social and medical needs are forced to turn to other forms of congregate living such as retirement homes, assisted living, and supportive housing, with their private payment implications. And more people have to rely on the unpaid work of family and friends, most of whom are women, and on out-of-pocket payment to others for intensified home and community care. As Muir (2017) shows, such private care is beyond the financial reach of many. The result is increasing inequality in access to care.

The extent to which the governments in our study pay for institutional care varies widely, with Sweden at the high end, covering close to 90% of the costs (Muir, 2017: Figure 8, Part B). In Norway, too, governments cover most of the costs. The US provides the least government funding. Even in the US though, the "majority of nursing home revenues came from Medicare (22.7 %) and Medicaid and other government programs (40.8 %) in 2012" (Harrington et al., 2016: 21). Long-term care coverage is mandatory in all German insurance schemes "so that the entire population is now protected against long-term-care costs" (Geraedts et al., 2016). The United Kingdom has devolved responsibility for residential care to the local level and both benefits and payments vary, as does the extent to which income and assets are taken into account (Gleckman, 2010: 17). Similarly, in Canada long-term residential care is a provincial and territorial responsibility, with variable fees and differences in whether income or assets are taken into account (MacDonald, 2015). In all of these Canadian jurisdictions, governments pay for the basic cost of care but charge what are called "accommodation fees." According to Muir (2017: Figure 11, Part B), the percentage of out-of-pocket costs still make care affordable in Sweden and Canada but not in the United States. In all of the countries in our study except for the United States, public payment covers the basic costs of care and these countries base admission mainly on health care needs, ensuring that low income is not a specific barrier to access. While we could find little analysis of the impact of these schemes on social locations beyond income, MacDonald's (2015: 11) research indicates that single senior women in particular benefit from the public payment schemes in Canada.

Given these complicated methods of public payment, it is not easy to track the extent to which costs have been shifted to individuals and families. In addition, the cost shifts we were told about in our ethnographic research were not primarily related to the monthly fees that could be tracked through public data, but to services beyond the basic minimum. These are much harder to document and to capture systematically. For example, in British Columbia we were told by a resident that he now had to pay for the physiotherapy his doctor recommended and for the transport to get him to the therapist. In an Ontario home, we were told by a family member that the home no longer provided the kind of shampoo the resident needed and so the family now had to cover the costs. Similarly, a family member reported that the new, cheaper laundry detergent used in the home gave her mother a rash, requiring the family to pay for an alternative laundry service. Laundry services had been reduced in other homes and so had other therapies, leaving residents or families to pay and creating inequities as a result.

But the much larger cost shifts we heard about were related to care. "There are not enough hands" was a common refrain, with families, residents, and staff telling us there were simply not enough people working in the home to provide the care residents require. Gaps in care are the result and the gaps are particularly obvious in relation to social care. For-profit managerial strategies, combined with detailed regulatory regimes, encourage a focus on tasks that can be counted and there is little time to chat, to listen, to take people for a walk, or even let a resident have a soak in the bath. In the German home we studied the gaps were, at least temporarily, filled by a large number of apprentices paid for through access to a government initiative. In Sweden and Norway, the significantly higher staffing levels helped make sure there were fewer gaps to fill. We did not encounter any privately paid companions in those countries, although we were told that a few had been hired in some places. But in the other three countries studied we saw a significant number of families paying privately for people to provide care within the nursing home. The hiring of these private companions has become widespread in some jurisdictions. In two of the Canadian homes we studied, the majority of residents had a private companion to help them eat, walk and talk.

These private companions create inequalities in access to care, given that many families cannot afford to pay for the additional care. But they also disrupt staffing and create tensions with employees who see some of the most rewarding aspects of the job done by someone else, someone who may not be there on a regular basis and may not have the skills or knowledge required (Daly, Armstrong, & Lowndes, 2015). These privately paid care providers also make planning difficult, as we heard from managers. Managers cannot, for example, be sure that there will be a private companion there to help a resident eat and must organize around that contingency. Authority lines are blurred, with families who are employing the companion directing the companion's work, and with staff often viewing the companions as spies for the family. For the private companions, the position is precarious. They have no authority, no job security or protections, and may be paid well below minimum wage (Brassolotto et al., 2017). Virtually all of the private companions we encountered were from immigrant/and or racialized communities and most were women.

Shifting Work

The hiring of private companions is one way the gaps in care are filled. Another way is through relatives and volunteers taking on the work. More difficult to see is the shift of care work to the unpaid labor of paid employees.

The shift in care work to families is particularly obvious in relation to clothes, laundry, food, and social activities but the work shift expands far beyond that, as Chapter 12 by Rachel Barken and Pat Armstrong explains. In a Canadian home, a daughter talked about how the high carbohydrate content in the diet meant that her mother went "from a size 10 up to a size 16 and that's a problem." Her mother regularly required new clothes, clothes that the daughter was expected to provide. Because her mother is in a wheelchair she needs special kinds of clothing, and the daughter had to hire a seamstress to deal with this growing and particular need. Her requests to the for-profit home for an alternative diet to limit the weight gain were refused. The daughter described another problem, with dental care. "I mean I do the Polident thing. I make certain she has her toothpaste, her toothbrush but I'm not there over her shoulder." When she talked to the nurse about dental care, the nurse "just shook her head." "They don't have the time either to stand over her shoulder and see that she's doing it properly." In order to have her mother's teeth cleaned, her daughter has to order and pay for transportation that can take a wheelchair and then travel with her mother to the dental hygienist. As this daughter explained, "even if they had a room set up so a dental hygienist could come and clean the teeth" it would save her time and money while making it much more comfortable for her mother. In other words, she was pressured to provide direct care as well as transportation, comfort, and money for services, as well as advocate on her mother's behalf.

Although relatives may be held responsible for some tasks, they are limited in the tasks they can provide and we saw a great deal of variation in what relatives were allowed to do. For example, a daughter in one home helped her mother bathe while in another this was defined as a risk and a daughter was prevented from helping with this task. Female relatives do most of this unpaid work and those without relatives, we were told, often simply go without. There are alternatives. In Sweden, for example, we were told that care aides could be paid to shop on behalf of those who required clothing and other supplies.

Volunteers may fill some of these gaps. In the UK, a man reported that he and his wife mainly fundraise to buy equipment for the home but recently have been involved in setting up a shop:

> which contains a few items which are convenient, mostly sweets and toiletries which is quite convenient for them to come and do their little bit of shopping here. Understandably very few of the residents are allowed out unaccompanied and there just aren't enough staff really to go around the village with them.

He went on to say: "My wife helps organize the bi-monthly bingo that they have here. That has a band of faithful, all local women, nearly all women, and that's quite a pleasant occasion." As he indicates, volunteers can make an important contribution to the home. However, we also heard that homes have come to rely more and more on these volunteers to take the place of paid workers. In addition to reducing the opportunities for paid employment, the volunteers do not necessarily have the skills required to work with the older population and they can be unreliable in terms of when they arrive and leave.

The low staffing levels and the pressure for paid employees to focus on countable tasks also serves to shift unpaid care work to those otherwise paid for the work. In an earlier survey conducted by some members of our team, nearly two-fifths of the Scandinavian care workers said they skip or shorten their lunch break at least once every week in order to get their work done, while 16% said they do so almost every day (Armstrong et al., 2009: 70–71). Among the Canadians surveyed, a majority of the Registered Nurses and Licensed Practical Nurses reported missing at least half of their scheduled breaks, as did 19% of personal support workers (Armstrong et al., 2009: Figure 10). The Canadians also reported coming in to work a half-hour early and leaving a half-hour late. In our current project, workers reported taking residents' laundry home with them and, on their own time, shopping for residents. They do so even though the majority report going home exhausted every day. It is women in particular who feel responsible (Baines, 2004), with almost a third of Swedish and nearly 40% of Canadian workers saying they go home feeling inadequate in terms of the care they provided (Armstrong et al., 2009: Table 19).

As is the case when tasks are not completed, workers are held responsible for the rising levels of violence. As more than one worker put it, we are told to "suck it up" (Braedley et al., 2017). At the same time, the new methods of work organization and reporting increases the control over workers (Baines & van den Broek, 2017), leaving those providing care without the autonomy or time to develop care relationships and to use their knowledge to prevent such situations from arising in the first place (Armstrong, 2013). Workers, however, often find ways to work around these restrictions. Take the case of limits placed on the number of diapers allowed per day per resident. Sitting in a wet diaper for hours, even if the manufacturer claims the diaper is fine until the urine reaches the blue line, can be uncomfortable and demeaning. It may even lead to violence as residents react to the indignity. Some workers we interviewed hid diapers in order to change them when, based on their knowledge, a resident needed a change.

Shifting the Dominant Discourse

As neoliberal approaches have gained dominance, so too has a new way of speaking about the right to care and about ways of organizing care. Residents become customers or consumers, rather than citizens with rights to care. This approach to nursing is nicely summed up by Goldmeier (2015) in his internet column on investment advice for the United States:

> The care of infirm people in special residential facilities who cannot be cared for at home is a multi-billion dollar industry. The 50 largest firms

account for 20% of the revenues the industry generates. Government reimbursements through Medicaid and Medicare, fee-for-service payments from states, and a mix of private insurance and self-pay are the primary sources of revenues.

The Competitions and Markets Authority (2016) in the UK announced in a press release that it would "examine how well care homes are complying with their obligations under consumer law." Consumer law, not the right to care, was how the issue was framed. As Chapter 9 by Ruth Lowndes, Jaqueline Choiniere, and Sara Erlandsson illustrates, homes are marketed like any other consumer good.

But it is not only those primarily focused on profits who think and talk in terms of business approaches to care. Government services are also called upon to require business plans and to focus on the bottom line. They embrace lean production and total quality management schemes drawn from industry. And, like businesses, when they restructure, reconfigure, or even reform, this typically means down-sizing. These moves are justified not just in terms of markets being better but in terms of a crisis created by the so-called "grey tsunami" that has to be addressed by alternatives to public care.

Shifting Decision-Making

Privatization shifts where, how, and on what basis decisions get made. For-profit companies are focused on the bottom line. Their main responsibility is to shareholders or owners. The arrangements they make with governments are often confidential, based on the argument that confidentiality is essential to competition. As Harrington and others (2017) show, some of these companies paid for through public funds do not even reveal all of their operations to governments and some governments do not reveal the information they do collect to the public. In the process, decision-making is privatized and the public cannot easily keep the corporations accountable. Meanwhile, free trade agreements may make it difficult for governments to reject takeovers, closures, and for-profit ownership, further limiting democratic decision-making.

Inadequate staff numbers also shift who decides about care. Families with economic resources can decide individually to hire a private companion for their relative. Volunteers can decide whether to show up or not. Families with time and skill can decide whether to provide extra services, although the pressures they face may leave them with little choice. Meanwhile, new work organization and reporting structures mean more surveillance of and less decision-making by those who provide care.

Patterns of Change

There are powerful forces within and outside government pushing for privatization and none of the six countries we studied has escaped this pressure. Across these countries, though, there are wide variations in the extent and nature of privatization, indicating there is little that is inevitable about the patterns of privatization. The effect, and indeed often the stated purpose, is to blur the lines between public and private organization and services.

Public payment for private delivery based on competition among suppliers is promoted as the best way to achieve the lowest cost for the best care while allowing consumer choice and reducing bureaucracy. This is based on the assumption that markets produce more innovation and efficiency. It is also based on the assumption that markets operate through some sort of invisible hand, as Adam Smith (1993) long ago argued when competition among small producers was replacing feudalism. These assumptions are particularly problematic in health care, which cannot be a market like any other, for several reasons. It is often a matter of life and death, and is dominated by natural monopolies such as regulated professions. It confronts tremendous difficulties in quantifying medical care, much less social care. It is characterized by asymmetrical information, with providers typically knowing much more about treatment possibilities than do the patients and residents they treat. The sector has to be managed and carefully controlled. When governments continue to own and deliver services, these services are increasingly required to adopt for-profit managerial strategies, based on the assumption that the old notion of public service is neither efficient nor responsive, and that for-profit organizations are both. Meanwhile, regulations, paid work, and government subsidies are frequently reduced to a minimum, shifting responsibility to corporations, families, volunteers, and individuals, based on the assumption that they will act appropriately.

In general, none of the assumptions on which privatization is based are supported by the evidence. This is not to say that there are no good care homes owned or operated by for-profit organizations or that all non-profit homes are ideal. Nor is it to say that all regulations are useful or government services non-bureaucratic. And it is not it to say that only governments rather than corporations, families, volunteers, and individuals should take any responsibility for appropriate care. However, there *is* compelling evidence that non-profit delivery and management tends to be better because it provides more democratic and accountable control, more protections for both residents and workers, and more possibilities for developing choices, as well as better care. Private corporations, in contrast, are difficult to monitor let alone control, especially when they operate internationally.

Our research, as we make clear in Chapter 13, indicates that there are promising practices offering alternatives to for-profit ownership and managerial practices, to detailed auditing and regulation, and to shifting responsibilities. Norway has demonstrated that for-profit ownership and delivery can be reversed through popular organizing, for example. And all countries in our study provide examples of ways to create the conditions that allow residents, workers, families, volunteers, and managers to have choices, to be treated with dignity and respect and to even experience joy.

Notes

1 According to the United Nations *Universal Declaration of Human Rights* (1948: Article 25a), "Everyone has the right to a standard of living adequate for the health and well-being of himself and of his family, including food, clothing, housing and medical care and necessary social services, and the right to security in the event of unemployment, sickness, disability, widowhood, old age or other lack of livelihood in circumstances beyond his control."
2 "Invisible Women: Gender and the Shifting Division of Labour in Long-term Residential Care," Tamara Daly, Principal Investigator. Funded by Canadian Institutes of Health Research (CIHR) – Institute of Gender and Health (2012–2014).

References

Ågotnes, G., Jacobsen, F. F., Harrington, C., & Petersen, K. A. (2016). A critical review of research on hospitalization from nursing homes; What is missing? *Ageing International*, *41*(1), 3–16.
Armstrong, P. (1997). The welfare state as history. In R. Blake, P. Brydon & J. F. Strain (Eds.), *The welfare state in Canada* (pp. 52–73). Concord, ON: Irwin.
Armstrong, P. (2013). Puzzling skills: Feminist political economy approaches. *Canadian Review of Sociology/Revue canadienne de sociologie*, *50*(3), 256–283.
Armstrong, P. & Armstrong, H. (2005). Public and private: Implications for care work. *Sociological Review*, *53*(s2) (December), 169–187.
Armstrong, P., Armstrong, H., & Scott-Dixon, K. (2008). *Critical to care: The invisible women in health services*. Toronto, ON: University of Toronto Press.
Armstrong P., Banerjee A., Szebeheky M., Armstrong H., Daly T., & Lafrance, S. (2009). *They deserve better: The long-term care experience in Canada and Scandinavia*. Ottawa, ON: Canadian Centre for Policy Alternatives.
Armstrong, P., & Day, S. (2017). *Wash, wear, and care: Clothing and laundry in long-term residential care*. Montreal, QC: McGill-Queen's University Press.
Auditor General. (2009). Report of the Auditor General. Chapter 5. https://www.gnb.ca/oag-bvg/2009v3/chap5e.pdf
Baines, D. (2004). Caring for nothing: Work organization and unwaged labour in social services. *Work, Employment and Society*, *18*(2), 267–295.
Baines, D., & van den Broek, D. (2017). Coercive care: Control and coercion in the restructured care workplace. *The British Journal of Social Work*, *47*(1), 125–142.
Bercovitz, K. L. (1998). Canada's active living policy: A critical analysis. *Health Promotion International*, *13*(4), 319–328.
Boyle, T. (2018) Axe for-profit nursing homes, Wettlaufer inquiry told. *Toronto Star*, September 18, A2.
Braedley, S., Owusu, P., Przednowek, A., & Armstrong, P. (2017). We're told, "suck it up": Long-term care workers' psychological health and safety. *Ageing International*, 1–19.

Bourbonniere, M., Feng, Z., Intrator, O., Angelelli, J., Mor, V., & Zinn, J. S. (2006). The use of contract licensed nursing staff in US nursing homes. *Medical Care Research and Review*, *63*(1), 88–109.

Brassolotto, J., Daly, T., Armstrong, P., & Naidoo, V. (2017). Experiences of moral distress by privately hired companions in Ontario's long-term care facilities. *Quality in Ageing and Older Adults*, *18*(1), 58–68.

Buchanan, D. (2011, June). The not-for-profit contribution and issues from the provider perspective. In *Reimagining Long-Term Residential Care Annual Meeting, Toronto* (Vol. 2).

Chase, S. (2016). Chinese company Anbang buys stake in B.C.-based retirement home chain. *The Globe and Mail*. November 28.

Choiniere, J. A., Doupe, M., Goldmann, M., Harrington, C., Jacobsen, F. F., Lloyd, L., Rootham, M. & Szebehely, M. (2016). Mapping nursing home inspections & audits in six countries. *Ageing International*, *41*(1), 40–61.

Cohen, M. G., & Cohen, M. (2004). *A return to wage discrimination: Pay equity losses through the privatization of health care*. Vancouver, BC: Canadian Centre for Policy Alternatives.

Competitions and Markets Authority. (2016). CMA launches review of UK care and nursing homes. Press release. December 2. https://www.gov.uk/government/news/cma-launches-review-of-uk-care-and-nursing-homes

Daly, T. (2015). Dancing the two-step in Ontario's long-term care sector: Deterrence regulation = consolidation. *Studies in Political Economy*, *95*(1), 29–58.

Daly, T., Armstrong, P., & Lowndes, R. (2015). Liminality in Ontario's long-term care facilities: Private companions' care work in the space "betwixt and between." *Competition & Change*, *19*(3), 246–263.

Day, S. (2014). *Making it work: A study of the decision-making processes of personal support workers in long-term residential care*. PhD dissertation, York University, Toronto.

Drury, J. (2017). Oswestry care home threat: Hopes of rescue deal fading. *Shropshire Star*. https://www.shropshirestar.com/news/health/2017/12/09/oswestry-care-home-threat-hopes-of-rescue-deal-fading/

Estes, C. L. (1979) *The aging enterprise* San Francisco, CA: Boyd and Fraser.

Estes, C. L. Biggs, S. & Phillipson, C. (2003) *Social theory, social policy and aging*. Berkshire, England: Open University Press.

Extendicare Management and Consulting Services. (2017). http://extendicareassist.ca/services.html

Geraedts, M., Harrington, C., Schumacher, D., & Kraska, R. (2016). Trade-off between quality, price, and profit orientation in Germany's nursing homes. *Ageing International*, *41*(1), 89–98.

Ginsburg, H. L., & Rosenthal, M. G. (2006). The ups and downs of the Swedish welfare state: General trends, benefits, and caregiving. *New Politics*, *11*(1), 70.

Gleckman, H. (2010). *Long-term care financing reform: Lessons from the US and abroad*. Washington, DC: Commonwealth Fund.

Goldmeier, H. (2015). Nursing home care industry is a solid investment. https://seekingalpha.com/article/3220236-nursing-home-care-industry-is-a-solid-investment

Gray, G. C. (2009). The responsibilization strategy of health and safety: Neo-liberalism and the reconfiguration of individual responsibility for risk. *The British Journal of Criminology*, *49*(3), 326–342.

Harrington, C., Armstrong, H., Halladay, M., Havig, A. K., Jacobsen, F. F., MacDonald, M., Panos, J., Pearsall, K., Pollock, A., & Ross, L. (2016). Comparison of nursing home financial transparency and accountability in four locations. *Ageing International, 41*(1), 17–39.

Harrington, C., Hauser, C., Olney, B., & Rosenau, P. V. (2011). Ownership, financing, and management strategies of the ten largest for-profit nursing home chains in the United States. *International Journal of Health Services, 41*(4), 725–746.

Harrington, C., Jacobsen, F. F., Panos, J., Pollock, A., Sutaria, S., & Szebehely, M. (2017). Marketization in long-term care: A cross-country comparison of large for-profit nursing home chains. *Health Services Insights, 10*, 1–23.

Laxer, K. (2015). Who counts in health care? Gender, power, and aging populations. In P. Armstrong & A. Pederson (Eds.), *Women's health: Intersections of policy, research, and practice*. (pp. 215–237) Toronto, ON: Women's Press.

Lloyd, L., Banerjee, A., Harrington, C. & Jacobsen, F. F., & Szebehely, M. (2014). It is a scandal! Comparing the causes and consequences of nursing home media scandals in five countries. *International Journal of Sociology and Social Policy, 34*(1/2), 2–18.

Longhurst, A. (2017). *Privatization and declining access to BC seniors' care*. Vancouver, BC: Canadian Centre for Policy Alternatives.

Macarov, D. (2003). *What the market does to people: Privatization, globalization and poverty*. London: Zed Books.

MacDonald, M. (2014). Cost of facility-based long-term care: Variations across provinces/territories and implications. Contract 4500309720 with Health Canada.

MacDonald, M. (2015). Regulating individual charges for long-term residential care in Canada. *Studies in Political Economy, 95*(1), 83–114.

Mayer, G. (2004). *Union membership trends in the United States*. Washington, DC: Congressional Research Service.

McGregor, M. J., & Ronald, L. A. (2011). *Residential long-term care for Canadian seniors: Nonprofit, for-profit or does it matter?* Montreal, QC: Institute for Research on Public Policy.

McGregor, M. J., Cohen, M., Stocks-Rankin, C. R., Cox, M. B., Salomons, K., McGrail, K. M., & Schulzer, M. (2011). Complaints in for-profit, non-profit and public nursing homes in two Canadian provinces. *Open Medicine, 5*(4), e183.

Muir, T. (2017). Measuring social protection for long-term care. OECD Health Working Papers, No. 93. Paris: OECD Publishing. http://dx.doi.org/10.1787/a411500a-en

OECD (Organization for Economic Cooperation and Development). (2011). *Help wanted? Providing and paying for long-term care*. Paris: OECD.

OECD (Organization for Economic Cooperation and Development). (2017). Health at a glance. http://www.keepeek.com/Digital-Asset-Management/oecd/social-issues-migration-health/health-at-a-glance-2017_health_glance-2017-en#.Wk-0wnkViUk#page209

Osborne, D., & Gaebler, T. (1992). *Reinventing government: How the entrepreneurial spirit is transforming the public sector*. Reading, MA: Addison-Wesley.

Peterson, M. (1997). Introduction to health care in the next century. *Journal of Health Politics, Policy and the Law, 22*(2), 291–313.

Power, M. (2003). Evaluating the audit explosion. *Law & Policy, 25*(3), 185–202.

Prada, G. (2011). *Innovation procurement in health care: A compelling opportunity for Canada*. Conference Board of Canada.

Sainsbury, D. (Ed.). (1999). *Gender and welfare state regimes*. Oxford, UK: Oxford University Press.

Smith, A. (1993/1776). *An inquiry into the nature and causes of the wealth of nations.* Oxford, UK: Oxford University Press.

Statistics Canada. (2012). Residential long-term care financial data tables. Statistics Canada, 2012. http://statcan.gc.ca

Statistics Canada. (2018). Data tables, 2016 Census. http://www12.statcan.gc.ca/census-recensement/2016/dp-pd/dt-td/Rp-eng.cfm?LANG=E&APATH=3&DETAIL=0&DIM=0&FL=A&FREE=0&GC=0&GI

Tanuseputro, P., Chalifoux, M., Bennett, C., Gruneir, A., Bronskill, A. E., Walker, P., & Manuel, D. (2015). Hospitalization and mortality rates in long-term care facilities: Does for-profit status matter? *Journal of the American Medical Directors Association, 16*(10), 874–883.

Toronto Central CCAC. (2017). Choosing a long-term care home.http://healthcareathome.ca/torontocentral/en/care/Documents/October-%20EN.pdf

United Nations. Universal Declaration on Human Rights. (1948). New York, NY: United Nations. http://www.un.org/en/universal-declaration-human-rights/index.html

Wahl, A. (2011). *The rise and fall of the welfare state.* London: Pluto Press.

Yalnizyan, A. (1994). Securing society: Creating Canadian social policy. In A. Yalnizyan, T. R. Ide, & A. J. Cordell (Eds.), *Shifting time: Social policy and the future of work* (pp. 17–71). Toronto, ON: Between the Lines.

Chapter 2

The Growth of the For-Profit Nursing Home Sector in Norway and Sweden
Driving Forces and Resistance

Gudmund Ågotnes, Frode F. Jacobsen, and Marta Szebehely

Introduction

Norway and Sweden have developed differently with regards to the expansion of for-profit actors in the nursing home sector. While a relatively large proportion of Swedish nursing homes have been contracted out to for-profit companies since the 1990s, the development has been slower and somewhat different in Norway. In this chapter, we ask why.

The Nordic countries are all commonly labelled as representatives of a Nordic or Scandinavian social democratic welfare regime in which citizens are secured universal access to welfare services such as childcare, disability services, and eldercare. Historically, a crucial aspect of this "service universalism" (Vabø & Szebehely, 2012) is that the services are not only publicly funded but publicly provided. However, in recent decades the provision of various forms of what has traditionally been considered part of welfare services, including schools, childcare, psychiatric care, disability services, and care for older people have been moved from the public to the private, for-profit sector.

This relatively recent change has occurred gradually and to varying degrees within different sub-sectors, but can still be considered a rather drastic change from the late 1980s and early 1990s when there were virtually no commercial providers, to the present where there is a substantial contribution from for-profit providers. While there are differences between the two countries (e.g., that publicly funded schools are allowed to make profit in Sweden), the overall development towards private provision is similar. These gradual processes have been accompanied by public awareness and debate, indicating an ideological "battle" between different stakeholders.

However, nursing homes in Norway seem to be somewhat of an anomaly (see Harrington & Jacobsen, this volume). While for-profit ownership was statistically insignificant in both countries in the early 1990s, for-profit ownership, primarily in the form of large, corporate chains, has risen to approximately 18 percent in Sweden and 6.2 percent in Norway. A gradual and slow increase in for-profit ownership in Norway seems to have stopped recently, suggesting that Norway will not reach the level of for-profit ownership in Sweden, at least not in the near future. Sweden, meanwhile, has been described as having undergone the largest change of the Scandinavian countries, from having the highest share of public welfare services to having the highest for-profit share (Sivesind, 2017). In brief, Norway may be considered as a sort of last outpost for continued public, institutional eldercare, not following trends either in Sweden or elsewhere in Europe.

In this chapter, we present a historical description of the development of privatization of nursing homes in Sweden and Norway, followed by a discussion of how the later developments can be explained.

"Privatization"?

The term "private nursing home" is used in different ways, sometimes referring to all private providers, including non-profit providers, sometimes exclusively to for-profit providers. In this chapter, we focus on the latter – the provision of nursing home care by companies seeking to make a profit. Researchers have highlighted quality differences between private for-profit and public-private non-profit nursing homes, arguing that for-profit nursing homes generally exhibit a lower quality of care (e.g., Harrington & Jacobsen, this volume). At the same time, privatization is not necessarily a question of either/or; it contains nuances, in a "complex interaction with public welfare" (Christensen, 2012). The process of privatization, therefore, does not necessarily follow a clear path from public to private, in which the entirety of services switches from one ownership type to the next. Also, the type of privatization might differ between and within countries, for instance in the form of: (a) the complete transfer of responsibility for delivering care from the public to the private sector (financing as well as provision); (b) contracting out of the care responsibilities for an institution (whereby a public administrative body leases contracts to private providers through arrangements such as bidding with specific timeframes); or (c) contracting out smaller parts of nursing home services, such as food or laundry.

In this chapter, we focus on (b): the contracting out of single nursing home institutions operated by and on behalf of a public system. The process in which a private for-profit company retains control of the operations of a nursing home can be described as relatively similar in Norway and Sweden: agents, for-profit, non-profit, or public, compete for contracts within a municipality. Generally, it is perceived that the tendering process is about "quality for the lowest amount of cost." However, cost rather than quality seems more significant in most cases, even if quality competition at a fixed price (in which case the municipalities set the price and the providers compete by arguing for best possible quality at that price) has recently become common in Sweden (Winblad, Blomqvist, & Karlson, 2017; Stolt, Blomqvist, & Winblad, 2011). The competition is in most cases over the operations of a nursing home, while ownership over the physical structure (buildings and other material assets) remains municipal (Stolt et al., 2011). The physical structure is also changing in the case of Sweden, where large corporations increasingly are building their own facilities and offer places (beds) to municipalities rather than compete for a contract in publicly owned nursing homes (Szebehely & Meagher, 2018). Similar developments have not (yet) reached Norway; perhaps, as we shall see, because of legislation and political and popular affinities towards the non-profit sector.

While ownership of nursing home provision varies between non-profit, for-profit, and public, as in most comparative countries the structure of financing remains more or less universal, regardless of provider ownership. The revenue providers receive is mainly public funding; the residents pay only a small fraction of the actual costs. Virtually all profit generated by for-profit nursing homes originates, therefore, from public funding. As such, the private, for-profit nursing home sector can be regarded as an integrated part of the public welfare system and not an alternative to it.

Historical Development of Privatization in Eldercare

While "privatization" in the form of contracting out nursing home provision after competitive tendering for a fixed period of time is a relatively new phenomenon in Scandinavia, both countries have had other forms of private eldercare provision, preceding even the public welfare model the countries are now renowned for. Private, non-profit providers, often in the form of religious and other mission-driven organizations, preceded the expansion of publicly run nursing homes (see also Chapter 8 by Jacobsen & Ågotnes, this volume). Private non-profit nursing home providers' share of homes has remained stable and comparatively low at 2.6 percent in Sweden (Winblad et al., 2017) and 5 percent in Norway (Statistics Norway, 2017).

The gradual move towards for-profit providers of nursing homes can be traced back to the 1980s. In the wake of a widespread financial recession, both Norway and Sweden implemented large-scale reforms in which the duties and responsibilities for providing a wide range of welfare services were moved from the state or regional level to the local/municipal level of governance. The reforms also included a reformatting of the financial structure of nursing homes. Now public financing is in the form of block grants provided to municipalities, providing them with complete autonomy in how to prioritize the funding. Nursing homes, then, became a matter of commitment for the municipalities, with prioritization in one area/sector affecting other areas/sectors. Simultaneously, the number of elderly residents increased in both countries, while the number of nursing home beds remained stagnant (Vabø & Szebehely, 2012).

In Sweden, these decentralization reforms coincided with political discussions concerning the reformatting of welfare services, led by the Social

Democratic government. Initiatives to promote competition within the welfare services were initiated (Meagher & Szebehely, 2013), leading, eventually, to the passing of a new Local Government Act by a Social Democratic government in 1991. The legislation allows private for-profit as well as non-profit agents to operate nursing homes through tendering processes initiated at the will of autonomous municipalities. At this time, there were no for-profit operators of eldercare in Sweden, but when some municipalities (following the new Act) initiated a tendering process, large corporations soon got a foothold in the Swedish nursing home sector. They had the capacity to manage the bidding procedure, partly because of economies of scale and partly because they had the economic ability to underbid to gain access to the market, paving the way for future growth. Later on, when the municipalities moved from competition purely based on price towards including quality measures, large actors continued to be favored, as they have resources to do the extensive paperwork in the bidding process (it has been estimated that the work involved in writing a bid corresponds to SEK 200,000 [about US$22,000]) (Szebehely, 2014).

Norway has to some degree followed the recent legislative changes seen in Sweden. An interesting difference is to be found in legislation and practices favoring private non-profit care providers. In 2006, legislation concerning long-term contracts with non-profit providers was established, in part to secure stability in services and in part to provide non-profits with a competition advantage compared to for-profits (Sivesind, 2017), although recent policy changes from the EU might alter such arrangements in the future (Segaard & Saglie, 2017). The legislation allowed non-profit organizations to receive contracts for the provision of nursing home care without timeframes, in contrast to contracts offered to for-profit providers. Similar to in Sweden, however, a purchaser-provider model – in which the role of the municipalities is split between them and potentially private third-party providers – has been implemented in Norway, albeit somewhat later (Harrington et al., 2017), and not to the same extent. The purchaser–provider model adopted in Norway has led to limited private for-profit provision, despite political pressure, especially from right-wing parties (Vabø & Szebehely, 2012) after the first case of competitive tendering of nursing homes in 1997. A few cities and their neighboring municipalities, particularly larger cities like Oslo, Bergen, Stavanger, and Trondheim, are the exception to the rule. However, after a recent scandal concerning workers' rights in for-profit institutions (Lloyd et al., 2014) and several negative media portrayals of for-profit providers, some contracts have been terminated or not renewed. In Oslo and Bergen, the two largest cities in Norway, this has coincided with a shift in local government, resulting in the termination of contracts with for-profit operators (Harrington et al., 2017). As the contracts are still active in 2018, the relative share of for-profit nursing homes in Norway is expected to fall in the near future. The proportion of private (for-profit and non-profit) operators of nursing homes in Sweden has increased from virtually zero before 1990 (Szebehely & Meagher, 2013) to 20 percent in 2017 (National Board of Health and Welfare, 2018), of which around 18 percent is for-profit and 2 percent to 3 percent is non-profit. In Norway, the proportion has gone from minuscule in the 1990s (statistics are not available) to around 6 percent for-profit and 5 percent non-profit in 2016 (Statistics Norway, 2017).

Privatization of nursing homes in the form of an increase of commercial provision has primarily taken place in the larger cities of both Norway and Sweden. In Sweden, with around 10 million citizens living in 290 municipalities, for-profit nursing homes are the majority in 20 municipalities. All nursing homes are public in almost two-thirds of the Swedish municipalities, especially in more sparsely populated areas. For-profit nursing homes are "clustered" around the capital Stockholm, particularly in municipalities characterized by high levels of urbanization, high incomes, and center-right local governments (Szebehely & Trydegård, 2018; Winblad et al., 2017).

Norway has 5.2 million inhabitants living in 428 municipalities. Each municipality is on average far smaller than in Sweden, although an ongoing reform will see the number of municipalities reduced to 387 in the near future. In Norway only a few municipalities have used the process of competitive tendering of nursing homes. Between 1997 and 2012 commercial companies won 38 of 47 tendering processes in Norway, in 15 different municipalities; none were won by non-profit providers (Herning, 2012; Szebehely & Meagher, 2013: 252). As in Sweden, commercial companies have primarily won the tendering processes in metropolitan areas, though, in contrast to Sweden, no municipality has a majority of for-profit NHs.

Among the private for-profit providers in both Sweden and Norway, multinational companies have been dominant. In Norway, four large international chains represent around 70 percent of all nursing home beds run by for-profit providers, or 4.8 percent of the entire sector. In Sweden, the five largest international chains control 70 percent of the private market, or 13.5 percent of the total sector. In both countries, these corporations are providing a variety of welfare services such as health care, disability services, addiction treatment, and child welfare, and are operating across national borders – three of the largest corporations in Sweden are among the four largest in Norway (Harrington et al., 2017).

Understanding the Differences Between Norway and Sweden

The historical development should be seen in relation to what has been described as a global wave of New Public Management, inspired by the political milieu, particularly in the US and the UK, from the 1980s onwards (see also Chapter 1 by Armstrong and Armstrong and Chapter 6 by Longhurst, Ponder, and McGregor, this volume). This political discourse, in which "care" is altered from a public responsibility to a commodity (Brennan et al., 2012), greatly affected the public sector in Sweden in the 1990s, and Norway some years later (Vabø & Szebehely, 2012). The impact was particularly strong in Sweden, but has met more resistance in Norway (Meagher & Szebehely, 2013).

With this backdrop, Sweden and Norway moved from more or less completely public and non-profit to partially for-profit private provision of eldercare within a publicly financed system. An unintended yet significant consequence of this move is de-universalization, affecting both how care is provided and equity among recipients. In short, care is not offered in the same way to all potential recipients; it is not based on an ideal of equal access (Szebehely & Meagher, 2018). As such, the privatization of welfare services is related to an important topic addressed elsewhere in this book: inequality in access to services. Here we ask why such a process of de-universalization has occurred differently in two seemingly similar countries. It has been argued that the process of marketization is influenced by contextual features and histories (Brennan et al., 2012), but how? We suggest four interrelated factors: the impact of the financial crisis, the "positioning" of political parties, the influence of unions and other interest groups, and finally, differences in the size and role of municipalities in the two countries, in particular how municipal autonomy is carried out in practice.

The Role of the Financial Crisis

Sweden was impacted by the financial recession in the early 1990s to a far greater extent than Norway (Szebehely & Meagher, 2018). Spending on the public sector, including eldercare, became an area of cost reduction in Sweden during this period, both at a national and at a municipal level. At the municipal level, local government officials and politicians saw cost-saving through competitive tendering of the various welfare services as promising. The recession impacted Norway later and to a much less significant extent (Gautun & Grødem, 2015; Szebehely & Meagher, 2018), particularly because of the relatively stable revenue provided by the dominant oil and gas industry. As a result, the overall financial situation (nationally and in the municipalities) and the political milieu surrounding it did not motivate local Norwegian politicians to the same degree as in Sweden.

The Role of Political Parties

Throughout and following the financial crisis, the two countries differed in the extent to which political parties related to the question of for-profit providers in the welfare sector, leading, we argue, to different overall political discourses.

In Sweden, center-right parties have been proponents of marketization and welcoming to for-profit actors in welfare services. The Social Democrats have been open to competition, choice, and New Public Management in general, and clearly ambivalent about the role of for-profit actors in the welfare sector (Meagher & Szebehely, 2019). In Norway, by contrast, during and after the financial crisis, the traditional left-right political axes remained more loyal to their respective political stances: right-wing parties in favor of increased privatization and the left supporting a continuous, generous public welfare system. The traditional center parties in Norway (particularly the Centre Party, whose main constituency is in rural areas and smaller municipalities, but also the Christian Democrats) have, in contrast to their Swedish sister parties, not favored for-profit actors in eldercare services. Interestingly, this ambivalence from the Norwegian political center mirrors, perhaps, that of the Social Democrats in Sweden, while the Social Democrats in Norway have remained opposed to increased privatization.

Thus, the overall political milieu in Norway can be described as being less favorable to privatization in general. This has led to concrete national legislation directly influencing (perhaps not intentionally) the stagnation of for-profit nursing homes. In Norway, legislation was passed favoring non-profit nursing homes (and other non-profit welfare providers) by the red-green coalition government in the early 2000s. The legislation allowed for open-ended contracts for non-profit but not for for-profit homes. Today, between 80 percent and 90 percent of non-profit nursing homes have long-term framework agreements (Sivesind, 2017). In Sweden, no such legislation has been implemented; instead, a very strict competition legislation demands competitive tendering of all non-public nursing homes, which, as we have seen, indirectly favors larger, for-profit corporations, as the model implies large administrative costs to "enter the market," and favors economy of scale.

The Role of Unions and Other Interest Groups

The "market" of welfare services, as seen from the perspective of for-profit providers, is both potentially rewarding in terms of profit (Harrington et al., 2016; Harrington et al., 2017) and risky at the same time. Political leadership can and does change, altering the conditions of the market. Particularly in Scandinavia, this is a significant factor for potential investors, as governance over the provision of eldercare is placed at a municipal level. The conditions under which for-profit providers operate can change relatively quickly and can be "fragmented" within even small geographical areas; one municipality might have a conservative local government while the neighboring municipality has a social democratic government. Such market mechanisms need "tending" from for-profit interest groups (Svallfors & Tyllström, 2018). In such a political environment, interest groups favoring or opposing for-profit privatization can influence its growth and/or stagnation.

Labor unions have had an important historical role in both countries, particularly through strong labor movements supported by traditionally strong social democratic parties. As such, one would assume that the process of marketization towards for-profit operators of welfare services would meet resistance at a political level. In Sweden, the labor unions have lost political capital since the 1980s while the employers' interest organizations have remained strong and powerful (Svallfors & Tyllström, 2018). Still, from an international perspective, Swedish labor unions remain large and influential. In Norway, there are close ties between the social democratic party, Arbeiderpartiet, which has maintained a relatively stable and large voter base, and the labor unions (Kjeldstadli & Helle, 2016). Also, the largest labor unions for employees at nursing homes, Fagforbundet and Sykepleierforbundet, have remained strong, both in actual numbers and in political influence.

Overall, labor unions in the two countries are similar, but with the significant difference that Swedish labor unions have been more open to for-profit operators than Norwegian unions. Particularly the Swedish public sector union, Kommunal, differs from its Norwegian counterpart, Fagforbundet. Kommunal was ambivalent to for-profit provision of the welfare services during the periods of fiscal austerity in the 1980s and 1990s (Ekdahl, 2010), and only recently started to oppose profits in the welfare services (Meagher & Szebehely, 2019). Conversely, the Norwegian union of care workers, Fagforbundet, has consistently opposed any form of privatization of the traditional publicly operated welfare services, particularly child- and eldercare (Vabø & Szebehely, 2012). Fagforbundet has also been a driving force behind the interest group "For the Welfare State" ("For Velferdsstaten"), a non-profit NGO funded by a number of unions that addresses issues across the various welfare services and has more than one million members. The organization has served as an influential lobby group against for-profit ownership of nursing homes and other welfare services. In Sweden, several smaller interest groups with a similar agenda to that of "For the Welfare State" are active, but have less union support and less success.

Conversely, interest organizations arguing for increased privatization have been successful in influencing the political milieu in Sweden, even within the Social Democratic party. After eight years in opposition, the Swedish Social Democrats came to power in 2014 and formed a minority government. The issue of profit and privatization was a heated topic in the election campaign and soon after the election the government established a commission to propose regulations limiting (but not forbidding) profit-making in welfare services and to suggest measures to improve the conditions for non-profit actors. The commission and its proposals have been forcefully attacked by the welfare service corporations and their business organizations, and the proposals did not lead to political action, partly as a result of these lobbying activities and partly because of the parliamentary situation in Sweden (Svallfors & Tyllström, 2018; Meagher & Szebehely, 2019). As such, interest and lobby groups arguing for the continued expansion of competition within the municipal health and care sector seem to have been more effectual in influencing this political landscape in Sweden than in Norway. This influence is perhaps amplified by more limited lobbying against privatization in Sweden, and in Norway an opposition that has remained loud and effective, and that has close ties to political parties and unions.

Popular opinion, as seen for instance through voter surveys, does not, however, seem to mirror that of the political elite or of lobby groups, particularly in Sweden. Voters in both countries express a clear disagreement with the notion of "profit for welfare providers." Between 60 percent and 80 percent (depending on the survey) of voters in Sweden express such a disagreement (Svallfors & Tyllström, 2018; Nilsson, 2017), signaling a definitive "distance" from the opinions of the political majority, particularly at the political center and right in Sweden (of which between 50% and 60% of voters oppose for-profits) (Nilsson 2016, 2017). Similarly, in 2017, 68 percent of voters in Norway completely or partially agreed that profit should be banned in the welfare services (www.fagforbundet.no). An interesting aspect of the Swedish surveys (more nuanced and detailed than the equivalents in Norway) lies in how voters express support for the notion of "freedom of choice" for "users" of the welfare services. Almost three quarters of Swedish voters express support for choice regarding provider of eldercare (Nilsson, 2017). It would appear that while support for freedom of choice remains significant in Sweden, for-profit providers are not considered an acceptable choice even by those who most favor "freedom of choice" (Nilsson, 2016, 2017; Svallfors & Tyllström, 2018).

In summary, the notion of market competition as a solution to the financial situation got a foothold in Sweden comparatively early (Szebehely & Meagher, 2018). The idea of competition as a mechanism for growth became a leading political discourse in Sweden *across* traditional political alliances (Szebehely, 2014), influenced by the wealthy and influential employers' interest organizations, and was not opposed by labor unions or other interest groups to the same extent as in Norway. Consequently, the financial crisis, and this political environment, led many local governments in Sweden to experiment with alternative forms of eldercare (Stolt et al., 2011), experiments that did not occur, at least not to the same extent, in Norway.

Municipalities in Sweden and Norway: Same, Same, But Different?

An essential point not thoroughly discussed so far is that the growth of commercial companies operating nursing homes has been limited by municipalities in Norway, and allowed or encouraged by Swedish municipalities. Studies tend to overlook this aspect, we argue, focusing more or less exclusively on the national context (Feltenius, 2017). It is tempting to hypothesize that the difference in nursing home provision between the countries is connected to more than the structural conditions to which municipalities relate. Perhaps the difference is more connected to the different form of Norwegian and Swedish municipalities.

Despite national legislation and oversight, the actual responsibility for the operation of nursing homes is placed at a municipal level in both Norway and Sweden. Consequently, there is considerable internal variation in both countries regarding coverage of, spending on, and ownership of nursing homes. In both countries, rural areas and/or smaller municipalities tend to have public nursing homes only, and in both countries, privatization has primarily occurred in metropolitan areas with conservative political majorities. Interestingly, neighboring municipalities tend to "follow suit," regardless of size or of political leadership, leading to a "geographical contagion," or a clustering of privatization (Stolt & Winblad, 2009) in areas surrounding larger cities. In general, the internal variation seen in Norway seems to mirror that of Sweden, although the trends in developments occur later and not to the same extent in Norway. "Geographical contagion," for instance, has occurred to some degree in eastern Norway, but not to the same extent as in the Stockholm area. Larger municipalities and metropolitan areas are, in other words, "attractive" to for-profit corporations and investment: they offer substantial potential for increased revenue in a market previously closed to them. If we transfer the previous argument about "politics matter" to a municipal level of governance, we find more correspondences than differences. Municipalities in both countries that have a conservative majority seem to be far more inclined to resort to competitive tendering and to proclaim for-profit providers as "winners." Rural areas in both Norway and Sweden – also those with a center, right, or center-right government – seem to be the exception.

However, a significant disparity for understanding the differences in the development of nursing homes, is, we argue, to be found in the rather prosaic fact that Norwegian municipalities are, on average, smaller and less urbanized than Swedish municipalities, thus representing a less promising market. There are more rural municipalities in Norway, which, as mentioned, tend to favor public welfare services. And the non-profit sector, having a traditionally important role in rural areas, has been and remains more significant in Norway than in Sweden (Sivesind, 2017).

Perhaps an answer to the question initially raised is, in part, to be found here; in the types and characteristics of the municipalities themselves. As seen, municipalities in Norway and Sweden have essentially the same or similar *formal* independence and maneuverability in relating to "the state"; they can both be described as autonomous regarding decisions concerning care provision. At the same time, they relate to these issues somewhat differently. Can Norwegian and Swedish municipalities be described as somewhat different in terms of their "distance" from dominant discourses as presented by the political elite and interest groups arguing for "choice" and "open markets" in their respective countries and in Europe in general?

Understanding Differences *and* Similarities

We do not propose a definitive answer to this difficult question, but suggest that it is an area in need of further analysis. Elsewhere, Norwegian municipalities have been described as being characterized by a distinct "culture of local democracy," in which the role of the local politician is still to protect the local constituency from "the outside," including the state (Vike, 2004). This role is maintained and perhaps even amplified by increased differences between local and central levels of governance. Connected to the historical significance of self-governance and autonomy at the municipal level of governance, which is similar in both Norway and Sweden, such a characteristic has taken on a new form, as more and more responsibility and tasks are delegated from the state to the municipality (Vike, 2004), and the economic situation for most municipalities is increasingly strained. This situation, we suggest, is perhaps more entrenched in the average, small, rural, Norwegian municipality, than in its larger Swedish counterpart.

On the other hand, the characteristics of Norwegian municipalities can be seen as only moderately different from those of Sweden. Norwegian and Swedish municipalities can be said to share more similarities than differences regarding provision of welfare services, an argument proposed by Feltenius (2017), who argues that they represent a welfare model adapted to "modern times," primarily characterized by regulations from the European Union.

This argument is contrasted to that of Sivesind (2017), who maintains that increasing differences between the Scandinavian countries regarding the mix of welfare providers (public, for-profit, non-profit), among other factors, question the very concept of a Nordic Welfare Model, concluding that the Scandinavian countries, rather, are moving towards Europe.

A Nordic Welfare Model notwithstanding, Sweden and Norway have developed somewhat differently regarding for-profit providers of nursing home care in recent decades, a development we believe is connected both to local and structural contextual features; legislation (favoring non-profits and for-profits differently); the effect of the financial recession; the positioning of political parties; the role and positioning of unions; the force of other interest groups, particularly those arguing for the right to make profits in welfare services; and, finally, to the characteristics of municipalities and local governance.

References

Brennan, D., Cass, B., Himmelweit, S., & Szebehely, M. (2012). The marketisation of care: Rationales and consequences in Nordic and liberal care regimes. *Journal of European Social Policy, 22*(4), 377–391. DOI:10.1177/0958928712449772

Christensen, K. (2012). Towards a mixed economy of long-term care in Norway? *Critical Social Policy, 32*(4), 577–596.

Ekdahl, L. (2010). *Välfärdssamhällets spegel: kommunal 1960–2010.* Stockholm: Premiss

Feltenius, D. (2017). Towards a more diversified supply of welfare services? Marketisation and the local governing of nursing homes in Scandinavian countries. In K. H. Sivesind & J. Saglie (Eds.), *Promoting active citizenship markets and choice in Scandinavian welfare* (pp. 117–156). Palgrave Macmillan. DOI:10.1007/978-3-319-55381-8

Gautun, H. and Grødem, A. S. (2015). Prioritizing care services: Do the oldest users lose out? *International Journal of Social Welfare, 24*(1), 73–80.

Harrington, C., Armstrong, H., & Halladay, M., et al. (2016). Comparison of nursing home financial transparency and accountability in four locations. *Ageing International, 41*(1), 17–39. https://doi.org/10.1007/s12126-015-9233-3

Harrington C., Jacobsen F. F., Panos J., Pollock A., Sutaria S., & Szebehely, M. (2017). Marketization in long-term care: A cross-country comparison of large for-profit nursing home chains. *Health Services Insights.* DOI:10.1177/1178632917710533

Herning, L. (2012). *Konkurranseutsatte sykehjem i Norge.* Notat. Oslo: For velferdsstaten.

Kjeldstadli, K. & Helle, I. (2016). Social democracy in Norway. In I. Schmidt (Ed.), *The three worlds of social democracy: A global view* (pp. 46–67). London: Pluto Press.

Lloyd, L., Banerjee A., Harrington C., Jacobsen F. F., & Szebehely, M. (2014). It is a scandal! Comparing the causes and consequences of nursing home media scandals in five countries. *International Journal of Sociology and Social Policy, 34*(1/2), 2–18.

Meagher, G., & Szebehely, M. (2013). *Marketisation in Nordic eldercare: A research report on legislation, oversight, extent and consequences.* Stockholm: Stockholm Studies in Social Work.

Meagher, G., & Szebehely, M. (2019). The politics of profit in Swedish welfare services: Four decades of Social Democratic ambivalence. *Critical Social Policy, 39*(3), 455–476.

National Board of Health and Welfare. (2018). *Statistik om äldre och personer med funktionsnedsättning efter regiform 2017.* https://www.socialstyrelsen.se/globalassets/sharepointdokument/artikelkatalog/statistik/2018-2-3.pdf

Nilsson, L. (2016). Välfärdspolitik och välfärdsopinion i Sverige och Västra Götaland 2015. In A. Bergström & A. Harring (Eds.), *Hållbarhetens horisont. Samhälle Opinion och Medier i Västsverige.* Gothenburg: SOM-institutet, Göteborgs universitet.

Nilsson L. (2017). Väljare och valda om vinster i välfärden. In U. Andersson, J. Ohlsson, H. Oscarsson, & M. Oskarson (Eds.), *Larmar och gör sig till.* Gothenburg: SOM-institutet, Göteborgs universitet.

Segaard, S. B., & Saglie, J. (2017). Education and elderly care in Denmark, Norway and Sweden: National policies and legal frameworks for private providers. In K. H. Sivesind & J. Saglie (Eds.), *Promoting active citizenship markets and choice in Scandinavian welfare* (pp. 75–114). Palgrave Macmillan. DOI:10.1007/978-3-319-55381-8

Sivesind, K. H. (2017). The changing roles of for-profit and nonprofit welfare provision in Norway, Sweden, and Denmark. In K. H. Sivesind & J. Saglie (Eds.), *Promoting active citizenship markets and choice in Scandinavian welfare* (pp. 33–74). London: Palgrave Macmillan. DOI:10.1007/978-3-319-55381-8

Statistics Norway (2017). *Helse- og omsorgsinstitusjonar, etter eigarforhold, statistikkvariabel og år.* https://www.ssb.no/statbank/table/09929/tableViewLayout1/?rxid=aff1c8cb-f3df-4858-b3ca-5a6675673d43.

Stolt, R., Blomqvist, P., & Winblad, U. (2011). Privatization of social services: Quality differences in Swedish elderly care. *Social Science and Medicine, 72*(4), 560–567.

Stolt, R., & Winblad, U. (2009). Mechanisms behind privatization: A case study of private growth in Swedish elderly care. *Social Science & Medicine, 68*(5), 903–911.

Svallfors, S. & Tyllström, A. (2018). Resilient privatization: The puzzling case of for-profit welfare providers in Sweden. *Socio-Economic Review*. February 14. https://doi.org/10.1093/ser/mwy015

Szebehely, M. (2014). Vinstyfte i äldreomsorgen. In J. Björkman, B. Fjæstad, & S. Alexius (Eds.), *Alla dessa marknader* (pp. 129–142). Gothenburg: Makadam förlag.

Szebehely, M. & Meagher, G. (2013). Four Nordic countries – four responses to the international trend of marketisation. In G. Meagher & M. Szebehely (Eds.), *Marketisation in Nordic Eldercare* (pp. 241–288). Stockholm: Stockholm University.

Szebehely, M., & Meagher, G. (2018). Nordic eldercare – weak universalism becoming weaker? *Journal of European Social Policy*, 28(3), 294–308.

Szebehely, M., & Trydegård, G.-B. (2018). Generell välfärd och lokalt självstyre – ett dilemma i den svenska äldreomsorgen? In *Äldreomsorger i Sverige: lokala variationer och generella trender* (pp. 21–40). Lund: Gleerups.

Vabø, M., & Szebehely, M. (2012). A caring state for all older people? In A. Anttonen, L. Häikiö, & K. Stefánsson (Eds.), *Welfare state, universalism and diversity*. Cheltenham: Edward Elgar.

Vike, H. (2004). *Velferd Uten Grenser: Den norske velferdsstaten ved veiskillet*. Oslo: Akribe Forlag.

Winblad, U., Blomqvist, P., and Karlson, A. (2017). Do public nursing home care providers deliver higher quality than private providers? Evidence from Sweden. *BMC Health Services Research*, 17(1), 487. https://doi.org/10.1186/s12913-017-2403-0

www.fagforbundet.no. *7 av 10 nordmenn mener det bør bli vanskeligere å ta ut profitt på velferdstjenester*. http://www.fagforbundet.no/forsida/7-av-10-nordmenn-mener-det-bor-bli-vanskeligere-a-ta-ut-profitt-pa-velferdstjenester/?article_id=144497.

Chapter 3

Privatization of Nursing Homes in the United Kingdom and the United States

Charlene Harrington, Allyson M. Pollock, and Shailen Sutaria

Introduction

The privatization of health and social services includes the delivery of commercialized services through competing private organizations (Meagher & Szebehely, 2013). In the United States (US) health care and long-term care services have historically been delivered by private organizations (both non-profit and for-profit), with only a very small number of long-term care services provided by city and county governments (Kaffenberger, 2000). Even though the US did not adopt a national health insurance program like other industrialized countries, over time various government programs have greatly expanded public funding for all health and long-term care.

In contrast, a national health service developed after World War II provided publicly funded and freely delivered comprehensive, universal health services throughout the United Kingdom (UK) (Pollock, 2005). Social care services, including long-term care, were the responsibility of local government authorities and most were subject to means-testing. In the 1990s, the UK adopted the New Public Management (NPM) approach that introduced new principles, practices, and regulations of competition and contracting into the public sector (Pollock, 2005). Reflected in the implementation of the National Health Service (NHS) and Community Care Act 1990, the NPM approach led to a dramatic increase in the growth of private for-profit long-term care homes and a withdrawal of government from the ownership and direct provision of long-term beds (Harrington & Pollock, 1998). This approach was adopted in spite of the historical and well-documented quality problems in for-profit delivery, limitations on access to care, as well as high costs and lack of public accountability and transparency.

Over the last few decades, many independently owned private nursing homes consolidated through mergers and acquisitions into for-profit chains (two or more homes owned by the same company) owned by large private companies and private equity funds in the US and UK. As a result of a process that began in the 1970s in the US (Banaszak-Holl et al., 2002) and since the 1990s in the UK, for-profit chains are now the dominant organizational form. For-profit chains were promoted as organizations that would improve profitability by economies of scale, standardization of services, brand-name recognition and visibility, and management expertise in competitive environments (Banaszak-Holl et al., 2002; Kitchener & Harrington, 2004). These dramatic changes in the ownership of nursing homes and the delivery of these services have negatively changed the amount, type, and quality of services in both the US and the UK (Ronald et al., 2016; Grabowski et al., 2013; Harrington et al., 2013; Stevenson, Bramson, & Grabowski, 2013).

What is remarkable is how the UK shifted from being a predominately publicly funded and delivered long-term care system from 1948 until the 1980s when it began to shift to a predominantly privately funded and delivered system. The extent of services delivered by for-profit companies and chains in the UK exceeds the delivery in the US and the public funding for services is lower than the funding in the US (Harrington et al., 2017). The UK and US are the industrialized countries that have gone the furthest in the use of privatized long-term care services (Harrington et al., 2017).

This chapter describes the policy changes that led to these developments and compares the nursing home delivery and funding in the UK with that in the US. It is based in part on a larger cross-country study showing the contextual differences and trends in growth of for-profit nursing home chains in Canada, Norway, Sweden, the UK, and the US (Harrington et al., 2017). This study draws on our previous analyses of data and secondary documents from multiple public and private sources as well as from a number of published studies in the two countries.

The Shift from Public to Private Nursing Home Services in the UK

After WWII, the United Kingdom established the National Health Service (NHS), which provided free universal health care to the population through a system of public hospitals and through primary care and community health clinics (Pollock, 2005). Following the creation of the NHS, the 1948 National Assistance Act placed a duty on local government authorities to provide social services, including residential/nursing home care and home care to those in need and allowed means-testing to obtain services (Harrington & Pollock, 1998). The 1972 Local Government Act weakened this statutory duty "to provide" to a "duty to make arrangements," which is legalese for contracting. This allowed local authorities to begin withdrawing from providing services and instead commission services from the private sector. Local authorities were reluctant to do this so it was not until the 1980s, when government introduced financial drivers and incentives that limited capital investment and upgrades of publicly owned facilities that in turn stimulated the rapid growth of private sector ownership of nursing homes accelerated.

The NHS and Community Care Act of 1990 fully devolved the funding responsibility of long-term care from central government NHS to local authorities and shifted the boundary between free NHS care and social care. This resulted in patients in free NHS long-stay beds being increasingly transferred into local authority long-stay social care beds which, unlike NHS beds, are means-tested and privately provided. With reductions in central government grants to local authorities and the need to manage the constraints of their budgets, local authorities had to reduce social care services and restrict access to those with the greatest need (Sutaria, Roderick, & Pollock, 2017; Burns et al., 2016b). These policies contributed to the rapid growth of the for-profit independent and chain nursing homes in the UK (Pollock, 2005).

Sutaria, Roderick and Pollock (2017) showed the dramatic shift from public to private beds after the passage of the NHS and Community Care Act of 1990. Total NHS long-stay beds (for all populations) decreased by 38 percent (from 106,173 in 1992–1993 to 65,764 in 2002–2003) and local government beds decreased by 53 percent while the number of private long-term care beds increased by 10 percent (Sutaria, Roderick, & Pollock, 2017). In the 1990s, following the transfer of funding responsibilities from central government to local authorities, local authorities were given incentives to utilize private providers of long-stay homes and to reduce their own long-stay beds. By 2014, the UK reported 86 percent of nursing homes were for-profit, 8 percent were nonprofit, and only 6 percent were government homes, surpassing the 70 percent for-profit homes in the US (Harrington et al., 2017). The steady reductions in government funding reduced services and entitlements, so that only individuals with the highest care needs and lowest income met the needs and means tested eligibility criteria to receive local authority funded services (Harrington et al., 2017).

Like most industrialized countries, the UK experienced a large growth in the population aged 65 and over. Specifically, the aged population in the UK grew from 18 to 20 percent (9.2 million to 11.1 million) between 2005 and 2014 (Harrington et al., 2017). In the UK, nursing homes for the aged increased by 6 percent between 2005 and 2014 (4853 to 5144 homes) and nursing home beds increased by 8 percent (from 201,200 to 217,700) (Harrington et al., 2017). Taking into account the growth in the aged population, however, the number of nursing home beds per 1000 aged population declined during the period from 21.9 beds per 1000 aged population to 19.6 beds. In 2014, the UK had a substantially lower overall rate of bed availability per 1000 aged population compared to the US, Canada, Norway, and Sweden (Harrington et al., 2017).

Since 2010, local authority expenditures on adult social care have decreased in total dollars, and spending on older people, adults with physical disabilities and mental health needs, and those with other needs decreased by 13 percent. Non-residential care services fell by 33 percent (Sutaria, Roderick, & Pollock, 2017). The financial crisis resulted in service cuts and serious problems in the availability of home care workers and providers (Burns et al., 2016b). With cuts in home care services as well as nursing home services, access and availability of long-term care services was limited overall.

Changes introduced to social care in 1972 are now being mirrored within the NHS. In the Health and Social Care Act of 2012, England changed the "duty to provide key services" to a duty to "arrange for provision" of services (Burns et al., 2016a; Pollock & Price, 2011a; Pollock, Macfarlane, & Godden, 2012). This is now resulting in the rapid privatization of the delivery of health care services. Combined with insufficient funding of NHS, increasingly only those individuals who can pay privately or who have private insurance have access to comprehensive health services while only those with the highest care needs have access to reduced government-funded health services, creating great disparities in access to care, increased costs, less efficient services, and the erosion of free universal services (Pollock, 2005; Pollock, MacFarlane, & Godden, 2012; Pollock & Price, 2011a; 2011b; Sutaria, Roderick & Pollock, 2017).

In the UK, total government expenditures for nursing homes for the aged increased from 6.2 billion pounds to 8.5 billion pounds between 2005 and 2014. At the same time, the proportion of residents paid for by government declined from 60 percent to 58 percent and was a lower percentage of total expenditures than in the US, Canada, Norway, and Sweden (Harrington et al., 2017). Thus, while government funding for the private nursing home sector grew steadily, the funding for individuals declined. These changes have clearly had a negative effect on access to nursing home/residential care services for the aged in the UK.

The US System of Private Nursing Home Services Remains Stable

The United States had an almshouse system for the poor in the 1800s, which was converted to boarding homes in the 1900s (Kaffenberger, 2000). After the enactment of the federal Old Age Assistance law in 1915 and the Social Security Acts in 1935, individuals were expected to pay for their own housing and care (Kaffenberger, 2000). Between the 1920s and the 1950s, the number of US nursing homes grew dramatically and ownership changed from small providers to larger for-profit companies.

In 1965, the Medicare and Medicaid programs were set up by federal legislation. Medicare only pays for the aged and disabled who need short-term rehabilitation services in nursing homes and home healthcare while Medicaid (a joint federal and state program) pays for individuals with low incomes (Kaiser Family Foundation, 2017). By default, the Medicaid program has become the major payer of long-stay nursing homes and home- and community-based services not covered by Medicare (Reaves & Musumeci, 2015). Under state Medicaid policies, individuals must meet state low-income eligibility and need criteria. There are wide variations in the level and type of Medicaid services available across states. Some states have Medicaid programs that are more generous in paying for nursing home care than other states that have strict asset and income requirements (Reaves & Musumeci, 2015).

After 1965, the growth in primarily private hospitals and nursing homes and the shift to for-profit companies was fueled by the steady source of government revenues from the Medicare and Medicaid programs and the Federal Housing Authority loan guarantee program (Kaffenberger, 2000). Major growth in for-profit nursing homes chains occurred in the 1990s with many acquisitions and mergers (Banaszak-Holl et al., 2002; Kitchener & Harrington, 2004).

Individuals not eligible for Medicare and Medicaid must pay for nursing home and other home and community services directly out-of-pocket, and this severely limits access to services. Only a few individuals have private long-term care insurance that will pay for services (Tumlinson, Aguiar & Watts, 2009). As nursing homes become more expensive, individuals are less likely to be able to afford institutional services, more likely to remain at home, and become impoverished from paying for their care.

In 2014, 70 percent of US nursing homes were owned by for-profit providers, 24 percent by non-profits, and 6 percent by government, a level that has been fairly stable since the 1990s (Harrington et al., 2016). Between 2005 and 2014, the number of US nursing home homes declined by about 2 percent (from 16,032 to 15,646) and the number of beds declined by 1 percent (from 1.7 million to 1.6 million) (Harrington et al., 2017; Harrington, Ross & Kang, 2015). As the US aged population grew from 12 to 15 percent (36.7 million to 46.2 million) during the same period, the beds per 1000 aged population dropped to an even greater extent (about 22 percent) (from 46.7 to 36.6 per 1000 aged population). The occupancy rates also steadily dropped, from 85.5 percent to 82.4 percent (Harrington et al., 2017), in part because of expanded Medicaid funding for home- and community-based services for low-income individuals that gave individuals options to remain at home (Ng et al., 2016).

Total US expenditures for nursing homes remained about the same between 2005 and 2014. The proportion of total nursing home residents funded by government was about 78 percent and the proportion of total nursing home expenditures paid for by government was 60 percent over the same period (Harrington et al., 2017).

Large For-Profit Nursing Homes Chains Dominate in the UK

In 2014, for-profit nursing home chains were the dominant provider in the UK and the US, unlike in Sweden, Canada, and Norway. The growth in chains occurred in all countries where data were available, with a large increase in chains in the UK (from 44 percent to 64 percent of nursing homes for the aged between 2005 and 2014, and 53 percent of beds in 2005 to 71 percent of beds in 2014) (Harrington et al., 2017).

In 2014, the five largest providers of nursing home care for the aged in the UK were Four Seasons Health Care, BUPA Care Homes, HC-One Ltd, Barchester Healthcare, and Care UK Health and Social Care Investment. They accounted for 35 percent of available beds in 2015–2016 (Harrington et al., 2017). Four companies were private limited companies, owned and controlled by private investment and equity groups and BUPA was owned by the British United Province Association. All except BUPA were registered in tax havens such as Guernsey, Jersey, or the Cayman Islands (Burns et al., 2016a).

Unable to pay the large debts taken on to fund rapid expansion and property development, the largest nursing home chain – Southern Cross, founded in 1995 – declared bankruptcy in 2011 and created financial instability in the market. Two-thirds of Southern Cross' facilities were sold to Four Seasons and one-third were purchased by HC-One Ltd, a new private company founded with equity investors in 2011 (Harrington et al., 2017; Burns et al., 2016a). Two companies showed growth (Four Seasons and Care UK) over the past ten years (Harrington et al., 2017). BUPA had a growth in beds over the 2005–2016 period but had a large financial loss in its UK care business in 2015 that resulted in plans to sell most of its care homes (Harrington et al., 2017). The five largest companies all had complex organizational structures, with the most prominent being Four Seasons, with over 185 companies owned by several holding companies (Burns et al., 2016a). A holding company usually does not produce goods or services but controls other companies to form a corporate group.

The largest chains used sale and leaseback arrangements, by splitting the operating and property holding companies into separate companies, and then leasing the property from the property company to the operating company, sometimes at artificially high rates (Burns et al., 2016a). The company strategies have been to restructure by selling less profitable homes and developing new care homes in more affluent areas and focusing on serving the private pay market. The companies have diversified and expanded into independent living and residential care, day care, palliative care, and other long-term care services. The five largest companies operated homes in England, Scotland, and Ireland, while BUPA had operations in Spain, Australia, and New Zealand (Harrington et al., 2017). These large companies have shifted their financing from equity to debt funding, where the interest payments are non-taxable and deducted before profits are taken (Burns et al., 2016a).

Revenues for the four largest chains ranged from 315 to 713 million pounds in 2015–2016 while BUPA had revenues of 55 million pounds in 2014 (Harrington et al., 2017). Three companies had 8 percent to 9 percent EBITDA (earnings before interest, taxes, depreciation and amortization) and 15 percent to 20 percent EBITDAR (earnings before interest, taxes, depreciation, amortization and rent costs) profits and one had a 3 percent profit in 2015. BUPA, however, reported a loss of 1.2 million in 2015 (Harrington et al., 2017). The demand for high profits while revenues are limited and costs increase appears to have resulted in a financially unsustainable situation for many chains (Plimmer, 2017). For example, in 2017, heavy debts at Four Seasons Health Care led to financial instability and potential bankruptcy (Plimmer, 2017).

Large For-Profit Nursing Home Chains Have Growing Market Share in the US

The US also saw a steady growth in nursing home chains from 52 percent of total homes in 2005 to 56 percent in 2014 (Harrington et al., 2017). In 2015, Genesis HealthCare was the largest for-profit chain and the only one of the five largest chains listed on the New York Stock Exchange (NYSE) but its controlling stock was owned by a private equity company (Provider Magazine, 2016). The next largest for-profit chains in the US were HCR ManorCare, Golden Living, and Sava SeniorCare, all owned by private equity firms. Only Life Care Centers of America (LCCA) was privately owned by an individual (Provider Magazine, 2016). Private equity firms provide financial backing and investments in operating companies and have been criticized because they lack expertise and long-term commitment to companies and are only looking for profit-making opportunities.

Over the decade, four of the five largest chains remained in the top five in 2015 although they changed positions, and one was replaced by Life Care Centers of America. Overall, the five largest for-profit chains had 10.3 percent of all nursing home beds and 9.2 percent of homes in the US in 2015 (Harrington et al., 2017). The four of the five largest chains (except LCCA) had complex ownership structures with multiple owners, holding companies, and subsidiary companies (Harrington et al., 2017; Stevenson, Bramson & Grabowski, 2013).

The four of the five large chains had moved their property ownership to either separate real estate investment trusts (REITs) or real estate companies with lease-back arrangements (Harrington et al., 2017). Their growth strategy was to acquire and merge with other nursing homes. Three chains showed a steady growth in beds and homes between 2005 and 2016. All of the largest chains were diversified to include assisted living, rehabilitation, home health, hospice, and other services. Three of the five chains provided management services to its own nursing homes, allowing profits to be shifted from the operation of homes to the owners' management companies. The five large chains had nursing homes in 21 to 34 states (Harrington et al., 2017). Each of the five chains was incorporated in the state of Delaware, known as the most favorable US state in terms of taxes (a tax haven) (Wayne, 2012).

The five chains had large revenues ranging from $1.3 billion to $5.6 billion in 2016 (Harrington et al., 2017). The four privately owned companies do not have to report revenues; only the publicly traded company, Genesis, had to publicly disclose its finances and its profits (EBTDAR of 12.4 percent in 2016) (Harrington et al., 2017).

The Negative Impacts of Privatization

The dramatic shift from government-owned and operated nursing homes to large for-profit chains in the UK and the steady increase in for-profit chains in the US have had negative consequences. We have described the dramatic decline in access to nursing home beds, especially for individuals with low incomes. In these countries, private companies have focused on the private pay market rather than relying on government payments for clients, creating serious access problems for individuals paid by government funds (Harrington et al., 2017).

Poor quality and low nurse staffing. There is strong evidence that for-profit nursing homes have poorer quality of care than government and non-profit nursing homes. Systemic reviews and meta-analysis show that for-profit nursing homes have poorer quality of care on average than not-for-profit homes (Comondore et al., 2009; Hillmer et al., 2005). In addition, homes with the highest profit margins have been found to have the worst quality in the US (O'Neill et al., 2003). Other studies have shown the poor quality of for-profit chains (Banaszak-Holl et al., 2002; Harrington, Ross, & Kang, 2015; Grabowski et al., 2016; US GAO, 2010). Ronald and others (2016) have argued that there is enough scientific evidence to suggest that for-profit nursing homes deliver inferior care and that policy changes are needed to move away from the use of for-profit nursing homes.

For-profit homes also have lower nursing staff levels than other types of homes (Harrington et al., 2012; McGregor et al., 2011). Nursing homes seeking high profit levels often reduce nurse staffing costs, especially RNs costs, and cut wages, benefits, and pensions, and hide low staffing levels (Lloyd et al., 2014; Harrington, Stockton, & Hooper, 2014; Rau, 2018b). In the US, the top ten for-profit chains and other for-profit homes had lower registered nurse and total nurse staffing hours than non profit facilities and government facilities in the 2003–2008 period. They also had more deficiencies than any other type of ownership group (Harrington, et al., 2012). Recent exposes and scandals have shown that quality and complaints about poor care have increased as profits have risen (Lloyd et al, 2014; Rau. 2018a,b).

In 2014, staffing hours of the five largest for-profit chains in the US were adjusted for resident acuity (the measurement of the intensity of care required for a patient accomplished by nurses). The measurement showed that nursing hours were significantly lower in three of the chains and total nursing hours were lower in all five of the largest chains than the average US nursing home (Harrington et al., 2017). With low staffing, it was not surprisingly that all the five largest chains (except one) had significantly higher quality deficiencies than the national average during 2009–2014 (Harrington et al., 2017). In the last ten years, all five of the largest US chains had been charged with fraudulent practices by the US Department of Justice (Harrington et al., 2017) and either had made large settlements with the government or had pending cases. The US government has rarely prohibited chains with poor quality from purchasing new homes or removed the chains from the government programs.

In the UK, quality concerns arose regarding care homes owned by corporate chains after scandals were widely reported by the media in Southern Cross's facilities in 2010–2011 (Lloyd et al., 2014). In 2016–2017, the Care Quality Commission (2017) adult social care home inspection reports found that 9 percent of all homes provided inadequate care and 32 percent needed improvement. No routine data, however, were collected on staffing levels or on categories of staff, and levels of training and data on residents are also limited. Thus it is difficult to look at resident care needs, staffing levels, and quality of care by ownership in the UK.

The US has federal standards that require nursing homes to provide adequate staffing to meet the highest care needs of residents but these standards lack adequate specificity and enforcement by regulators (US GAO, 2009b). The UK also does not have clear minimum staffing standards. (See Chapter 10.)

Many research studies have shown the need for minimum staffing standards because higher registered nurse and certified nursing assistant staffing has been associated with improved quality indicators, fewer deficiencies, less rehospitalization and other benefits (Castle & Anderson, 2011; Castle & Engberg, 2008; Dellefield et al., 2015; US CMS, 2001; Schnelle et al., 2004). As Chapter 10 explains in greater detail, many organizations in the US have endorsed mandating minimum staffing levels (Institute of Medicine, 2004; Harrington, Schnelle, McGregor & Simmons, 2016). If detailed staffing standards were adopted as recommended by experts, then it would be much more difficult for nursing home chains to reduce staffing levels below minimal accepted levels and this would protect residents.

Lack of transparency. Because the largest for-profit nursing home chains are primarily owned by private equity companies and investors, they are not required to publicly report on their financing and operations – in contrast to publicly traded companies. This limits financial transparency and accountability for government funds, which pay about half of the revenues for care homes. The UK and US governments have not attempted to collect data on costs or quality or to limit further growth and marketization of large for-profit nursing home companies and their related-party and real estate companies, although the US does require extensive cost reporting on individual nursing homes at the federal and state levels regardless of ownership type (Harrington, Armstrong et al., 2016; Harrington, Jacobsen et al., 2017; Grabowski et al., 2016). In the US, the Affordable Care Act of 2010 (Obama Care) did strengthen the ownership and financial reporting requirements for individual nursing homes but the federal government does not have a system for ensuring the accuracy and auditing of the ownership and financial reports at the federal level (Grabowski et al., 2016; Harrington et al., 2017; Stevenson, et al., 2013; US GAO, 2010; 2016; Wells & Harrington, 2013).

There is a remarkable lack of government information on the ownership and operation of UK nursing homes and nursing home chains Clearly, the UK needs to develop more detailed ownership and financial reporting requirements for individual nursing homes and both countries should require ownership and financial reporting for chains and the large private companies that own nursing homes (US GAO, 2010; 2016). Transparency in reporting and regular auditing would help ensure greater accuracy and information for the public and policy makers.

Lack of financial and regulatory accountability. Government payers in the UK and US have not established financial limits on administration and profits and have not required public financial transparency of administrative costs and profits by individual nursing homes or their corporate owners (Harrington, Armstrong, et al., 2016). Nor have they ensured that government funds are used for nurse staffing and direct care services. In California, nursing homes spent about 35 percent of revenues on nursing and direct services in 2012, a level that had declined by 11 percent over the previous six years (Harrington, Armstrong et al., 2016; Harrington, Ross & Kang, 2015; Harrington, Ross, Mukamel & Rosenau, 2013). Although actual financial data were not available in England, industry reports recommended that only 35 percent of total expenditures be allocated for all nursing care services in 2012, an 8 percent decline over a five-year period (Harrington, Armstrong et al., 2016). In contrast, Norway reported 60 percent of its expenditures were for nursing care services.

Numerous investigations by the government agencies have found that nursing homes routinely violate federal nursing home regulations in the US. In addition, violations are frequently under-identified and serious violations are under-rated by state surveyors (US GAO, 2009a,b; 2011; US OIG, 2013; 2014). Facilities often are not given penalties for serious violations or the penalties are so minimal that enforcement does not result in compliance (Harrington et al, 2014; US GAO, 2009b; 2011; US OIG, 2013; 2014). Moreover, nursing homes are seldom terminated from the Medicare/Medicaid programs as a result of violations. Because government has not had an effective regulatory system, civil litigation remedies have been very important in the US (Harrington, Ross & Kang, 2015; Harrington et al., 2014; Harrington, Armstrong et al., 2016; US GAO, 2009a, 2009b).

In the US there have been many calls by government agencies, research experts, consumer advocacy organizations, congressional members, and others to improve the regulatory oversight and enforcement systems for nursing homes (Harrington et al, 2014; US GAO 2009b, 2011; US OIG, 2013; 2014). Rather than strengthening regulatory oversight, the current US administration has taken actions to reduce regulatory "burdens" at the request of the nursing home industry (Center for Medicare Advocacy, 2018; Rau, 2017).

In the UK serious questions have been raised as to whether private nursing homes are amenable to judicial review or to a human rights or freedom of information challenge, which are remedies against public bodies. Outsourcing of public services to private and voluntary bodies has led to several cases where the courts have had to wrestle with where and how to draw the line.[1] For example, under the Human Rights Act of 1998 in the UK residents have a right to a home but could not challenge a chain's decision to close and sell off their nursing home. Private care homes funded through local authority contracts were held by the House of Lords in 2007 not to be exercising functions of a public nature under the Human Rights Act 1998,[2] and this had to be reversed seven years later by primary legislation.[3] One approach for the UK may be to address access and quality issues through litigation remedies, such as has been done in the US (Harrington, Stockton & Hoopers, 2014).

The US does not have legislation comparable to the European and UK Human Rights Acts but the federal Medicaid legislation guarantees that low-income individuals eligible for Medicaid will receive nursing home services in nursing homes that meet federal standards. Research however shows that individuals receiving Medicaid payments for care and individuals who are ethnic minorities are living in nursing homes with the poorest quality of care (Smith et al., 2007; Li et al., 2015a,b). In addition, Medicaid home and community based services are optional so that states without adequate availability of home and community based services may unnecessarily force individuals into nursing homes to receive services (Ng, Wong & Harrington, 2014).

Higher costs of services. Research has found that private for-profit companies often have higher operating and total income margins, as well as higher operating costs than other nursing homes. As a result, these companies may not be financially sustainable over the long term (Burns et al., 2016a). A lack of stability in many chain owners and investors was evident from the frequent buying and selling of companies, nursing homes and businesses (Grabowski et al., 2016; Harrington et al., 2017). The problem has been made worse by the use of triple-net lease agreements with real estate companies that make individual nursing homes responsible for net real estate taxes on the leased assets, net building insurance, and net common area maintenance (Burns et al., 2016a). These types of lease agreements have been problematic for some large chains, as in the example of Southern Cross's bankruptcy, and for the Four Seasons in the UK (Plimmer, 2017). Adopting restrictions on the use of such nursing home lease agreements in the UK and US would help protect nursing home residents.

Failure to pay taxes. Large nursing home chains pay little in taxes. Taxes for property companies are generally lower than for other types of companies and interest rates on loans and property rental rates can be artificially inflated to benefit the property owners (Burns et al., 2016a; Pradhan et al., 2013). The largest for-profit nursing home chains are often heavily debt-financed by obtaining cash through loans from banks or investors (Burns et al., 2016a; Pradhan et al., 2013). Interest payments are non-taxable and are deducted before profit is declared. In addition, many of the large nursing home chains in the UK used tax havens, which offered investors low or no taxes on profits while chains in the US used Delaware, a state with minimal corporate taxes. The problem of tax havens is not unique to nursing home corporations.

Excess profit-taking. Nursing home companies have been attractive to private investors, because they often have high rates of return. With a few exceptions, the profits by the largest nursing home chains were high, ranging from 6 percent to 28 percent, in spite of financial market fluctuations. The high profit margins were an expectation of private investors (LaingBuisson, 2015). At the same time, the profits of nursing home chains are under-reported and hidden in chain management agreements and fees, lease agreements, interest payments to owners, direct withdrawals by owners, and purchases from related party companies (Burns et al., 2016a; Harrington et al., 2013; Harrington, Ross & Kang, 2015; Rau, 2018a; Stevenson et al., 2013). Moreover, profits can be manipulated over time to reduce taxes and pay dividends.

One policy option is to establish limits on profits and administrative costs to ensure that adequate resources are spent directly on care. Increasing the financial accountability of nursing homes can help assure that government funds are used for care rather than to enhance shareholder and owner values (Harrington, Armstrong et al., 2016; Harrington, Ross, Mukamel & Rosenau, 2013). There is a US precedent for such a policy. Restrictions on profits and administrative costs to no more than 20 percent of premiums were placed on health insurance plans in the US under the Affordable Care Act and these resulted in billions in consumer refunds (Harrington, Ross, Mukamel & Rosenau, 2013).

Reconsidering Privatization

As large for-profit nursing home chains grow in dominance in the marketplace and political arena, the UK and US have exerted little control over the amount, type, and quality of nursing home services. Government policies have largely shifted the responsibility for nursing home and long-term care/social services from government to individuals as a means of reducing government costs. As the UK and US governments become more dependent on large nursing home chains for services, they are less able to terminate contracts, remove residents from or apply protective measures in poorly performing facilities, ensure that standards are maintained, and control the costs of care.

If the UK and US continue their policies of privatized long-term care, there are policies that clearly are necessary. Government should establish criteria regarding the purchase of nursing homes to ensure that new owners have a history of providing high quality homes and have financial stability rather than allowing poor quality chains to buy more nursing homes (Grabowski et al., 2016). Stronger regulatory approaches are essential: to ensure adequate staffing levels are met, to enforce existing laws and regulations, to ensure quality, and to limit profit taking and excess administrative costs. Government should focus on transparency and accountability in financial and ownership reporting. Oversight is needed to address the challenges of privatization and marketization of nursing home and other long-term care services.

We argue that the policies of privatization need to be reconsidered. Norway offers a valuable example of a country that provides its citizens with comprehensive publicly owned and delivered nursing home and home health care. By maintaining municipal ownership of nursing home properties, Norway is able to limit the growth of for-profit nursing homes and control the quality of its services as well as the costs (see Chapter 2).

In the US, recently government have had to take over management of failing homes putting them into government receiverships. This would be an ideal time for government to purchase or nationalize these private companies and convert them to public ownership and management. In addition, government should take steps to protect nursing homes currently owned by public or non-profit organizations from shifting to for-profit ownership. Government loans, bonds, financial incentive systems, and other means can be used to stabilize the existing public and not-profit facilities.

As the rest of the NHS undergoes a similar assault on ownership and control that occurred with nursing homes, there are now new calls to renationalize social services and social care and establish them under the framework and legislation of a national health service. Currently a Bill is in parliament to reinstate the NHS (www.nhsbillnow.com). However, the debate needs to extend to the most frail and vulnerable in our society by restoring ownership and control over services to the public for the public. This will involve mapping the private sector and opening all the contracts that government and local authorities have with the private sector with a view either to termination and to buying or taking back ownership and control. Most of these contracts are short term so can be taken back in-house.

The problem is that there is a tight web of interests resisting such change. Given the cost of buying back the capital estate, the first place to start would be with the workforce. Reinstating the workforce into a National Health and Social Care Service would require training, job security, restoration of national terms and conditions, funding for career development opportunities, and, at the very least, establishing professional norms and standards for staffing levels and training for care as well as requiring routine data collection for administrative and audit purposes. In time, land, buildings and estate services could also be renationalized. With less ability to gouge out profits from staff costs which are the highest proportion of expenditure, investors and shareholders may be encouraged to divest themselves and relinquish their contracts.

All these initiatives require two things in sequence. First, the political will – to dare to dream and then to act to take moral responsibility for protecting the public. Second, changes to public expenditure rules which currently favor the private sector are necessary to allow this to happen. Only the sort of radical thinking that allowed the welfare state to come into being will result in radical change for the better – all the rest is tinkering around the edges of a very bad system.

Notes

1 R v Panel on Take-Overs and Mergers, ex parte Datafin [1987] QB 815; R v The Insurance Ombudsman Bureau ex parte Aegon Life [1994] CLC 88; Hampshire County Council v Graham Beer (t/a Hammer Trout Farm) [2003] EWCA Civ 1056, available at: http://www.bailii.org/ew/cases/EWCA/Civ/2003/1056.html; Holmcroft Properties Ltd, R (on the application of) v KPMG LLP & Ors [2016] EWHC 323 (Admin), available at: http://www.bailii.org/ew/cases/EWHC/Admin/2016/323.html
2 YL (by her litigation friend the Official Solicitor) (FC) (Appellant) v. Birmingham City Council and others (Respondents) [2007] UKHL 27, available at: http://www.bailii.org/uk/cases/UKHL/2007/27.html
3 Care Act 2014, section 73, available at: http://www.legislation.gov.uk/ukpga/2014/23/section/73

References

Banaszak-Holl, J., Berta, W. B., Bowman, D. M., Baum, J. A., & Mitchell, W. (2002). The rise of human service chains: Antecedents to acquisitions and their effects on the quality of care in US nursing homes. *Managerial and Decision Economics, 23*(4–5), 261–282.

Burns, D., Cowie, L., Earle, J., Folkman, P., Froud, J., Hyde, P., & Williams, K. (2016a). *Where does the money go? Financialised chains and the crisis in residential care*. Manchester, UK: Centre for Research on Socio-Cultural Change (CRESC).

Burns, D., Earl, J., Folkman, P., Froud, J., Hyde, P., Johal, S., & Williams, K. (2016b). *Why we need social innovation in home care for older people*. Manchester, UK: Centre for Research on Socio-Cultural Change (CRESC).

Care Quality Commission. (2017). The state of health care and adult social care in England 2016/17. *Care Quality Commission.* http://www.cqc.org.uk/sites/default/files/20171123_stateofcare1617_report.pdf

Castle, N. G., & Anderson, R. A. (2011). Caregiver staffing in nursing homes and their influence on quality of care. *Medical Care, 49*(6), 545–552.

Castle, N. G., & Engberg, J. (2008). Further examination of the influence of caregiver staffing levels on nursing home quality. *Gerontologist, 48*, 464–76.

Center for Medicare Advocacy (2018). Administration and nursing home industry: Lockstep in deregulating nursing home facilities and reducing resident protections. January. http://www.medicareadvocacy.org/alert-tax-cut-harm-just-got-worse-this-week-in-sabotage-cms-pushing-ma-plans-snf-deregulation/

Comondore, V. R., Devereaux, P. J., Zhou, Q., Stone, S. B., Busse, J. W., Ravindran, N. C., et al. (2009). Quality of care in for-profit and not-for-profit nursing homes: Systematic review and meta-analysis. *Research, Policy and Planning, 28*(1), 1–13.

Dellefield, M. E., Castle, N. G., McGilton, K. S., & Spilsbury, K. (2015) The relationship between registered nurses and nursing home quality: An integrative review (2008–2014). *Nursing Economic$, 33*(2), 95–108, 116.

Grabowski, D. C., Feng, Z., Hirth, R., Rahman, M., & Mor, V. (2013). Effect of nursing home ownership on the quality of post-acute care: An instrumental variables approach. *Journal of Health Economics*, *32*(1), 12–21.

Grabowski, D. C., Hirth, R. A., Intrator, O., Li, Y., Richardson, J., Stevenson, D. G., & Banaszak-Holl, J. (2016). Low-quality nursing homes were more likely than other nursing homes to be bought or sold by chains in 1993–2010. *Health Affairs*, *35*(5), 907–914.

Harrington C., Armstrong, H., Halladay, M., Havig, A., Jacobsen, F. F., MacDonald, M., Panos, J., Pearsal, K., Pollock, A., & Ross, L. (2016). Nursing home financial transparency and accountability in four locations. *Ageing International*, (1), 17–39.

Harrington, C., Jacobsen, F. F., Panos, J., Pollock, A., Sutaria, S., & Szebehely, M. (2017). Marketization in long-term care: A cross-country comparison of large for-profit nursing home chains. *Health Services Insights*, *10*, 1178632917710533.

Harrington, C., Olney, B., Carrillo, H., & Kang, T. (2012). Nurse staffing and deficiencies in the largest for-profit nursing home chains and chains owned by private equity companies. *Health Services Research*, *47*(1pt1), 106–128.

Harrington, C., & Pollock, A. M. (1998). Decentralization and privatization of long-term care in UK and USA. *The Lancet*, *351*, 1805–1808.

Harrington, C., Ross, L., & Kang, T. (2015). Hidden owners, hidden profits, and poor nursing home care: A case study. *International Journal of Health Services*, *45*(4), 779–800.

Harrington, C., Ross, L., Mukamel, D., & Rosenau, P. (2013). *Improving the financial accountability of nursing facilities*. Washington, DC: Kaiser Commission on Medicaid and the Uninsured.

Harrington, C., Schnelle, J. F., McGregor, M., & Simmons, S. F. (2016). The need for minimum staffing standards in nursing homes. *Health Services Insights*, *9*, 13–19.

Harrington, C., Stockton, J., & Hooper, S. (2014). The effects of regulation and litigation on a large for-profit nursing home chain. *Journal of health politics, policy and law*, *39*(4), 781–809.

Hillmer, M. P., Wodchis, W. P., Gill, S. S., Anderson, G. M., & Rochon, P. A. (2005). Nursing home profit status and quality of care: Is there any evidence of an association? *Medical Care Research and Review*, *62*(2), 139–166.

Institute of Medicine. (2004). *Keeping patients safe: Transforming the work environment of nurses*. Washington, DC: National Academy of Medicine.

Kaffenberger, KR. (2000). Nursing home ownership: An historical analysis. *Journal of Aging & Social Policy*, *12*(1), 35–48.

Kaiser Family Foundation. (2017). An overview of Medicare. Issue Brief. November. http://files.kff.org/attachment/issue-brief-an-overview-of-medicare.

Kitchener, M., & Harrington, C. (2004). The US long-term care field: A dialectic analysis of institution dynamics. *Journal of Health and Social Behavior*, *45*, 87–101.

LaingBuisson. (2015). *Fair price for care: Calculating a fair price for nursing and residential care for older people and people with dementia*. (6th Ed.). London: England.

Li, Y., Harrington, C., Mukamel, D. B., Cen, X., Cai, X., and Temkin-Greener, H. (2015a). Nurse staffing hours at nursing homes with high concentrations of minority residents, 2001–11. *Health Affairs*, *34*(12), 2129–2137.

Li, Y., Harrington, C., Temkin-Greener, H., Cen, X., Cai, X., and Mukamel, D. B. (2015b). Deficiencies in care at nursing homes and in racial/ethnic disparities across homes fell, 2006–11. *Health Affairs*, *34*(7), 1139–1146.

Lloyd, L., Banerjee, A., Harrington, C., F. Jacobsen, F., & Szebehely, M. (2014). It is a scandal! Comparing the causes and consequences of nursing home media scandals in five countries. *International Journal of Sociology and Social Policy, 34*(1/2), 2–18.

McGregor, M. J., Cohen, M., Stocks-Rankin, C. R., Cox, M. B., Salomons, K., McGrail, K. M., & Schulzer, M. (2011). Complaints in for-profit, non-profit and public nursing homes in two Canadian provinces. *Open Medicine, 5*(4), e183.

Meagher, G., & Szebehely, M. (2013). Marketisation in Nordic eldercare: A research report on legislation, oversight, extent and consequences. *Stockholm Studies in Social Work, 30*. Sweden: Stockholm University.

Ng, T., Harrington, C., Musumeci, M., & Reaves, E. L. (2016). Medicaid home and community-based services programs: 2013 data update. Washington, DC: Kaiser Family Foundation. https://www.kff.org/medicaid/report/medicaid-home-and-community-based-services-programs-2013-data-update/

Ng, T., Wong, A., and Harrington, C. (2014). Trends in Olmstead litigation against state Medicaid programs. *J. of Social Work Disability and Rehabilitation, 13* (1–2), 97–109.

O'Neill, C., Harrington, C., Kitchener, M., & Saliba, D. (2003). Quality of care in nursing homes: An analysis of relationships among profit, quality, and ownership. *Medical Care, 41*(12), 1318–1330.

Plimmer, G. (2017). Care home crisis deepens under private equity owners. *Financial Times*, December 15. https://www.ft.com/content/330fde3c-e187-11e7-a8a4-0a1e63a52f9c

Pollock, A. M. (2005). *NHS Plc: The privatization of our health care.* (2nd Ed.). London: Verso.

Pollock, A. M., Macfarlane, A., & Godden, S. (2012). Dismantling the signposts to public health? NHS data under the Health and Social Care Act 2012. *BMJ, 344*, e2364.

Pollock, A. M., & Price, D. (2011a). How the secretary of state for health proposes to abolish the NHS in England. *BMJ, 342*, d1695.

Pollock, A. M., & Price, D. (2011b). The break up of the English NHS: The new market bureaucracy needs information systems based on members and not geographic populations. *Michael Q, 8*, 460–475.

Pradhan, R., Weech-Maldonado, R., Harman, J. S., Laberge, A., & Hyer, K. (2013). Private equity ownership and nursing home financial performance. *Health Care Management Review, 38*(3), 224–233.

Provider Magazine. (2016). Top 50 largest nursing facilities companies. *Provider Magazine*, 48–51.

Rau, J. (2017). Trump administration eases nursing fines in a victory for the industry. *New York Times*. December 24. https://www.nytimes.com/2017/12/24/business/trump-administration-nursing-home-penalties.html

Rau, J. (2018a). Care suffers as profits rise. *New York Times*. January 7, A1.

Rau, J. (2018b). Nursing homes routinely mask low staff levels. *New York Times*. July 8. A1.

Reaves, E. L., & Musumeci, M. (2015). Medicaid and long-term services and supports: A primer. Kaiser Family Foundation. https://www.kff.org/medicaid/report/medicaid-and-long-term-services-and-supports-a-primer/

Ronald, L. A., McGregor, M. J., Harrington, C., Pollock, A., & Lexchin, J. (2016). Observational evidence of for-profit delivery and inferior nursing home care: When is there enough evidence for policy change? *PLOS Medicine, 13*(4), e1001995.

Schnelle, J. F., Simmons, S. F., Harrington, C., Cadogan, M., Garcia, E., & Bates-Jensen, B. (2004). Relationship of nursing home staffing to quality of care? *Health Services Research, 39*(2), 225–250.

Smith, D. B., Feng, Z., Fennell, M. L., Zinn, J. S., Mor, V. (2007). Separate and unequal: Racial segregation and disparities in quality across U.S. nursing homes. *Health Affairs* (Millwood), *26*(5): 1448–1458.

Stevenson, D. G., Bramson, J. S., & Grabowski, D. C. (2013). Nursing home ownership trends and their impacts on quality of care: A study using detailed ownership data from Texas. *Journal of Aging & Social Policy, 25*(1), 30–47.

Sutaria, S., Roderick, P., & Pollock, A. M. (2017). Are radical changes to health and social care paving the way for fewer services and new user charges? *BMJ, 358*, j4279.

Tumlinson, A., Aguiar, C., & Watts, M. O. M. (2009). *Closing the long-term care funding gap:* https://kaiserfamilyfoundation.files.wordpress.com/2013/01/closing-the-long-term-care-funding-gap-the-challenge-of-private-long-term-care-insurance-report.pdf

US Centers for Medicare and Medicaid Services (US CMS), Prepared by Abt Associates Inc. (2001). *Appropriateness of minimum nurse staffing ratios in nursing homes. Report to Congress: Phase II Final. Volumes I–III.* Baltimore, MD: CMS.

US Government Accountability Office (US GAO). (2009a). *CMS's specific focus facility methodology should better target the most poorly performing facilities which tend to be chain affiliated and for-profit.* Washington, DC. http://www.gao.gov/new.items/d09689.pdf

US Government Accountability Office (US GAO). (2009b). *Nursing homes: Addressing the factors underlying understatement of serious care problems requires sustained CMS and state commitment.* GAO-10-70. Washington, DC: GAO.

US Government Accountability Office (US GAO). (2010). *Nursing homes: Complexity of private investment purchases demonstrates need for CMS to improve the usability and completeness of ownership data.* GAO-10-710. Washington, DC: GAO.

US Government Accountability Office (US GAO). (2011). *Nursing homes: More reliable data and consistent guidance would improve CMS oversight of state complaints investigations.* GAO-11-280. Washington, DC: GAO, April.

US Government Accountability Office (US GAO). (2016). *Skilled nursing facilities: CMS should improve accessibility and reliability of expenditure data.* GAO-16-700. Washington, DC: GAO, September.

US Office of the Inspector General (US OIG). (2013). *Medicare nursing home resident hospitalization rates merit additional monitoring.* OEI-06-11-00040. November. Washington, DC: OIG.

US Office of the Inspector General (US OIG). (2014). Adverse events in skilled nursing facilities: National incidence among Medicare beneficiaries. OEI-06-11-00370. February. Washington, DC: OIG.

Wayne, L. (2012). How Delaware thrives as a corporate tax haven. *The New York Times*, June 30. http://www.nytimes.com/2012/07/01/business/how-delaware-thrives-as-a-corporate-tax-haven.html

Wells, J., & Harrington, C. (2013). *Implementation of Affordable Care Act provisions to improve nursing home transparency and quality.* Washington, DC: Kaiser Commission on Medicaid and the Uninsured.

Chapter 4

The Marketization and Commodification of Long-Term Care in Germany
Effects on Work and Relationship-Based Care in Nursing Homes

Beatrice Müller

Marketization in the German long-term care sector is not characterized by the privatization of former public care provision. Rather, it is accompanied by the development and expansion of publicly funded long-term care services that in the past were mainly provided by female family members and private non-profit welfare organizations. Even though the long-term care sector has been formalized and extended, this family-oriented focus has remained largely intact (Auth, 2017). Although the orientation today is towards an adult worker model, with women integrated into the labor market, elder care remains largely an unpaid duty that women are responsible for (Auth & Rudolph, 2017). At the same time, competition is the new regulation mode that increases not only for-profit provision but changes the logic within non-profit homes in the long-term residential care sector.

This chapter focuses on these political-economic changes within the German long-term residential care (LTRC) infrastructure and its consequences for practices that allow the development of care relationships in long-term care residences. It demonstrates the main forms of marketization in Germany. Providing a conceptualization of this marketization, it argues that marketization and commodification reduce the possibility for such care, which not only has negative effects for residents in nursing homes, but results in deteriorating working conditions for nursing home staff. These tendencies affect women at a greater scale, because they account for the majority of residents in nursing homes and of the workforce.

Method and Theoretical Approach

The argument is based on a literature and document analysis as well as on interviews and fieldnote data obtained from our rapid ethnographies, as described in the Introduction to this book.

The German case differs somewhat from other countries. Because elder care has never been a public responsibility, privatization is not the most accurate term to describe the main processes of transformation in the German long-term care sector. Although there are aspects of privatization, neoliberal transformations in LTRC are most commonly described as marketization. Marketization is defined broadly as the "use of managerial-economic and market-based methods and regulation mode with the goal of increasing efficiency" (Maurer, 2015: 180, translation B. M.). It includes the implementation of competition and contract management as well as an increase in for-profit providers (Pfau-Effinger, Och, & Eichler, 2008). This broad understanding of marketization is used in this chapter as an umbrella term and as an initial concept, defined to include the processes of cost-containment, commodification, and privatization.

The focus of this analysis is on the relation between marketization and relationship-based care. It is argued that care is a necessity for all human beings and that there is a contradiction between the logic of care and market logic (see also Haug, 1996a; Haug, 1996b; Mol, 2008). The first contradiction is based on the understanding of subjectivity. Neoclassic and market-oriented perspectives draw on a conceptualization of subjectivity as autonomous and rational. In contrast, from an ethics of care perspective, human beings live in a network of mutual dependency and vulnerability (Tronto, 1993). The practice of care is understood as care that encompasses more than just task-oriented services. It is understood as a relationship based on mutuality and trust (Armstrong & Braedley, 2013), embodied work, or as "thickly embodied labour" (Lanoix, 2013), and as a very complex process that involves specific skills (Tronto, 1993; Lanoix, 2013; Armstrong & Braedley, 2013; Müller, 2016).

In particular, care as a relationship is based on attentiveness, responsibility, competence, and responsiveness (Tronto, 1993). These qualities constitute the second contradiction with regards to the logic of marketization. This type of care can hardly be measured and thus efficiency cannot be improved through the kind of measurement common in market systems. For example, attentiveness (e.g., "being there," listening to the needs of residents, realizing if somebody needs help) or responsiveness (flexibility to readjust care to the desires and needs of residents, being aware of responses) lose their main quality if they have to be provided in a cost- and therefore time-efficient manner (Tronto, 2011).

Relationship-based care applies to both residents and care workers. As we will see in the following, marketization has led to a deterioration in working and caring conditions, reducing the possibility for care relationships to develop.

Historical Background

The German conservative welfare state is characterized by social insurance based on the Bismarck model, which covers all wage workers who pay a wage share, as opposed to a tax-based model that covers the entire population. Until the 1970s, this was complemented in western Germany by a strong male breadwinner model that enforced a clear gender-based division of labor (Seeleib-Kaiser & Toivonen, 2011; Auth, 2017). During that time, care for the elderly was largely provided by women in private households and female labor force participation rate was low. Public care was mainly provided by non-profit organizations called welfare associations, such as the *Arbeiterwohlfahrt* (Worker Welfare), which has ties to the Social Democratic Party (*Sozialdemokratische Partei Deutschlands, SPD*), or the Catholic *Caritas* association, which has ties to the Christian Democratic Union (*Christlich Demokratische Union Deutschlands, CDU*).

The close relations between the state and welfare organizations were based on the concept of subsidiarity, which gave primary responsibility to local and non-public organizations and institutions. This close cooperation between the state and welfare organizations was a characteristic of the German welfare regime and has existed since the Weimar Republic. It was strengthened after the Second World War (Theobald, 2012: 65). Welfare organizations provided care and were compensated by public funds. The emphasis was clearly based on needs. The relation between state and welfare organizations can be labelled, according to the model of Anttonen and Meagher (2013), as outsourcing to welfare associations *without* competition. But the relation wasn't one-dimensional. State and welfare organizations had a cooperative relationship because welfare organizations were supposed to influence policy development from the perspective of care receivers, advocating for the most vulnerable parts of society (Theobald, 2012: 67; Meyer, 1996). Nevertheless the traditional organization of care depended heavily on women's unpaid work, and welfare organizations have been widely criticized for their hierarchical structure and paternalistic understanding of care in which care receivers' autonomy, choice, and preferences were not the main focus (Heinze & Olk, 1984; Meyer, 1996).

Between 1980 and 1990, this welfare regime and its emphasis on local autonomy was challenged. As in many other countries, public administrations were criticized for being too expensive and inefficient or for representing the "organized irresponsibility" of municipal organizations (Banner, 1991: 6), instead of resembling modern service companies. Reforms were implemented, including the introduction of a new regulation mode in the social sector as well as related reforms in health care and later in long-term care (Theobald, 2015: 27).

Within the long-term care sector, the background for this welfare state critique was a so-called care crisis. As women increasingly entered the formal employment sector on a greater scale, albeit mostly as part-time workers, the former acceptance of unpaid care work was challenged. Against the background of demographic and social transformations, public care provision became increasingly necessary and in demand, which in turn led to a shortage of nursing homes. At the same time, the growing demand was seen as being too expensive for the welfare state because residents in nursing homes were mostly funded by health care insurance and social welfare.

After a 20-year debate, long-term care insurance coverage was finally implemented.[1] In this debate, the need to introduce long-term care coverage was a common concern but diverse interest groups, including welfare organizations, care associations, physician associations, quasi-public organizations such as the health insurance funds that purchase services, political parties, employer associations and trade unions (Meyer, 1996), argued about where responsibility for the costs should fall. Other questions included which costs should be covered and who should regulate care provision (Meyer, 1996). More generally, the political argument and struggle hinged on the question of whether long-term care coverage should be developed from a fiscal point of view or from a social policy perspective (Auth, 2017; Naegele, 2014). For example, the (neo)liberal Free Democratic Party (*Freie Demokratische Partei*, FDP) fought at the beginning of the debate for a completely private solution, with citizens covering their care risk through market-based private insurance. Welfare organizations and the Social Democratic Party, along with the trade unions, fought for a comprehensive social insurance solution to cover all care needs and opposed long-term care insurance based on cost-containment.

Long-Term Care Insurance

The long-term care insurance (LTCI) law introduced in 1994 was shaped by the FDP in alliance with employer associations (Lessenich, 2003). Long-term care insurance was introduced as the fifth pillar of the German social insurance system, which is based on the statutory social insurance pillars of pension insurance, unemployment insurance, health care insurance, and accident insurance. Its introduction as social insurance, rather than based on a tax model, corresponded with German welfare state tradition but was contentious because employer associations and the FDP favored a private capital-based solution to minimize costs (Meyer, 1996).

The new law profoundly changed the regulation mode and the relationship between state, market, and welfare organizations (Theobald, 2012: 65). At first glance, the results were an expansion of targeted public LTRC provisions and seemed to represent continuity with German welfare provision. One example of this continuity is the conservative focus on family care. By pushing for family and home care and through the implementation of a very narrowly defined understanding of care dependency, LTCI kept the conservative focus on family care intact (Auth, 2017), while not contradicting a neoliberal approach.

The introduction of LTCI had significant consequences not only for the provision of long-term care but for the social sector in general. It appeared to be a traditionally recognized instrument. But according to Stephan Lessenich, it was used on these grounds as a tool to transform the entire welfare regulation system. The goal was to redefine care provision to enable more efficient services that corresponded with cost-containment, and to provide users with free choice (Theobald, 2012: 65). LTCI is therefore seen as a "Bismarckian camouflage" that served to profoundly restructure the German welfare state (Lessenich, 2003).

The Design of LTCI: Budgeting and Standardization

The objective of cost-containment led to an insurance design that is not needs-based. Instead, the insurance pays a lump sum for strictly defined care tasks, tasks that do not necessarily cover the care needs of residents. Residents then have to pay the costs that are not covered as their equity share. The need for additional private payment to cover all care needs is a significant departure from the former social insurance system, which is either needs-based as health care insurance or equivalence-based as pension or unemployment insurance (Lessenich, 2003: 223).

The statutory definition of "care dependency" also represents strategies of cost-containment. The German model is known for its classification of care on a physical basis and according to strictly defined tasks. Between 1995 and 2017, the three levels of care dependency applied to instrumentally oriented, basic nursing, and body care-oriented tasks; for example, taking a shower, combing hair. These were defined within four areas: nursing care, nutrition, mobility, and housekeeping assistance. To be eligible for funding by LTCI, care receivers must have basic nursing care needs (at least 45 minutes for the first level, 120 minutes for the second level, and 240 minutes for the third level of care dependency) and housekeeping needs (45 minutes for the first level of care dependency) (see Schulz, 2010).

Until 2008, those with social care needs such as emotional support were not eligible for financial assistance unless they had other needs, such as for support with activities of daily living. In turn, beneficiaries (care receivers) were only categorized into a care level due to their physical needs even if their needs for social assistance made supporting them with activities of daily living much more extensive. For example, showering can be a much more time-consuming activity if the beneficiary has a cognitive impairment.

Since staffing is provided according to the level of care dependency, a higher care level leads to higher staffing ratios in nursing homes and vice versa (see Effects on Care Staff and Residents, on p.76). Thus, the initial exclusion of social care needs from the three levels of care became particularly problematic. Nevertheless, the recognition of social care needs subsequently changed as a result of a long-lasting struggle and debate. Welfare organizations and especially dementia associations and the service union Ver.di (the second-largest German trade union) have strongly criticized the understanding of care and care dependency embedded in LTCI. Many studies have illustrated the problematic and excluding effects of the assessment criteria and demonstrated the need for a different care dependency term (Landtag NRW, 2005; Ministry of Health, 2017b; Wingenfeld et al., 2007).

Social care needs due to cognitive impairments have been slowly included in the social insurance scope[2] but only in 2017 was a more fundamental transformation established: the implementation of a new statutory term of "care dependency." The three levels of care dependency were changed to five care grades and a new assessment introduced that included the need for social care. Therefore the funding situation for residents with cognitive impairments (i.e., with dementia) has improved but the staffing regulations in nursing homes remain the same and funding is still a lump sum that doesn't cover all the costs of care needs.

Commodification: Price Competition and the Rise of For-Profit Companies

The introduction of a care market in 1995 was another step towards marketization. Nullmeier describes the LTCI law as a "market-creating law" ("*Marktschaffungsgesetz*") (Nullmeier, 2002: 273, translation B. M.) because a welfare market was established, giving equal access to for-profit providers for the first time. (Moreover, the equal recognition of for-profit and non-profit providers was subsequently adopted in other social insurance laws.) With this change the former practice of cooperation between the state and welfare organizations ended. In the new marketized arrangement, LTRC is outsourced to welfare organizations *and* for-profit providers and this outsourcing is based on the explicit goal of introducing competition between them (Theobald, 2012). Competition to attract residents in this customer choice model is expected to be around nursing home quality and care rates/prices. In fact, competition around prices is the central competitive factor and has led to a transformation of the LTRC sector.

Price competition can be best described as *commodification of long-term care*. Commodification is here understood as a socio-economic process of transformation that changes access to care from being a social right provided by the welfare state (in cooperation with welfare organizations) to a commodity that is partly regulated by markets (Chorus, 2013). Thus long-term care becomes a quasi-commodity, even if the provider is a non-profit organization. Because the insurance pays only a lump sum, a high-equity ratio of nursing home costs are paid by private households (42.8%, Weiß, 2016). And because many residents and their relatives are in need of inexpensive services, non-profit organizations also have to keep their prices low to compete in the care market. Hence, price competition in particular is responsible for a commodification of care that blurs the lines between non-profit and for-profit.

A low price strategy and cost-containment are the reasons why non-profit providers apply strategies similar to those of the for-profit sector. Lower prices demand new forms of rationalization, strategies that have negative effects on work and care because cost savings mostly affect staffing and consequently the quality of work and care (Hielscher et al., 2013).

However, market logic does not apply completely. Care markets in Germany are described as quasi-markets because the LTCI law *prescribes* long-term care services, and care prices are not set by market principles of demand and supply but are *negotiated* between quasi-public organizations such as long-term care insurance funds and provider organizations in a process described as contract management.

Regulated and Forced Commodification

Since 1995, contract management as the new regulation mode between the state, market, and welfare associations has been introduced and defined in the LTCI law. Regional long-term care insurance funds are responsible for the negotiation of the contracts and care rates/prices with all care providers that meet the preconditions, such as the qualification of staff and cost-efficient services (Theobald, 2012: 65).[3]

Long-term care insurance funds negotiate with nursing home providers or welfare associations. In these negotiations, care prices (rates) are discussed and determined, with adaptions for the single nursing home or organizations like Caritas that negotiate for all their members. Nursing homes are required to be oriented towards standard market prices. In practice, all providers try to make sure that prices are high enough to cover their costs or to make a profit, while at the same time that they are not too high to assure a good position in a competitive care market (see Müller, 2018).

Due to the price negotiations and the delineation of long-term care services by public and quasi-public institutions, the outsourcing of LTRC to a for-profit provider is somewhat regulated. This means their autonomy as a market player is to some extent limited, and I suggest we should understand this as *regulated commodification*. Outsourcing to non-profit organizations, in turn, pushes for a market orientation and managerial practices. It can be most appropriately understood as *forced commodification*, because the logic of welfare has to be adjusted and oriented towards a market logic. This commodification and enforced competition blurs the lines between for-profit and non-profit but it does not constitute them as equals. The for-profit providers, especially nursing home chains, push for more market practices and fewer political regulations that limit profit. Furthermore, they offer lower nursing home rates/prices that put pressure on other nursing homes.

According to a study commissioned by an employer association, the increase of for-profit homes leads to a successive lowering of prices by non-profit homes in the same region (Rhine Westphalia Institute for Economic Research, 2011: 50). The low price strategy of for-profits leads as a result to a general price limitation in long-term care that reduces costs for residents and the public purse but also limits the income of nursing homes. Thus, to have a balanced budget, non-profit organizations that offer low care rates/prices also need to lower their expenses, which they often achieve by employing a particular mix of staff that is less expensive. Outsourcing of whole departments such as housekeeping within residential care homes to for-profit companies is also a strategy to limit expenses. In general it is evident that lower prices are often related to lower quality (Comondore et al., 2009; Harrington et al., 2012; Harrington, Ross, & Kang, 2015; Geraedts et al., 2016).

Furthermore, for-profit nursing home providers are often not unionized and thus pay wages that do not abide by collective wage agreements in order to afford lower prices (Rhine Westphalia Institute for Economic Research, 2011; Hielscher et al., 2013; Geraedts et al., 2016; Schleitzer, 2016; Auth, 2017; Müller, 2018). A union study found that workers in care organizations (e.g., nursing homes, hospitals) that adhere to collective wage agreements earn 24 percent more than colleagues in facilities that don't follow such agreements (Bispinck et al., 2013). The consequences are mainly felt by women, because women make up a significant majority of the labor force.

Although there are some similarities between for-profits and non-profits, their underlying differences are evident in the concepts of *regulated commodification* and *forced commodification*. It is obvious that for-profit employers, especially nursing home chains, follow a different logic than non-profit organizations. Their logic is capital accumulation and the search for profit (e.g., see the nursing home rating report, Augurzky et al., 2015: 16). Financial investors increasingly regard the German nursing home sector as a promising investment target (Schwaldt, 2015). In contrast, welfare organizations follow – or at least used to follow – the logic of care or welfare needs, which can be paternalistic and problematic but nevertheless implies a different course of action (see Mol, 2008 on the logic of choice versus the logic of care; Haug, 1996a, 1996b on different time logics; Meyer, 1996 on the logic of welfare organizations). In addition, welfare organizations face different conditions. They often use and move funding between facilities that belong to the same organization (cross-subsidization) and gain money through donations, and are therefore able to balance the marketization pressure differently (Hielscher et al., 2013).

Increase in For-Profit Provision

The commodification of long-term care has also led to an expansion of for-profit LTRC providers. With the introduction of LTCI, for-profit providers were recognized as being on equal terms with welfare organizations. In contract negotiations, they are equally favored, based on the concept of subsidiarity. This recognition, along with the introduction of price competition, led to a care market expansion based on for-profit ownership of home care agencies and nursing homes. In 1992, only 15 percent to 20 percent of long-term care residences and about 20 percent of home care agencies were owned by for-profit agencies (Rothgang, 1997). After the introduction of LTCI, the number of residential care homes more than tripled from about 4,300 in 1992 (Hielscher et al., 2013) to about 13,600 in 2015 (Federal Statistical Office, 2017). For-profit provision increased steadily, so that by 2015 for-profit providers held a 42 percent share of residential care and 65 percent of home care (Federal Statistical Office, 2017). Thus the main transformations in Germany are not the privatization of former public or non-profit services, but an expansion of LTRC services based on for-profit provision.

Privatization and Individualization of Costs

A form of privatization applies to the financing structure of LTCI. Usually, social insurance in Germany is co-paid by employees and employers. LTCI is paid in the same way, but the employers successfully negotiated to cut a public holiday as compensation for their share. Therefore, according to Rothgang, co-payment is only a "fiction" (Rothgang, 1994; Lessenich, 2003: 225; Naegele, 2014). In the context of a debate about the competitiveness of Germany as a business location, this new regulation evolved into a master standard for all subsequent social policy decisions. Under this approach, reforms should be cost-neutral, or at least should not increase costs for the employer[4] (Lessenich, 2003). In this way legislation privatized costs by shifting the responsibility to individuals. Compensation for the employers' share was the main point of controversy between the conservative-liberal government and the social democratic opposition in the long process preceding implementation of long-term care insurance. The FDP pushed for an even larger compensation for employers that included cutting two public holidays and introducing unpaid sick days. Unions were strongly opposed to employer compensation since co-payment between worker and employer is symbolic for the German welfare state (Meyer, 1996).

See Table 4.1 for a summary of the various processes of marketization, commodification, and privatization in Germany.

Effects on Care Staff and Residents

These new forms of marketization and commodification have effects on working and caring conditions in long-term residential care, with negative consequences for workers and residents. In this section the focus is on the effects of commodification at the level of the nursing home and on care interactions within nursing homes.

The Taylorization and Standardization of Care

Financial restrictions led to a restrictive insurance design that pays only part of the care needs and is oriented to strictly defined care tasks. Competition is also aimed at reducing expenses in long-term care. This cost-containment policy,

Table 4.1 Forms of marketization in Germany

	For-profit actors can be involved	Beyond ownership
Market Practices/Competition	**1 Commodification** Outsourcing with competition: *Regulated commodification* for for-profit providers *Forced commodification* for non-profit providers Customer choice models	**2 Managerial practices** Importation of managerial practices into the non-profit and public sector: Efficiency, contract management, competition, budgeting, task-orientation, standardization
No market practices	**3 Privatization** Co-payment; only a fiction Reliance and support of (unpaid) care/family care	**4 Traditional** Outsourcing without competition (doesn't exist today) Unpaid family care

Source: Based on Anttonen & Meagher, 2013; modified for Germany

accompanied by a resident population with increasingly complex care needs, had led to underfunding and understaffing in German residential care homes. This resulted in a Taylorization and standardization of care, that in some examples make care work look like assembly-line work (Interview with a care worker, Müller, 2018; Armstrong et al., 2009; Matuschek et al., 2008: 50). There is often a strict division of labor, with clinical care (*Behandlungspflege*) carried out by those defined as highly skilled, and with basic body care and social care frequently left to low-paid staff members who have little formal training (Hielscher et al., 2013).

The workload for qualified care workers and assistive staff has increased due to decreased staffing levels and work tasks shifted between occupational groups. Time pressure is thus a common concern in the nursing home sector (Hielscher et al., 2013). While the resident-staff ratio was 2.37 in Germany in 2003, it decreased to 2.46 in 2013 (Greß & Stegmüller, 2016). It is important to stress that the data do not include the increased workload due to an older and sicker resident population, an increased demand to provide high-quality care with increased requirements for quality management, and especially the need for documentation (Lloyd et al., 2014; Choiniere et al., 2015). A nurse supervisor for a non-profit long-term care home explains:

> The tension is that the level of quality the government expects us to maintain and the regulations [are] increasing but we get the same amount of money as before. So the regulation is more and more and more but they didn't tell us you get 10 per cent more money. So this regulation forces us to have a lot of people [responsible for] quality management but we didn't get money for this. So the expert standards that we have that were created require us to train people. For example when it comes to food we have people trained especially how to create food that is especially for people suffering from dementia or people who have problems swallowing. We train the people but we don't get money for the training. So higher expectations. We need to train more and more people and get no money for this. No extra money.
>
> (Interview with Nurse Supervisor)

Increased regulation also led to work intensification and less time for direct resident care. Moreover, the increased demands for quality management and documentation[5] ties care staff to management positions even if this is not recognized in the formal staff calculations. According to German national law 50 percent of staff must be nurses or elder carers with a three-year qualification. Nevertheless, numbers are lower in some jurisdictions (Greß & Stegmüller, 2016). And this regulation has no effect on the number of paid personnel or the staff–resident ratio. Staffing is not set by law and not calculated in a formal resident assessment; instead, regional gross staffing guidelines are formulated in relation to five levels of care. While the care levels/care grades are set nationally, the staffing guidelines are different in every jurisdiction, so staff numbers differ greatly and are not regulated on the basis of everyday care needs[6] (Greß & Stegmüller, 2016). Therefore residents with the same care needs are attended by different numbers of staff, depending on the jurisdiction. For example, for 80 residents with an average acuity level, the jurisdiction Brandenburg requires 27.1 full-time equivalents (FTEs) whereas Saxony requires 34.5 FTEs (Greß & Stegmüller, 2016). Work intensification and time pressure lead to the accumulation of overtime (Theobald et al. 2013). Workers with a migrant background provide way more unpaid extra hours than care staff without a migration background (Theobald 2018).

Additionally, according to the management and staff at a long-term care facility we studied, the position of a quality manager, for example, in practice decreases the resident–care staff ratio because the quality manager is included in the calculation even though this manager does not provide direct care (Management Interview, Germany). A study in 2009 demonstrated that the time provided for resident care in German LTRC facilities is very low. If only the interaction between residents and care workers (nursing and social care; resident-related housekeeping included; administrative work excluded) is taken into account, then only one hour per resident per day is provided (Stenger & Kirchen-Peters, 2011; Hielscher et al., 2013).

These cost-containment strategies not only affect caring conditions negatively but influence individual care workers and residents.

An Education in Markethood

On a subjective level, forced commodification can be understood as an "education in markethood." Individuals learn to act like market-subjects and understand they are responsible for their own fate (Nullmeier, 2004; Bröckling, Krasmann & Lemke, 2000). Both care workers and management in non-profit care homes experience this form of education and thus are forced to apply a market-logic. However, some nursing homes react with creative coping strategies or even resistance. They figure out ways to employ more staff without undermining collective wage agreements (Müller, 2018; Müller, Goldmann & Theobald, 2017).

The managing director of one of these non-profit homes criticizes the standardizing of care that is labeled as consumer protection. This standardization takes away staff autonomy and time. Before the introduction of long-term care insurance with its accompanying risk management, a care worker was able to provide care based on their skills and the needs of residents, but nowadays the standardization and the forced following of so-called expert standards requires them to first think about these standards. "So I think in terms of the quality of care or the substance of people's care, it has tended to get worse" (Interview with Management, Germany). According to this managing director, the quality of care has deteriorated due to the priority given to quality management.

Precarious Working Conditions and the Increasing De-Qualification of Care Work

The conditions of work are also negatively affected by the implementation of marketization strategies. The formal care work workforce increased from approximately 320,000 in 1995 to approximately 1.1 million in 2015, with a rise in employment rates for both those with and without significant formal training (Federal Statistical Office, 2015; Oschmiansky, 2010; Theobald, 2012).

This increase is based mainly on non-standard and precarious working conditions that are attributable to cost-containment and price competition. In residential care, part-time work rose from 39.1 percent in 1995 to 63 percent in 2015. Eight and a half percent of care workers hold a marginal employment contract, with a low absolute earning level and low social security standards compared to full-time and part-time employees. According to Theobald, care workers who have no (or no recognized) formal training are often marginally employed (Theobald, 2012: 69; Federal Statistical Office, 2017). In a different study Theobald demonstrates that care staff with low formal training and a migrant background often have work arrangements with fewer work hours than care staff with low formal training without a migrant background (Theobald, 2018).

Additionally, marketization has led to a hierarchization of employment groups, and social and relational elements of care have become increasingly delegated to low-paid care workers such as social care aides. At the same time, the volunteers—most of whom are women—are increasingly taking over social care duties. Also, refugees are explicitly targeted as possible resources to provide volunteer work. In general, marketization has led to a deregulation of collective bargaining policy and in that context to an overall pressure on wages, especially for less formally trained staff (Dahme & Wohlfahrt, 2007; Kühnlein, 2007). In short, the marketization and commodification of long-term residential care in German nursing homes has led to a decline in working and caring conditions.

Marketization Marginalizes Care Relations and Impairs Working Conditions

Cost-containment was the main reason for the development of LTCI in its present design. The restriction of public payment to a lump sum was justified on the basis of fiscal constraint. The intended competition between provider organizations is also justified as a way to reduce costs. Mosebach (2010) used the term "competitive cost-containment" to describe such processes within the German health care sector, a description that is effective in conveying an understanding of the two commodification processes that are prevalent in the LTRC sector.

We are witnessing a forced commodification with regard to non-profit ownership and a regulated commodification with regard to for-profit ownership.

Marketization is now a widespread phenomenon in Germany. More concretely, cost-containment, regulated and forced commodification and privatization are the main processes that have led to the marginalization of care as a relationship and to a decline in working conditions. This has an impact especially on women as the main professional caregivers because they make up the biggest part of the work force and the residents in nursing homes. Additionally, women mostly are responsible for unpaid care work, which fills the care gap that is a result of marketization and commodification of care.

Acknowledgments

I'd like to thank the interview participants for sharing their stories. Many thanks also to Pat Armstrong, the principal investigator, and Wendy Winters the project coordinator of the Reimagining long-term care project of which the research of this chapter has been part of. I am also grateful for very helpful comments and suggestions on different versions of this chapter and want to thank Pat Armstrong, John Kannankulam, Hildegard Theobald, and members of our team who participated in the book workshop.

Funding

This research was supported by the Social Sciences and Humanities Research Council of Canada as part of their Major Collaborative Research Initiative.

Notes

1 A report written by an influential organization in the German elder care sector (*Kuratorium Deutsche Altenhilfe*, KDA) in 1974 was the starting point of the debate about long-term care coverage. The report recommended that statutory health care insurance should cover complete residential care costs, and relieve social assistance insurance of the high expense (Meyer, 1996).
2 In various reforms, care receivers with such needs were funded on a very basic level but to a gradually increasing extent. In a 2002 reform, beneficiaries with supplementary social care needs were able to get an additional 460 euros a year. In a reform called *Pflege-Weiterentwicklungsgesetz* in 2008, this allowance increased to 100 to 200 euros a month (home-based care) and the employment of low formally trained social care aides (initially to take care of residents with dementia) in nursing homes was funded (Ministry of Health, 2017a). Moreover, this reform included care receivers who were not previously eligible for a level of care dependency by introducing a new level of care dependency for them called level 0 (TNS, 2011).
3 There is also no regulation of care provision that assesses regional needs, which is the case in other health care- related areas, for example, of family physicians in private practice. Even if there are many care service companies or long-term care residences operating in a region, every new provider has to be considered, which increases the competition between nursing homes. Thus, further regional concentration of nursing homes is expected, which will be an additional competitive advantage for nursing home chains (Lennartz, 2011, p. 4).
4 Nevertheless, increases in long-term care insurance share rates since 2008 are paid by the employer and employee alike.
5 A new documentation system is being developed to reduce the time needed for documentation.
6 For example, the actual staffing guidelines in North-Rhine Westphalia are: 1: 8 (care grade 1, lowest care needs); 1:4.66 (care grade 2); 1:3.05 (care grade 3); 1:2.24 (care grade 4); 1:2 (care grade 5) (Tillmann & Sloane, 2017). But these numbers include vacations, sick days, and further training so the actual ratio is lower (Hielscher et al., 2013). However, the introduction of a resident assessment instrument is planned for 2020.

References

Anttonen, A. & Meagher, G. (2013). Mapping marketization: Concepts and goals. In G. Meagher & M. Szebehely. (Eds.), *Marketization in Nordic eldercare: A research report on legislation, oversight, extent and consequences*. Stockholm: Department of Social Work, Stockholm University.

Armstrong, P., Banerjee, A., Szebehely, M., Armstrong, H., Daly, T. & Lafrance, S. (2009). *They deserve better: The long-term care experience in Canada and Scandinavia.* Ottawa, ON: Canadian Centre for Policy Alternatives.

Armstrong, P. & Braedley, S. (Eds.). (2013). *Troubling care. Critical perspectives on research and practices.* Toronto, ON: Canadian Scholars' Press.

Auth, D. (2017). *Pflege in Zeiten der Ökonomisierung. Wandel von Care-Regimen in Großbritaniennen, Schweden und Deutschland.* Münster. [Transformation of Care Regimes in Great Britain, Sweden and Germany. Munster.]

Auth, D. & Rudolph, C. (2017). Care im sozialinvestiven Wohlfahrtstaat – Mehr Geschlechtergerechtigkeit oder mehr Krise? Einleitung. In: Femina Politica: Care im (sozialinvestiven) *Wohlfahrtstaat*, 2, 26, 9–19. [Care in the social investment welfare state – more gender equity or more crisis? Introduction. Femina Politica: Care in (the Social Investment) *Welfare State*, 2, 26, 9–19.]

Augurzky, B., Heger, D., Hentschker, C., Krolop, S. & Stroka, M. (2015). Pflegeheim rating report 2015 executive summary. http://www.rwi-essen.de/media/content/pages/publikationen/sonstige/pflegeheimratingreport2015_execsum.pdf

Banner, G. (1991). Von der Behörde zum Dienstleistungsunternehmen – Die Kommunen brauchen ein neues Steuerungsmodell. In: *VOP – Fachzeitschrift für die öffentliche Verwaltung*, 1, 6–11. [From public authority to a service company – municipalities need a new regulative model. In: *VOP – Journal of Public Administration*, 1, 6–11.]

Bispinck, R., Dribbusch, H., Öz, F. & Stoll, E. (2013). Einkommens- und Arbeitsbedingungen. In Pflegeberufen. Eine Analyse auf Basis der WSI-Lohnspiegel-Datenbank, Arbeitspapier 21. [Income and working conditions within the long-term care profession. An analysis based on WSI-Wage-Data Bank, Working Paper 21.]

Bröckling, U., Krasmann, S. & Lemke, Th. (Eds.) (2000). *Gouvernementalität der Gegenwart. Studien zur Ökonomisierung des Sozialen.* Frankfurt a.M. [*Contemporary governmentality. Studies on marketization of the social.* Frankfurt.]

Choiniere, J. A., Doupe, M., Goldmann, M., Harrington, C., Jacobsen, F. F., Lloyd, L., Rootham, M. & Szebehely, M. (2015). Mapping nursing home inspections and audits in six countries. *Ageing International*, 41(1), 40–61. doi: 10.1007/s12126-015-9230-6

Chorus, S. (2013). *Care Ökonomie im Postfordismus. Perspektiven einer integralen Ökonomie-Theorie.* Munster. [*Care economy in postfordism. Perspectives of an integrative economic theory.* Munster]

Comondore, V. R., Devereaux, P. J., Zhou, Q., Stone, S. B., Busse, J. W., Ravindran, N. C. et al. (2009). Quality of care in for-profit and not-for-profit nursing homes: Systematic review and meta-analysis. *British Medical Journal*, 339, b2732.

Dahme, H. J., & Wohlfahrt, N. (2007). Vom Korporatismus zur Strategischen Allianz von Sozialstaat und Sozialwirtschaft. Neue 'Sozialpartnerschaft' auf Kosten der Beschäftigten? In: Dahme, Heinz-Jürgen/Trube, Achim/Wohlfahrt, Norbert (Hg.): *Arbeit in sozialen Diensten: flexibel und schlecht bezahlt? Zur aktuellen Entwicklung der Beschäftigungsbedingungen im Sozialsektor.* Schorndorf, 22–34. [From Corporatism to Strategic Alliances between the Social State and the Social Economy. New 'Social Partnerships' at the Expense of Employees? Dahme, Heinz-Jürgen/Trube, Achim/Wohlfahrt, Norbert (eds.): *Labour in Social Services: Flexible and Poorly Paid? About the actual Development of Working Conditions in the Social Sector.* Schorndorf, 22–34.]

Germany, Federal Statistical Office. (2001–2017). *Long-term care statistics in the context of the long-term care insurance (various years).* Wiesbaden.

Geraedts, M., Harrington, C., Schumacher, D. & Kraska, R. (2016). Trade-off between quality, price, and profit orientation in Germany's nursing homes. *Ageing International*, 41(1), 89–98. https://doi.org/10.1007/s12126-015-9227-1

Greß, S. & Stegmüller, K. (2016). Gesetzliche Personalbemessung in der stationären Altenpflege.[Statutory Resident Assessment in residential Elder Care]. https://gesundheit-soziales.verdi.de/++file.../pgp_2016_01_gress_stegmueller.pdf

Harrington, C., Olney, B., Carrillo, H. & Kang, T. (2012). Nurse staffing and deficiencies in the largest for-profit nursing home chains and chains owned by private equity companies. *Health Services Research*, 47, 106–128.

Harrington, C., Ross, L. & Kang, T. (2015). Hidden owners, hidden profits, and poor nursing home care: A case study. *International Journal of Health Services*. doi:10.1177/0020731415594772

Haug, F. (1996a). Knabenspiele und Menschheitsarbeit. Geschlechterverhältnisse als Produktionsverhältnisse. In Dies.: *Frauen-Politiken*. Berlin, 125–154. [Boys games and men's work. Gender relations as relations of production. Id: *Women's Politics*. Berlin, 125–154.]

Haug, F. (1996b). Ökonomie der Zeit, darin löst sich schließlich alle Ökonomie auf. Herausforderungen für einen sozialistischen Feminismus. In Dies.: *Frauen-Politiken*. Berlin, 105–124. [Economy of time, to this all economy ultimately reduces itself. Id: *Women's Politics*. Berlin, 105–124.]

Heinze, R. G. & Olk, T. (1984). Sozialpolitische Steuerung: Von der Subsidiarität zum Korporatismus. In M. Glagow (Hg.), *Gesellschaftssteuerung zwischen Korporatismus und Subsidiarität*. Bielefeld, 162–194. [Social political regulation: From subsidiarity to corporatism. M. Glagow (ed.): *Regulation of society between corporatism and subsidiarity*. Bielefeld, 162–194.]

Hielscher, V., Nock, L., Kirchen-Peters, S. & Blass, K. (2013). *Zwischen Kosten, Zeit und Anspruch: das alltägliche Dilemma sozialer Dienstleistungsarbeit*. Wiesbaden. [*Between costs, time and demand: The daily dilemma of social service work*. Wiesbaden.]

Kühnlein, G. (2007). Auswirkungen der aktuellen arbeitsmarkt- und tarifpolitischen Entwicklungen auf die Arbeits- und Beschäftigungsverhältnisse von Frauen in der Sozialen Arbeit. In Dahme, H.-J./Trube, A./N. Wohlfahrt (Eds.): *Arbeit in sozialen Diensten: flexibel und schlecht bezahlt? Zur aktuellen Entwicklung der Beschäftigungsbedingungen im Sozialsektor*. Schorndorf, 35–46. [Consequences of the recent labour market and tariff political developments on working and employment relations of women in social work. Dahme, H.-J./Trube, A./N. Wohlfahrt (Eds.): *Labour in social services: Flexible and poorly paid? About the actual development of working conditions in the social sector*. Schorndorf, 35–46.]

Landtag NRW. (2005). *Enquete-Kommission. Situation und Zukunft der Pflege in NRW*. Düsseldorf. [*Enquete Commission. Situation and future of long-term care in North-Rhine Westphalia*. Dusseldorf.]

Lanoix, M. (2013). Labour as embodied practice: The lessons of care work. *Hypatia: A Journal of Feminist Philosophy*, 28, 85–100.

Lennartz, Peter. (2011). Aktuelles aus dem Gesundheitswesen. Stationärer Pflegemarkt im Wandel – Gewinner und Verlierer 2020. In: Ernst & Young. http://www.paritaet-lsa.de/cms/files/pflegemarktstudie_2011_ernst___young.pdf [News from the Health sector. Residential long-term care market in transformation. Winner and Loser 2020. Ernst & Young. http://www.paritaet-lsa.de/cms/files/pflegemarktstudie_2011_ernst___young.pdf]

Lessenich, S. (2003). *Dynamischer Immobilismus: Kontinuität und Wandel im deutschen Sozialmodell.* Frankfurt/Main, New York. [*Dynamic immobility: Continuity and change in the German social model.* Frankfurt/ New York.]

Lloyd, L., Banerjee, A., Harrington, C., Jacobsen, F. F. & Szebehely, M. (2014). "It is a scandal!" Comparing the causes and consequences of nursing home media scandals in five countries. *International Journal of Sociology and Social Policy, 34*(1/2), 2–18. doi:10.1108/ijssp-03-2013-0034

Maurer, A. (2015). Dominanz von Markt, Wettbewerb und Kostenoptimierung: Ökonomisierung. In H. Brandenburg & H. Güther, *Lehrbuch Gerontologische Pflege.* 1. Aufl. Bern.

Matuschek, I., Kleeman, F. & Voß, G. (2008). Subjektivierte Taylorisierung als Beherrschung der Arbeitsperson. *Prokla* 150: Umkämpfte Arbeit. 38. Jg. Vol. 1, 49–65.[Subjectivated Taylorism as domination of workers. *Prokla* 150: Contested Work. 38. Jg. Vol. 1, 49–65.]

Meyer, J. (1996). *Der Weg zur Pflegeversicherung. Positionen – Akteure – Politikprozesse.* Frankfurt a/M. [*Development of the long-term care insurance. Positions – actors – policy processes.* Frankfurt.]

Ministry of Health. (2017a). Zusätzliche Betreuungskräfte. https://www.bundesgesund heitsministerium.de/themen/pflege/pflegekraefte/zusaetzliche-betreuungskraefte. html (Access 4.12.2017). [Additional social care aides. https://www.bundesgesundheits ministerium.de/themen/pflege/pflegekraefte/zusaetzliche-betreuungskraefte.html (Access 4.12.2017)]

Ministry of Health. (2017b). Die Pflegestärkungsgesetze – Hintergründe zu den Neuregelungen in der Pflege. [Care strengthening act – Background to the new legislation in long-term care.] https://www.bundesgesundheitsministerium.de/index.php?id=684#c4070 (Access 4.12.2017).

Mol, A. (2008). *The logic of care: Health and the problem of patient choice.* Abingdon, Oxon: Routledge.

Mosebach, K. (2010). Kommerzialisierung und Ökonomisierung von Gesundheitssystemen. Ein essayistischer Problemaufriss zur Identifizierung möglicher Felder zukünftiger medizinsoziologischer Forschung, Diskusionspapier 2. [Commercialization and marketization of health care systems. A problem oriented essay to identify possible fields of future medical-sociological research. Discussion paper] https://publikationen.ub.unifrankfurt. de/frontdoor/index/index/year/2012/docId/27712

Müller, B. (2016). *Wert-Abjektion. Zur Abwertung von Care-Arbeit im patriarchalen Kapitalismus.* Münster. [*Value-abjection. On the devaluation of care in patriarchal capitalism.* Münster.]

Müller, B. (2018). Privatization and marketization in long-term residential care in Germany: Effects on care and care work. *Politiche Sociali/Social Policies, 1.*

Müller, B., Goldmann, M., & Theobald, H. (2017). Apprentices: More hands are necessary but not sufficient. In P. Armstrong & T. Daly (Eds.), *Exercising choice in long-term residential care.* Ottawa, ON: Canadian Centre for Policy Alternatives.

Naegele, G. (2014). *20 Jahre Verabschiedung der Gesetzlichen Pflegeversicherung. Eine Bewertung aus sozialpolitischer Sicht. Wiso Diskurs.* Friedrich Ebert Stiftung. Bonn. [*20 years statutory long-term care insurance. An evaluation from a social political perspective. Wiso discourse.* Friedrich Ebert Foundation. Bonn.]

Nullmeier, F. (2002). Auf dem Weg zu Wohlfahrtsmärkten. In W. Süß (Ed.), *Deutschland in den Neunziger Jahren. Politik und Gesellschaft zwischen Wiedervereinigung und Globalisierung.*

Opladen. [On its way to welfare markets. W. Süß (Ed.), *Germany in the nineties. Politic and society between reunification and globalization*. Opladen.]
Nullmeier, F. (2004). Vermarktlichung des Sozialstaats, WSI-Mitteilungen, 9. [Marketization of the social state, WSI-Notice, 9.] https://www.boeckler.de/wsi-mitteilungen_24363_24370.htm
Oschmiansky, H. (2010). Wandel der Erwerbsformen in einem Frauenarbeitsmarkt. Das Beispiel "Altenpflege". *Zeitschrift für Sozialreform (ZSR), 56*(1), 31–57. [Change of employment patterns in a women's labour market. The example "elder care". *Journal of Social Reform (JSR), 56*(1), 31–57.]
Pfau-Effinger, B., Och, R. & Eichler, M., (2008). Ökonomisierung, Pflegepolitik und Strukturen der Pflege älterer Menschen. In Evers, A./Heinze, R. G. (Eds.), *Sozialpolitik. Ökonomisierung und Entgrenzung.* Wiesbaden, 88–98. [Marketization, Care policy and Structures of Care for the Elderly. In Evers, A./Heinze, R. G. (Eds.), *Social politics, marketization and blurred boundaries.* Wiesbaden, 88–98.]
Rhine Westphalia Institute for Economic Research (Eds.) (2011). *Faktenbuch Pflege –Die Bedeutung privater Anbieter im Pflegemarkt*, Endbericht September 2011 Forschungsprojekt im Auftrag des Arbeitgeberverbandes Pflege. [*Fact book long-term care – the meaning of private provider within the care market*, Final Report September 2011 Research Project on behalf of the Employer Association Long-Term Care.]
Rothgang, H. (1994). Die Einführung der Pflegeversicherung – Ist das Sozialversicherungsprinzip am Ende? In Riedmüller, B./Olk, T. (Eds.), Grenzen des Sozialversicherungsstaats. *Leviathan, 14,* Special Issue, Opladen, 164–187. [The Introduction of the Statutory Long-Term Care Insurance – Is the Social Insurance Model at a Final Stage? Riedmüller, B./Olk, T. (Eds.) Limits of the Social Insurance State. *Leviathan, 14,* Special Issue, Opladen, 164–187.]
Rothgang, H., (1997). *Ziele und Wirkungen der Pflegeversicherung. Eine ökonomische Analyse.* Frankfurt/New York. [*Goals and Effects of the Long-Term Care Insurance. An Economic Analysis.* Frankfurt/New York.]
Schleitzer, E. (2016). Das Geschäft mit den alten Menschen. Investmentgesellschaften dominieren die Altenpflege, in: *Sozialismus* 5, Hamburg. [The Business with the Elderly. Investment Companies Dominating the Elder Care Sector. *Socialism* 5, Hamburg.]
Schulz, E. (2010). *The long-term care system in Germany.* German Institute for Economic Research (DIW Berlin).
Schwaldt, N. (2015). Mit Pflegeheimen lässt sich reichlich Profit machen. [Long-Term Care Homes are very Profitable.] https://www.welt.de/finanzen/immobilien/article139642076/Mit-Pflegeheimen-laesst-sich-reichlich-Profit-machen.html
Seeleib-Kaiser, M. & Toivonen, T. (2011). Between reforms and birth rates: Germany, Japan, and family policy discourse. *Social Politics, 18*(3).
Stenger, J. & Kirchen-Peters, S. (2011). Finanzierung von ambulanten und stationären Pflegeleistungen nach SGB XI. In: Aktion Psychisch Kranke (Eds.). *Projektbericht. Entwicklung eines Konzeptes quartiersorientierter integrierter Versorgung für pflegebedürftige Menschen mit psychischen Beeinträchtigungen, insbesondere Demenz.* Bonn. [Financing of Home (Ambulatory) and Residential Long-Term Care Services according to the Social Code Book XI. Action Mentally Ill (Eds.), *Project report. Development of a concept of district oriented and integrative care provision for care dependents with mental impairments, especially dementia.* Bonn.]

Theobald, H. (2012). Combining welfare mix and new public management: The case of long-term care insurance in Germany. *International Journal of Social Welfare, 21*, 61–74.

Theobald, H. (2015). Marketization and managerialization of long-term care policies in a comparative perspective. In T. Klenk and E. Pavolini (Eds.), *Restructuring welfare governance: Marketization, managerialism and welfare state professionalism* (pp. 27–45). Northampton, MA: Edward Elgar Publishing.

Theobald, H. (2018). *Pflegearbeit in Deutschland, Schweden und Japan. Wie werden Pflegekräfte mit Migrationshintergrund und Männer in die Pflegearbeit einbezogen?* Düsseldorf: Hans-Böckler-Studie [*Long-term care work in Germany, Sweden and Japan. How are care staff with migrant background and man integrated in care work?* Dusseldorf : Hans-Böckler-Study.] (https://www.boeckler.de/pdf/p_study_hbs_383.pdf).

Theobald, H., Szebehely, M. & Preuß, M. (2013). *Arbeitsbedingungen in der Altenpflege. Die Kontinuität der Berufsverläufe – ein deutsch-schwedischer Vergleich.* Berlin. [*Working conditions in elder care. The continuity of career paths – a German Swedish Comparison.* Berlin.]

Tillmann, R. & Sloane, K. (2017). Nord-Rhein Westfahlen: Personalschlüssel werden angepasst. *Care Konkret, 17,* 6. [North Rhine Westphalia: Adjusting the staff ratio. *Care Konkret, 17,* 6.]

TNS (2011). *Abschlussbericht zur Studie, Wirkungen des Pflege-Weiterentwicklungsgesetzes. Bericht zu den Repräsentativerhebungen im Auftrag des Bundesministeriums für Gesundheit.* München. [*Final report about the study, effects of the act concerning the further development of care. Report to the representative survey on behalf of the Ministry of Health.* Munich.]

Tronto, J. (1993). *Moral boundaries: A political argument for an ethics of care.* New York, NY: Routledge.

Tronto, J. (2011). A feminist democratic ethics of care and global care workers: Citizenship and responsibility. In R. Mahon & F. Robinson (Eds.), *Feminist ethics and social policy: Toward a new global political economy of care.* Vancouver, BC: University of British Columbia Press.

Weiß, C. (2016). *Vergütung der stationären Langzeitpflege. Leistungsgerechtigkeit – Wettbewerbsneutralität – Dynamische Effizienz.* Münster. [*Payment of Residential Long-Term Care. Service Equity, Competitive Neutrality – Dynamic Efficiency.* Munster.]

Wingenfeld, K., Büscher, A., & Schaeffer, D. (2007). *Recherche und Analyse von Pflegebedürftigkeitsbegriffen und Einschätzungsinstrumenten.* Bielefeld. [*Review and analysis of care dependency and assessment instruments.* Bielefeld.]

Chapter 5

Privatization of Long-term Residential Care in Canada
The Case of Three Provinces

Pat Armstrong, Hugh Armstrong, Martha MacDonald, and Malcolm Doupe

---

Canada's federal system leaves the primary responsibility for healthcare services to the provinces and territories, which in turn transfer some responsibilities to municipalities. The federal government has, however, played a major role in funding healthcare through various transfer programs over the years (currently through the Canada Health Transfer). In 1984 the *Canada Health Act* was introduced to ensure some consistency across the country in return for federal money. However, the *Act* is focused primarily on medically necessary hospital and physician care. For these insured services covered by the *Act*, federal funding is conditional on the provinces and territories complying with five principles. Their public health insurance schemes must cover everyone and do so without imposing fees for any of the insured services. In addition to these principles of universality and accessibility, the *Act* specifies that services must be comprehensive, defined as covering "all insured health services provided by hospitals, medical practitioners or dentists, and where the law of the province so permits, similar or additional services rendered by other healthcare practitioners" (Government of Canada, 1985). The coverage must also be portable outside the jurisdiction and the public health insurance scheme must be administered by a non-profit organization (although there is no mention of non-profit or for-profit delivery of the covered services).

Since its origin, the suite of services comprising the older adult care continuum, such as home-based services, nursing homes, and more recently some community-based housing with health services options introduced as an alternative to nursing home care, have been excluded from this *Act* and the national standards it provides, as limited as these standards may be. This, in turn, has led to major differences in the organization of and access to these care options across Canada, with almost no evidence establishing their various merits and challenges. Furthermore, the nomenclature used to describe these baskets of services varies widely across Canada and leads to challenging cross-jurisdictional discussions. As the remainder of this chapter demonstrates, the exclusion of continuing care from the *Canada Health Act* has also led to vast additional inter-provincial differences as it relates to the supply and mix of services offered, to the staffing levels provided, and to regulatory (or in some instances, lack thereof) policies. As a case in point, nursing home bed supply is shown to vary substantially across Canada, from a high of 363.2 beds per 1,000 people 85+ years old in Prince Edward Island to as few as 264.1 beds in British Columbia. This diversity is unrelated to additional provincial differences such as home care expenditures, and greater supply is positively associated with reductions in alternative level of care hospital days, further highlighting the need to evaluate more critically the diverse continuing care options that exist across Canada, including policies said to ensure their equitable application.

A variety of factors have contributed to the rate and nature of privatization in continuing care across Canada. Beginning in the 1990s, the federal government began cutting funding transfers as it followed neoliberal approaches to deficits and to government programs. But this reduction in federal funding was not the sole factor. Partly in response, the provinces and territories in turn adopted, to varying degrees, their own versions of neoliberal governance. The familiar arguments of the need to cut government spending and to improve both efficiency and quality through market strategies were certainly invoked. But these were combined with arguments from community organizations and researchers that pointed to the risks of hospitalization, the oppressiveness of institutions, and the preference for care at home. The number of beds in acute care hospitals was reduced starting in the early 1990s (CIHI, 2005: Figures 1 and 12). Beginning in the early 1980s, numerous psychiatric, chronic care and rehabilitation hospitals were closed or reclassified as residential care facilities (CIHI, 2005: Table 1.9). Because the principles of the *Canada Health Act* apply most clearly to hospitals and doctors, this movement of care outside their services created more opportunities for privatization. It also meant greater demand for care in nursing homes. This, coupled with preferences of most people to remain in the community for as long as possible, has resulted not only in the growth in home care, but has also affected nursing home use patterns. Individuals are now admitted into nursing homes older, frailer and with more complex needs (Menec et al., 2002; Sharkey, 2008). There was increasing talk of the need for individuals and families to take responsibility for their own health, talk that usually ignored the fact that most of this responsibility was assigned without discussion to women. The popularity of Canada's medicare system meant that changes were primarily justified, in gender-blind fashion, as a means of saving this public system of hospital and doctor care.

This chapter provides examples of privatization related to nursing home care in three of the four Canadian provinces in our study. It sets out both commonalities and differences among Nova Scotia, Manitoba and Ontario, identifying factors that contribute to these commonalities and differences within a single federation. The British Columbia case is discussed in the chapter by Andrew Longhurst and colleagues in this volume. All three provinces discussed here provide public funding for the care of nursing home residents (provided by nurses, care aides, physicians and some therapists) while charging what are sometimes called accommodation or per diem fees associated with room and board. However, as a study for our project shows, there is inconsistency across jurisdictions in what is considered 'care', and in how much public coverage there is for capital costs, therapies and other services (MacDonald, 2015).

Privatizing Ownership and Delivery

Before neoliberal approaches began to take serious hold in the 1990s, nursing home care was provided in all three provinces by a mixed collection of for-profit, non-profit and publicly owned homes (Tarman, 1990: Table 1). The for-profit homes were, for the most part, small and owned by a family or a nurse, while many of the non-profit homes were owned by religious organizations. Hospitals provided much of the care for those with clinical and significant cognitive impairment. The distribution by ownership differed substantially by region, with Atlantic Canada having many small for-profit nursing homes and the prairie provinces having more publicly owned homes, a pattern that continues into this century (Berta et al., 2006). As an article by Charlene Harrington and colleagues (2016) on for-profit ownership points out, it is not easy to get current detailed data on the ownership of nursing homes in Canada, and as the chapter in this volume by Tamara Daly makes clear, big data may conceal as much as they reveal. The difficulty of obtaining data suggests that there is little official interest in supporting the investigation of how different ownership patterns influence care. However, we do have quantitative data from earlier surveys, from our analytical mapping, and from some provincial studies that indicate both a move to private for-profit delivery and a tendency to concentrate for-profit nursing homes where large populations (and therefore resources) exist that can encourage economies of scale in care services (Harrington et al., 2017). We also have evidence that quality care tends to be lower in for-profit versus non-profit and public homes (McGregor & Ronald, 2011; Ronald et al., 2016; Doupe et al., 2011; Tanuseputro et al., 2015). For example, Berta et al. (2006: Table 4) found that within each Canadian jurisdiction, total direct hours of care were lowest in for-profit homes versus non-profit, government and religious facilities. See also the chapter by Charlene Harrington and Frode Jacobsen in this volume. We did not undertake site visits at any large national corporate chains because none were suggested to us by those we consulted in governments, unions and community organizations, when we asked about promising practices. However, we did study one large regional chain that is growing rapidly and, more significantly, we saw multiple examples of services contracted out to the for-profit sector that impeded the quality of resident care.

Ontario, by far the largest of the three provinces both geographically and by population size, also has the highest proportion of for-profit and chain ownership of nursing homes across Canada. According to Baum (1999: 544), chain-owned nursing homes operated only 8% of Ontario nursing homes beds in 1971 but held the majority (54%) of beds just 20 years later. Extendicare is the largest of these chains in Canada (Harrington et al., 2017: 4), with 112 seniors' centres in Ontario as of 2015 (CTV News, 2015). Based in Ontario, in 2014 Extendicare agreed to pay $38 million in response to charges that it provided poor care and inappropriately billed for physiotherapy in its US homes (Thomas, 2014). According to Joyce R. Branda, an acting assistant attorney general, "These problems stemmed in large part from Extendicare's business model — a model that was driven more by profit and less by the quality of care it provided" (quoted in Thomas, 2014). In the US and in Canada, for-profit ownership is associated with lower quality care, as noted above (McGregor: Ronald, 2011).

Growth in the delivery of for-profit nursing homes has received considerable support from the Ontario government. In the mid-1990s, the Conservative government announced a massive expansion in long-term residential care. Committed to the notion that markets produce the best quality for the lowest price, it introduced a competitive bidding process. But this process was in reality an affirmative action plan for corporate chains. Conditions required the bidders to have access to sufficient capital to create new buildings or to substantially retrofit existing ones to meet new building standards. Small, family-owned companies did not have the capital resources, access or expertise to invest in such projects, and neither did most charitable or cash-strapped municipal homes. While the Conservative government committed to the repayment of at least some of these capital costs, this was paid out at a rate of $10.35 per day over 20 years, to an overall maximum of $75,555 per bed. As a result, two-thirds of the 20,000 new nursing home beds were awarded to for-profit nursing home chains. The top five municipal and charity-based nursing home operators were awarded 2,049 new beds while the top five for-profit companies were allocated 6,573 new beds (McKay, 2003).

With a Liberal government in power from 2003 to 2018 (when a new Conservative government was elected), non-profit homes remained under threat. According to the organization that represents non-profit homes, "long-term care facilities in central Toronto can't meet the government's requirements for more space on their existing properties, and buying more land is too expensive" (referenced in Crawley, 2017). As we saw in our site visits, the central location of nursing homes allows workers and family members (a majority of whom are women) to use public transit to get quickly and cheaply to a home, while at the same time allowing residents to feel part of the community even if they can no longer get out to visit shops. Moving homes to where land is less expensive can thus lower the quality of resident life, although it can be attractive to homes searching to make a profit from selling more centrally located land.

In general, Ontario provides the same kinds of financial support for all licensed beds in the home regardless of ownership. All homes receive operating funds for food, nursing care, supplies and programs. Although people applying for nursing home beds show a strong preference for non-profit facilities – perhaps reflecting the larger number of verified complaints in for-profit homes (McGregor et al., 2011) – long waiting lists for non-profit homes means that for-profit owners are guaranteed both a full house and full payment. There is, then, little support for the claim that competition for 'customers' will ensure high quality. Nor is there support for the notion that competition will increase transparency and accountability. Research by our team shows that, although Ontario requires financial reports from these companies, it does not require information on profits and does not make the data it does collect public (Harrington et al., 2016).

The ownership pattern in Manitoba differs substantially from that in Ontario. Manitoba has a population of 1.3 million people dispersed across five geographically diverse healthcare regions. Four of these regions are rural or remote and almost two-thirds of Manitoba's residents reside in the Winnipeg Health Region (i.e., the city of Winnipeg; population 767,000) (Manitoba Health, 2016a). Manitoba has one of the highest supplies of nursing home beds in Canada (338 beds per 1,000 population 85+ years old), second only to Prince Edward Island at 363 beds (Sivananthan et al., 2015). The current distribution of nursing home beds in Manitoba matches that of the population, with 38 facilities comprising 5,506 beds located in Winnipeg (Manitoba Health, 2016b). Accordingly, the size and type of nursing home structure varies considerably across this province. Approximately 40% of the care homes in Winnipeg and Brandon, the province's second city, are for-profit while outside these health regions "relatively few are proprietary" (Currie & De Coster, 2005: 2). Most rural nursing homes in Manitoba are small (e.g., 20–40 bed facilities) and almost half are linked to a hospital. Conversely, while fewer in number, Winnipeg nursing homes are free standing and tend to be much larger in size (ranging from 57 to 317 beds). While only 19 of the 125 nursing homes (15.2%) in Manitoba are for-profit, these facilities tend to be large and comprise about 25% of all nursing home beds in the province. Fourteen of these for-profit facilities are located in Winnipeg, and these facilities comprise about 35% of all nursing home beds in this region.

Eight of the for-profit nursing homes in Manitoba are owned and operated by Central Park Lodge, while four are owned and operated by Extendicare (Ernst & Young, 2014). Some research shows that these for-profit homes tend to have lower staffing levels and higher rates of antipsychotic medication dispensing (Currie & De Coster, 2005). It appears that this trend for non-profit nursing homes will continue in Manitoba. Despite having an already relatively large supply of beds, a recent mandate letter from the Conservative Premier has directed the Minister of Health in Manitoba to develop a funding model to fast-track the construction of an additional 1,200 nursing home beds with "nonprofit organizations, faith-based groups and community leaders" (Premier of Manitoba, 2016).

Like most provinces, Manitoba cost shares the nursing home operation budget. Residents pay a standard per diem fee (adjusted for people's marital and net income status) to help cover their room and board, and the remaining operational costs are paid for by government. Both of these revenue sources have increased similarly with time. Government funds to support nursing home care has risen in Manitoba from $54,500 annually per bed in 2011, to $63,600 in 2016, while the fee structure charged to residents has increased from a range of $31.30–$73.40 daily in 2010, to $36.40–$85.00 in 2016 (Manitoba Health, 2017). It is important to note that these per diem fees in Manitoba, as in most of Canada, are standard irrespective of nursing home type, and provincial policy prohibits nursing homes from charging additional resident fees (MacDonald, 2015).

Given these standard fees, it is challenging to understand how for-profit nursing homes in Manitoba maintain their profit margins. Despite having consistent funding policies in Manitoba, from the publicly available financial statements in Winnipeg, the costs incurred by for-profit nursing homes in this region are, on average, almost $2,200 higher per bed than non-profit facilities (Ernst & Young, 2014). Despite these increased costs, evidence shows that for-profit nursing homes in Manitoba tend to have higher rates of select adverse events (e.g., hip and non-hip fractures, hospitalized falls, skin ulcers, and respiratory infections) as compared to non-profit facilities (Doupe et al., 2011), and that residents in for-profit nursing home are at least 50% more likely both to transition to hospital in their last six months of life and to die in an acute care setting (Menec et al., 2009).

There are some similarities and some differences in ownership trends in Nova Scotia. Like Ontario, most for-profit homes were traditionally small, single location operations. In 2005–2006, 68% of 'homes for the aged' with 1–19 beds were proprietary, compared to only 29% of those with over 100 beds (Statistics Canada, 2007: calculated from Table 1-4). During the first decade of this century about 51% of 'homes for the aged' were private while the percentage of beds that were private was lower, at around 41% (Statistics Canada cat. 83-237-X, various years). It should be noted that the category of 'homes for the aged' in Nova Scotia includes publicly funded lower level 'residential care facilities' as well as nursing homes (resident fees are lower for the former). Figures on nursing homes alone provided by Nova Scotia's Department of Health and Wellness showed that 39% of the 6,902 beds and 41% of the 90 facilities were for-profit in 2013. Clearly a higher proportion of the lower level facilities are for-profit (again, often small single location homes). While changes in ownership status have not necessarily occurred, the character of the for-profit sector has changed, with a trend toward more multiple-facility companies.

Like Ontario, Nova Scotia undertook a long-term residential care expansion program in the first decade of the century. The Continuing Care Strategy, launched in 2006, aimed to add about 800 new beds plus replace another 800 beds (Nova Scotia Department of Health, 2006). Like Ontario, the new beds were handled through a Request for Proposals (RFP) process, which began in 2007. There were very specific design standards and new staffing models for the new buildings and replacement facilities. For the new builds, 14 providers were selected to construct 24 facilities (19 of which were nursing homes). The model was to have smaller facilities, mostly in the 36–66 bed range. Of the 19 nursing homes actually constructed, 13 (68%) were private, representing 93% of beds added. This also represented an increase in the role of chains in the private sector. These large firms were able to handle the complicated RFP and construction process. For example, the largest private chain, Shannex, got almost 50% of the contracts (building 9 of the 19 new facilities). Like other large companies in the sector, Shannex operates senior housing outside of the public sphere (large independent and assisted living complexes) and was well positioned to participate in the nursing home expansion. Indeed, the mandated model of smaller homes makes it challenging for stand-alone facilities to compete, as they lack the economies of scale of the large multi-facility companies.

Interestingly, as noted in the Nova Scotia Auditor General's report, the replacement bed component of the strategy did not favour the private sector to the same extent, as the department dealt with existing providers rather than using a tendering process (Nova Scotia Office of the Auditor General, 2011). The Auditor General thought the latter process should have been undertaken, which would have further skewed provision toward the private sector.

As noted, the data available on ownership are inconsistent across Canada. Statistics Canada has replaced the Residential Care Facilities survey with its "Residential Long-Term Financial Data Tables". Tables based on the 2015 version of the new survey report total revenues, plus expenses for public and private facilities (Statistics Canada, Cansim Tables 107-0001 and 107-0002). Overall, in Canada operating revenues of private facilities represented 38% of the combined revenues. In Ontario this share was 55%, compared to 41.5% in Nova Scotia and 18% in Manitoba. This is consistent with the general point that the supply of for-profit nursing home beds is much greater in Ontario than Manitoba. The tables also give profit rates, with Nova Scotia having a higher rate (9.1%) than Ontario (7.6%) or Manitoba (6.9%). The Nova Scotia budgeting process allows a profit margin to be factored into a facility's budget (interview with key informant).

While it is difficult to track ownership patterns, it is even harder to track the extent to which non-profit nursing homes have contracted out services. Under pressure to reduce costs and often with support from government, homes have turned to the for-profit sector to provide services within their facilities. As previously indicated, we did not undertake site visits at any large corporate chains.

Ontario law requires that every municipality of a certain size establish a municipal nursing home, and a non-profit home cannot transfer its licensed beds to a for-profit home, except under limited circumstances (Government of Ontario, 2013). However, this legislation does not prevent for-profit companies from managing other (including non-profit) homes. According to its website, Extendicare (2017) manages as many homes as it owns. The promise is quality and efficiency for non-profit homes. "Our resources help you provide care and services to those who depend on you, while maintaining a close eye on your bottom line" (Extendicare Assist, 2017). In a non-profit site visit for a sister research project, we interviewed a mid-level manager about the impact of for-profit management of his non-profit home. One example he gave for reduced costs was the elimination of composting, which was seen as too expensive because it meant sorting food waste into relatively small bags. Leaving aside the environmental impact, the saving led to more injuries as workers had to lift heavy bags of waste as a result. Another example he gave concerned the impact of food on residents. Meals were central to the cultural group served by this home and soup at lunch and dinner were considered essential by the residents but defined as waste by the new managers. A huge outcry from residents and families ensued, resulting in the return of the soup.

The privatization of food services either through contracting out or through following for-profit managerial strategies was evident in one of the non-profit homes we studied in Ontario. Here, the food was prepared in an off-site, centralized kitchen, with full plates delivered on carts. Residents had no tempting cooking smells and no choice about portions. The food had to be consumed in a specified, limited time so the plates could be put back on the carts to be returned to the off-site kitchen. A similar process existed in a private for-profit facility we visited in Nova Scotia, where the company operated a central industrial kitchen from which meals were delivered to various facilities to be reheated and plated. Although in these cases the food was served by employees, in some other places with outsourced services that we visited the dietary staff was employed by the food service and did not know the residents very well. Indeed, at some sites the residents were actively discouraged from even talking to the contracted-out dietary workers. Our interviews supported the research finding that, although contracting out services may have some positive results, in general it means poorer working conditions, lower salaries, fewer benefits and entitlements, and reduced job satisfaction for workers whose jobs have been contracted out (Vrangbaek, Petersen & Hjelmar, 2015). It also undermines continuity in care.

Privatization and Regulation

Neoliberal strategies tend to promote deregulation on the grounds that markets will ensure quality (though in practice it is often more about reregulation than deregulation). However, healthcare services in general do not operate like a free market model would predict. Leaving aside the question of whether this theory ever works in practice, it is clear that it does not work in the case of Canadian nursing homes, where demand almost always exceeds supply, where the price is regulated and does not respond to supply and demand, where governments control supply while guaranteeing payment, and where 'customers' have few choices and little decision-making power. The media and advocacy groups in several countries have exposed abuse and poor quality care, demanding government action. Research by our team (Lloyd et al., 2014) shows that scandals publicized in the media, along with public protests, have contributed to the detailed regulation that has become common in the sector in five countries, especially where for-profit, chain ownership is common. Yet to some extent this detailed regulation has served to provide an advantage to the chains. As another study (Daly, 2015: 49) for our project explains, the regulatory burden of reporting and managing data puts small operators at a disadvantage. The chains can benefit from economies of scale and their corporate expertise, while single owner and charitable groups struggle under the administrative burden, a struggle the chains are eager to address through contracting out to their management subsidiaries.

This is especially the case in Ontario, where for-profit ownership is highest and the regulations are the most detailed. There are, for example, 117 regulations on health and safety alone (Government of Ontario, 2013). While each of these makes sense when considered individually, too often their net effect is to increase the burden on the care workers and limit their autonomy. Reporting requirements are also heavy. Ontario requires homes to use the RAI-MDS reporting system, a mandate that means hiring a coordinator to handle the administrative load and, as we heard in the homes we studied, which also means time away from care for the licensed nursing staff who are the only ones allowed to enter the data. This, too, limits the workers' autonomy, limiting their possibilities for responding to individual resident needs (Armstrong, Daly and Choiniere, 2016). At the same time though, in keeping with neoliberal approaches the province does not regulate larger structural factors such as ownership or even staffing levels (Banerjee and Armstrong, 2015). Indeed, the Conservative government that came to power in the mid-1990s removed the requirements to have a Registered Nurse (RN) on every shift and to provide a minimum of 2.5 hours of direct care per resident per day. Although the Liberal government that followed did reinstate the requirement for an RN on every shift, it did not reinstate the minimum, let alone raise it to the 4.1 hours recommended in the research (Harrington et al., 2012). Companies searching for profit were particularly likely to take advantage of this lack of regulation. For-profit "chain members have the lowest staffing level in Ontario's LTC sector, at 2.63 hours of direct care per resident, per day" (Hsu et al., 2016: 182).

Nova Scotia also does not have regulated minimum staffing, other than the requirement to have an RN on duty at all times. However, the funding formula for the homes built under the Continuing Care Strategy discussed above allows for 4 hours of care per resident-day, including 1 hour of licensed RN or LPN care and 3 hours of Continuing Care Assistant (CCA) time, using the 'augmented traditional model' where the CCAs' role includes housekeeping tasks as well as direct care (Curry, 2015: 30). This is not in the regulations, however, and the funding for staff differs for other types of homes (discussed below). Nursing homes in Manitoba are regulated to provide, on average, 3.75 hours of care per resident-day (nurses and healthcare aides combined), although it is unclear is this figure represents paid or worked hours of care (Manitoba Health, 2012). At least one nursing staff is required to be on site at all times.

Ontario, unlike other provinces, differentiates between a basic rate charged for shared rooms and a higher rate for private rooms, with its inequitable impact on female and male residents. It also sets the proportion of rooms that must be provided at the basic rate. Other provinces charge the same rate regardless of type of room. While this fee exceeds what low-income Canadians receive from the combination of Old Age Security (the universal public pension plan) and the income-based Guaranteed Income Supplement, income-based subsidies are available that ensure access to long-term care, in shared rooms, independent of income. There is no asset-stripping in order to pay for long-term care. Access is thus largely based on healthcare needs, not on income or wealth. In keeping with neoliberal approaches, however, the previous Conservative Government had allowed Ontario owners to designate a higher proportion of single rooms with their higher accommodation rates (McKay, 2003), and to charge a small supplement for all rooms in the newer facilities.

The Ontario government seeks to ensure that most of the public money goes to care rather than to profits by allocating funding in envelopes designed for specific purposes such as raw food and nursing care. Although regulations require that any unspent envelope money must be returned, a manager we interviewed informed us about creative ways of squeezing profits from these envelopes. For example, by hiring temporary nurses through an agency the home owns, the home can make a profit while still spending the money on nurses.

In Nova Scotia, as in all other provinces except Ontario, the maximum fee and fee reductions are independent of the type of room or facility. In terms of government funding, one result of the Continuing Care Strategy is that the nursing home sector in Nova Scotia now has two models of funding, creating a two-tier system. All homes constructed under the expansion and replacement programs are funded by an envelope system similar to Ontario's, with protected (care and raw food costs) and unprotected (administration, accommodation costs, food prep, capital funding for 25-year mortgage) envelopes. The latter can be carried over. There is also a separate model of practice for the care aides (CCAs) in the new and replacement homes, as noted above. The old homes follow a traditional staffing model (with CCAs providing only direct care) and line budgeting, where essentially the budget is based on what the home in question had last year. Various key informant interviewees expressed concern with this two-tier system. The new homes have all single rooms, while the older homes have mostly shared rooms. There have been budget freezes under the traditional funding model, and older homes find it hard to maintain their existing facilities, let alone see any prospect for replacement now that the Continuing Care Strategy building spree has ended. As mentioned previously, residents in Manitoba are charged a standard per diem fee based on their net income and marital status, independent of nursing home type (Manitoba Health, 2017).

Privatization of Costs

One of the main ways provincial governments privatize cost is by failing to provide enough spaces in subsidized homes to fill the demand or enough home care to support the care work. As a result, many who need 24-hour care or support have no alternative but to seek space in a retirement home, to use an Ontario term, or in another form of supportive housing or assisted living. Whatever the form, costs for residents are higher in these private sector alternatives than they are in nursing homes, again with negative implications for women, who tend to arrive with fewer financial resources than men.

In Ontario, the vast majority of these retirement homes are privately owned and mainly for-profit. Sun Life Insurance Company (2016) estimates that the cost of the private room in an Ontario retirement home ranges from $1,360.00 to $7,000 a month, with a median rate of $2,900. But this fee does not include the 24-hour nursing care, personal support, laundry, recreational and other services included in the $2,563.22 a month for a private room in a publicly subsidized nursing home. Shared accommodation in an Ontario nursing home is $1,794.28 a month, and also includes all the services left out of the retirement home fees. Comfortlife (2017) estimates that memory care for residents with dementia that includes meals, housekeeping, bathing and medication administration in a retirement home would cost $6,500 a month in Toronto. And it is important to note that even this does not include the full extent of services provided in a nursing home.

Although care within Ontario nursing homes is heavily regulated, this is not the case with retirement homes. In response to scandals, Ontario moved in 2010 to provide some limited regulation and inspection under the direction of an independent agency. "In the first year the Retirement Homes Regulatory Authority [RHRA] was established, it had to inspect approximately 150 homes due to complaints with 50 having multiple complaints and unresolved problems" (RNAO, 2015), suggesting that this regulation was long overdue. The RHRA is funded entirely by fees from the 733 retirement homes themselves (RHRA, 2017) but it does not regulate prices, admission, or eviction. One retirement home we visited as part of a related project contracted out all its employees, save for senior management.

The story is similar in Nova Scotia, where a private sector operates alongside the publicly-funded and regulated long-term care sector. In independent and assisted living facilities the basic fees typically cover room and board, with residents purchasing additional services as needed. It is important to note that the operators of these private sector alternatives also often run nursing homes that are part of the public system, so the two sectors can be integrated. The campus model (found in many jurisdictions) may include seniors' apartments, independent living units, assisted living (all outside the public system) and a publicly funded nursing home. Indeed, sometimes the company also has a fully private nursing home with the full suite of care services, which they upsell to their residents and to which they directly control entry. This integration makes it hard to disentangle the finances and profit generation of the components.

A similar scenario exists in Manitoba, where community-based supportive housing (called assisted living in many provinces and the United States) has for some years been implemented as an alternative to nursing home care. A recent report released in this province demonstrates that the admission guidelines for nursing home care are vastly outdated and that those defining supportive housing use are also vague (Doupe et al., 2016). Except for a small number of supportive housing facilities that are owned and operated by the province, authors also report that the majority of supportive housing in Winnipeg is private and for-profit. As compared to the highly regulated standards and audited procedures that exist for nursing homes in Manitoba, these same procedures for supportive housing in Manitoba are virtually non-existent. While the government costs for supportive housing are less than half of that for nursing homes, the median costs to users are much higher ($1,886 per month for supportive housing tenants versus $1,146 per month for nursing home residents), meaning that transition across the care continuum is based on a combination of people's needs and their ability to pay. Lastly, despite having relatively minor health challenges (at least versus nursing home residents), Doupe et al. (2016) show that supportive housing tenants tend to have far higher transfers rates to emergency departments than their much sicker nursing home counterparts, and that transitions from supportive housing to nursing homes are often accompanied by a long hospital stay, with a median of 60 days. Collectively, this evidence supports the notion that ongoing reform in Manitoba needs to address the inequities and inefficiencies built into the current continuing care model.

Conclusions

This comparison of three jurisdictions within Canada offers several lessons. First, the pressures towards privatization in terms of the ownership and delivery of long-term care are powerful across the country, and can have negative consequences, particularly for women. Second, evidence has not been the primary basis on which privatization has spread. Third, and more promising, the variations among provinces suggest that there are sound alternatives to the for-profit, chain ownership of nursing homes and the care delivered in nursing homes.

References

Armstrong, H., Daly, T. and Choiniere, J. A. (2016). Policies and practices: The case of RAI-MDS in Canadian long-term care homes. *Journal of Canadian Studies,* 50(1), 348–367.

Banerjee, A. and Armstrong, P. (2015). Centring care: Explaining regulatory tensions in residential care for older persons. *Studies in Political Economy,* 95, 7–28.

Baum, J. (1999). The rise of chain nursing homes in Ontario, 1971–1996. *Social Forces* 78(2), 543–583.

Berta, W., Laporte, A., Zarnett, D., Valdmanis, V. & Anderson, G. (2006). A pan-Canadian perspective on institutional long-term care. *Health Policy,* 79(2–3), 175–194.

CIHI (2005). *Hospital trends in Canada.* Ottawa: Canadian Institute for Health Information.

Comfortlife (2017). *Cost of retirement homes in Ontario.* http://www.comfortlife.ca/retirement-community-resources/retirement-costs-ontario. Accessed December 30, 2017.

Crawley, M. (2017). Nursing homes 'intending to leave' Toronto over rebuilding costs CBChttp://www.cbc.ca/news/canada/toronto/ontario-long-term-care-renewal-construction-subsidy-1.4360276

CTV News (2015). Extendicare to buy three retirement communities in Saskatchewan, Ontario November 11. https://regina.ctvnews.ca/extendicare-to-buy-three-retirement-communities-in-saskatchewan-ontario-1.2653951

Currie, R. & De Coster, C. based on a study by M. Doupe et al. (2005). *Assessing Manitoba nursing homes: Is good good enough,* Manitoba Centre for Health Policy. http://mchp-appserv.cpe.umanitoba.ca/reference/pch.qi_summ.pdf

Curry, P. (2015). *Broken Homes.* Nova Scotia Nurses Union. Dartmouth, NS.

CIHI (2005). *Hospital trends in Canada.* Ottawa: Canadian Institute for Health Information.

CIHI (2005). *Hospital trends in Canada.* Ottawa: Canadian Institute for Health Information.

Daly, T. (2015). Dancing the two-step in Ontario's long-term care sector: Deterrence regulation=consolidation (1940–2013). *Studies in Political Economy,* 95, 29–58.

Doupe, M., Finlayson, G., Khan, S., Yogendran, M., Schultz, J., McDougall and Kulbaba, C. (2016). *Supportive housing for seniors: Reform implications for Manitoba's older adult continuum of care.* Winnipeg, MB: Manitoba Centre for Health Policy.

Doupe, M., Brownell, M., St. John, P., Strang, D. J. G., Chateau, D. & Dik, N. (2011). Nursing home adverse events: Further insight into highest risk periods. *J Am Med DirAssoc.,* 12(6), 467–474.

Ernst & Young (2014). Consolidated financial statements of the Winnipeg Regional Health Authority. http://wwwwrhambca/healthinfo/reports/files/AuditedFS_1314pdf. 2014.

Extendicare (2017). *Find an Extendicare location.* https//www.extendicare.com/contact/find/ Accessed December 29, 2017.

Extendicare Assist (2017). *Management and consulting services* http://extendicareassist.ca/services.html. Accessed December 29, 2017.

Government of Canada (1985). *Canada Health Act* (R.S.C., 1985, c. C-6) http://laws-lois.justice.gc.ca/eng/acts/C-6/page-2.html#h-6

Government of Ontario (2013). *O. Reg. 67/93: Health care and residential facilities* https://www.ontario.ca/laws/regulation/930067 April 8, 2013 117 regulations. Accessed December 30, 2017.

Harrington, C., Jacobsen, F., Panos, J., Pollock, A., Sutaria, S. & Szebehely, M. (2017). Marketization in long-term care: A cross-country comparison of large for profit nursing home chains. *Health Services Insights*, 10, 1–23.

Harrington, C., Armstrong, H., Halladay, M., Havig, A., Jacobsen,F., MacDonald, M., Panos, J., Pearsall, K., Pollock, A. & Ross, L. (2016). Comparison of nursing home financial transparency and accountability in four locations. *Ageing International*, 41(1), 17–39.

Harrington, C., Choiniere, J., Goldmann, M., Jacobsen, F., Lloyd, L., McGregor, M., Stamatopoulos, V. & Szebehely, M. (2012). Nursing home staffing standards and staffing levels in six countries. *Journal of Nursing Scholarship*, 44(1), 88–98.

Hsu, A., Berta, W., Coyte, P. & Laporte, A. (2016). Staffing in Ontario's long-term care homes: Differences by profit status and chain ownership. *Canadian Journal on Aging / La Revue canadienne du vieillissement* June, 35(2), 175–189.

Lloyd, L., Banerjee, A., Harrington, C., Jacobsen, F. & Szebehely, M. (2014). It is a scandal!: Comparing the causes and consequences of nursing home media scandals in five countries. *International Journal of Sociology and Social Policy*, 34 (1–2), 2–18.

MacDonald, M. (2015). Regulating individual charges for long-term residential care in Canada. *Studies in Political Economy*, 95, 83–114.

Manitoba Health. (2012) Annual Report 2011–2012. 2012; http://www.gov.mb.ca/health/ann/docs/1112.pdf.

Manitoba Health (2016a). Population Report: June 1, 2016. http://www.gov.mb.ca/health/population/pr2016.pdf 2016.

Manitoba Health (2016b). Annual Statistics 2015–2016. 2016; https://www.gov.mb.ca/health/annstats/as1516.

Manitoba Health (2017). *Personal care services: Residential charges in Manitoba – Information Manual*, Aug 1, 2017 – Jul 31, 2017. https://www.gov.mb.ca/health/pcs/docs/guide.pdf 2017.

McGregor, M. & Ronald, L. (2011). *Residential long-term care for Canadian seniors. Nonprofit, for-profit or does it matter?* IRPP Study 14 (January) (Ottawa: IRPP).

McGregor, M. J. et al. (2011). Complaints in for-profit, non-profit and public nursing homes in two Canadian provinces. *Open Medicine*, 5(4), 183–192.

McKay, P. (2003). Taxpayers finance construction boom. Ontario's nursing home crisis — Part 4. *Ottawa Citizen* (April 29, 2003), A1.

Menec, V., MacWilliam, L., Soodeen, R. A. et al. (2002). *The health and health care use of Manitoba's seniors: Have they changed over time?* http://wwwumanitobaca/centres/mchp/reports,htm#46 [serial online].

Menec, V. H., Nowicki, S., Blandford, A. & Veselyuk, D. (2009). Hospitalizations at the end of life among long-term care residents. *J GerontolA BiolSci Med Sci.*, 64(3), 395–402.

Nova Scotia Department of Health (2006). *Continuing care strategy: Shaping the future of continuing care.*

Nova Scotia Office of the Auditor General (2011), Chapter 5, Health and Wellness: Longterm care – New and replacement facilities. *Report of the Auditor General*. https://oag-ns.ca/sites/default/files/publications/2011%20-%20May%20-%20Ch%2005%20-%20DHW%20-%20Long%20Term%20Care.pdf

Premier of Manitoba. (2016). Ministerial mandate letter – Province of Manitoba. https://wwwgovmbca/asset_library/en/executivecouncil/mandate/hon_kelvin_goertzenpdf

Registered Nurses Association of Ontario (RNAO) (2015). *The Retirement Homes Act Review*. http://rnao.ca/policy/letters/retirement-homes-act-review

RHRA [Retirement Homes Regulatory Authority] (2017). *Annual report 2016/17*. Accessed January 1, 2018.

Ronald, L., McGregor, M., Harrington, C. & Pollock, A. (2016). Observational evidence of for-profit delivery and inferior nursing home care: When is there enough evidence for policy change? *PLoS Medicine*, 13(4), e1001995.

Sharkey, S. (2008). *People caring for people: Impacting the quality of life and care of residents of long-term care homes*. 2008. Toronto, Ontario, Ontario Ministry of Health and Long-Term Care.

Sivananthan, S., Doupe, M., & McGregor, M. (2015). Exploring the ecology of Canada's publicly funded residential long-term care bed supply. *Canadian Journal on Aging*, 34(1), 60–74.

Statistics Canada. *Table 107-0001 – Public nursing and residential care facilities, summary statistics, annual (dollars)*, CANSIM database. Accessed February 9, 2018.

Statistics Canada. *Table 107-0002 – Private nursing and residential care facilities, summary statistics, annual (dollars unless otherwise noted)*, CANSIM database. Accessed February 9, 2018.

Statistics Canada (2007). *Residential Care Facilities 2005/2006*. [Cat. No. 83-237-X]. Ottawa: Minister of Industry.

Sun Life Insurance Company (2016). *Long-term care in Ontario in 2016*. https://www.sunnet.sunlife.com/files/advisor/english/PDF/Completereport-LTC-Costs-ON.pdf

Thomas, K. (2014). Chain to pay $38 million over claims of poor care, Business Day. *New York Times* October 10. https://www.nytimes.com/2014/10/11/business/extendicare-agrees-to-pay-38-million-over-inadequate-nursing-home-care.html

Tarman, V. (1990). *Privatization and health care: The case of Ontario nursing homes*. Toronto: Garamond Press.

Tanuseputro, P., Chalifoux, M., Bennett, C., Grunier, A., Bronskill, S., Walker, P. & Manuel, D. (2015). Hospitalization and mortality rates in long-term care facilities: Does for-profit status matter? *JAMDA*, 16(10), 874–83.

Vrangbaek, K., Petersen, O. H. & Hjelmar, U. (2015). Is contracting out bad for employees? A review of international experience. *Review of Public Personnel Administration*, 35(1), 3–23.

Chapter 6

Labor Restructuring and Nursing Home Privatization in British Columbia, Canada

Andrew Longhurst, Sage Ponder, and Margaret McGregor

In 2007, 450 care aides who provided intimate personal care to frail seniors living in long-term residential care (LTRC) in Vancouver, British Columbia (BC), lost their unionized jobs in a mass firing. The abrupt termination of their employment and the disruption in care was the result of far-reaching legislation that eliminated job security protections negotiated through collective bargaining (HEU, 2007). Earlier that same month, 168 care aides, primarily women from immigrant backgrounds, had been fired just one week after ratifying a new collective agreement (HEU, 2007). This was the third firing in three years. The increasingly unstable working conditions for frontline care workers – who build long-term relationships with residents – is the result of government-led program of labor restructuring and fiscal austerity in the seniors' LTRC sector initiated in the early 2000s. In this chapter, we show how a series of neoliberal reforms restructured a stable, unionized labor regime in favor of "flexible" employment relations by providing private LTRC operators with unprecedented rights and labor law exemptions to contract out unionized work to subcontractors and re-tender commercial contracts at will. We explain how LTRC privatization – defined as the shift to for-profit ownership and care delivery – has been advanced through labor reforms and justified in the name of fiscal austerity. This chapter reviews academic and grey literature, government documents, and media articles, and also draws on key informant interviews conducted as part of a university ethics-approved study.

Long-Term Residential Care in BC

British Columbia is Canada's western-most province with over 4.6 million residents. In Canada, provinces have statutory responsibility for the planning, design, and public administration of hospital and physician services, which must be consistent with national legislation, including universal access free at the point of delivery. Although provinces are not required to provide universal, publicly funded LTRC, BC does maintain a publicly funded LTRC system. It was established in the late 1970s (Hollander & Pallan, 1995), although charitable and faith-based nursing facilities have existed for much longer (Davies, 2003). To this day, government health authorities maintain coordinated access and referral to publicly funded LTRC delivered across three facility ownership types: government health authority; charitable, cultural, or faith-based non-profit; and single-site or chain-owned for-profit. Since the creation of the publicly funded LTRC sector, the BC government has contracted with non-profit and for-profit-owned entities to deliver publicly funded care. Non-profit and government-owned facilities have historically provided over two-thirds of publicly funded care. However, in this chapter, we explain how neoliberal fiscal and labor policies led to greater for-profit LTRC ownership and delivery of care. This process of privatization undermined the stable conditions of work that are a precondition relational care and better outcomes for nursing home residents.

The Backdrop to Restructuring: Neoliberalism and Fiscal Austerity

Over the last three decades, a large body of research from middle and high income countries has mapped the effects of neoliberalism on different state governments and welfare and labor regimes (Peck & Tickell, 2002; Bondi & Laurie, 2005; Brenner, Peck, & Theodore, 2010), including the impact of neoliberal reforms on public health care services (Armstrong & Armstrong, 2010; Whiteside, 2015) and, specifically, LTRC (Meagher & Szebehely, 2013; Armstrong & Day, 2017: 20–26; Mercille, 2017). In North America and Western Europe neoliberalism has been conceptualized as a process rather than an end-state, with the "roll back" of Keynesian welfare institutions and social rights, and the "roll out" of market-oriented regulatory change intended to expand the role of the private sector – often through privatization and labor market "flexibility." In Canada, throughout the 1980s, and primarily the 1990s, well-established welfare state policies were delegitimized and defunded, constituting the roll back of Keynesian regulatory institutions and norms, including social welfare programs and stable labor regimes based on the "standard employment relationship," typically with union coverage (Vosko, 2006). For feminist scholars, neoliberal reforms have significant gendered implications. In the Canadian postwar context, women working in publicly funded sectors achieved greater recognition and pay, and moved closer to the standard employment relationship, especially in areas that were traditionally seen as unpaid women's work performed in the private sphere (Armstrong, 2010). These gains were often achieved through collective bargaining and labor standards legislation, but have been undermined by privatization resulting from successive rounds of roll-back and roll-out neoliberal reforms.

In Canada, the roll back of collective gains have typically been rationalized in the name of fiscal austerity and normative claims that governments must prioritize deficit and debt reduction by cutting social spending. Fiscal austerity has been a key part of neoliberal governance and can be defined as "a composite of policies, including fiscal consolidation, structural reforms of the public sector, and flexibilization of labour markets" (Evans & McBride, 2017: 3). Throughout the 1990s, deficit and debt concerns dominated public discourse across Canada. In 1994, a federal credit rating downgrade and the depreciation of the Canadian dollar were used as evidence that the federal Liberal government needed to reduce deficits and debt through social spending cuts in order to maintain the confidence of credit rating agencies and financial markets (Russell, 2014: 38). The 1995 federal cutbacks are a definitive moment in the roll back of Canada's Keynesian welfare state, and provincial governments were left with dramatically reduced federal funding for social programs at a time when provincial governments were expected to assume greater responsibility for program delivery (McBride & Whiteside, 2011: 64). In health cost-sharing, the federal contribution declined from a 50:50 split in the 1970s and is now closer to 80:20, with provinces paying the larger share. Although many OECD countries successfully eliminated deficits in the 1990s without dramatic cuts, Canada was an outlier in pursuing a path of fiscal austerity and deep social program cuts. Canada's fiscal approach was more of an ideological commitment to austerity than sound fiscal policy (Stanford, 2001: 154; Stiglitz, 2010; Russell, 2014).

Federally imposed austerity created major challenges for Canadian provinces, including BC (Armstrong & Armstrong, 2010: 155), where federal transfer payments to provinces declined from $19.3 billion in 1994–1995 to $12.5 billion in 1997–1998 (Lee, Klein, & Murray, 1999: 3). The left-leaning BC New Democratic Party (NDP), which governed during the 1990s, buffered the province from the federal cuts and maintained health care spending (Lee et al., 1999). In the LTRC sector, the NDP increased operational spending during the 1990s (Figure 6.1). However, capital expenditures in health care – necessary to maintain and develop new public and non-profit LTRC facilities – suffered as a result of the 1995 cuts. Capital spending in BC fell from an historic high of 3.6% of total health spending in 1991 to 2.1% in 1998 (authors' calculation of CIHI, 2017).

The drop in capital spending from 1996 to 1998 (Figure 6.1) was triggered by federal cuts. However, it also reflected the NDP's effort to keep debt off government books – consistent with principles of neoliberal fiscal "discipline" and the "received understandings of what the ... credit rating agencies [and] the 'markets' will bear" (Peck, 2001: 446). The BC NDP positioned itself in conservative fiscal terms especially after 1995, with a focus on deficit and debt reduction. This was in part a political response to a hostile corporate sector and a right-leaning press (Sigurdson, 1996), but also a reflection of what is perceived to be possible under neoliberal constraints (e.g., Carroll & Ratner, 2005). Debt reduction and credit ratings were principal concerns of the government. Although the BC NDP

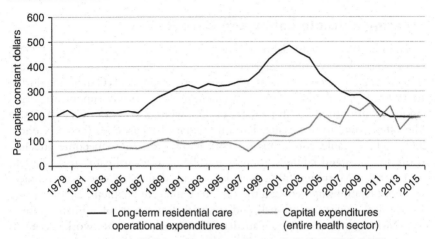

Figure 6.1 Government spending by sub-sector in British Columbia, 1979–2015

Note: LTRC operational expenditures also includes a small amount of spending on care facilities for persons with physical disabilities, psychiatric disabilities, and alcohol and drug problems. 2015 constant dollars calculated using the BC Stats Consumer Price Index.

Sources: Authors' calculations of CIHI National Health Expenditure Trends, 1975–2017, Series D3 and Appendices; BC Stats Consumer Price Index.

maintained health care operational spending following the 1995 federal cuts, the provincial government responded with its own cutbacks: downsizing the civil service; reducing government fiscal capacity through tax cuts; and declaring a capital spending freeze (Ministry of Finance and Corporate Relations, 1996).

In fact, the BC government ended direct capital grants to non-profit LTRC operators, a move that required non-profit agencies to seek private financing – or simply forego capital upgrades and new development – in an effort to move debt off government books. Capital restraint in the latter half of the decade meant that new non-profit and public LTRC construction could not keep up with the LTRC needs of a growing population. From 1996 to 1999, only two non-profit facilities were constructed – and no new government-owned care homes were opened during this period (authors' calculations from Office of the Seniors Advocate, 2016). By 1999, the Ministry of Health concluded that nearly 4,500 new beds were needed by 2001 and nearly 1,400 beds annually were required to maintain service levels (Cohen, 2003: 14). That a social-democratic government could not resist pressures of fiscal retrenchment during the late 1990s – when the province had the second-lowest debt-to-GDP ratio in the country (Lee et al., 1999: 3) and even as austerity policies were discredited (Stanford 1995) – speaks to the ideational power of neoliberal austerity. The political aversion to debt-financed capital expansion – embedded in the provincial government in the 1990s – would become even stronger in the 2000s.

Creating a Stable Labor and Care Regime

In the mid-1990s, a stable labor and care regime was established in the LTRC sector as a result of women's gains achieved through collective bargaining under a pro-labor government, evident in increased per capita LTRC spending during the 1990s (Figure 6.1). LTRC employment provided family-supporting wages and job security to a workforce of over 85% women (Statistics Canada, 2018) who often come from racialized and immigrant backgrounds (Lee & Cohen, 2005). These stable conditions of work allow workers to become attached to the residents and families, thereby enabling "relational care" (e.g., Jansen, 2011: 10–14; Murphy, 2006). Relational care, defined as one that embraces the entire relationship between the caregiver and care recipient, encompassing the physical, social, emotional, and spiritual dimensions of human connection (McGilton et al., 2005; Canadian Aboriginal AIDS Network, 2008), is considered increasingly important in the care quality literature and in turn is associated with residents' improved quality of life (Ramage-Morin, 2006). Conversely, the empirical health services literature demonstrates inferior outcomes associated with higher staff turnover in LTRC (Barry et al., 2005; Castle et al., 2005; 2007).

In BC, this stable labor/care regime was based on a sectoral bargaining model that maintained parity in worker compensation and working conditions across all publicly funded facilities. Frontline care workers were entitled to standardized compensation and workplace rights based on a 'master' collective agreement across government, non-profit, and for-profit-owned facilities alike. The creation of this sectoral structure flowed from the recommendations of the 1991 Royal Commission on Health Care and Costs. BC, not unlike other provinces, adopted a "closer to home" agenda to health care restructuring, with a focus on shifting away from more costly and institutional hospital-based care. This policy direction required a simplified labor relations regime with broad-based bargaining structures in order to facilitate uniform working conditions and standards of care:

> In general, [the Commission] support[s] a move toward one independent agent bargaining for management, and a significantly reduced number of bargaining units acting for the unions. Such a move would increase the flexibility of the system as it places greater emphasis on providing services in the home and in the community. A myriad bargaining agents do not foster mobility and multi-skilled services. Nor does a number of associations bargaining on behalf of employers encourage uniformity of working conditions.
>
> (BC Royal Commission on Health Care and Costs, 1991: D-27)

Accepting these recommendations, the BC NDP government implemented labor reforms that included the LTRC sector. Better population health outcomes and cost-savings were anticipated by a "closer to home" approach; however, the NDP's initiation of health care restructuring was not a moment of rollback neoliberalism. As we will show, health care workers would, in fact, benefit from the changes that provided better employment security and working conditions. New legislation designated five multi-employer and multi-union bargaining units that applied to health care workers in publicly funded hospitals, community health services, and LTRC facilities. The facilities health support subsector covered all publicly funded LTRC facilities, meaning that unionized workers were covered by the same industry-wide master collective agreement. In technical terms, sectoral bargaining occurred between multi-employer and multi-union associations. In 1993, the Health Employers Association of British Columbia (HEABC) was formed by amalgamating three separate employer associations that bargained independently with unions. HEABC was established to bargain on behalf of its government, non-profit, and for-profit employer-members. What was particularly novel about this new sectoral bargaining structure was that all publicly funded facilities were required to be HEABC member-employers. As the exclusive bargaining agent, HEABC negotiated the master collective agreement for all LTRC facilities with the single bargaining agent for all unions – an association of unions called the Facilities Bargaining Association, led by the Hospital Employees' Union (HEU).

Over the course of the 1990s, HEU used its increased bargaining power through the sectoral structure with a pro-labor government to make impressive gains and raise standards of care. Strengthening no contracting-out protections in the master collective agreement was an ongoing strategy to prevent privatization. This strong no-contracting-out language would later become the target of the BC Liberal government in the early 2000s:

> The Employer agrees that they will not contract out bargaining unit work that will result in the lay-off of employees within the bargaining unit during the term of this agreement. The Employer will discuss with representatives of the local in a timely manner, functions they intend to contract out after the date of signing this collective agreement that could otherwise be performed by Union members within the facility, except where an emergency exists.
> (Health Services & Support Facilities Subsector Collective Agreement, 2001: 41)

In addition to contracting-out protections, BC's health care unions negotiated an employment security program in the mid-1990s that supported health care workers laid off due to service changes with retraining and continued health sector employment. These improvements in wages and working conditions achieved through the sectoral bargaining model meant material gains for the female-dominated workforce. In 1998, the starting wage for a care aide was about $19 an hour – more than double the $7.15/hour minimum wage at the time. The master collective agreement also provided health support workers with one of the best benefit and pension plans in Canada. For thousands of women, health support occupations provided well-paid employment – critical to maintaining a stable labor regime that allowed frontline caregivers to maintain long-term relationships with residents. For public finances, this stable labor regime required increased government spending at a time of federal austerity – LTRC funding that increased by 54% from 1995 to 2001 (Figure 6.1). Despite the growth in spending, it remained overall a very small share of the provincial economy (peaking at 1.17% of GDP in 2002) (calculated from CIHI, 2017). Nonetheless, for the new BC Liberal government elected in 2001, this stable labor/care regime – characterized by its politicized working-class union members – would become the target of government reforms that would seek to cut public LTRC spending by stripping union rights and encouraging the privatization of care delivery and facility ownership.

Rolling Back a Stable Labor and Care Regime

In 2001, the BC Liberal party came to power in a landslide victory (winning 77 of 79 seats in the provincial legislature) with an ambitious neoliberal agenda (McBride & McNutt, 2007). The BC Liberals' agenda of tax cuts, competitive procurement for public services, increased private sector investment, enhanced labor market flexibility and an end to sectoral bargaining (BC Liberals, 2001) would have a profound effect on the LTRC sector. Although the Liberal government committed to building 5,000 new non-profit LTRC beds (Cohen, 2003: 13) deep personal and corporate tax cuts of 25% and 5%, respectively, and the ensuing fiscal "crisis" created the political context for privatization (Klein, 2002; Cohen, 2006: 233). In 2002, the government began the biggest downsizing of public beds in the province's history, closing thousands of beds that were to be replaced with 4,000 assisted living and supportive housing units built outside the sectoral bargaining structure and with much lower staffing levels (Cohen 2003: 14). From 2001 to 2004, over 2,500 beds in 26 facilities were closed, most of them in government and non-profit facilities (Cohen et al., 2005).

In January 2002, nine months after coming into office, the new BC government passed Bill 29: the Health and Social Services Delivery Improvement Act (hereafter, Bill 29). Bill 29 unilaterally removed negotiated job security and contracting-out protections from master collective agreements, affecting approximately 100,000 workers in health care and social services (Fairey, 2005; McBride & McNutt, 2007: 191–194). HEABC employers that were part of the sectoral bargaining structure could lay off their existing "non-clinical" staff – such as care aides, housekeepers, and food service workers – with minimum notice, and subcontract the work to a third-party commercial provider, while voiding union rights for the collective agreement to follow the work, known as union successorship rights (Cohen, 2003; Stinson, Pollak & Cohen, 2005; McBride & McNutt, 2007: 191–192). The definition of "non-clinical" included care aides who provide most direct resident care but who are not designated health professionals under legislation. The elimination of "no contracting-out" provisions from the master collective agreement drastically undermined the stable unionized labor regime that supported continuity of care – a pre-condition for relational care.

Bill 29 cancelled two sections of the BC Labour Relations Code ("the Code") that maintained union successorship rights that discouraged subcontracting as a cost-cutting union evasion strategy. Both provisions fostered workforce stability. The first provision, Section 35 (successor rights and obligations), ensured that

> if a business or a part of it is sold, leased, transferred, or otherwise disposed of, the [new employer] is bound by all proceedings ... [and] if a collective agreement is in force, it continues to bind [the new employer] to the same extent as if it had been signed by [new employer]...
> (Labour Relations Code, 1996)

Overnight health care workers lost union successorship rights. In addition, Bill 29 cancelled section 38 of the Code (several businesses treated as one employer, referred to as "common employer"), which provided that

> if in the [Labour] board's opinion associated or related activities or businesses are carried on by or through more than one corporation, individual, firm, syndicate or association, or a combination of them under common control or direction, the board may treat them as constituting one employer for the purposes of this code ...
> (Labour Relations Code, 1996)

Therefore, companies and their subcontractors would not be treated as a single "common" employer, meaning that unions would always need to organize and negotiate a new collective agreement, no matter the extent to which a company and its subcontractors operate as a single entity. In effect, Bill 29 provided HEABC employers under the sectoral bargaining structure the ability to get out of no- contracting-out (subcontracting) and job security provisions in the master collective agreement as well as sections of the Labour Relations Code that discouraged subcontracting by providing union successorship rights. This created new employment and business relationships that had not existed in the sector previously. Bill 29 rolled out unprecedented legal rights for LTRC operators to subcontract-out care work without union protections in place to safeguard work against this form of privatization.

In total, the initial wave of contracting out resulted in the firing of 9,000 unionized health care workers, mostly women working in hospital cleaning, laundry, and food service occupations. Many were rehired as private-sector employees with substantially reduced wages, benefits, and workplace rights (Stinson et al., 2005; see also Zuberi, 2011a, 2011b). Initially, some of the largest contracts, for housekeeping and food services in government hospitals and LTRC facilities, were awarded to Compass, Sodexo, and Aramark – the three largest multinational service corporations in the world at the time (Cohen & Cohen, 2004: 12; Cohen, 2006). The provincial government justified the introduction of Bill 29 because of "rigid collective agreements," the need for greater labor flexibility and reducing health labor costs that were placing the "viability of public health care ... in jeopardy" (Ministry of Skills Development and Labour, 2002: 2). The government argued that the "province's health labour costs [were] among the highest in Canada ... [and] [f]or support services staff, BC's wage rates are up to 30 per cent higher than the rest of Canada" (Ministry of Skills Development and Labour, 2002). However, this argument ignored the evidence that wages were consistent with BC's higher general labor costs and higher costs of living (Cohen & Cohen, 2004). The rationale for cutting government expenditure by privatization and rolling back compensation did not apply to doctors, for whom compensation increased on average by $50,000 during the BC Liberals' first term in office. The doctors' salary increase was more than the annual salary of a care aide (Cohen, 2006: 633).

At the same time, the new government was moving quickly on its commitments to "restore open tendering on government contracts to allow for fair competition for businesses and provide better value for taxpayers" (BC Liberals, 2001: 4). As part of its efforts to encourage private sector involvement in publicly funded service delivery, the 2003 Procurement Services Act required government health authorities to align their procurement policies with "best practices [that] promote fair and open procurement, competition ... value for money, transparency and accountability" (Procurement Services Act, 2003). The provincial government gave itself new powers to establish government-wide policy directives and procurement practices that applied to public contracts for LTRC services. One of the policy directives, the Capital Asset Management Framework, encouraged "non-traditional" procurement models, including public–private partnerships (P3s) in the health sector (Whiteside, 2015). This policy shift meant that health authorities were required to use request for proposal (RFP) processes in an effort to obtain lowest-cost bids, typically from for-profit companies. This was a significant departure from the first half of the 1990s, when the provincial Ministry of Health partnered with non-profit organizations to develop new LTRC facilities and provided construction and development expertise to the non-profit sector.

As LTRC procurement responsibilities devolved to newly established regional health authorities in the late 1990s, the bureaucratic expertise and support for non-profit LTRC development ended. The RFP process under the Liberals in the 2000s required non-profit and for-profit operators alike to competitively bid against one another by preparing administratively complex proposals that relied on private capital financing. Consistent with the use of competitive procurement for publicly funded LTRC delivery in other jurisdictions (e.g., Meagher & Szebehely, 2013), the RFP process tends to benefit well-capitalized for-profit companies (and large non-profit organizations) with the technical capacities and economies of scale. A health authority administrator admitted that the RFP process represented a big shift for non-profit organizations, which often lacked the necessary skills to prepare bids that would be successful (Key informant interview, Jan. 2018). These changes in procurement encouraged private sector involvement and complemented labor reforms rolled out under Bill 29 and the subsequent Bill 94.

In late 2003, the BC Liberal government passed another significant bill intended to facilitate labor restructuring and privatization, and specifically targeted at the LTRC sector. Bill 94, the Health Sector Partnerships Agreement Act (hereafter, Bill 94), extended the legal rights under Bill 29 to non-HEABC employers and granted new – mainly for-profit – entrants to the LTRC sector the economic advantage of unrestricted rights to subcontract and flip commercial contracts. The new government saw this legislation as an opportunity to expand public-private partnerships (P3s) in the LTRC sector where facility owners and their investors would bring the capital and the government guaranteed long-term operational funding. In the words of then-Labour Minister Graham Bruce, Bill 94 "encourages much greater participation by the private-sector community within the whole [public-private partnership] process in British Columbia" (Rud, 2003). In a 2003 government document, the use of private financing to deliver new capital infrastructure was identified as the primary benefit to government:

> [Bill 94] ... [ensures] that partners who finance, design and build or renovate facilities will be able to operate under the same rules that currently apply to other health employers ... Partnerships are a way to add capacity to the health-care system and create improved facilities for patients. The partner takes on the risk of designing and building the facility – at its cost – and then contracts with government to provide non-clinical services over a longer term.
>
> (Ministry of Skills Development and Labour, 2003)

Specifically, unionized workers in these P3-designated facilities also lost their rights under sections 35 (successor rights and obligations) and 38 (common employer) of the Code while employers gained new rights unavailable in any other industrial sector. With Bill 94 (and Bill 29), the government opened the door for new employment and business relationships in the LTRC sector, relationships that had never existed before.

LTRC operators were encouraged to establish business relationships with third-party subcontractors. It was a significant rupture from a labor regime based on a traditional funding and service-provider relationship: Government health authority (funder) → contracted non-profit or for-profit service provider. The legislation created a (third) subcontracting tier, depicted as follows: Government health authority (funder) → contracted non-profit or for-profit service provider → subcontractor(s).

Since 2003, 65 new publicly funded for-profit and non-profit operated LTRC facilities have opened in BC. More than half of these facilities (35) have been designated P3s under Bill 94 (Table 6.1). None of the designated P3 facilities are part of the sectoral bargaining structure. Frontline care workers in these facilities, if they are unionized, have a stand-alone collective agreement, with lower wages, reduced benefits, and no public-sector pension (see Fenn & Katic, 2017). Bill 94 entrenched subcontracting in the sector and allowed these employers to engage in "contract flipping," a practice in which the facility owner/operator may terminate a commercial contract, the subcontracted workforce is laid off, the operator re-tenders the contract, and a new subcontractor is hired with a new (non-union) workforce with lower wages and benefits (Cohen, Tate & Baumbusch, 2009: 27; HEU, 2009). If those workers decide to unionize, the union must negotiate a new collective agreement.

For an LTRC administrator with decades of experience, Bill 94 marked a decisive shift in the labor regime: "[I]t changed the landscape quite a bit, both for unions and the employers ... It changed the landscape of how people did business." Subcontracting placed downward pressure on wages and working conditions as a strategy to encourage private capital investment. Economist David Weil (2014: 77–78) refers to this phenomenon as workplace "fissuring," defined as "the increasing use of contracting and outsourcing and contingent work arrangements" as businesses seek to avoid unionization, employer-paid premiums (e.g., workers' compensation), and liability. The effect is downward pressure on the subcontractor and its workforce. For workers, the threat of subcontracting serves as a powerful union deterrence strategy. In some cases, workers decertified from their union out of fear that unionization would make their jobs a target for contracting out (Key informant interviews, Jan. and Feb. 2018). More often, the threat of subcontracting and contract flipping had more subtle effects by disciplining a feminized and predominately racialized workforce that might otherwise be more assertive. As one union representative noted, "In many cases there was not a bottom people wouldn't have gone to [in order] to stay working and not ... deal with the stress of going through contracting out" (Key informant interview, Feb. 2018).

Subcontracting and contract flipping served the provincial government's fiscal austerity objectives by placing downward pressure on health sector labor costs – and using the for-profit sector (and to a lesser extent, the non-profit sector) to achieve these goals. Government health authorities – subject to the provincial government's fiscal restraint – were not increasing funding levels to account for increased LTRC labor and operating costs. Fiscal austerity imposed by the provincial government was used to impose labor restructuring and encourage subcontracting of care work – evident in the steep drop in LTRC operational expenditures after 2002 (Figure 6.1). According to a union representative, many facilities, especially non-profit operators and mom-and-pop companies, tried to maintain their in-house care staff. However, the provincial government imposed labor restructuring through its power as the funding provider:

> The thing that I saw happening again and again with employers that did not want to contract out their staff, [and] wanted to maintain them. They were told [by the government health authorities] you're not going to get any more [funding] increases, we're not going to give you more money ... and you have to contract out ... and if you don't you are going to run into a deficit ... The [government was] starving them ... And then you had some of those employers [that welcomed subcontracting] where it was all about maximizing profit.
> (Key informant interview, Feb. 2018)

In many respects, these business practices achieved what was intended. They suppressed worker compensation, including benefits. With contract flipping, workers must re-unionize and begin the process of negotiating a new collective agreement since successorship exemptions mean that the existing collective agreement does not follow them. For example, at one facility, where the commercial contract has been flipped six times since 2003, care aides earn $18.11/hour or $5.07/hour less than the $23.18/hour that they would earn in the same role working for an HEABC employer covered by the master agreement – a wage differential of 28 percent. In BC today, government has designated care aides as priority health professions due to staffing shortages and recruitment and retention challenges (Ministry of Advanced Education, Skills and Training, 2017) that can be linked to the erosion of working conditions (HEU, 2014).

Subcontracting and contract flipping undermine the continuous employment relationship that is a pre-condition for relational and intimate care to frail seniors. For example, in 2003, frontline care workers at the for-profit Willingdon Park facility were the first care aides to be contracted out to a third-party subcontractor. Fifty-five care aides were terminated, abruptly ending the employment relationship that had allowed them to build long-term relationships with residents:

> Raj Atwal [...] who has worked for 16 years at the facility, appealed to [politicians] to consider what it will mean for residents to lose the familiar, trusted relationships they have with ... the care aides. ... "Most have worked at Willingdon Park for more than 10 years," she said. "We're

there because we want to be, because we love working with seniors and because we are doing useful, important work."

(HEU, 2003)

In another example, 450 care aides employed by a subcontractor were terminated across multiple facilities when the commercial contract ended. At one care home, staff had been fired three times in three years. A union representative lamented that the long-term relationship between care aides and residents that develop over years was lost:

> The ... government has handed these for-profit companies license to make a quick buck off publicly-supported seniors' care. But it's seniors and their caregivers who will pay the highest price. The close personal bonds that are critical to good care will be sacrificed.
>
> (quoted in HEU, 2007)

Bill 29 and Bill 94 served pivotal roles in the government's program of labor restructuring and privatization. Bill 29 rolled out the legal right for existing LTRC employers who were part of the sectoral bargaining structure to be exempted from no contracting-out and employment security protections that had been negotiated in the master collective agreement under the left-leaning BC NDP government in the 1990s. Bill 29 was primarily a mechanism for existing health sector employers to escape collective agreement obligations while also receiving labor law exemptions that were not available in any other industrial sector. Bill 94 extended these same labor law exemptions to facilities designated by government as P3s, along with their business partners, including investors and subcontractors. These P3 designations have been applied to many new facilities built by some of the largest corporate chains operating in BC. The exemptions for these private sector entities provided unprecedented legal rights for subcontracting, contract flipping and labor union evasion. For both Bill 29 and Bill 94, legislation *rolled out* new rights for employers and *rolled back* the rights of health care workers achieved through free collective bargaining.[1]

In the early 2000s, the BC government also restructured the relationship between publicly funded LTRC operators and HEABC that undermined the sectoral bargaining structure. Following successful lobbying from industry, the Liberal government allowed voluntary HEABC membership for new publicly funded LTRC employers/facilities (and designated P3s under Bill 94), meaning that they were not subject to the master collective agreement and bargained individually with unions. In 2009, the government went a step further. Existing HEABC member-employers – part of the sectoral bargaining structure – could terminate their HEABC membership and leave the sectoral structure. These operators sometimes utilized their new subcontracting rights in order to "free" themselves from the master collective agreement. As a former LTRC administrator indicated, these operators could reduce labor costs and increase profitability:

> Now [operators] don't have to be members of HEABC, it's much easier, you're not tied into the [Facilities Bargaining Association]. If you were a [HEABC] member, you couldn't get out of it. A lot of it had to do with the fact that there was such strong union influence in that sector that [...] once you were sunk in, it was like quick sand, you could not get out. It got to the point where it was so bad that you couldn't do your business.
> (Key informant interview, Jan. 2018)

This was a watershed moment in dismantling the sectoral bargaining structure. When the sectoral bargaining structure was established in the mid-1990s, LTRC facilities could only receive public funding if they were HEABC members. The advent of voluntary HEABC membership for new facilities, combined with the government decision to allow existing HEABC employers to terminate their membership, further eroded the sectoral bargaining structure and stable labor and care regime.

These changes to HEABC membership requirements – in addition to Bill 29 and Bill 94 – have facilitated a notable shift in facilities and LTRC work out of the sectoral bargaining structure and master collective agreement. By 2016, 42% of publicly funded LTRC facilities, mostly for-profit employers, were no longer part of the sectoral bargaining structure that maintained a stable labor and care regime (Table 6.1) – compared to the mid-1990s when all publicly funded LTRC employers were party to the master collective agreement. Most notably, 75% of facilities built since 2003 were established outside the sectoral bargaining structure and without any barriers to subcontracting and contract flipping. Forty-seven of these 59 new facilities are owned and operated by for-profit companies, often corporate chains (Table 6.1). The BC Liberal government's legislative and policy reforms were successful at encouraging greater for-profit sector involvement through a program of labor restructuring through subcontracting and contract flipping. Combined with an RFP process that benefited corporations, the restructuring of the LTRC labor regime has facilitated a notable shift to for-profit provision in a short period of time.

Between 2001 and 2016 the number of beds delivered by government health authorities and non-profit organizations declined at a rate of 11%. Over the same period, the number of beds in the for-profit sector increased by 42% – from 6,211 beds in 2001 to 8,832 beds in 2016 (Longhurst, 2017). This increasing ownership share of LTRC by the for-profit sector is especially concerning, given the published evidence demonstrating superior quality in government and non-profit-owned facilities in the empirical health services literature (McGregor et al., 2006; Comondore et al., 2009; McGregor

Table 6.1 Publicly funded long-term residential care facilities covered by industry-wide master collective agreement, British Columbia, 2016

	No. of facilities in BC	% of total facilities	No. of facilities opened since 2003	% of total facilities
Covered by master collective agreement	168	58%	20	25%
Health authority (government)	109	37%	14	18%
For-profit	4	1%	1	1%
Non-profit	55	19%	5	6%
Not covered by master collective agreement	124	42%	59	75%
Health authority (government)	0	0%	0	0%
For-profit	95	33%	47	59%
Non-profit	29	10%	12	15%
Total facilities	**292**	**100%**	**79**	**100%**

Source: Authors' calculations from Health Services & Support Facilities Subsector Collective Agreement (2014) and Office of the Seniors Advocate (2016).

et al., 2010; Tanuseputro et al., 2015; Ronald et al., 2016). The main reason for the quality advantage of publicly owned facilities is improved levels and mix of staff. The labor restructuring not only drove down remuneration and benefits for this work, but also reduced staffing levels at a time when residents' medical complexity was increasing (McGregor et al., 2010) due to stricter criteria for who qualified for publicly funded residential care introduced in 2002 (Cohen et al., 2005: 13). Low staffing levels have been associated with inferior quality in nursing care practices (Schnelle et al., 2004) and higher turnover in the health services literature (Harrington & Swan, 2003). Indeed the Office of the Seniors Advocate has since its inception consistently reported on the failure of facilities to meet the staffing standard of 3.36 hours of resident care per day (Longhurst, 2017: 15). In a survey of care aides, more than half said that they did not have enough time to adequately meet the needs of their residents, with most identifying low staffing and heavy workloads as barriers to improved care (HEU, 2014).

Challenging Fiscal Austerity, Reimagining Stable Labor Regimes and Relational Care

In British Columbia, labor restructuring has been used to advance long-term residential care privatization. Restructuring this stable labor regime along neoliberal lines of flexibility and precarity has been achieved through successive rounds of neoliberal legislative and policy reforms, and rationalized by discourses of fiscal austerity – a tenet of neoliberal governance. Although the stable labor regime that fostered continuity of care based on strong, long-term relationships between elderly residents and care workers has been fundamentally altered, privatization of the LTRC sector remains an unfolding story. The history of labor restructuring and privatization in British Columbia's LTRC sector illustrates the importance of sectoral collective bargaining structures that create stable labor regimes and improved standards of care. Even after unprecedented legal rights and labor law exemptions were rolled out to the for-profit industry, the majority of publicly funded care is still provided by government and non-profit-owned organizations. Unionized nursing home care workers – predominately women – are remarkably resilient in the face of a very challenging labor relations environment, and they continue to organize for improved conditions of care. And although the broad-based labor relations model has been eroded, it maintains the stable high-quality caring conditions for thousands of older British Columbians. The province's sectoral labor structure provides lessons for other jurisdictions looking to foster a stable labor/care regime as a precondition for relational care. Perhaps the most significant lesson is the need to challenge discourses of fiscal austerity that are often used to justify privatization and the erosion quality nursing home care.

Acknowledgments

The authors would like to thank the individuals who agreed to be interviewed for this research. They also thank staff at the Hospital Employees' Union, Pat Armstrong, and Marcy Cohen, and Seth Klein for their helpful comments on previous versions of this chapter. The usual disclaimers apply.

Note

1 In 2002, health care unions, led by the Hospital Employees' Union, BC Government and Service Employees' Union, and the BC Nurses' Union, launched a court challenge against Bill 29, arguing that it violated two sections of the Canadian Charter of Rights and Freedoms. Ultimately, the challenge was appealed to the Supreme Court of Canada, which rendered its decision in 2007. The Supreme Court ruled that the Charter-protected "freedom of association" extends to free collective bargaining. It was a partial victory for the unions as certain sections in Bill 29 and Bill 94 were struck. However, health sector employers, including the LTRC sector, still retained important Labour Relations Code exemptions that would allow them to continue subcontracting and flipping contracts in order to avoid unionization. In sum, employers retained their rights to contract-out work and flip the commercial contracts. However, the Supreme Court ruled that employers had to consult with unions in advance if they planned to contract out and restructure workplaces. The Court ruled that the "no contracting-out" protections – negotiated through free collective bargaining – are protected Charter rights and should not have been stripped by government.

References

Armstrong, P. (2010). Neoliberalism in action: Canadian perspectives. In S. Braedley & M. Luxton (Eds.), *Neoliberalism and Everyday Life* (pp. 184–202). Montreal: McGill-Queen's University Press.

Armstrong, P., & Armstrong, H. (2010). *Wasting away: The undermining of Canadian health care*. Don Mills, ON: Oxford University Press.

Armstrong, P., & Day, S. (2017). *Wash, wear, and care: Clothing and laundry in long-term residential care*. Montreal, QC: McGill-Queen's University Press.

Barry, T. T., Brannon, D. & Mor, V. (2005). Nurse aide empowerment strategies and staff stability: effects on nursing home resident outcomes. *Gerontologist*, 45(3), 309–317.

BC Liberals. (2001). *A new era for British Columbia: A vision for hope & prosperity for the next decade and beyond*. https://www.poltext.org/sites/poltext.org/files/plateformes/bc2001lib_plt._27122008_141728.pdf

BC Royal Commission on Health Care and Costs (1991). *Closer to home: The report of the British Columbia Royal Commission on Health Care and Costs, Volume 2*. https://www.llbc.leg.bc.ca/public/pubdocs/bcdocs/53108/closertohomevol2.pdf.

Bondi, L., & Laurie, N. (2005). Introduction. In L. Bondi & N. Lauri (Eds.), *Working the Spaces of Neoliberalism* (pp. 1–8). Chichester, UK: John Wiley and Sons.

Brenner, N., Peck, J. & Theodore, N. (2010). Variegated neoliberalism: Geographies, modalities, pathways. *Global Networks*, 10(2), 182–222.

Canadian Aboriginal AIDS Network. (2008). *Relational care: A guide to health care and support for aboriginal people living with HIV/AIDS*. http://caan.ca/wp-content/uploads/2012/05/Relational-Care-20081.pdf

Canadian Institute for Health Information (CIHI). (2017). *National health expenditure trends, 1975–2017*. https://www.cihi.ca/en/national-health-expenditure-trends

Carroll, W. K., & Ratner, R. S. (2005). The NDP regime in British Columbia: A post-mortem. *Canadian Review of Sociology*, 42(2), 167–196.

Castle, N. G. & Engberg, J. (2005). Staff turnover and quality of care in nursing homes. *Medical Care*, 43(6), 616–626.

Castle, N. G., Engberg, J. & Men, A. (2007). Nursing home staff turnover: Impact on nursing home compare quality measures. *Gerontologist*, 47(5), 650–661.

Cohen, M. (2003). *Health care restructuring in BC*. Vancouver, BC: Canadian Centre for Policy Alternatives – BC Office.

Cohen, M. (2006). The privatization of health care cleaning services in southwestern British Columbia, Canada: Union responses to unprecedented government actions. *Antipode*, 38(3), 626–644.

Cohen, M. G. & Cohen, M. (2004). *A return to wage discrimination: Pay equity losses through the privatization of health care*. Vancouver, BC: Canadian Centre for Policy Alternatives – BC Office.

Cohen, M., Murphy, J., Nutland, K. & Ostry, A. (2005). *Continuing care renewal or retreat? BC residential and home health care restructuring, 2001–2004*. Vancouver. BC: Canadian Centre for Policy Alternatives – BC Office.

Cohen, M., Tate, J. & Baumbusch, J. (2009). *An uncertain future for seniors: BC's restructuring of home and community health care, 2001–2008*. Vancouver, BC: Canadian Centre for Policy Alternatives – BC Office.

Comondore, V. R., Devereaux, P. J., Zhou, Q., Stone, S. B., Busse, J. W., Ravindran, N. C. et al. (2009). Quality of care in for-profit and not-for-profit nursing homes: Systematic review and meta-analysis. *British Medical Journal, 339*, b2732.

Davies, M. (2003). *Into the house of old: A history of residential care in British Columbia.* Montreal & Kingston, ON: McGill-Queen's University Press.

Evans, B. E. & McBride, S. (2017). Austerity as lived experience: An introduction. In B. E. Evans & S. McBride, *Austerity: The lived experience* (pp. 3–19). Toronto, ON: University of Toronto Press.

Fairey, D. (2005). *Eroding worker protections: British Columbia's new "flexible" employment standards.* Vancouver, BC: Canadian Centre for Policy Alternatives – BC Office.

Fenn, S. & Katic, G. (2017). A bath a week: One look at privately run seniors care. *The Tyee.* October 26. https://thetyee.ca/News/2017/10/26/A-Bath-a-Week-Privately-Run-Seniors-Care/

Harrington, C. & Swan, J. H. (2003). Nursing home staffing, turnover, and case mix. *Medical Care Research & Review, 60*, 366–392.

Health Services & Support Facilities Subsector Collective Agreement. (2001).

Health Services & Support Facilities Subsector Collective Agreement. (2014). https://www.heu.org/sites/default/files/imce-uploads/FBA%202014-2019%20collective%20agreement.pdfhttp://www.lrb.bc.ca/cas/WQL20.pdf

Hollander, M. J. & Pallan, P. (1995). The British Columbia continuing care system: Service delivery and resource planning. *Aging Clinical and Experimental Research, 7*, 94–109.

Hospital Employees' Union (HEU). (2003). Burnaby council supports Willingdon Park care aides. Newsletter. June 14. https://www.heu.org/news-media/newsletters/publications/burnaby-council-supports-willingdon-park-care-aides.

Hospital Employees Union (HEU). (2007). 450 Care aides terminated in largest mass firing of health care workers since BC Liberal's first term in office. Press release. May 31. https://www.heu.org/news-media/news-releases/450-care-aides-terminated-largest-mass-firing-health-care-workers-bc-libera.

Hospital Employees' Union (HEU). (2009). *Quality of care in BC's residential care facilities: A submission to the office of the BC Ombudsman on Seniors' Care*, p. 20. http://www.heu.org/sites/default/files/uploads/2010%20seniors/HEU%20submission%20to%20Ombudsperson.pdf.

Hospital Employees' Union (HEU). (2014). Care aides under pressure, and at risk, in efforts to provide quality care to nursing home residents and patients, according to poll. https://www.heu.org/sites/default/files/uploads/Backgrounder%20for%20care%20aide%20poll%2010-16-14.pdf.

Jansen, I. (2011). *Residential long-term care in Canada: Our vision for better seniors' care.* Ottawa: Canadian Union of Public Employees.

Klein, S. (2002). *Reckless and unnecessary: CCPA's analysis, facts, and figures for understanding and challenging BC's January 17 budget and job cuts.* Vancouver: Canadian Centre for Policy Alternatives – BC Office.

Labour Relations Code, Revised Statutes of British Columbia (1996, c. C-45). BC Laws website: http://www.bclaws.ca/civix/document/id/complete/statreg/96244_01

Lee, M. & Cohen, M. (2005). *The hidden costs of health care wage cuts in BC.* Vancouver: Canadian Centre for Policy Alternatives – BC Office.

Lee, M., Klein, S. & Murray, S. (1999). *Behind the headlines: A review of public policy in BC.* Vancouver: Canadian Centre for Policy Alternatives – BC Office. https://www.poli

cyalternatives.ca/sites/default/files/uploads/publications/BC_Office_Pubs/headlines. pdf.

Longhurst, A. (2017). *Privatization and declining access to BC seniors' care: An urgent call for policy change*. Vancouver: Canadian Centre for Policy Alternatives – BC Office.

McBride, S. & McNutt, K. (2007). Devolution and neoliberalism in the Canadian welfare state: Ideology, national and international conditioning frameworks, and policy change in British Columbia. *Global Social Policy*, 7(2), 177–201.

McBride, S. & Whiteside, H. (2011). *Private affluence, public austerity: Economic crisis & democratic malaise in Canada*. Black Point, NS: Fernwood Publishing.

McGilton, K. S., Pringle, D. M., O'Brien-Pallas, L. L., Wynn, F. & Streiner, D. (2005). Development and psychometric testing of the Relational Care Scale. *Journal of Nursing Measurement*, 13(1), 51–64. PMID: 16315570 PLOS Medicine.

McGregor, M., Tate, R. B., McGrail, K. M., Ronald, L. A., Broemeling, A. M. & Cohen, M. (2006). Care outcomes in long-term care facilities in British Columbia, Canada: Does ownership matter? *Medical Care*, 44(10), 929–935.

McGregor, M. J., Tate, R. B., Ronald, L. A., McGrail, K. M., Cox, M. B., Berta, W. & Broemeling, A. M.. (2010). Staffing in long-term care in British Columbia, Canada: A longitudinal study of differences by facility ownership, 1996–2006. *Health Reports*, 21, 1–7.

Meagher, G. & Szebehely, M. (Eds.). (2013). *Marketisation in Nordic eldercare: A research report on legislation, oversight, extent and consequences*. Stockholm, Sweden: Stockholm University.

Mercille, J. (2017). Neoliberalism and health care: The case of the Irish nursing home sector. *Critical Public Health*. doi:10.1080/09581596.2017.1371277

Ministry of Advanced Education, Skills and Training. (2017). *British Columbia labour market outlook*. Victoria: Government of BC. https://www.workbc.ca/getmedia/66fd0e7c-734e-4fcb-b1a6-0454862525a6/BC_Labour_Market_Outlook_2017_Edition_Nov_2017.PDF.aspx

Ministry of Finance and Corporate Relations. (1996). *Budget 96: Jobs up, taxes down, debt reduced, budget balanced*. Government of BC. http://www.fin.gov.bc.ca/archive/budget96/brochure.htm

Ministry of Skills Development and Labour. (2002). *Health and Social Services Delivery Improvement Act*. Media backgrounder, January 25. Government of BC. https://archive.news.gov.bc.ca/releases/archive/2001-2005/2002sdl0034-001028-attachment2.htm

Ministry of Skills Development and Labour. (2003). *Legislation clarifies rules for health partnerships*. Information bulletin, November 19. Government of BC.

Murphy, J. (2006). *Residential care quality: A review of the literature on nurse and personal care staffing and quality of care*. Report prepared for Nursing Directorate, BC Ministry of Health. http://www.health.gov.bc.ca/library/publications/year/2006/residential-care-quality-a-review-of-the-literature-on-nurse-and-personal-care-staffing-and-quality-of-care.pdf

Office of the Seniors Advocate. (2016). *British Columbia residential care facilities quick facts directory*. Victoria: Government of BC.

Peck, J. (2001). Neoliberalizing states: Thin policies/hard outcomes. *Progress in Human Geography*, 25(3), 445–455.

Peck, J. & Tickell, A. (2002). Neoliberalizing space. *Antipode*, 34(4), 380–404.

Procurement Services Act, Statutes of British Columbia (2003, C-22). BC Laws website: http://www.bclaws.ca/Recon/document/ID/freeside/00_03022_01.

Ramage-Morin, P. (2006). Successful aging in healthcare institutions. Statistics Canada 2006; Report # 82–003. https://www.statcan.gc.ca/pub/82-003-s/2005000/pdf/9089-eng.pdf

Ronald, L. A., McGregor, M., Harrington, C., Pollock, A. & Lexchin, J. (2016). Observational evidence of for-profit delivery and inferior nursing home care: When is there enough evidence for policy change? *PLOS Medicine, 13*(4), 1–12.

Rud, J. (2003). Province, HEU face off over hiring policy set out in Bill 94. *Times Colonist*, November 20, C3.

Russell, E. (2014). The strategic use of budget crises. In D. Baines & S. McBride, *Orchestrating austerity: Impacts & resistance* (pp. 34–49). Black Point, NS: Fernwood.

Schnelle, J. F., Simmons, S. F., Harrington, C., Cadogan, M., Garcia, E. & Bates-Jensen, M. (2004). Relationship of nursing home staffing to quality of care. *Health Services Research, 39*: 225–250.

Sigurdson, R. (1996). The British Columbia New Democratic Party: Does it make a difference? In K. Carty, *Politics, policy and government in British Columbia* (pp. 310–337). Vancouver, BC: UBC Press.

Stanford, J. (1995). The economics of debt and the remaking of Canada. *Studies in Political Economy, 48*, 113–135.

Stanford, J. (2001). The economic and social consequences of fiscal retrenchment in Canada in the 1990s. In K. Banting, A. Sharpe & F. St-Hilaire, *The review of economic performance and social progress*. Ottawa, ON: Centre for the Study of Living Standards and the Institute for Research on Public Policy.

Statistics Canada (2018). Labour force characteristics by occupation, annual. Table 14-10-0297-01.

Stiglitz, J. E. (2010). The dangers of deficit reduction. *The Economist's Voice, 7*(1), 1–3.

Stinson, J., Pollak, N. & Cohen, M. (2005). *The pains of privatization: How contracting out hurts health support workers, their families, and health care*. Vancouver, BC: Canadian Centre for Policy Alternatives – BC Office.

Tanuseputro, P., Chalifoux, M., Bennett, C., Gruneir, A., Bronskill, S. E., Walker, P. & Manuel, D. (2015). Hospitalization and mortality rates in long-term care facilities: Does for-profit status matter? *Journal of the American Medical Directors Association, 16*, 874–883.

Vosko, L. F. (2006). Precarious employment: towards an improved understanding of labour market insecurity. In L. F. Vosko, *Precarious employment: Understanding labour market insecurity in Canada* (pp. 3–39). Montreal and Kingston: McGill-Queen's University Press.

Weil, D. (2014). *The fissured workplace: Why work became so bad for so many and what can be done to improve it*. Cambridge, MA: Harvard University Press.

Whiteside, H. (2015). *Purchase for profit: Public–private partnerships and Canada's public health care system*. Toronto, ON: University of Toronto Press.

Zuberi, D. (2011a). Contracting out hospital support jobs: The effects of poverty wages, excessive workload, and job insecurity on work and family life. *American Behavioral Scientist, 55*(7), 920–940.

Zuberi, D. (2011b). The deleterious consequences of privatization and outsourcing for hospital support work: The experiences of contracted-out hospital cleaners and dietary aids in Vancouver, Canada. *Social Science & Medicine, 72*, 907–911.

Part 2
Key Issues

Chapter 7

Public Funds, Private Data
A Canadian Example

Tamara Daly

For privatization to occur, something must be moved from the public to the private, commercial, non-profit, or individual spheres. For public health systems, privatization commonly occurs through shifts from public funding, delivery, or administration. While the Canada Health Act (1984) publicly covers administration and funding of hospital and physician services, delivery is largely private, with mostly non-profit hospitals and independent physicians in private practice. In contrast, long-term residential care (LTRC) is an extended health service, meaning there is no stipulation that it receive public funding. In fact, levels of public funding vary across each of Canada's provinces and territories, although all these jurisdictions fund some aspects of LTRC.

In Ontario, delivery (ownership) of LTRC is mixed, although each municipality must provide at least one facility. As a service delivered outside of the stipulations of the Canada Health Act (1984), LTRC is subject to the terms of the North American Free Trade Agreement (1994). This is reflected in the largely private, commercial composition of the sector in Ontario (Daly, 2015), with mostly public funding for the care services and private costs for residents' accommodation. Indirect shifts to funding, like limiting the number of publicly funded beds and encouraging private responsibility through home care, also constitute a shift. Unlike more obvious forms, the privatization of administration can be quite subtle and require different approaches to identify it.

Following an overarching shift to neoliberalism, the administration of Ontario's health care system operates under New Public Management (NPM) discourses and mechanisms; this shift progressed with the advent of the Health System Restructuring Commission (1998). According to Larbi (1999), key elements of NPM include various forms of decentralizing management within public services (e.g., the creation of autonomous agencies and devolution of budgets and financial control); increasing use of markets and competition in the provision of public services (e.g., contracting out and other market-type mechanisms); and increasing emphasis on performance, outputs, and customer-orientation.

Importantly, NPM has opened endless new spaces for the privatization of administration. This chapter argues that the emphasis on performance, outputs, and customer-orientation via "person-centered care" is encapsulated in the province's approach to "quality," one that is more often associated with consumer-oriented spaces. However, unlike the more straightforward metrics associated with measuring privatization of funding (changes to funds coming from governments) or delivery (changes in ownership), the privatization of administration is subtle and must be explored via means that include the re-organization of work, the influence of dominant discourses, and shifts to relations of ruling in terms of policy and practice.

To understand the privatization of administration, this chapter takes up the following questions: how is Ontario's quality project in long-term care operationalized? In what ways does this project represent a shift towards privatization? I apply Donabedian's framework to the LTRC quality project in Ontario, focusing on how the use of the Resident Assessment Instrument-Minimum Data Set 2.0 (RAI-MDS 2.0) administrative tool has shaped structures, processes, and outcomes in LTRC. In terms of methodology, I employ feminist political economy – which situates everyday experiences within the overarching economic and political system and explores power relations shaping how decision-making is exercised – as a way of addressing the need for the type of multi-scalar method Donabedian (1966) advocates. Feminist political economy (Armstrong & Connelly, 1989: 5–12; Andrew et al., 2003; Vosko, 2002) directs analytical attention to the neoliberal governance that sets the context for Ontario's health system and promotes the use of New Public Management (NPM) reforms such as the RAI-MDS 2.0. The chapter's method of data collection involved a review of grey and academic literature related to the tool and its use.

The chapter argues that NPM principles, facilitated by the quality discourse, have resulted in the privatization of administration. Understanding the theory and politics behind the privatization of administration on the one hand and the discourse, policy, and practice on the other is important for seeing this form of stealthy privatization in action. The next section outlines the structure afforded by quality theory and politics in the province of Ontario, with a focus on the use of the RAI-MDS 2.0 instrument and the big data collection and analysis that it promotes; it situates the instrument's use within a larger New Public Management context. The next two sections focus first on process, by outlining the discourse, policy, and practice of using the tool, and second, on the outcomes from the privatization of this data. The final section concludes that our current quality regime is only a proxy for quality, given the limits on what is measured, how, and for what ends.

Structure: Quality Theory and Quality Politics

There is a difference between the theory and politics of quality and its discourse, policy, and practice. In terms of its theorization, there is a sizable literature related to quality measurement in health care, with Donabedian's (1966; see also 1988) *Structure, Process, Outcomes Framework* derived from his study of physician care in hospitals the classic model. Donabedian acknowledges that quality care is extremely difficult to define, involving a combination of values and goals within the care system as well as society at large. He cautions that the "multitude of possible dimensions and criteria ... selected to define quality will, of course, have profound influence on the approaches and methods one employs in the assessment of medical care" (Donabedian, 1988: 167).

In Donabedian's framework, structure involves the context as well as administrative and related processes that support and direct health care provision and that include adequacy of staffing, buildings, and human resources. Process, in contrast, is what actions are undertaken, while outcomes are the results or effects. Outcome indicators are often treated as the most valid quality measures, but Donabedian points out that relevancy, the impact of factors outside of care provision, and the difficulty of pinpointing the sources of deficiency or strength all mean that outcome indicators must be used with caution. In addition, process indicators can be less stable and final but may be better indicators of the extent to which care has been properly provided. The assessment of structure indicators assumes that "given the proper settings and instrumentalities, good ... care will follow" (p. 170). The advantage is that structure addresses information that is both concrete and accessible. The major limitation is that "the relationship between structure and process or structure and outcome, is often not well established" (p. 170). Consequently, quality in health care as theorized by Donabedian must be assessed with a multi-scalar approach, though he does not resolve the methodology for how to do so.

According to Ikegami, Hirdes, and Carpenter (n.d.) in a report for the OECD, quality in long-term care is difficult to measure but there are four general approaches: compare it to the "tender loving care" from family; apply "service industry standards" of friendliness and cleanliness; invoke "traditional" standards including staffing levels and professional qualifications; and finally, use "professional standards" of quality designed to slow rates of decline and improve quality of life.

In North America, efforts to measure quality in LTRC increased in the early 1990s. The resident assessment quality measurement structure was implemented in 1991 in United States nursing homes in receipt of government funding for Medicare and Medicaid following a series of scandals (Carpenter & Hirdes, 2013). Following implementation there, interRAI, an international registered non-profit group of more than 40 researchers and clinicians – mostly medical doctors and researchers with doctorates – stepped up efforts to convince governments around the world to implement a modified RAI tool in provincial and national LTRC systems. The group owns the international rights to the RAI-MDS. Their stated purpose is to conduct multinational and collaborative research to develop, implement, and evaluate the RAI-MDS. The group claims that their validated and reliable tool is "designed for clinical and administrative use," provides facility-level "benchmarks," can "track individuals" between community and residential care, and is "more efficient if also used for payment purposes" (Ikegami, et al., n.d.). The interRAI tool is described as a third-generation tool because unlike first-generation ones that were singular scales or second-generation multidimensional tools that crossed clinical areas, they incorporate multi-dimensionality but also cover multiple care settings, such as hospital, home care, and residential care (Carpenter & Hirdes, 2013). The authors argue that prior to its implementation, there had been few academic assessments of quality in long-term care when compared with hospital care.

Importantly, NPM principles, particularly those emphasizing performance and measurement, are enmeshed in the tool. The interRAI group has identified the following quality indicators in the tool: outcome indicators (e.g., falls prevalence, prevalence of behaviors towards others, and incidence of cognitive impairment); process (e.g., use of 9+ medicines, prevalence of daily physical restraints, and prevalence of indwelling catheters); combined (e.g., prevalence of occasional / frequent bladder / bowel incontinence with no toileting plan, and insulin-dependent diabetes with no foot care); and other (e.g., prevalence of tube feeding, and prevalence of little or no activity). It is notable that most indicators derived from this tool focus on clinical outcomes.

Ontario used the Alberta Classification, a Canada assessment and funding tool, until the provincial Harris Conservative government established the Hospital Services Restructuring Commission (HSRC) with the controversial mandate to cut and redesign hospital and long-term care services. In 1998, the HSRC recommended implementation of the RAI-MDS tool for long-term care. To transition to the use of the RAI-MDS system, a "high touch approach" was adopted by Community Care Information Management – formerly the Continuing Care e-Health Program – in their leadership role on the Long-term Care Homes Common Assessment Project team (CCIM, 2011). They were responsible for rolling out the tool starting in 2005, first to 20 early adopter homes (Phases 1 and 2) and then to 197 more homes once alignment was made between RAI-MDS 2.0 and ministry standards.

A total of 36 percent of homes were submitting quarterly assessment data to CIHI by Spring of 2009. In September of the same year, the last set of 411 homes began using the tool. Rollout involved face-to-face education and training for the first 200+ homes over a three-year period. These first homes were also transitioned from Community Care Information Management to the ministry's Health Data Branch on April 1, 2010, to support facilities' questions about "data accuracy," "home process," and "other general questions" (CCIM, 2010). The additional 411 homes were trained and on-boarded in 18 months, by using electronic means of training, including WebEX, teleconferencing, and a web portal. Homes were provided with a $385 per bed staff replacement and training cost, and subsequently, the cost of a full-time RAI coordinator (approximately $65,000 plus benefits) (Niagara Region, 2008). The remaining 411 homes were transitioned to the Health Data Branch on April 1, 2011.

In a document archived on the Canadian Gerontological Nursing Association website (n.d.) and written when only 35 percent of homes had implemented RAI-MDS, three nurses describe their experiences with using the tool. One nurse notes that "Due to a more detailed approach to assessing each resident, we have found that there is now a more holistic approach to caring for the resident." Another explains: "Front-line staff are more involved during the assessment process, which ultimately empowers them and makes them realize how important they are in the team." A third says:

> As nursing staff get familiar with the new assessment tool, they also acquire an asset that helps their career going forward ... It allows nurses to have current up-to-date computer skills, which makes them more marketable. More and more homes will be using RAI-MDS 2.0. If a nurse has to relocate for personal or professional reasons, it will be an easier transition.

In other publications, staff involved in the tool's rollout were quoted. For instance, at the 2011 conclusion of the Long-Term Care Homes Common Assessment Project (CAP), Tim Burns, former Steering Committee Chair of the project, then Director of the Performance Improvement and Compliance Branch, and now a LTC facility administrator indicates that:

> I've been a huge fan of this project because of the significant difference it has made for residents and how much it has enabled a positive change in the sector, and continues to do so. This positive change is driven by the measurements captured through the RAI-MDS 2.0 assessments, which can now be used to identify trends as well as provide a means for residents and care providers to speak for themselves.
>
> (CCIM, 2011)

Burns further notes:

> The LTCH CAP project has allowed us to *collaborate with the system to implement change and standardize on best practices* in a way that would not have been possible even five years ago ... I would have said there was every reason this ambitious enterprise would fail. *There was little history of system-wide implementation, huge variation across the sector in core processes of care, assessment methods and technologies.* Some very humble, *tactical decisions were made along the way that resulted in massive changes and a project that delivered staying power.* The bang for the buck on this early "listen and learn effort" was spectacular.
>
> (CCIM, 2011, emphasis added)

The language about the RAI-MDS tool from frontline staff and a CAP project chair reflect several key themes: promotion of teamwork; provision of transferable assessment and computer skills as career assets; facilitation of a more holistic approach to care; allowing residents and providers to have a voice; and changes in the form of standardization and best practices as opposed to variation based on context.

The standardized RAI-MDS 2.0 instrument was fully implemented in Ontario long-term care in 2011. Although the tool does not measure structure, in many ways the instrument now forms a quintessential part of the backbone of the NPM administrative structure governing LTRC.

Process: Quality in Discourse, Policy, and Practice

Accompanying the shift from old-style public administration to NPM and facilitated by lowering costs of technology and growing technological literacy amongst the workforce, the administrative restructuring has included the large-scale adoption of information technology systems. In its wake is a fundamentally changed administration of health systems. Armstrong, Daly, and Choiniere (2016) invoke Foucault's notion of governing from a distance to characterize it.

Discourse: New Public Management and Data Privatization in Long-Term Care

NPM emphasizes discourses of quality and performance; the example of long-term care reveals the ways in which the discourse is operationalized and how the overarching structure operates to produce a privatized administrative structure in LTRC. Applying NPM tools and approaches in social and health services is about increasing efficiencies and effectiveness, reducing costs and then measuring quality. As Hoffman and Leichsenring (2011) argue, when users contribute higher levels of out-of-pocket payments, they want to be able to purchase "quality," which arguably reflects a customer orientation. Assessment systems such as the RAI-MDS apply statistical measures as opposed to agreement among raters or what is known as inter-rater reliability and other validity measures to data that are used by the province to avoid rowing but to maintain steering through measuring quality and determining funding (Osborne & Gaebler, 1992).

Policy: Harnessing Regulatory Power and the Collection of Big Data

The RAI-MDS 2.0 tool operates effectively as a relation of ruling (Smith, 1987; 1996) and a new public management "structure" (Donabedian, 1966) of administration within health care that must be accounted for. Relations of ruling are the "[i]nstitutional complexes (emerging from the development and elaboration of capitalist economies) that coordinate the everyday work of administration and the lives of those subject to administrative regimes" (Smith, 1987: 18). For instance, policy requirements to collect large volumes of data – to produce so-called "big data" – enhance the provincial government's regulatory and funding powers and control from afar the everyday work practices within publicly funded organizations and services and the everyday lives of recipients.

There are several powerful yet nearly invisible ways in which the government's mandated collection of big data constitutes a tool of New Public Management: it standardizes workers' practices and residents' late life by determining what data are collected and the timing of collection, and by extension what matters within care work; it allows for the application of algorithms and weightings to the data to derive "quality" indicators; it facilitates governments' abilities to attribute quality performance and quality care to very selective "quality indictors"; it enables governments to align "quality indicators" to their allocation and administrative decision-making for funding and accountability; and it privatizes access to the data collected. Privatization occurs because of the requirement for frontline staff to undertake training and for facilities to purchase private hardware and software technology. This privatization effectively removes the data from wholesale public scrutiny and limits what is publicly reported to (highly stylized) information available on websites for the computer literate. Privatization also cedes very limited access to the data for independent research and analysis purposes, while creating a huge repository of data about our most vulnerable citizens that is held by private firms who run third-party software and are licensed by CIHI to integrate with the RAI-MDS 2.0.

In order to collect the big data, facilities require big technology. In many cases, LTRC homes have purchased expensive third-party hardware and software technology from private software vendors to facilitate data collection and integration with the RAI-MDS 2.0 tool. The Continuing Care Reporting System licensed eight third-party companies in 2017/18: Anzer IT Solutions; B Sharp Technologies Inc.; Clarity Health Inc.; HI Next Inc.; Med2020 Healthcare Software Inc.; Meditech (Medical Information Technology Inc.); Momentum Healthware Inc.; and Point Click Care. Licensees must renew on a three-year basis and complete the "selection of products form" each year. CIHI then distributes products that align with the RAI-MDS 2.0 to licensed vendors, which in turn design their graphical user interface for frontline care and internal organizational management.

Data collection technology has been directly inserted into frontline work. In increasing numbers of LTRC homes, tablet-style devices are purchased from vendors and then mounted on hallway walls or behind nursing stations, which enables data collection to be integrated into frontline care. These software systems normally include electronic care plans and enable tabulations from personal support workers documenting daily bodily and behavioral functions and care needs for individual residents. Instead of doing "ticky box" paper sheets at the end of a shift, personal support workers / care aides are required to input data throughout the day, even receiving red signals if the data entry is delayed by care work (Daly, Choiniere & Armstrong, forthcoming). To support the tool's use, LTRC homes also purchase privately produced training materials from the interRAI organization, as well as licenses to reproduce the tool. They send employees to training sessions to learn about the tool and to conferences to report on the use of the tool.

Practice: Standardizing Collection and Applying Algorithms

The Ontario provincial government requires frontline care workers to apply the standardized instrument to measure resident outcomes and then to compile the measurements for the Canadian Institute for Health Information (CIHI), an independent body funded by government. The collected data are aggregated, adjusted using regression analysis and weighting, compiled into indicators, analyzed, and returned to facilities. Highly stylized data, displayed using infographics, are reported on public websites as well as sent to government departments for funding decision-making. LTRC facilities are funded and administered based on the provincial government's analysis because the data collected are central in shaping resource allocation decisions.

As Figure 7.1 shows, Ontario's LTRC data privatization process involves six key steps (outlined below). The roughly 300-item assessment is conducted and data are collected on each resident upon admission, if/when a significant change of status occurs, and quarterly. An "event" such as on admission, every 90 days, or in the case of a significant change or hospitalization prompts frontline workers, primarily nurses, to complete RAI-MDS 2.0 resident assessments. The RAI-MDS 2.0 assessments involve a seven-day

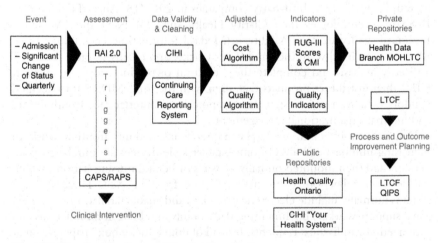

Figure 7.1 The Ontario Cost and Quality Data Trail

lookback to document primarily medical but some social capacities. These assessments trigger Resident Assessment Protocols (RAPS) for a specific clinical intervention to be performed by care staff. Data validity is shaped by sending the data to CIHI, where they are questioned and returned to facilities or cleaned and uploaded to the Continuing Care Reporting System (CCRS), the data repository held by CIHI. Following their insertion into the CCRS, the data are adjusted. This involves the application of weightings as well as specific and complex cost and quality algorithms. In the first instance, CIHI produces Resource Utilization Group-III (RUG-III) and Case Mix Index (CMI) scores for each facility. In addition, CIHI produces comparative quality indicators at the level of the facility, region, and province. Raw data are weighted to produce the comparisons. The indicators housed on public and private repositories are represented by highly stylized infographics and are sent back to LTRC facilities for process and outcome improvement planning within individual facilities (CIHI, 2015; 2017a; 2017b; 2017c).

Once collected, these agency-wide data are gathered by a RAI-MDS Coordinator and input into two algorithms that are guided by provincial cost and quality mandates. The CIHI collects the raw RAI-MDS data directly from long-term care facilities (LTCFs), performs both data validity checks and data cleaning, and then inputs the data into a cost algorithm to compute RUG-III (Resource Utilization Group-III scores) (CIHI, 2014), before transferring the data to the CIHI Continuing Care Reporting System (CCRS) database to compute a quality algorithm.

How are algorithms applied? InterRAI research on risk adjustment, which it claims are based on more than 3000 facilities in six US states and 92 facilities in Ontario and Nova Scotia, was used to create a standard reference population. The specified indicators are calculated using logistic regression and a weighted average to enable comparison between facilities with a standard reference risk profile of its residents; and to adjust the facility's quality indicator results to match the standard reference population. Facilities are then stratified into three risk groups: high, medium, and low.

Each LTRC home's CMI or case mix index (score of the facility's medical care complexity), is based on its aggregated RAI-MDS scores translated into scaled RUG-III scores to assess the resources utilized to meet the recorded needs. Importantly for our discussion, neither unmet needs, nor time-consuming (but not medically complex) behaviors are captured. In Ontario, these scores are translated into long-term care facility budgets for nursing and personal care, paying for frontline care staff, with significant consequences for staffing levels.

These Ontario RAI-MDS data are transposed into highly stylized infographics of LTRC indicators that are housed on public internet sites such as CIHI "Your Health System" and Health Quality Ontario.[1] As Figure 7.2 demonstrates, CIHI publicly reports on the following adjusted quality indicators:

Figure 7.2 Public LTC Data Available to Ontarians

safety including falls in last 30 days and worsened pressure ulcers; appropriateness and effectiveness (inappropriate use of anti-psychotics, and restraint use); and health status (improved physical functioning, worsened physical functioning, worsened depressive mood, experiencing pain, and experiencing worsened pain). These weighted scores are subsequently returned to each facility and sent to the Health Data Branch at Ontario's Ministry of Health and Long-Term Care. For Health Quality Ontario, the publicly reported quality indicators are falls, pressure ulcers, antipsychotic medication use, physical restraints use, pain, depression, and wait times. Facility and individual level data are also housed at the Health Data Branch of the Ministry of Health and Long-Term Care. Finally, weighted data are returned to long-term care facilities to inform their organization-level quality indicator process system. The infographics are used by CIHI and Health Quality Ontario to publicly rank facilities on "quality." What is very clear is that the reported indicators are largely limited to what Donabedian refers to as outcome quality indicators. The Ontario Ministry of Health and Long-Term Care also reports on failures to comply with regulations and any notifications. However, considering there are 333 regulations in Ontario, managers have reported that it is impossible to escape a compliance review without more than ten violations cited as a matter of course even though some of these may not have significant consequences for the quality of care.

What is fascinating – given the tool's origins in the United States – is that the province of Ontario has designed its quality system very differently to the system employed south of the border. Specifically, the province has eschewed the more holistic approach favored in the United States, which takes into consideration structure, process, and outcome measures of quality. In the US, the internet site Nursing Home Compare presents data from their Minimum Data Set tool (Nursing Home Compare, 2018). The system publicly reports more extensive outcome quality indicators than Ontario. Figure 7.3 shows the range of quality indicators reported in the US. The left-hand column

Public Funds, Private Data | 135

- **Outcome Quality Indicators**
  - Falls with major injury
  - Urinary tract infection
  - Moderate to severe pain
  - High rish residents with pressure ulcers
  - Lose control of their bowel or bladder
  - Catheter inserted and left in bladder
  - Physical restraints
  - Ability to move independently worsened
  - Increased help with activities of daily living
  - Lose too much weight
  - Depressive symptoms
- **Process Quality Indicators**
  - Received an antianxiety or hypnotic medication
  - Assessed and given, appropriately, the seasonal influenza vaccine
  - Residents assessed and given, appropriately, the pneumococcal vaccine
  - Got an antipsychotic medication

- **Star Ranking**
- **Inspections and complaints**
  - Fire
  - Health
- **Staffing**
  - Staffing intensity (Staff hours per resident per day)
    - Self-reported data 2 weeks prior to annual inspection
    - Registered nurses, licensed practical or vocational nurses, physical therapists and nursing assistants
- **Penalties from last 3 years**
  - Fines
  - Payment denials

https://www.medicare.gov/nursinghomecompare

Figure 7.3 US Nursing Home Compare

includes outcome and process indicators. The right-hand column includes structure indicators such as staffing intensity, inspection, complaint, and penalty indicators.

The choice to limit the nature and number of quality indicators reported in Ontario is the responsibility of the Expert Panel to Produce LTRC Indicator Benchmarks. More than one-third of the members of the expert panel are research-affiliated: Natalie Damiano (CIHI), Dr. John Hirdes (University of Waterloo), Dr. Walter Wodchis (University of Toronto), and Dr. Diane Doran (University of Toronto). Two individuals have positions that involve data quality and informatics (Shelby Poletti and Debbie Johnston). There are three clinicians: two are physicians, with one representing Ontario LTRC physicians and the other the chief of staff of a large facility providing a continuum of care for seniors, while the other holds a position as a Director of Care. Another member is Chief Executive Officer of a hospital, while another is an Assistant Administrator of a nursing home. Finally, there is a Manager of an area office of the Ministry of Health and Long-Term Care. The clinical outcomes focus of the indicators is not surprising, given the composition of the panel. What is surprising is the notable lack of structure and process indicators to enable the province to provide to the public a more robust quality profile, given the amount of public funds invested in LTRC.

Outcome: Public Funds, Private Data

In reviewing complex systems as disparate as teaching and policing, O'Neil (2016) argues that policy and personal decisions are being made based on analysis of big data and algorithms that are flawed and create at least three main problems: opacity, scale, and damage. Opacity is about a lack of transparency. Scale is about the ability to spread systems and ideas across multiple organizations. Damage is about making poor decisions with huge consequences. In Ontario's application of big data in LTRC, all three of these outcomes are present.

In terms of data collection, complex algorithms that require specialized statistical knowledge are used. This is done to ensure statistical reliability and validity as opposed to the more costly inter-rater reliability, which also relies on expert knowledge. In addition, the scoring algorithms are hidden or extremely complex, requiring highly specialized knowledge and time to interpret in ways that the data can be used directly by facilities. Managers complain that it's not clear how the calculations are made or what the numbers really mean. For instance, there is confusion amongst managers and their boards about how to reconcile adjusted with unadjusted numbers. Also, because RUGS-III is used for costing, it removes managers' ability to plan budgets into the future. Furthermore, funding is based on services provided, rather than on services needed by residents that could not be provided by staff.

The fact that the RAI-MDS tool is rolled out everywhere, to everyone, and standardizes "best practices" is emblematic of what O'Neil refers to when she cites the problem of scale. In particular, the system has collected millions of bits of data, which affect the everyday lives of residents and workers. Because the data are collected about individuals and reward certain types of care that directly translate into certain behaviors, the tool has stepped in as a proxy quality discourse for "person-centered care." The tool invokes an individualized care terminology, though interestingly the tool's utility for frontline care work has been repeatedly questioned. It is not used clinically, in an everyday way, except when there is a significant "trigger" that alerts staff to the need for a clinical intervention. It has also been accused of breaking up teamwork, with nurses more focused on filling out forms and frontline staff left to do the care (Daly et al., forthcoming). In other ways, it is the absolute opposite of individualized, personalized care because it categorizes large swaths of people into boxes, and erases individuals and contexts. In this way, it is more fit as a tool for administrators and researchers than clinicians. As Sharon Warren (2000) writes: "The benefits of high quality databases for health care planning and research have been recognized for years" (p. vi), but she is assuming the quality of the data and failing to take into account what happens in the daily lives of residents and staff.

Finally, like other "weapons of math destruction," the tool inflicts massive damage. It affects staffing levels by changing the division of labor between nurses and PSWs (care aides), it interrupts teamwork between professional and non-professional staff, and it reinforces hierarchies as well as downloading skilled nursing tasks. It concentrates decisions about care in the hands of a few "experts," those with quantitative research, medical, and computer software system skills, creating little room for dissention. The tool's use creates pernicious feedback loops within the system because funding can decrease if there is not enough time to properly do the data entry when workload increases but staffing does not. If homes focus overtly on quality indicators for which they are being measured other important aspects of care may be neglected.

Quality as Proxy

Quality indicators are proxies. They are thus stand-ins, but for "quality of what" is the important question. Are we measuring quality care, quality of life, quality of work, or quality of administration? For instance: is a home with fewer falls of better quality if by quality we mean quality of life? How do we measure quality of life if maintaining mobility is the quality indictor? Is quality of life improved if we take time to measure violent behaviors or work hard to problem-solve around these behaviors? How is quality of life improved if residents and families have no idea what the data are being used for?

We must return to ask these questions: What is the purpose of quality measurement in health care? Do we report on quality of long-term care in Ontario? Harrington (n.d.) argues for "quality indicators" for long-term care because they inform professionals and advocates; encourage providers to improve; enable "consumers" to make choices; and assist governments in contracting out services. Donabedian (1966), using the example of medical care, argues that

> the distinction between values, and elements of structure, process or outcome, [must be] recognized and maintained; and ... [be] subjected to equally critical study. Partly to achieve this kind of orientation emphasis must be shifted from preoccupation with evaluating quality to concentration on understanding the (medical) care process itself.

Donabedian guides us to pay attention to the importance of the kinds of indicators used, by whom, how, for what purpose, and under what conditions.

The current system in Ontario uses primarily health outcome measures. Relying on Donabedian for guidance, it is clear that we cannot simply use health outcome measures as a proxy for overall quality. We must include structure and process measures as well. We must also acknowledge how power as well as private interests and ideas fuel the NPM RAI-MDS 2.0 approach. If we are measuring the quality of publicly funded health care for purposes of public accountability, then we cannot privatize data collection, analysis, and reporting. As a matter of public interest, we must question the ends to which we are collecting, analyzing, and reporting on the big data collected in long-term care.

Atul Gawande's book, *The Checklist Manifesto* (2010), represents an increasingly popular approach to improving quality. Using examples from a range of diverse fields – construction, aviation, and medicine – he addresses how to avoid failure. He shows that distilling very complex and high pressure tasks into constituent steps leads to radical improvement in outcomes. This chapter has outlined the steps we currently take to administer public funds in long-term care in Ontario. It is clear from this review that the current steps lead to subtle but important ways in which data about residents are privatized, the work of frontline care is narrowed and specified from afar, and the ownership of the tools and technology rest in private hands. It is, as Siddhartha Mukherjee says in *The Laws of Medicine* (2015) a clear challenge because "big data is not the solution to the bias problem; it is merely the source of more subtle (or even bigger) biases." In other words, numbers also have values and assumptions embedded within them.

Note

1 Canadian Institute for Health Information https://yourhealthsystem.cihi.ca and Health Quality Ontario http://www.hqontario.ca/

References

Andrew, C., Armstrong, P., Armstrong, H., Clement, W. & Vosko, L. F. (Eds.). (2003). *Studies in political economy: Developments in feminism*. Toronto: Women's Press.

Armstrong, P. & Connelly, M. P. (1989). Feminist political economy: An introduction. *Studies in Political Economy, 30*, 5–12.

Armstrong, H., Daly, T. & Choiniere, J. (2016). Policies and practices: The case of RAI-MDS in Canadian long-term care homes. *Journal of Canadian Studies*, Re-imagining the house of old: Promising practices in Canadian long-term residential care, *50*(2), 348–367.

Canada Health Act. (1984). http://laws-lois.justice.gc.ca/eng/acts/c-6/

Canadian Institute for Health Information (CIHI). (2014). Continuing care reporting system: Case mix resource utilization groups version 3 and RUG weighted patient days—resource materials and FAQ, 2014–2015. https://www.cihi.ca/en/ccrs_materials_2014_15_en.pdf

Canadian Institute for Health Information (CIHI). (2015). CCRS profile of residents in continuing care facilities 2015–2016, CCRS Quick Stats, 2015–2016. https://www.cihi.ca/sites/default/files/document/ccrs_quick_stats_2015-2016_en-web.xlsx

Canadian Institute for Health Information (CIHI). (2017a). Continuing care metadata. https://www.cihi.ca/en/continuing-care-metadata.

Canadian Institute for Health Information (CIHI). (2017b). CCRS quality indicators risk adjustment methodology. https://www.cihi.ca/en/ccrs_qi_risk_adj_meth_2013_en.pdf

Canadian Institute for Health Information (CIHI). (2017c). Resource Utilization Group III (RUG-III) (34-Group) grouping methodology: Flowcharts, SAS code and CMI values, CCRS version. https://secure.cihi.ca/estore/productSeries.htm?pc=PCC503

Canadian Gerontological Nursing Association. (n.d.). Raising the bar: Common assessment instrument benefits long-term care residents. http://www.cgna.net/uploads/RAIStory.pdf

Carpenter, I. & Hirdes, J. (2013). Using interRAI assessment systems to measure and maintain quality of long-term care. In *A good life in old age? Monitoring and improving quality in long-term care.* OECD Health Policy Studies. Paris: OECD Publishing. http://dx.doi.org/10.1787/9789264194564-en

Community Care Information Management Connections (CCIM). (2010). RAI-MDS 2.0 benefiting residents in all Ontario long-term care homes. Newsletter. http://www.nwlhin.on.ca/forhsps/CommunityCareInformationManagement.aspx

Community Care Information Management Connections (CCIM). (2011). Long-term care homes project puts focus on nursing and resident needs. Newsletter.

Daly, T. (2015). Dancing the two-step: Deterrence-oriented regulation = ownership consolidation in Ontario's long-term care sector. *Studies in Political Economy*, 95, 29–58.

Daly, T., Choiniere J. Toronto: University of Toronto Press & Armstrong H. (forthcoming). Code work: RAI-MDS, measurement, quality and work organization in long-term care facilities in Ontario. *Health Matters*. Mykhalovskiy, E. et al. (Eds.). Toronto: University of Toronto Press.

Donabedian, A. (1966; reprinted 2005). Evaluating the quality of medical care. *The Milbank Memorial Fund Quarterly*, 44(3, Part 2), 166–206. http://aulavirtual.iberoamericana.edu.co/recursosel/documentos_para-descarga/EVALUATING%20THE%20QUALITY%20OF%20MEDICAL%20CARE.pdf

Donabedian, A. (1988). Quality assessment and assurance: Unity of purpose, diversity of means. *Inquiry*, 25(1), The Challenge of Quality, 173–192. http://www.jstor.org/stable/29771941?seq=1#page_scan_tab_contents

Gawande, A. (2010). *The checklist manifesto: How to get things right.* London: Profile Books.

Harrington, C. (n.d.) Public reporting of nursing home quality in California. Presentation to California Department of Health Care Services. http://www.dhcs.ca.gov/services/medical/Documents/SNF%20Quality%20Workgroup/Charlene%20Harrington.pdf

Hoffman, F. & Leichsenring, K. (2011). *Quality management by result-oriented indicators: Towards benchmarking in residential care for older people.* Policy brief. Vienna: European Centre for Social Welfare Policy and Research. http://www.euro.centre.org/publications/detail/398

Ikegami, N., Hirdes, J. & Carpenter, I. (n.d.), Measuring the quality of long-term care in community and institutional settings. Health Canada/OECD. http://www.oecd.org/els/health-systems/1960045.pdf?TSPD_101_R0=d2307b6b2a8e561a42d8c3f19fda053bo030000000000000000a91f65dcffff00000000000000000000000005a8655e0001f5ffa18

Larbi, G. (1999). *The new public management approach and crisis states.* Discussion Paper. Geneva: United Nations Institute for Social Development.

Mukherjee, S. (2015). *The laws of medicine: Field notes form an uncertain science.* New York: TED Books, Simon and Schuster.

Niagara Region. (2008). Report to co-chairs and members of public health and social services committee, application of provincial funding for an automated common Resident Assessment Instrument – Final Phase, COM 67-2008, December 9.

North American Free Trade Agreement. (1994). https://www.nafta-sec-alena.org/Home/Texts-of-the-Agreement/North-American-Free-Trade-Agreement/mvid/2

Nursing Home Compare. (2018). Official U.S. Government Site for Medicare.

O'Neil, C. (216) *Weapons of math destruction: How big data increases inequality and threatens democracy.* Largo: Crown Books https://www.medicare.gov/nursinghomecompare

Osborne, D. & Gaebler, T. (1992). *Reinventing government: How the entrepreneurial spirit is transforming the public sector.* New York, NY: Addison-Wesley.

Smith, D. (1987). *The everyday world as problematic: A feminist sociology.* Boston, MA: Northeastern University Press.

Smith, D. (1996). The relations of ruling: A feminist inquiry. *Studies in Cultures, Organizations and Societies, 2*(2), 171–190.

Vosko, L. F. (2002). The pasts (and futures) of feminist political economy in Canada: Reviving the debate. *Studies in Political Economy, 68,* 55–83.

Warren, S. (2010). Editorial: Resident assessment instruments: Their use for health care planning and research. *Canadian Journal on Aging,* Special InterRAI issue, *19* (S-2 Fall), i–vii.

Chapter 8

Accountable For-Profits in Nursing Home Services?

Frode F. Jacobsen and Gudmund Ågotnes

Introduction

A nursing home scandal that emerged in 2011, involving a Swiss-based multinational for-profit company, intensified an ongoing debate in Norway about privatization and exposure to tender for nursing homes in particular and welfare services in general. As will soon be dealt with in more detail, the company was ousted from the Norwegian nursing home sector following a scandal (Lloyd et al., 2014). The privatization of nursing homes and other welfare services is still much debated in the Norwegian mass media. However, what privatization means and what characterizes the for-profit sector is not often addressed. A distinction between non-profit and for-profit providers is not always made by the mass media, where the term "private" frequently is employed indistinctively. Moreover, the differences in types of for-profits the companies are seldom explained to the public. All this is highly relevant to the issue of accountability, in terms of both the extent and means by which the companies are made accountable to the authorities and the general public.

In the late 1990s, supported mainly by political parties to the right of the political spectrum, several of the largest municipalities in Norway introduced a purchaser–provider split, implying an 'internal' administrative split between purchasing and providing units within the municipalities. Since then, competitive tendering and free provider choice have been gradually introduced among a minority of the municipalities. As recently as 2012, 7% of the municipalities had competitive tendering for nursing homes and 4% free provider choice (Vabø et al., 2013).

Public health care services in Scandinavian and other countries are, as will be dealt with below, relatively recent. Hence, alternatives to government services in a welfare state like that in Norway, do not in themselves represent a radical break if we take a longer historical perspective, although in several ways this history influences the present situation of public welfare. However, the types of present-day alternatives do not mirror the state of affairs in the past, where non-government organizations used to play a vital role. The present involvement of for-profits in the health and care services poses some new challenges with regard to accountability, the main theme of this chapter. Those challenges relate to both the nature of the dominant for-profits and to the traits of Norwegian culture and society.

A Brief Historical Account

Over the greater historical span, social and health care services have mostly been provided within the household circle. Even today, some researchers such as the medical anthropologists Arthur Kleinman (see e.g., Kleinman, 1980; 1988), Lisbeth Sachs (Sachs, 1992) and Carol Mendelson (Mendelson, 2003) believe individual households and personal networks (including family, relatives, neighbours and friends) are the largest provider of care across the world. In the context of the current pressure on public services in Scandinavian and other welfare states, household and informal network-based care seems to be on the increase both in terms of work volume and proportion of total care offered (Berven & Selle, 2001; Christensen, 2003; Stamsø, 2009; Støkken, 2002).

More recent than the private household-based care is the care provided by the so-called "third sector", constituted by private secular and religious voluntary organizations. Such care work by non-profit organizations precedes the state services in Norway and many other European countries, frequently forming the basis of the historical establishment of the state health and social services. As an example, the secular Norwegian Women's Public Health Association (Norske Kvinners Sanitetsforening, NKS) mobilized one quarter of all women between the age of 20 and 70 years in the 1960s. Among its victories are establishing nurse education in Norway in 1898, founding the first local health centre for infants in 1914 and building and running more than half of such centres available in 1974 (at which point the Norwegian government took over), pioneering elderly care work from 1950–1970, and establishing the first education for auxiliary nurses (LPNs/LVNs) in 1963 (Bjarnar, 2001). This organization is not merely an important part of Norwegian history. In 2001 the organization had around 120,000 members, of a total Norwegian population of about 4.6 million people (ibid.). Although the number of members has declined to around 40,000 today (www.sanitetskvinnene), NKS is still one of the major Norwegian voluntary organizations. More generally, voluntary organizations are still managing several institutions within health and social services, currently accounting for about 5.0% of Norwegian nursing homes (SSB, 2019).

The For-Profit in Present-Day Norway

Although for-profit private services in the health care sector in Scandinavia have gained the attention of social scientists primarily since the beginning of the 1980s (Askildsen & Haug, 2001; Lorentzen, 1984), commercial services have been provided for a longer time by professionals like physicians, psychologists, pharmacists, physiotherapists and dentists (Stamsø, 2009). However, commercialization in the health sector since the 1980s has some specific traits that differ from earlier for-profit ventures.

First, commercial activities have entered previously public and non-profit institutions in the primary care level, including services for the elderly. Second, for-profit enterprises in the health and social care sector are mainly run based on public funding. Still, like for all commercial enterprises, economic surplus is not channelled back into the organization but rather is shared among investors (Meagher & Szebehely, 2013). Third, and of particular importance for the current discussion, for-profit companies in the health care sector are, in Scandinavia and beyond, mostly part of large multi-national chains dealing with a broad range of activities within welfare services, from nursing homes and specialist clinics to kindergartens and rehabilitation facilities for drug addicts, in addition to non-welfare activities like running hotels (Herning, 2015). Fourth, a few companies dominate the nursing home market. Almost 70% of for-profit nursing home beds in Norway are administered by large chains (Harrington et al., 2017). There are only four chains operating in Norway, namely Aleris, Norlandia, UniCare and Attendo, three of them among the top five in Sweden (ibid.). Fifth, the commercial firms almost exclusively invest in cities, and most are in the bigger cities (Meagher & Szebehely, 2013). Finally, there seem to be some special traits with regard to staffing policy which set them apart from other organizers within the care sector, such as a lower coverage of registered nurses (RNs). The Norwegian economist Anders Kvale Havig found, based on analysis of 21 nursing homes, a tendency for for-profit management to mean fewer RNs, a lower staffing level, lower pension costs and more use of short work shifts (Havig et al. 2011).

In the context of the more recent Scandinavian tradition of universal, tax-financed care services, centred on public provision, this increase of marketization and the growing role of for-profit companies in residential care for older people might be considered unexpected. However, Sweden and Norway, with fairly similar welfare models are not affected to the same extent (see the chapter by Ågotnes, Jacobsen and Szebehely, this volume). In Norway, approximately 6% of a total of 41,000 beds in residential care are run by for-profit providers (SSB, 2017) while in Sweden this is the case for about 18% of 90,000 beds (Harrington et al., 2017).

Even if the proportions are comparatively small compared to Anglo-Saxon countries such as Great Britain where approximately 86% of nursing home beds are run by for-profits (ibid.), the growth is considerable given that there were almost no for-profit actors in Scandinavia before the beginning of the 1990s. Although for-profit providers have been present in Norway since the early sixties, they were family-run companies hardly making any profit. Of particular importance is that in both countries, large international corporations increasingly dominate the market. Starting in Sweden about 2005, these corporations were bought up by private equity firms, a process that has been to some extent reduced in recent years as lower shares go to private equity. The ownership structure of the corporations is, in any case, very complex. This presents a situation where complex company structures make financial and other forms of transparency difficult. This lack of transparency has been pointed out as a prevailing challenge with regard to for-profits welfare services in Norway (Choiniere et al., 2015; Herning, 2015). As will soon be discussed, accountability and transparency are topics closely related. Moreover, the extent to which the companies are made accountable to government and to the wider society also depends on the regulatory environment.

The Regulatory Environment in Norway

Daly et al. (2016) distinguish between two main types of regulatory systems in the nursing home sector and other welfare services; prescriptive versus interpretive regulation. Prescriptive regulation denotes a tendency to specify what work is to be performed when, how and by what staff. Interpretative regulation denotes a tendency to broadly define care without making the above mentioned specifications. The latter seems to be a fitting description of the regulatory system in Norway, which also could be described as having a 'framework regulation', where there is a low degree of formalization in the system of oversight (ibid.). In contrast to a so-called deterrence approach, where compliance and formal legal regulations are important, the regulatory environment in Norway concerning audits and inspections of welfare services can be characterized as involving a more supportive approach, where the institutions are assisted in improving quality, rather than being obliged to do so (Harrington et al., 2015; Ågotnes, 2017b). Ethnographic fieldworks in Norwegian nursing homes have also documented such a supportive, and to some extent permissive, approach to regulations at the level of individual facilities, leading to a considerable degree of both municipal and institutional autonomy (Jacobsen, 2005; Ågotnes, 2017a).

At a national level, the Norwegian Board of Health Supervision (NBHS) is responsible for the audit of nursing homes. It pays particular attention to how facilities monitor risks, ensure that health and safety are maintained, and that potential problems are corrected for residents and staff. The NBHS performs informal inspections of selected NHs in each municipality annually, in addition to responding to complaints. The focus of inspection varies from year to year. As an example, in 2011 they investigated the use of restraints in dementia care (Choiniere et al., 2015). The guidelines from national authorities are mainly perceived by municipal authorities and agencies as recommendations. Moreover, respecting the autonomy of the municipalities is a very strong tradition in Norway. Hence, national agencies like the Health and Care

Department (HOD) and the Directorate of Health are hesitant to enforce local standards (Harrington et al., 2015).

Audits are also performed at the municipal level. Even though the Norwegian Association of Local and Regional Authorities (KS) proposes guidelines for the municipalities, the municipalities differ significantly in what and how they do oversight (Choiniere et al., 2015). The nursing home inspections tend to follow a cooperative and supportive pattern, with few opportunities for and little will to sanction individual homes not performing up to standards (ibid.). The standards are, in short, not very precise, following the interpretive approach. There are few guidelines for staffing levels and staff competence, with the exception of a requirement to have a medical doctor and a registered nurse on hand (but not necessarily on site) around the clock with 'sufficient staffing' and 'professional staffing' (Harrington et al., 2012).

Norway has a limited national system for quality indicators, where all municipalities report on eight to ten nationally established quality measures. The information on quality indicators is only available for the national authorities at the municipal level, precluding oversight of individual nursing homes. Until recently most of the indicators have been structural indicators, not including staffing level (Harrington et al., 2015). In the last couple of years, more process indicators have been introduced, a development much supported by the major employers' organizations in Norway and by the for-profits themselves, a topic to which we will return. No outcome indicators are included.

The interpretive and supportive regulatory environment in Norway relates to a long historical tradition of trust between government and the general population, including non-government organizations (Jacobsen & Mekki, 2012). The interpretive regulatory environment also means few precise guidelines and requirements for for-profit actors in the nursing home sector. Perhaps not surprisingly given the strong tradition for public provision, the Norwegian government has been hesitant about placing a limit on profits made by companies running nursing homes and other welfare services. Moreover, as already pointed to, there is a dearth of quality indicators for monitoring the performance of the companies. Combined with certain characteristics of the dominant for-profits operating in Norwegian nursing homes, this make the issue of accountability of for-profits in the sector at best challenging.

A dearth of quality indicators and of regulations seems in particular to be the case of the "care sector", including nursing homes and homebased care, and where for-profits encounter fewer regulations (Herning, 2015). This seems to relate to a so-called "feminization" of the sector (Christensen, 2012) in public opinion and political debates, a sector where the workers primarily are women and a majority of persons cared for are women (ibid.; see also chapter by Harrington and Jacobsen, in this volume).

Trade Unions Keeping For-Profits in Welfare Services at Bay

Trade unions have played a vital part in counteracting the influence and position of for-profit in Norwegian welfare services. Unions have, historically and currently, a strong position in Norway. Norway and the Nordic countries are, together with Belgium, the leading countries with regard to unionization rate (Nergaard, 2016). In the Norwegian public sector, every four out of five workers are unionized (Nergaard, 2017). Since close to 90% of Norwegian nursing home facilities are public (Harrington et al., 2017), this implies that the majority of their staff are union members. RNs and LPNs (LVNs, auxiliary nurses) each tend to stick mainly to one union. The membership of practising RNs in the Norwegian Nurses' Association is as high as 83%, while the rate of LPNs in their main union, *Fagforbundet* (the Norwegian Union of Municipal and General Employees), is around 50%. The high unionization rate contributes to the bargaining power of those major unions with regard to issues of working conditions in the health and care sector.

The Norwegian Confederation of Trade Unions (LO), the largest Norwegian workers' organization with nearly a million workers as members, has, in general, taken a critical stance towards marketization and for-profits in eldercare and other welfare services (see also the chapter by Ågotnes, Jacobsen and Szebehely, this volume). In particular, *Fagforbundet*, a major union in LO, has made it a main priority to limit privatization (Vabø et al., 2013).

The Adecco Scandal and the Quest for Transparency

Trade unions like Fagforbundet have proved to be instrumental in exposing scandals in eldercare public such as the 2011 scandal about Adecco, a Swiss-led multinational for-profit running four nursing homes in Norway. The scandal revealed that workers' rights were systematically violated. Staff lived in bomb shelters, did not get pensions they were entitled to, worked more than 80 hours a week without overtime pay, received insufficient holiday pay and did not have valid contracts. Moreover, the nursing homes had a lower percentage of skilled workers and fewer RNs than agreed upon in the contracts with the municipalities. Soon deficiencies in care for residents came to light as well (Lloyd et al., 2014). Curiously, one of the Adecco nursing homes, Ammerudlunden in the capital of Oslo, was at the time rated as one of the best facilities by the Oslo municipality, based on available quality indicators. This result did not go unnoticed by Norwegian employers' organizations and by the leader of the conservative party, Erna Solberg, the present prime minister of Norway. In 2009, in her private blog, she highlighted Ammerudlunden nursing home as one of the best available nursing homes, adding that "the oldest old deserves the very best". "The present red-green government want a care monopoly where we have to make do with government-run services", she continued (Solberg, 2009). Ammerudlunden was the facility where the Adecco scandal was first revealed, a scandal resulting in the ousting of the Adecco company from the nursing home sector and also from some other businesses in Norway, such as the slaughterhouse industry.

The Adecco scandal became a turning point with regard to the interest of unions and the mass media (see also the chapter by Harrington and Jacobsen). After this multinational private equity company was ousted from the health and care sector in Norway, Norwegian unions, including the Norwegian Nurses Association, have followed the for-profits in eldercare and other welfare services closely, revealing several other nursing home scandals. While the Adecco scandal focused mostly on workers' rights and working conditions, an increasing number of scandals have revealed low quality of care for residents in for-profit nursing homes.

As an example, several instances of care and harm/jeopardy deficiencies in one of the Norlandia care homes – one of four major for-profit firms in the Norwegian nursing home sector – became public in the Fall of 2017 (Harrington et al., 2017). The first scandal concerned a male resident. In 2016 his family discovered maggots in a wound not properly treated by the staff. Some days later, the resident was left to die alone by staff who appeared to have given up on him, after he experienced increasing problems in breathing. A year later *Fagforbundet* learned about the incidence and immediately alerted the mass media (Winstad & Mortensen, 2017a).

This scandal was soon to be followed by other scandals involving Norlandia and the Moss facility. Several relatives of present and former residents of the facility came forward with their stories. For example, a 92-year-old woman who experienced severe pain was left alone in her room for several days before her daughter and son managed to get her transferred to a hospital, where she eventually died (Mortensen & Winstad, 2017). Another example concerns a report from a former employee of a resident suffering from severe amyotrophic lateral sclerosis (ALS). The resident experienced severe health issues on two occasions where the vital cannula connecting her with the respirator was pulled out by accident, a potential life-threatening incident that the staff appeared to not be properly trained for handling. This deficiency was not reported to the municipal authorities as required by law. The former employee added several other dangerous incidents concerning the same residents, relating the serious deficiencies to lack of properly trained staff (Tømmerås, 2017).

The relatives did not blame individual staff members, but instead said that

> We saw that they were understaffed. We also knew that they were less well paid than in government facilities. We also came to the conclusion that the leadership quite often let their staff down and did not offer them sufficient support.
>
> (Winstad & Mortensen, 2017b)

They ended the interview by asking the question, "Could it be that lack of competence among the employees results from bad working conditions, since highly competent health care staff would prefer to work elsewhere?" (ibid., authors translation)

After other similar stories were revealed, the Fagforbundet, a major union within LO, tried to get in contact with members working for Norlandia. Their chief employee representative found that most members were afraid to speak to him and to other people in the union, for fear of retribution from Norlandia (Winstad, 2017). By the end of September 2017, the Moss municipality decided to end all contracts with Norlandia (Winstad & Mortensen, 2017b).

"We Are Fully Transparent"

The for-profits operating in Norway frequently stress than their actions and transactions are fully transparent to the public and to municipal governments. As an example, Aleris states in their public website that they promise municipalities that want to work with them "full transparency as to routines and actions", adding, "if wanted" (Aleris, 2017), a transparency promised by Norlandia and the other two major for-profit actors as well.

An economist working for the Norwegian union Fagforbundet, Fanny Voldnes, has made a model of the ownership structure of Norlandia as it was in 2014 (Voldnes, 2017). At the very top of the model, the four major investors appear: Bent Eidisson, Even Carlsen, Roger Adolfsen and Kristian A. Adolfsen. The yellow circle represents the Norlandia Care Group Ltd, the part of the company structure directly involved in running nursing homes, along with several other welfare services. Although Norlandia appears as a limited company, links to private equity funds are made clear. Norlandia Care Group officially pay taxes to Norway, although the drawing points to links to companies based in tax havens. Similarly to the three other major for-profit players in the Norwegian nursing home industry, Norlandia has diversified its services by operating in various areas like health and social care, child protection, preschools, patient hotels, and other welfare services. That the company is operating in several countries further increases the complexity of the corporate structure of Norlandia.

The model in Figure 8.1 represents a simplification of the ownership structure of the Norlandia company.

Transparency may be defined as "complete and accurate information to provide a clear understanding of ownership and financing, while financial accountability is answerability and account-giving for public funding" (Harrington et al., 2015). "Following the money" has proved an arduous task for the national government and the Norwegian municipal governments who have made an attempt at it (Herning, 2015). A highly complex and non-transparent company structure is part of the explanation for this. Repeatedly, for-profits appeal to politicians and to the general public not to look exclusively at

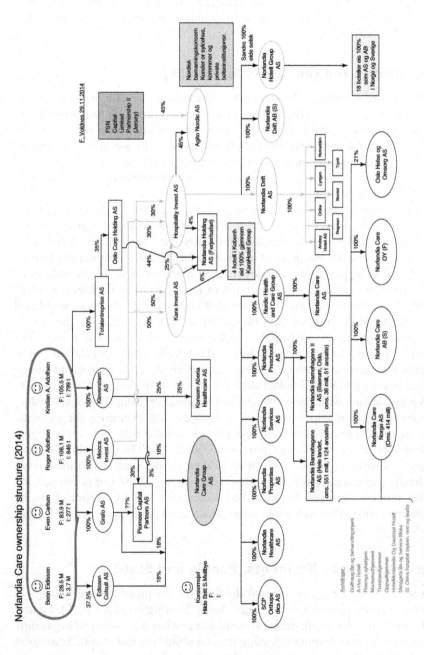

Figure 8.1 Norlandia company structure

finances and earnings of the companies, but to focus on the quality of care that they deliver (ibid.). As already alluded to, documenting quality is scarcely possible given the lack of relevant quality indicators for nursing homes, and in particular, outcome indicators.

For-profits and the Quest for Quality

While many outcome indicators such as the occurrence of pressure ulcers are care sensitive, process indicators lend themselves more easily to manipulation. In addition, the quality indicators are not facility-specific, but are only reported at the municipal level. Still, the for-profits advocate the use of existing quality indicators for documenting how the companies perform, and together with the employers' organizations work actively on influencing the composition of national quality indicators.

NHO and the Enterprise Federation of Norway (Virke), the second largest employers' organization, have been active in influencing the government's policies towards for-profits in eldercare. They have also sought several times to influence the development of national quality indicators for nursing homes. Rather than opposing the employment of more national quality indicators, they have strived to affect which types of indicators to be deployed. In 2013 both organizations worked together with The Norwegian Association of Local and Regional Authorities (KS) on quality indicators, publishing the widely distributed booklet suggesting the employment of more national quality indicators, in particular, process indicators (NHO, Virke & KS, 2013). The publication was aimed at municipal leaders and staff involved in economic planning. Only two pages of the booklet deal with issues of quality, in comparison to 23 pages dealing with economy and budget planning. Still, the booklet makes strong recommendations as to quality measure and indicators, for example, stating that "user satisfaction surveys provides a solid basis for ... developing the quality of (care) in service provision" (ibid.: 12). The possibility of introducing outcome indicators, which up to now are not used at a national level, is briefly mentioned, while the authors argue strongly in favour of introducing more process measures. As pointed to earlier, they argue in favour of quality indicators where they may more easily obtain good results without much effort and investment.

Accountable to Residents, Family and Staff?

As already mentioned, almost two thirds of the for-profit nursing home beds in Norway are administered by large chains (Harrington et al., 2017). Hence, the question of for-profits being accountable in what way and to whom mainly concerns the four dominating, complex and multi-national chains. Since most of the funds of the companies are public, ultimately generated from taxpayers, they are also, by the nature of their funding, accountable to residents, family and staff, as members of the Norwegian public. To what extent they respond to the general public and are held accountable for their actions, is a matter for discussion.

An older research report by the economists Dahle and Bjerke, documenting how for-profits generate profit through a reduction of pensions, work shift reorganization, and individualized wage differences, still seems valid (Dahle & Bjerke, 2001). They documented several instances where private companies in the nursing home sector offered lower pensions than the public sector, started pension payments at a higher age and stopped at a certain age, and required five years of employment to receive pensions. This is in stark contrast to public homes, where pension payments start earlier and last for a lifetime. The Adecco scandal alerted the general public about both pension reduction and withdrawal by a for-profit company (Lloyd et al., 2014). Both public sector and non-profits guarantee a relatively high pension level for their staff (66% of earnings), while the for-profit sector does not guarantee a fixed pension level (Vabø et al., 2013) and generally still tends to pay lower pensions than in the public sector (Herning, 2015). In addition, the companies also generate profit by lower average staff formal training (in Norway: fewer RNs), lower staff coverage, additional fees for "extra services" and tax evasion (ibid.).

A story that illustrates the lack of accountability concerning staff of the for-profits is told by the RN Birgit Berg, a nurse for forty-three years. In 2011, she complained about being treated badly by management after becoming a scapegoat due to a press leakage. The press leakage revealed lack of qualified staff, malnourishment, and outdated equipment at an Attendo home in the capital of Oslo. After the press leakage, the manager of the nursing home, Midtåsen, and the senior executive of Attendo Norway, held individual talks in the chapel in the dark nursing home basement with each nurse to find out who went public. They failed to identify the "culprit", and Birgit Berg, being the local union representative, became the scapegoat (Herning, 2015: 113–118).

How does the accountability towards residents and family play out? A recent letter to a Norwegian newspaper's editor from the son of a mother in a for-profit nursing home may illustrate problems in this regard. In the letter, the son, Kristian Thunes, voiced concerns about treatment at an Attendo nursing home in Oslo, the Attendo Paul nursing home (Thunes, 2016). Amongst other points, he presented a personal note he made in January 2016: "Today the staff helped her with hairdressing, at the extra cost of 1.650 NOK (150 GBP) and cut her nails, costing 400 NOK (thirty-seven GBP)". In government or non-profit nursing homes, this is all free. He moreover complained about excessive use of psychotropic drugs (specifically mentioning Sublimaze/fentanyl, Heminevrin/clomethiazole, Imovane/zoplicone and Risperdal/risperidone) keeping his mother asleep most of the day, in order to decrease the work burden of the staff. She did not demonstrate agitation before this "cocktail" was introduced. His mother moved to another NH where they ended use of psychotropic drugs: "She used to sleep the whole day (...) Now she rises from her chair and walks around by herself along the corridors. The risk of falls is greatly reduced" (his personal notes from summer 2016).

Concluding Thoughts

The two stories above, by the son of a nursing home resident and an experienced RN, aptly illustrate that even though the for-profits are accountable to residents, family and staff, they seem to discourage actions by workers and family aimed at holding the companies responsible and accountable. The complex ownership structure combined with a seeming unwillingness of the for-profits to disclose all their transactions, makes full transparency to the authorities and the general public difficult to achieve (Herning, 2015). Combined with the interpretive regulatory environment of Norway, this makes it easy for the companies to make substantial surplus with few legal restraints and at a rather low risk of government sanctions. However, unions have proved capable of providing quite effective resistance, as illustrated by their role in revealing the Adecco scandal and later care home scandals.

Could a greater share of for-profits alter the regulatory environment in the direction of making the companies more accountable? Comparative research indicates that with the higher for-profit share of the NH market came a more prescriptive regulatory environment, and more extensive and complex systems of accountability (Choiniere et al., 2015). Interestingly, the largest employers' organization in Norway, the NHO, acknowledges both the role of for-profits in increasing oversight and uses this connection as one of their arguments for involving more for-profits in care. In a recent publication, NHO argues that "the municipalities will achieve better control over the running [of the welfare services], since involvement of for-profits makes it necessary to establish routines of control" (NHO, 2017: 5).

Would an increase of the for-profit share of the nursing home market then mean that they become more accountable? There seems to be no evidence to support such a claim. Evidence from countries such as the United States shows that a stricter and more complex regulatory environment, although an important government tool for controlling the companies, is also exploited by companies as they become increasingly skilled at manipulating quality indicators for their own benefit (Choiniere et al., 2015; Harrington et al., 2017).

References

Ågotnes, G. (2017a). *The institutional practice: on nursing homes and hospitalizations.* PhD dissertation. Bergen, Norway: University of Bergen.

Ågotnes, G. (2017b). Same but different: Norwegian nursing homes between equality and autonomy. *Ageing International*, online publication, https://link.springer.com/article/10.1007/s12126-017-9292-8, last accessed 28 February 2018.

Aleris (2017). *For the municipalities: with Aleris as partner (For kommunene: Med Aleris som samarbeidspartner):* https://www.aleris.no/Vi-tilbyr/barnevern-rus-psykisk-omsorg-bpa/Brukerstyrt-assistanse/For-kommuner/, last accessed 14 January 2018.

Askildsen, J. E. & Haug, K. (eds.) (2001). *Helse, økonomi og politikk: utfordringer for det norske helsevesenet* (Health, economy and politics: challenges for the Norwegian health care system). Oslo, Norway: Cappelen Academic Publishing.

Berven, N. & Selle, P. (eds.) (2001). *Svekket kvinnemakt? De frivillige organisasjoner og velferdsstaten.* Oslo: Gyldendal Akademisk,

Bjarnar, O. (2001). Sanitetskvinnene "lot alltid skje i stillhet" – var det riktig? In Berven, Nina & Selle, Per (eds.), *Svekket kvinnemakt? De frivillige organisasjoner og velferdsstaten.* Oslo: Gyldendal Akademisk, pp. 64–83.

Choiniere, J., Doupe, M., Goldmann, M., Harrington, C., Jacobsen, F. F., Lloyd, L., Rootham, M. & Szebehely, M. (2015). Mapping nursing home inspections & audits in six countries, *Ageing International*, published online 03 Nov 2015, DOI 10.1007/s12126-015-9230-6.

Christensen, K. (2003). De stille stemmer – om kønsrelatert magt i offentlige omsorgstjenester. In Isaksen, L. W. (ed.), *Omsorgens pris. Kjønn, makt og market i velferdsstaten.* Oslo: Gyldendahl Akademisk, pp. 22–48.

Christensen, K. (2012). Towards a mixed economy of care in Norway? *Critical Social Policy*, Vol. 32(4), pp. 577–596.

Dahle, T. & Bjerke, P. (2001). *Private sykehjem. En rapport om kommersiell sykehjemsdrift.* (Private nursing home. On commercial provision). DeFacto Publishers.

Daly, T., Struthers, J., Müller, B., Taylor, D., Goldman, M., Doupe, M. & Jacobsen, F. F. (2016). Prescriptive or interpretive regulation and the care work frontlines in the "three worlds" of Canada, Germany and Norway. *Labour / Le Travail*, Vol. 77, pp. 37–71.

Harrington, C., Armstrong, H., Halladay, M., Havig, A. K., Jacobsen, F. F., McDonald, M., Panos, J., Pearsall, K., Pollock, A. & Ross, L. (2015). Comparison of nursing home financial transparency and accountability in four locations, *Ageing International*, online publ. DOI 10.1007/s12126-015-9233-3.

Harrington, C., Jacobsen, F. F., Panos, J., Pollock, A., Sutaria, S. & Szebehely, M. (2017). Marketization in long-term care: a cross-country comparison of large for-profit nursing home chains, *Health Services Insights*. DOI: 10.1177/1178632917710533.

Harrington, C., Choiniere, J., Goldman, M., Jacobsen, F. F., Lloyd, L., McGregor, M., Stamatopoulos, V. & Szebehely, M. (2012). Nursing home staffing standards and staffing levels in six countries, *Journal of Nursing Scholarship*, Vol. 44, No. 1, pp. 88–98.

Havig, A. K., Skogstad, A., Kjeksus, L. E. & Romoren, T. I. (2011). Leadership, staffing and quality of care in nursing homes, *BMC Health Services Research*, Vol. 11, pp. 327–340.

Herning, L. (2015). *Velferdsprofitørene. Om penger, makt og propaganda i de norske velferdstjenestene.* Oslo: Tanum.

Jacobsen, F. F. (2005). *Cultural discontinuity as an organizational resource. Nursing in a Norwegian nursing home.* Bergen, Norway: NLA-Forlaget.

Jacobsen, F. F. & Mekki, T. E. (2012). Health and the changing welfare state in Norway. A focus on municipal health care for elderly sick. *Ageing International*, Vol. 37, No. 2, pp. 125–142.

Kleinman, A. (1980). *Patients and healers in the context of culture: an exploration of the borderland between anthropology, medicine, and psychiatry*. Berkeley: University of California Press.

Kleinman, A. (1988). *The illness narratives: Suffering, healing, and the human condition*. New York: Basic Books.

Lloyd, L., Banerjee, A., Harrington, C., Jacobsen, F. F. & Szebehely, M. (2014). It is a scandal! Comparing the causes and consequences of nursing home media scandals in five countries, *International Journal of Sociology and Social Policy*, Vol. 34, No. 1/2, pp. s.2–18.

Lorentzen, H. (ed.) (1984). *Privat eller offentlig velferd? Privatisering i helse- og sosialsektoren*. Oslo: Universitetsforlaget.

Meagher, G. & Szebehely, M. (eds) (2013). *Marketisation in Nordic eldercare: A research report on legislation, oversight, extent and consequences*. Stockholm Studies in Social Work 30. Stockholm: Stockholm University

Mendelson, C. (2003). 'Creating healthy environments: Household-based health behaviors of Mexican American women', *Journal of Community Health Nursing*, Vol 20, No. 3, pp. 147–159.

Mortensen, Y. & Winstad, Ø. (2017). Nye avsløringer om Norlandia Skoggata bo- og servicesenter (New disclosures on Norlandia Skoggata bo- og servicesenter). *Fagbladet* 30.08.17: https://frifagbevegelse.no/nyheter/-mor-la-alene-pa-rommet-med-store-smerter-hun-ringte-etter-ansatte-men-ingen-kom-6.158.484378.fca0ed88cd, last accessed 14 February 2018.

Nergaard, K. (2016). *Hvem er organisert – og hvor? (Who is unionized, and where?)* Oslo: FaFo, http://www.arbeidslivet.no/Lonn/Fagorganisering/Hvem-er-organisert---og-hvor/, last accessed 22 January 2018.

Nergaard, K. (2017). Antall fagorganiserte og organisasjonsgrad i Norge (The number of union members and union coverage in Norway), Oslo: FaFo. http://www.arbeidslivet.no/Lonn/Fagorganisering/Antall-fagorganiserte-og-organisasjonsgrad-i-Norge/, last accessed 22 January 2018. (50.5% 2006, 49% 2016)

NHO. (2017). *Myter og fakta (Myths and facts)* file://hvl.no/tilsett/privat/ffj/Documents/Skrivebord-22-02-2010/Privatizing%20care%20book%202017-/nho-myter-og-fakta%20konkurranseutsetting-2017-brosjyre-106x149_f41_web.pdf, last accessed 13 January 2018.

NHO, Virke, & KS. (2013). *Beregning av enhetskostnader i pleie og omsorg: Grunnlag for vurderinger av kostader og kvalitet (Estimation of cost per unit in the care servicers: a basis for evaluation of costs and quality)*: www.ks.no/globalassets/blokker-til-hvert-fagomrade/beregning-av-enhetskostnader-pleie--og-omsorgstjenester---hefte.pdf, last accessed 11 January 2018, in Norwegian.

Sachs, L. (1992). *Vårdens etnografi: om hälsa, sjukdom och vård i sitt kulturella sammanhang* [The ethnography of care: on health, illness and care in cultural context]. Stockholm: Almqvist & Wiksell.

Solberg, E. (2009). De eldste fortjener det beste (The oldest old deserves the very best). http://erna.vgb.no/2009/08/14/de-eldste-fortjener-det-beste/, last accessed 14 January 2018.

SSB (Statistics Norway). (2019). Care services: https://www.ssb.no/en/helse/statistikker/pleie, last accessed 10 July 2019.

Stamsø, M. A. (2009). *Velferdsstaten i endring. Norsk sosialpolitikk ved starten av et nytt århundre*. Oslo: Gyldendal Norsk Forlag.

Støkken, A. M. (2002). Privatisering – nye rammevilkår for velferdsprofesjoner. In Børre Nylehn & Anne Marie Støkken (eds.), *De profesjonelle*. Oslo: Universitetsforlaget, pp. 108–125.

Thunes, K. (2016). Hvordan tjene penger på eldreomsorg' [How to make money on eldercare]. *Aftenposten* 25 August 2016: https://www.aftenposten.no/meninger/debatt/i/QE3L4/Hvordan-tjene-penger-pa-eldreomsorg--Kristian-Thunes, last accessed 15 February 2018.

Tømmerås, O. (2017). ALS-rammede Berit Tellmann må ha respirator for å leve. To ganger er den livsviktige kanylen dratt ut ved et uhell. Avviket ble ikke rapportert til kommunen. (Berit Tellmann, suffering from ALS, needs a respirator to stay alive. Two times, the vital cannula was pulled out by an accident. This deficiency was not reported to the municipal authorities). *Fagbladet* 9 September 2017: https://fagbladet.no/nyheter/alsrammede-berit-tellmann-ma-ha-respirator-for-a-leve-to-ganger-er-den-livsviktige-kanylen-dratt-ut-ved-uhell-avviket-ble-ikke-rapportert-til-kommunen-6.91.485922.8b2a6f5a95, last accessed 15 February 2018.

Vabø, M., Christensen, K., Jacobsen, F. F. & Trætteberg, H. D. (2013). Marketisation in Norwegian Eldercare: preconditions, trends and resistance. In Meager, G. & Szebehely, M. (eds.), *Marketization in Nordic eldercare*. Stockholm Studies in Social Work no.30. Stockholm: Stockholm University, pp.163–202.

Voldnes, F. (2017). Hvorfor er ULLR viktig for fagbevegelsen? (Why is extended country-by-country reporting so important for Fagforbundet?) http://www.publishwhatyoupay.no/sites/all/files/Se%20presentasjonen%20til%20Fanny%20Volndes%20her.pdf, last accessed 14 January 2018.

Winstad, Ø. (2017). Ansatte i Norlandia er redde for å kontakte fagforeningen sin (Norlandia employees are afraid to contact their union). *Fagbladet* 8 September 2017: https://frifagbevegelse.no/nyheter/-ansatte-i-norlandia-er-redde-for-a-kontakte-fagforeningen-6.158.485944.fa612fcdbc, last accessed 14 February 2018.

Winstad, Ø. & Mortensen, Y. (2017a). Åge hadde levende fluelarver i sårene før han døde (Åge had live maggots in his wounds before dying). *Fagbladet* 24 August 2017: https://fagbladet.no/nyheter/age-hadde-levende-fluelarver-i-sarene-for-han-dode-6.91.483228.c783dcb97b, last accessed 14 February 2018.

Winstad, Ø. & Mortensen, Y. (2017b). Moss kommune kaster ut privat omsorgsselskap etter avsløringene (Moss municipality have ousted a private care company after disclosures). *Fagbladet* 22.09.17: https://fagbladet.no/nyheter/moss-kommune-kaster-ut-privat-omsorgsselskap-etter-avsloringene-6.91.488810.84e39584f6, last accessed 14 February 2018.

Chapter 9

Marketing Long-Term Care
Website Analysis of For-Profit Corporations in Sweden and Canada

Ruth Lowndes, Jacqueline Choiniere, and Sara Erlandsson

In North America, since the late 1960s and early 1970s, health services have increasingly been subjected to commercialization, with "care services" the product being marketed. As Pat and Hugh Armstrong discuss in Chapter 1, the move towards privatization of health services came as a result of reduced government funding, a conviction that for-profit ways were superior, and political decisions to offload government responsibility for health care, all of which have led to health providers entering the competitive market. In 1986, Lar wrote that health care services "are recognized like any other commodity, something to be bought, sold, and traded in business terms" (p. 3). In Sweden, privatization started in the mid-1980s (Szebehely, 2016). By 2012, 86 percent of private residential care facilities were being operated by for-profit companies (Erlandsson, Storm, Stranz, Szebehely & Trydegard, 2013). For more detail on the privatization of LTRC in Sweden see Chapter 2 and for Canadian details see Chapters 5 and 6.

LTRC homes are increasingly being bought, managed, and built by large corporations that see an expanding business opportunity with the aging population and growing longevity. These demographics are used by corporations to sell their services. In Canada, as one for-profit company puts it,

> For the first time in the country's history, there are more citizens over the age of 65 than under 15. And this wave will only accelerate as the baby-boomer generation advances into their 70s with life expectancies reaching new highs.
>
> (Extendicare, Annual Report, 2016: 14)

Similarly, in Sweden, a corporation draws attention to the fact that "Today, over half a million Swedes are over 80 years old and that figure will increase steadily over the next 20 years" (Attendo, About Attendo, 2018).

Marketing is defined in the related literature as "the successful interchange of goods or services which gives satisfaction to both producer and user" (Lar, 1986: 4). In the body of literature on marketing long-term care, audiences are told that "competition for patients is intense, and more effective marketing is essential for survival" (Cooper & Cronin, 2000: 177). Recommended marketing strategies include positively representing the facility within the community; developing relationships both in the community and between administrators, staff, and residents and their families; and carefully choosing the wording in advertisements (Laurence & Kash, 2010). Target groups include those who require immediate and significant levels of care due to failing health and the inability of families to provide that care, and those who are aging (or have a family member or friend who is aging). The facility wants to convince these individuals to move into their agency.

Thornton (1995) expands on this by suggesting that community efforts as part of marketing strategies need to "encompass as many target market groups as possible" (p. 30). Marketing is a strategic endeavor and is taken up in a large way by private companies, to achieve buy-in, to sell their product – senior care – and to generate as much revenue as possible. Marketing is both internal and external (Laurence & Kash, 2010), targeting not only prospective residents, but their families, administrators (often employees of the corporation rather than the LTRC home), care and ancillary staff, and current and prospective shareholders. Senior care is a thriving business for large, private corporations and is marketed as such.

In Canada, LTRC facilities operate at full capacity, so why market them? For-profit senior care corporations market for a number of reasons, including: to sell management and consulting services, to recruit staff, and to link privately funded accommodations and extra services to the wealthy. As argued elsewhere (Armstrong & Braedley, 2013; Suek, 2009), privatization in care introduces inequity, as the more affluent are able to access the marketed additional services. Rather than being offered to all as part of routine care practices, some services (such as private rooms, therapies, and hair care) are provided at an additional cost, which some people cannot afford. Moreover, service provision, staff, residents, and families are represented in a way similar to other products and services on the market, illustrating the emergence of market language and principles in the privatization of care. Finally, staff, residents, and families are often unknowingly drawn into and/or participate in this marketing agenda, which is problematic in a number of ways as we show in our website analysis. Our research explores these issues, pointing out what is missing in the website accounts and representations.

Website Selection and Analysis

For the Canadian part of this study, we purposely selected three of the largest for-profit chain corporations that combined have a major presence across the provinces of Ontario, British Columbia, Alberta, Quebec, Manitoba, and Nova Scotia. One of the three also has interests in the United States and the United Kingdom. For the Swedish component, we selected the two largest for-profit companies, which are also spread across several Nordic countries.

The third company, although not in the top five in size (it is the seventh largest), was selected because it represents itself as "the Hilton of elder care" (Kavat Vård, About us, 2018); its facilities are marketed as having a language and culture profile, such as Persian and Spanish homes, or a lifestyle profile, such as hotel models and spas. None of the facilities owned or operated by the companies on the websites were part of the Reimagining LTRC project. These websites and the information found on them were all publicly available and accessible through the Internet.

The websites were analyzed using an iterative approach. We examined the written materials and the images on each of the websites, both individually and as a collective grouping, in order to capture similarities and differences across companies in how they market and represent themselves. Themes were generated from the data reviewed across the websites, and include "quality," "trust," "choice," and "growth," and we present findings under these headings. Pictures and video representations were examined and are described throughout the chapter and in a section on representations of residents, families and staff. Finally, we analyze the websites' text and visual representations to establish compatibility with our research findings from the Reimagining LTRC Project.

Quality

The term "quality" is very common on all of the for-profit LTRC websites we examined. Quality is not only about resident care and the organization's care practices, but is connected to revenue generation. For example, on the Extendicare website, the following is included in the corporate governance statement: "We believe that good governance is good business ... Our commitment to ... the delivery of quality services while building shareholder value, is well established and enduring" (Extendicare, Investors-Corporate Governance, 2018). Quality care is part of Extendicare's business strategy: "Quality is our Focus" (Extendicare, Annual Report, 2016: 12).

> We will emphasize quality, transparency and communication with our customers and stakeholders in order to continue to be viewed as a leader in the Canadian senior care sector ... By executing this strategy effectively, we believe we can provide an appropriate and consistent return to our shareholders who have demonstrated their belief in our mission by investing in Extendicare.
>
> (Extendicare, Annual Report, 2016: 20)

In their annual report to shareholders, they describe their marketing and sales efforts:

> As leaders in the senior care sector in Canada, with brands that have earned the trust of seniors and their families through our commitment to quality

care and services, we are well positioned to meet the growing needs resulting from the massive demographic transition under way in our country.
(Extendicare, Annual Report, 2016: 14)

Chartwell, another large, for-profit corporation in Canada, directly links quality to revenue in one of their financial reports: "Guided by our Vision, Mission and Values of Respect, we focus on providing exceptional services and quality care to our residents which we believe will translate into sustainable long-term value creation for our unitholders" (Chartwell, Annual Report, 2016: i). Revera, the third company included in our analysis, does not have any investor/shareholder or financial information on its website so the link to revenue generation cannot be made.

Swedish private companies engage in similar marketing strategies, focusing on "quality" to sell health care services and to draw in potential business partners. On Ambea's website, where the claim is made that it is "one of Sweden's largest private operators in age care, with approximately 80 residential homes throughout the country" (Ambea, Vardaga Division, 2018), the success of the company is accomplished "through investing in employee skills development, health promotion activities, and continuous quality improvement" (Ambea, Growth, 2018). Under the "Investor Relations" tab, quality is marketed as a key element and reason to invest in this growing company. They report to have "industry-leading quality" leadership and "quality is [a] central part of Ambea's vision, values, strategy and operations" (Ambea, Investor Relations, 2018). Under the "Attractive financial profile and value creation" section their "strategic shift in business mix towards residential care, disabled care with high care content and own management improves profitability and quality of earnings" (Ambea, Investor Relations, 2018).

Quality Measurement

The private companies market quality measurement tools such as "National Quality Framework," with words like evidence-based, best practices, standardization, proven methodologies and protocols (Extendicare, Long Term Care: Commitment to Quality Care, 2018), Qualimax (Ambea, Quality and Sustainability, 2018), and "the quality wheel" (Attendo, About Attendo: Focus on Quality, 2018). The companies also report which quality indicators they work with. In Canada, the concentration is on quality indicators connected to the Resident Assessment Instrument-Minimum Data Set (RAI-MDS): improving function, minimizing falls, restraints and pressure ulcers, improving continence, administering appropriate medications and managing pain. We agree that it is important to assess these physiological aspects of resident care, and in some provinces they are required measures and linked to funding allotments. However, measurements that are directly linked to funding are problematic because they are prioritized often to the exclusion of other important aspects of care quality such as building relationships and ensuring meaningful engagement in daily life.

The Swedish providers highlight indicators related to care plans, risk assessment, meals and nutrition. These areas are also measured in the annual survey on quality of eldercare carried out by the National Board of Health and Welfare. The results from the survey, although not linked to funding, are publicly available on the National Board of Health and Welfare website with the purpose of making it easier to choose residential care. However, it is not known if users and their relatives actually access this information (Erlandsson et al., 2013).

Family and resident surveys are another strategy used to market quality care. Positive comments are showcased on websites and in shareholders' annual reports (see Extendicare, Annual Report, 2016). The Swedish providers we analyzed present results from national user surveys in their annual reports. Such surveys can provide useful information, but we do not have any way of assessing response rate, or whether the users fill out the surveys by themselves or with help from next-of-kin or staff.

Trust

Trust is another theme on the websites. According to the marketing literature, the long-term care business is based on building relationships with potential buyers of senior care (Laurence & Kash, 2010). Some websites indicate their organization has been in existence for many years, a message often used in businesses to convey trustworthiness (Ambea, About Ambea: The History of Ambea, 2018; Attendo, About Attendo, 2018; Chartwell, Annual report, 2018; Extendicare, About Extendicare, 2018; Revera, About Revera, 2018). Most websites highlight trust as an important consideration (Attendo, Vision and Values, 2018; Extendicare, 2018; Revera, 2018). Chartwell lists trust as a core value (Chartwell, About us, 2018). On the Extendicare website, both consumers and shareholders are targeted in the following statement: "As a provider of health care and services to seniors, we are particularly aware of the value of trust and transparency" (Extendicare, Investors-Corporate Governance, 2018). The display of third-party accreditation indicates regulatory requirements have been met, and thus may also build trust (Attendo, About Attendo, 2018; Extendicare, Long Term Care: Commitment to Quality Care, 2018; Revera, Long Term Care: Quality Care, 2018).

Words such as "family," "home," "relax," and "comfort" are all used in the websites. Phrases that link emotionality to service provision include "meaningful interactions," "person-centred care is at the heart of all we do" (Revera, Long Term Care: Quality Care, 2018), "quality is at the heart of everything we do" (Extendicare, Care and Services: Long Term Care, 2018). "We want family members to feel reassured that their loved ones are secure, active and engaged while living in one of our retirement or long term care residences"

(Chartwell, About us, 2018). The phrasing evokes images of family, connectedness, memories, and home. For example, "Every family has a story, let us be part of yours" (Extendicare, 2018). A further marketing strategy is to sell culturally specific accommodations: "language, food and a sense of community creates a feeling of safety and security ... you are also met with an atmosphere and sense of 'home to Iran'" (Kavat Vård, Our Facilities: Persikan, 2018). The same company also markets "Spanish profile" (Kavat Vård, Our Facilities: La Casa, 2018), and "Arab profile" care homes (Kavat Vård, Our Facilities: Bejtona, 2018).

Websites also offer resident and family testimonials, often found on dedicated scroll-down tabs and in video format, suggesting that services are of high quality and the home can be trusted to meet residents' individual needs. Residents are portrayed on the websites as smiling, engaging in various activities, and often accompanied by family and staff members. One website includes videos of "Edna," an animated, white, seemingly wealthy resident, describing different positive aspects of Chartwell homes in a funny, engaging manner (see https://chartwell.com/about-us/ask-edna).

Choice

Choice is another marketing term used across sites, giving viewers the impression that resident choice is prioritized. For example, "Revera is committed to providing residents with choices to meet their unique personal care needs and preferences" (Revera, Long Term Care: Quality Care, 2018). One of the for-profit Swedish companies uses their website to make the claim that privatization provides more choice (benefiting consumers and employees alike), and higher quality services than the public social care system, while saving tax dollars (Attendo, About Attendo, 2018). Attendo reports that as a private care company it "[c]ontributes to freedom of choice and quality development in the care sector" and so municipalities are choosing to cooperate with them (Attendo, About Attendo, 2018). Customers have the ability to choose their LTRC home of preference, for example, based on special interests, and care workers have numerous employers to choose from (Attendo, About Attendo, 2018). Privatization is marketed as the optimal choice for all.

The websites collectively claim that residents and families are given freedom of choice in picking a home. Viewers see phrasing such as, "You're not just choosing a home, you're choosing the right home" (Extendicare, Where to Begin – Choosing a Home, 2018). They are then drawn further into the website to search for "home locations" from a list that contains only the homes that the particular company is affiliated with (i.e., manages and/or owns). The home page of Extendicare's locations states: "Today, there are more options than ever when looking for care. We try to make your decision easier by offering helpful information and resources to answer your questions ... Extendicare's home locator is a good place to start" (Extendicare York, 2018). So, in this case, and in the other for-profit websites, the choice becomes which Extendicare home to pick from, because options for all other homes, including non-profit facilities, are not provided. Moreover, the websites convey a simplified picture of the extent of choice within residential care, not mentioning that choice is limited by waiting lists and availability of beds. In Ontario, for example, the admission process for LTRC is controlled by Home and Community Care, which assesses potential residents and adds them to a waiting list if eligibility criteria are met. Although they can indicate their first (up to) five choices, potential residents must take the first available home from those selected or be removed from the waitlist (Central Community Care Access Centre, 2015). They have 24 hours to accept the bed offer and five days to move in, during which time they are charged the accommodation fee, otherwise the potential resident's file is closed (Central Community Care Access Centre, 2015). Thus in reality, choice in LTRC placement is extremely limited.

Growth

> Long term care is growing. Join us!
> (Extendicare York, Student Placement, 2018)

In their website materials private companies emphasize their potential for growth – owing to senior demographics, facility development/expansions, partnerships, diversifying of portfolios – in relation to revenue generation. On the Canadian websites we studied, the concept of company growth is also directed to prospective employees, students, and volunteers, as indicated in the above quote.

Investors are reassured that their money is growing:

> Extendicare's revenue from continuing operations for 2017 grew to $1.10 billion, up 3.4% over 2016, driven by growth in our home health care business volumes, funding enhancements and higher preferred accommodation in our long-term care operations, and continued growth of our retirement living operations. These factors contributed to the growth in net operating income from continuing operations of 4.4% to $135.8 million for the year.
> (Extendicare, Financial Reports, 2018)

Expansion across the country is identified as a further promise of revenue generation. "As we embark on the new and exciting chapter of our journey in Canada we look forward to working together toward the bright future that lies ahead" (Extendicare, Investors – Corporate Governance, 2018). Revenue is generated through LTRC and other related senior care services such as retirement communities (Chartwell, Retirement residences, 2018; Extendicare, 2018; Revera, 2018), home health care (Attendo, Home care services, 2018; Extendicare, 2018), training (Ambea, 2018; Extendicare, 2018; Revera, About Revera, Careers: Career Development, 2018), policy and program development (Extendicare, Long Term Care: Commitment to Quality Care, 2018), staffing (Ambea, 2018; Attendo, Our services, 2018), service provision (food, housekeeping, laundry, maintenance, recreational, and therapy programs) (Extendicare, Group Purchasing, 2018), equipment and supplies (i.e., incontinence products) (Extendicare, Group Purchasing, 2018), and other partnerships (Ambea, About Ambea, 2018; Chartwell,Investors, 2019; Extendicare, Group Purchasing, 2018; Revera, 2018). All of the for-profit websites display their business strategies, intent on expanding and diversifying to generate more revenue moving forward.

Representations of Residents, Families, and Staff

Residents

From the perspective of the for-profit companies, residents are the buyers or consumers of senior care. They are represented as "customers" (Attendo, About Attendo, 2018) and "clients" (Extendicare, 2018; Revera, 2018) who are presented with purchasing choices offered by the companies as something they need.

Facilities are described as "home" and are sometimes marketed as being based on "hotel" or "spa" concepts (Kavat Vård, Our Facilities: Persikan, 2018). Mission statements focus on the individual and how much better they will be in their new "home": "We make the world a better place, one person at a time" (Ambea, About Ambea, 2018); "Residents will have something to look forward to every day" (Kavat Vård, Our Facilities: Persikan, 2018); "celebrate the ageless spirit of people through service and innovation" (Revera, About Revera. 2018); "Making people's lives BETTER" (Chartwell,Retirement residences, 2018); and "Helping people live better, one life at a time" (Extendicare, 2018). "Welcome home" greets viewer on the webpage of each particular home location of one company (Extendicare York, 2018).

Websites of LTRC corporations offer a variety of images to represent residents, often accompanied by staff members, and sometimes with testimonials written by residents and families. The majority of the websites show images of relatively young, smiling residents, beside a care worker who is also smiling, often holding the resident's hand, resting an arm over the resident's shoulder, reading with them, or kneeling beside a resident in a wheelchair. These images convey the sense of a personal relationship between the resident and care worker. Sometimes residents are pictured with a family member (usually a younger female, suggesting a daughter visiting her mother).

Residents are also presented as engaged in various activities such as reading a newspaper or book, playing a piano and singing along, watching movies, gardening, and enjoying a hot beverage outdoors. Images show a physiotherapist facilitating a group resistance training exercise with small hand weights (Revera, Long Term Care, 2018) or residents stretching (Chartwell, Active Living, Recreation, 2018) and socializing (Chartwell, About us, 2018). Dining is marketed as being "healthy, nutritious and delicious ... [with] diverse food choices" (Revera, Retirement Living, 2018) and "should be an exceptional experience you look forward to each day" (Chartwell, Care and Services, Dining, 2018). Some visual representations show gourmet meals, a smiling chef, and residents eating while laughing and socializing (Chartwell, Care and Services, Dining, 2018). Extendicare (2018) also has a sample menu on each location's website.

Families

Families are also depicted on the websites in photographs and in testimonials. They are represented as being relaxed and happy, smiling as they stand or sit beside their also smiling, senior relative. The representation of family members gives the impression that they are confident that their relative is being cared for, has meaningful activities in which to engage, and is safe and comfortable. On Canadian websites, testimonials are always positive and praise the facility for the care provided (Revera, Videos and Testimonials, 2018).

Staff

In addition to the images of workers caring for residents in various ways, staff on the for-profit websites are represented as an extensive, unified, competent and happy workforce. For instance, Extendicare website indicates, "Our qualified and highly trained workforce of 23,700 individuals is dedicated to helping people live better through a commitment to quality service and a passion for what we do" (Extendicare, Care and Services, 2018). This representation suggests that the employees who are directly involved in providing senior services are strong in numbers and trained to deliver the product, quality care, as promised.

Instead of focusing on individual employees, websites show what they offer for services, and how they achieve success in service delivery, which ties in with their overall business strategies. "Our strategy is to be a leading provider of care and services to seniors in Canada. To do this, we strive to provide quality, person-centred care through compassionate caregivers across the continuum of care" (Extendicare, Annual Report, 2016: 20). Websites indicate that "detailed and documented care plans" are used via a "team approach." In addition, "each resident benefits from having a consistent personal care team" and "ALL staff members are fully qualified according to provincial requirements" (Extendicare, Programs and Services, 2018). Kavat Vård (About us, 2018) summarizes the organization's work ethics as "in addition to knowledge and competence, we are known to always have a friendly response."

What's Missing?

In keeping with neoliberal approaches, these websites make it clear that nursing home care is understood as a service to customers and with responsibility to shareholders. There are questions to be raised about these messages. Some of these are prompted by findings from the Reimagining LTRC project, along with other ethnographic studies in long-term care (Baum, 1977; Clough, 1981; Davies, 2003; Diamond, 1992; Foner, 1994; Gass, 2004; Gubrium, 1975; Johnson, Rolph & Smith, 2010; Kayser-Jones, 1990; McLean, 2007; Meacher, 1972; Parker, 1987; Stafford, 2003; Tobin & Lieberman, 1976; Willcocks, Peace, & Kellaher, 1987), and some by the broader literature comparing for-profit and not-for-profit homes (e.g., Harrington et al., 2017; McGregor & Ronald, 2011). Although there are undoubtedly for-profit homes that provide good care, the research suggests a pattern of lower quality in care homes seeking a profit (Baum, 1977; Harrington et al., 2017; Johnson, Rolph & Smith, 2010; Kayser-Jones, 1990; McGregor & Ronald, 2011; Stafford, 2003). In their study of 173 non-profit and for-profit care homes in England in Wales, tracing Townsend's ethnographic work, Johnson, Rolph, and Smith (2010) found,

> [T]hat overall the quality of care provided in the voluntary sector homes is higher than that in the private sector, and that the best homes by and large are to be found in the voluntary sector, particularly those that originated in the voluntary sector, whereas the worst homes are to be found in the private sector.
> (p. 186)

Kayser-Jones (1990) confirmed,

> [N]ursing home care has become a commercial enterprise, and profit making, even at the expense of the disabled aged, is considered a legitimate goal. Profit making is the primary goal at [name of US nursing home] where accountability to the proprietor is a major concern for the administrative staff. Unfortunately for the aged, the emphasis on financial gains often directly opposed to high-quality care.
> (pp. 125–126)

We described how for-profit LTRC companies market their services using words such as quality, trust, choice, and growth. Simply put, their marketing sites communicate a growing need for their "product" and make it clear that the sites are intended for potential purchasers and current and future investors. Residents and families may be drawn in by images and phrases depicting caring relations, and investors by financial reports, along with business strategies showing a return on investment dollars. Given the research on factors that contribute to quality, accessible care, it is useful to ask what is missing from these advertisements.

What Is the Cost of Care?

The costs for all services and accommodations, a detail that might deter people from browsing and considering senior care services, are missing across the private company websites. Not only are costs omitted, some websites indicate that "Long-term care can be afforded by everyone" (Extendicare, Where to Begin, Frequently Asked Questions, 2018). Another company's website reports, "Retirement living, an affordable option worth exploring" and beside this is a "budget assistant tool" that the customer can use to estimate their current living expenses and projected income from the sale of their home (Chartwell, Finance, 2018).

There are fees associated with residing in a LTRC home in both Canada and Sweden. For example, co-payments for accommodations are required and can vary with the home classification, the type of room (basic, semi-private, or private), and amenities offered. Depending on the jurisdiction, for example in Ontario, necessary services such as hair care, dentistry/denturistry, physiotherapy, and foot care are paid out-of-pocket by the resident and/or family. Residents and/or families must also bear the burden of paying for wheelchairs and other aids, some medications/treatments, body care products, and transit to and from doctors' appointments, among other necessities. Additional fees often include recreational outings and some in-house events, telephones, cable television, and internet access (if available). In Sweden, the care fee is the same, regardless of provider. Residents also pay for food and rent: the amount varies between different providers and there is some variation on what services are included in the rent. Medical and dental care, medications, foot care, hairdresser, and other services are paid by the individual.

Where Are the Staff?

On the websites, the companies market themselves as having vast, qualified workforces. For example, "A total of 20,000 employees in approximately 500 units in the Nordic countries" (Attendo, About Attendo, 2018). However, staffing ratios and hours of care per resident are omitted. Staffing levels in LTRC are known to be critically low (Armstrong, 2015; Laxer, 2013). As Chapter 3 makes clear, for-profit chains tend to have the lowest staffing levels and may well have a greater proportion of staff with less formal education. While all nursing homes need to "stay in the black" (p. 63) and "comply with regulations" (p. 63) the large chains, in particular, "must also be profitable and satisfy their shareholders in today's competitive economy. This means trimming costs wherever possible, including the direct caregiving staff, one of the costlier items" (McLean, 2007: 63). Erlandsson et al. (2013) report lower staffing levels and smaller numbers of full-time staff in Swedish residential homes that are privately managed. Moreover, there is no mention on the websites of the precarious working conditions, often resulting from the for-profit companies' attempts to reduce staffing costs. An increasing reliance on casual and part-time staff positions serves to undermine the quality of care that is claimed (Laxer, 2013). For "customers" to assess care effectively, they would need to know the distribution of RNs, LPNs, and care aides, the proportion who are full-time or permanent part-time, the numbers actually on shift at any time, and the number of residents for whom they provide care. According to the websites, staff are responsible for carrying out the promised high-quality, personalized care and maintaining positive attitudes regardless of the working conditions with which they are faced.

An Extendicare core value is staff attitude: "We have the ability to choose our attitude every day and we choose to be helpful, approachable and positive in tone, body language and appearance" (Extendicare, About Extendicare, 2018). "Everyone works diligently to go the extra mile to help ensure the quality of care we provide and the level of service we deliver is truly exceptional" (Extendicare, About Extendicare, 2018). However, the individual care worker who is continually working short-staffed and burdened with a heavy workload will find these promises extremely challenging if not impossible. In the Reimagining LTRC project, a Canadian care aide told us, "[T]his job is physically hard ... It's very hard, very rushed every day. Job load is really, really hard for us," a concern that we repeatedly heard from staff, residents and families alike. A registered practical nurse expressed, "Yeah, this is a stressful environment especially with Alzheimer's. It takes a lot of tolerance and patience and all of that to work in this environment so it's stressful, very stressful." In another Canadian province, a care aide explained how emotionally taxing the job can be:

> When the residents are very agitated some days my patience is uncontrolled because sometimes [you've] had it. Like if you have six days straight and you have ... seven [residents] to give the pills, help them with daily needs, you know, and their meals, everything.

Psychological stress, emotional exhaustion, and burnout from work overload are workplace hazards found in LTRC that often go unrecognized and/or are considered to be an individual problem rather than a systemic or structural problem (Braedley, Owusu, Przednowek & Armstrong, 2017).

Some of the websites indicate that training is provided (Ambea, 2018; Extendicare, Career Centre, 2018; Revera, Careers: Career Development, 2018). From the Reimagining LTRC project, however, we have learned that training on aspects of care varies from facility to facility, is organized differently in each place, and is frequently squeezed into an already busy work schedule or during a worker's time off (Lowndes & Struthers, 2017). Instead of interactive, hands-on sessions, training is often provided via individually accessed computer programs (Lowndes & Struthers, 2017). Participants in the Reimagining LTRC project also shared that training is not always geared towards necessary skills development, for instance, on dementia and/or relational care provision. Rather, risk and task-oriented, clinically based care and documentation procedures are frequently the focus of training (Lowndes & Struthers, 2017). Other ethnographers (Gass, 2004; Johnson, Rolph & Smith, 2010; McLean, 2007) also found that training and care work is often task-oriented and medicalized, rather than being focused on emotional and social care needs.

In order to appropriately assess these website claims about training we need to know what kind of training is provided to how many and for what designations of staff. The for-profit websites point to the primary focus of the organizations, ensuring that regulations such as pain management and falls prevention are covered. This suggests that training revolves around these government-mandated indicators rather than other relational aspects of care that are part of everyday practice. Customers may want to know what kind of training staff have in establishing care relationships and how this is supported by working conditions.

The depiction of care work on the websites does not coincide with what we saw in the places we visited, whether for-profit or not-for-profit. For instance, Extendicare uses a video on each location's home page, "Day in the Life," which is narrated by a care aide, and navigates the viewer through a "typical day in the life of an Extendicare resident." The residents are depicted as being busy, enjoying a social meal, gardening, etc., and the staff have ample time to accommodate individual needs and desires. While we certainly visited homes where staff worked hard to engage and entertain residents and accommodate individual needs, staffing levels, among other barriers, made this difficult. Real-life residents have more extensive care needs than the relatively young and healthy seniors depicted on the websites. Moreover, the care work that staff members perform every day is essentially missing in this video. A more accurate account would demonstrate the intensity of required care, the necessary rush to carry out the many, competing mandated tasks and to complete them on schedule, often with inadequate staff. We saw numerous promising practices in the Reimagining LTRC project: for example, when the philosophy of care that put the resident first was embedded in practice; when there was commitment to continuous care by ensuring adequate staffing and less reliance on casual and agency staff; and when physical spaces allowed for resident involvement and freedom of movement (Armstrong & Braedley, 2016; Baines & Armstrong, 2015).

"A giant thumb looms over us all" (Gass, 2004: 60). Although the websites do not point to surveillance as being an objective of the companies, there are phrases indicating that staff are monitored, such as

> We have a corporate team of experts, including nurses, dietitians, infection control and environmental health specialists, fire safety experts, policy and program consultants and others that support our homes on a daily basis, helping to identify and implement best practices.

and "Our systems allow us to monitor the key risk areas in our homes… to identify where we need to focus our improvements" (Extendicare, Long Term Care: Commitment to Quality Care, 2018). And in the North American homes we studied, staff members are surveilled through such devices as computer programs that track data in alignment with resident assessment and inspection criteria (Armstrong, H., Daly & Choiniere, 2016; Choiniere et al., 2016). In discussion with a Canadian care aide, a researcher captured in a fieldnote, "it is frustrating because there is time pressure to get things put in on time, throughout the day (because this is tracked) and you cannot enter things early, 'cannot cheat' as [the care aide] put it." A manager of another Canadian care home reported, "[E]verything has to be documented for [RAI:]MDS purposes … They have all sorts of flow sheets that they have to [complete]." Much of staff work time, and their sometimes unpaid overtime, is used to document care (Armstrong, H., Daly & Choiniere, 2016) because timely ongoing record keeping is mandatory, for example, for RAI:MDS.

Another central element missing on the websites is a focus on care as a relationship. Aside from the closeness and touching depicted in the visual representations, there is no indication of how relational care will be achieved. As Chapter 3 shows, the for-profit companies tend to spend a significantly smaller portion of their budgets on staff and have lower staffing levels, so it is difficult to see how there will be time to develop care relations. The quality measures the websites describe are quantitatively focused and include pain management, falls prevention, skin and wound care, and continence care (Extendicare, Long Term Care: Commitment to Quality Care, 2018). These quality indicators, while important in their own right, and aligned with regulatory requirements, fail to capture emotional/relational aspects of care.

Our findings demonstrate that when quantitatively assessed, clinical, quality indicators are prioritized, the more relational, social aspects of care are neglected. Care is a relationship (Armstrong & Braedley, 2013) and relational care practices need to take priority. In the Reimagining LTRC project, participants often voiced concerns about having no time to spend with residents in a relational way (Lowndes & Struthers, 2017). Residents too expressed their desire for staff to spend quality time with them. As a Canadian resident explained to us,

> [T]hey don't always pay attention to you. That's because they don't have enough staff. Not enough people to talk to you, just talk to you, just listen to you. You know, just listen to me. That's not easy. Not easy.

For instance, mealtimes, which can provide the opportunity for socialization (Armstrong, 2013; Lowndes, Armstrong & Daly, 2015; Lowndes, Daly, & Armstrong, 2017), are often rushed. This rushing is even more pronounced in homes where food services are contracted out to for-profit companies which operate on minimal staff and restricted dining times, and provide lower-quality food in order to increase profit margins (Lowndes, Daly & Armstrong, 2015). Moreover, although the websites indicate food is delicious, and there are plenty of choices, we found this is often not the case when food services are outsourced (Lowndes, Daly & Armstrong, 2017; Lowndes, Armstrong & Daly, 2015).

How Do Families Fit In?

Families are visible in the website images and in testimonials, and are presented as relaxed and happy. The viewer is given the impression that families are confident that their relative is being cared for, has meaningful activities in which to engage, and is comfortable. As we confirmed in the Reimagining LTRC project, family members often continue to provide care to their relative in the LTRC home (Barken, Daly & Armstrong, 2017), with some family carers visiting often and over mealtimes because they are concerned that staff levels are insufficient and basic needs may not be met (Barken, Daly, & Armstrong, 2017; Lowndes, Daly & Armstrong, 2017). There is often role confusion (Barken & Lowndes, 2017) and the perception that staff sometimes come to rely on family members to perform care (Barken, Daly & Armstrong, 2017). Family members essentially can become supplementary, albeit unpaid, help, along with students and volunteers, instead of the care home company being held accountable and hiring additional, sufficient levels of permanent staff. (See Chapter 12 for a detailed discussion of family involvement in LTRC within the context of privatization.) In the Reimagining LTRC project, we saw many instances of promising family engagement and our research is extending into this area in the Changing Places Project.[1]

Is there Freedom of Choice?

Choice and freedom of choice are prioritized on all of the websites we studied, but clearly they are not necessarily delivered. First, the respective websites only market their own facilities and omit all other choices, including public, not-for-profit, and charitable organizations. Research indicates that the longest wait times in Ontario are for the not-for-profit homes (Buchanan, 2011), which suggests that for-profit homes are not the first choice. In the U.K. in 2005, a market study of care report was issued by the Office of Fair Trading, and a key concern

> was whether older people were provided with reliable information about a home and its providers, their rights within the home and a clear, fair contract to help them come to a good, initial decision at a time when they were likely to feel particularly vulnerable.
> (Johnson, Rolph & Smith, 2010: 33)

Further, LTRC homes are offered based on availability and first choices are difficult or even impossible to obtain. Location is another factor to consider in the notion of "consumer choice" because people do not want to reside in LTRC homes located at a distance from family, friends, and other support networks. Moreover, the websites do not always offer an account of everyday life in a nursing home that is compatible with our research. Freedom of choice varies from care home to care home and we argue that exercising choice in a meaningful sense needs to be considered within all contexts (Armstrong & Daly, 2017).

Senior Care as a Commodity

> One of our nursing-home brochures invites potential customers to "imagine yourself in a fine resort." Come on. This is not a vacation spot. We are a business, and businesses are designed to make money. And naturally, our top staff needs to attract customers. We expect salespeople to put the best spin on facts, but we at the front know that our stock-in-trade is human misfortune. In practice we see these two realities clash every day.
> (Gass, 2004: 54–55)

Senior care, once a public responsibility, is increasingly being privatized in Canada and Sweden, and other countries. Care for seniors is being treated like other commodities that are bought and sold on the competitive market. Our analysis of for-profit websites suggests there is content intended to attract "customers," such as future residents, their families, and potential employees, alongside other content that is focused on attracting investors. In Canada, even though LTRC homes operate to full capacity and have long wait-lists, there is incentive for the for-profit companies to market their services: they advertise access to seamless care by linking their LTRC services to their privately funded, independent and assisted living accommodations and extra services that are geared to the wealthy. They also advertise management and consulting services, investment opportunities and partnerships, and staff recruitment. In Sweden, companies have incentives to engage in marketing to get users to choose their services, to affect public opinion on private providers, to encourage municipalities to cooperate with them, and to attract investors and employees. Not only are there tensions between these objectives, but the notion of marketing care for those who can afford to pay conflicts with the goal that all citizens should have the right to access needed care. Moreover, the written and visual materials depicting the quality of care and of care work contrast sharply with our research findings, suggesting there are essential pieces missing on these websites. The ability of future residents, families, and workers to make informed decisions in relation to LTRC is significantly compromised by these gaps in information. Important questions need to be asked, and information made available to answer them, in order to make truly informed choices.

Note

1 The SSHRC-funded "Changing Places: Unpaid Work in Public Spaces" project, led by Dr. Pat Armstrong, uses team-based rapid ethnography within a feminist perspective to examine how the paid and unpaid work involved in care changes with a person's transition into long-term residential care.

References

Ambea. (2018). Accessed from: https://www.ambea.com/ on February 23, 2018.

Ambea. (2018). About Ambea. Accessed from: https://www.ambea.com/about-ambea/ on February 23, 2018.

Ambea. (2018). About Ambea: The history of Ambea. Accessed from: https://www.ambea.com/history/ on February 23, 2018.

Ambea. (2018). Growth. Accessed from: https://www.ambea.com/growth/our-own-care-homes/ on February 21, 2018.

Ambea. (2018). Investor relations. Accessed from: https://www.ambea.com/investor-relations/ambea-as-an-investment/ on February 21, 2018.

Ambea. (2018). Quality and sustainability. Accessed from: https://www.ambea.com/quality-sustainability/quality-policy/ on February 21, 2018.

Ambea. (2018). Vardaga division. Accessed from: https://www.ambea.com/divisions/vardaga/ on January 5, 2018.

Armstrong, H., Daly, T. J. & Choiniere, J. A. (2016). Policies and practices: The case of RAI-MDS in Canadian long-term care homes. *Journal of Canadian Studies, 50*(2), 348–367.

Armstrong, P. (2013). Skills for care. In P. Armstrong & S. Braedley (Eds.), *Troubling care: Critical perspectives on research and practices* (pp. 101–112). Toronto, ON: Canadian Scholars' Press.

Armstrong, P. (2015). Conclusion: Where do we go from here? In P. Armstrong & D. Baines, *Promising practices in long-term care: Ideas worth sharing* (pp. 73–79). Ottawa: Canadian Centre for Policy Alternatives. Available at: https://www.policyalternatives.ca/publications/reports/promising-practices-long-term-care

Armstrong, P. & Braedley, S. (Eds.). (2013). *Troubling care: Critical perspectives on research and practices.* Toronto, ON: Canadian Scholars' Press.

Armstrong, P. & Braedley, S. (Eds.). (2016). *Physical environments for long-term care: Ideas worth sharing.* Ottawa, ON: Canadian Centre for Policy Alternatives. Available at: https://www.policyalternatives.ca/publications/reports/physical-environments-long-term-care

Armstrong, P., & Daly, T. (Eds.). (2017). *Exercising choice: Ideas worth sharing.* Ottawa, ON: Canadian Centre for Policy Alternatives. Available at: https://www.policyalternatives.ca/publications/reports/exercising-choice-long-term-residential-care

Attendo (2018). About Attendo. Accessed from: https://www.attendo.se/om-attendo on February 23, 2018.

Attendo (2018). About Attendo: Focus on quality. Accessed from: https://www.attendo.com/content/focus-on-quality-1 on April 27, 2018.

Attendo (2018). Home care services. Accessed from: https://www.attendo.se/Hemtj%C3%A4nst on February 25, 2018.

Attendo. (2018). Our services. Accessed from: https://www.attendo.com/sv/content/attendos-verksamheter on February 25, 2018.

Attendo. (2018). Vision and values. Accessed from: https://www.attendo.com/content/vision-and-values-1 on February 23, 2018.

Baines, D. & Armstrong, P. (Eds.). (2015). *Promising practices in long-term care: Ideas worth sharing.* Ottawa, ON: Canadian Centre for Policy Alternatives. Available at: https://www.policyalternatives.ca/publications/reports/promising-practices-long-term-care

Barken, R., Daly, T. & Armstrong, P. (2017). Family matters: The work and skills of family/friend carers in long-term residential care. *Journal of Canadian Studies, 50*(2), 321–347.

Barken, R. & Lowndes, R. (2017). Supporting family involvement in long-term residential care: Promising practices for relational care. *Qualitative Health Research.* doi:10.1177/1049732317730568

Baum, D. (1977). *Warehouses for death: The nursing home industry.* Don Mills: Burns & MacEachern.

Braedley, S., Owusu, P., Przednowek, A. & Armstrong, P. (2017). We're told, 'suck it up': Long-term care workers' psychological health and safety. *Ageing International.* https://doi.org/10.1007/s12126-017-9288-4

Buchanan, Dan. (2011). The not-for-profit contribution and issues from the provider perspective. Presentation to the "Re-imagining Long-Term Residential Care", annual conference, Toronto, Ontario, June 2.

Central Community Care Access Centre (2015). Planning for long-term care: A practical guide. Accessed from: http://healthcareathome.ca/central/en/care/Documents/LongTerm%20Care%20Flip%20Guide_2015.pdf on April 24, 2018

Chartwell. (2018). About us. Accessed from: https://chartwell.com/about-us/welcome on April 27, 2018.

Chartwell. (2018). Active living: Recreation. Accessed from: https://chartwell.com/active-living/recreation on April 26, 2018.

Chartwell. (2016). Annual report, 2016. Accessed from: http://investors.chartwell.com/Cache/1500102760.PDF?Y=&O=PDF&D=&fid=150010760&T=&iid=4100072 on January 2, 2018.

Chartwell. (2018). Annual report, 2018. Accessed from: http://investors.chartwell.com/QuarterlyResults on July 8, 2019.

Chartwell. (2018). Care and services: Dining. Accessed from: https://chartwell.com/care-and-services/dining on February 22, 2018.

Chartwell. (2018). Chartwell retirement residences. https://chartwell.com/index

Chartwell. (2018). Finance. Accessed from: https://chartwell.com/finance/budget-assistant-tool on February 22, 2018.

Chartwell. (2019). Investors. Press releases June 7, 2016. Accessed from http://investors.chartwell.com/News on July 9, 2019.

Choiniere, J., Doupe, M., Goldmann, M., Harrington, C., Jacobsen, F., Lloyd, L., Rootham, M. & Szebehely, M. (2016). Mapping nursing home inspections and audits in six countries. *Ageing International, 41*(1), 40–61. https://doi.org/10.1007/S12126-015-9230-6

Clough, R. (1981). *Old age homes*. London: George Allen & Unwin Ltd.

Cooper, J. & Cronin, J. (2000). Internal marketing; A competitive strategy for the long-term care industry. *Journal of Business Research, 48,* 177–181.

Davies, M. (2003). *Into the house of old: A history of residential care in British Columbia*. Montreal, Quebec: McGill-Queen's Press.

Diamond, T. (1992). *Making gray gold: Narratives of nursing home care*. Chicago, IL: University of Chicago Press.

Erlandsson, S., Storm, P., Stranz, A., Szebehely, M. & Trydegard, G. (2013). Marketising trends in Swedish eldercare: Competition, choice and calls for stricter regulation. In G. Meagher & M. Szebehely, *Marketisation in Nordic eldercare: A research report on legislation, oversight, extent and consequences* (pp. 23–75). Stockholm: US-AB.

Extendicare. (2018). https://www.extendicare.com

Extendicare. (2018). About Extendicare. Accessed from: https://www.extendicare.com/about-extendicare/ on February 22, 2018.

Extendicare. (2016). Annual Report. Accessed from: https://www.extendicare.com/investors/financial-reports/ on January 5, 2018

Extendicare. (2018). Care and services: Long term care. Accessed from https://www.extendicare.com/care-and-services/long-term-care/long-term-care/ On February 21, 2018.

Extendicare. (2018). Career centre. Accessed from: https://www.extendicare.com/careers/working-at-extendicare/ on April 26, 2018.

Extendicare. (2018). Financial reports. Accessed from: https://www.extendicare.com/investors/financial-reports/ on February 22, 2018.

Extendicare. (2018). Group purchasing. Accessed from: https://www.extendicare.com/care-and-services/group-purchasing/ on April 26, 2018.

Extendicare. (2018). Investors. Accessed from: https://www.extendicare.com/investors/about-extendicare/ on February 22, 2108.

Extendicare. (2018). Investors – Corporate governance. Accessed from: https://www.extendicare.com/investors/corporate-governance/ on February 21, 2018.

Extendicare. (2018). Long term care: Commitment to quality care. Accessed from: https://www.extendicare.com/care-and-services/long-term-care/commitment-to-care/ on February 21, 2018.

Extendicare. (2018). Programs and services. Accessed from: https://www.extendicare.com/care-and-services/long-term-care/programs-and-services/ on February 22, 2018.

Extendicare. (2018). Where to begin – Choosing a home. Accessed from: https://www.extendicare.com/where-to-begin/choosing-a-home/ on February 21, 2018.

Extendicare. (2018). Where to begin, frequently asked questions. Accessed from: https://www.extendicare.com/where-to-begin/faqs/ on February 22, 2018.

Extendicare York. (2018). http://www.extendicareyork.com/

Extendicare York. (2018). Student Placement. Accessed from: http://www.extendicareyork.com/careers/student-placement/ on February 22, 2018.

Foner, N. (1994). *The caregiving dilemma: Work in an American nursing home*. University of Berkeley and Los Angeles, CA: California Press Ltd.

Gass, T. (2004). *Nobody's Home: Candid reflections of a nursing home aide*. Ithaca: Cornell University Press.

Gubrium, J. (1975). *Living and dying at Murray Manor*. Charlottesville: University Press of Virginia.

Harrington, C., Jacobsen, F., Panos, J., Pollock, A., Sutaria, S. & Szebehely, M. (2017). Marketization in long-term care: A cross-country comparison of large for-profit nursing home chains. *Health Services Insights*, 10. doi:10.1177/1178632917710533

Johnson, J., Rolph, S. & Smith, R. (2010). *Residential care transformed: Revisiting the last refuge*. Basingstoke, Houndsmills: Palgrave Macmillan Press.

Kavat Vård (2018). About us. Accessed from: http://www.kavatvard.se/om-oss/ on February 23, 2018.

Kavat Vård. (2018). Our facilities: Bejtona. Accessed from: https://www.kavatvard.se/portfolio_page/bejtona/ on April 28, 2018.

Kavat Vård. (2018). Our Facilities: La Casa. Accessed from: https://www.kavatvard.se/portfolio_page/la-casa/ on April 28, 2018.

Kavat Vård. (2018). Our facilities: Persikan. Accessed from: http://www.kavatvard.se/portfolio_page/persikan/ on February 23, 2018.

Kayser-Jones, J. (1990). *Old, alone, and neglected: Care of the aged in United States and Scotland*. Berkeley: University of California Press.

Lar, R. (1986). Marketing for senior care services. Do-it-yourself marketing for long-term care administrators. *Health Marketing Quarterly*, 4(1), 3–11.

Laurence, J. & Kash, B. (2010). Marketing in the long-term care continuum. *Health Marketing Quarterly*, 27, 145–154.

Laxer, K. (2013). Counting carers in long-term residential care in Canada. In P. Armstrong & S. Braedley (Eds.), *Troubling care: Critical perspectives on research and practices* (pp. 73–88). Toronto, ON: Canadian Scholars' (Eds.) Press.

Lowndes, R., Armstrong, P. & Daly, T. (2015). The meaning of dining: The social organization of food in long-term care. *Food Studies*, 4(1), 19–34.

Lowndes, R., Daly, T. & Armstrong, P. (2017). "Leisurely dining": Exploring how work organization, informal care, and dining spaces shape residents' experiences of eating in long-term residential care. *Qualitative Health Research*, 28(1), 126–144. doi:10.1177/1049732317737979.

Lowndes, R. & Struthers, J. (2017). Changes and continuities in the workplace of long-term residential care in Canada, 1970–2015. *Journal of Canadian Studies*, 50(2), 368–395.

McGregor, M. & Ronald, L. (2011). Residential long-term care for Canadian seniors: Nonprofit, for-profit or does it matter? *IRPP Study, 14(January)*. Ottawa: IRPP.

McLean, A. (2007). *The person in dementia: A study of nursing home care in the US*. Ontario, CAN: Broadview Press.

Meacher, M. (1972). *Taken for a ride: Special residential homes for confused old people*. London: Longman Group Limited.

Parker, R. (1987). *The elderly and residential care: Australian lessons for Britain*. Aldershot, England: Gower Publishing Company Limited.

Revera (2018). http://www.reveraliving.com

Revera (2018). About Revera. Accessed from: https://www.reveraliving.com/about-revera/about-revera on April 26, 2018.

Revera (2018). About Revera, Careers: Career development. Accessed from: https://www.reveraliving.com/about-revera/careers/career-development on April 26, 2018.

Revera (2018). Long term care. Accessed from: https://www.reveraliving.com/long-term-care on April 26, 2018.

Revera (2018). Long term care: Quality care. Accessed from: https://www.reveraliving.com/long-term-care/care on February 22, 2018.

Revera (2018). Retirement living. Accessed from: https://www.reveraliving.com/retirement-living on February 22, 2018.

Revera (2018). Revera videos and testimonials. Retrieved on January 5, 2018 from http://www.reveraliving.com/about-revera/videos-testimonials/testimonials-en

Stafford, P. (2003). *Gray Areas: Ethnographic Encounters with Nursing Home Culture*. Santa Fe, New Mexico: School of American Research Press.

Suek, B. (2009). A dream retirement community: Long-term care options. In P. Armstrong, M. Boscoe, B. Clow, K. Grant, M. Haworth-Brockman, B. Jackson, A. Pederson, M. Seeley & J. Springer (Eds.), *A place to call home: Long-term care in Canada* (pp. 79–88). Blackpoint, NS: Fernwood Publishing.

Szebehely, M. (2016). Residential care for older people: Are there lessons to be learned from Sweden? *Journal of Canadian Studies, 50*(2), 499–507.

Thornton, P. (1995). New twists on an old marketing standby. *Nursing Homes: Long Term Management Care, 44*(5), 30–34.

Tobin, S. & Lieberman, M. (1976). *Last home for the aged: Critical implications of institutionalization*. San Francisco, CA: Jossey-Bass, Inc., Publishers.

Willcocks, D., Peace, S. & Kellaher, L. (1987). *Private lives in public places: A research based critique of residential life in local authority old people's homes*. New York, NY: Tavistock Publications.

Chapter 10

Nurse Staffing in Nursing Homes in Industrialized Countries

Charlene Harrington and Frode F. Jacobsen

Nursing care, provided by registered nurses, licensed vocational or practical nurses, and nursing assistants or aides, is the fundamental service provided to individuals living in nursing homes (also called long-term residential care in some countries). Nursing is of critical importance regardless of whether residents receive short-term post-acute care or long-stay care for assistance with activities of daily living, medications, treatments, and rehabilitation. Nursing homes have often been found to have poor quality of care and this is directly associated with inadequate nurse staffing levels and the training and competence of nurses. Conversely, higher nurse staffing levels are essential to ensure adequate quality of care.

This chapter is based on a synthesis of the existing literature as well as the findings from many studies conducted by the Reimagining Long-Term Residential Care project studying nursing homes in Canada, Germany, Norway, Sweden, the UK, and the US. Our collaborative research has directly examined staffing standards and levels across countries, the trends in the privatization of nursing home care, the impact of large for-profit chains on staffing and quality, the financial oversight and transparency of nursing homes across countries, and related issues. Fundamental to these studies is the finding that privatization of nursing home care has had a negative impact on staffing and quality. The political actions by nursing home associations to prevent increased staffing requirements are reviewed and contrasted with those of professional organizations, unions, and consumer organizations, along with a positive example of union actions in Norway. Policy approaches are discussed as ways to mitigate the impact of privatization.

Higher Staffing Levels Are Related to Better Quality

Many research studies on nursing home staffing have been conducted in the US and other industrialized countries. Most studies show positive relationships between higher staffing and better quality (Bostick et al., 2006; Castle, 2008; Dellefield et al., 2015). Higher registered nurse (RN) and certified nursing assistant (CNA) staffing has been associated with improved quality indicators, including physical restraints, catheter use, pain management, and pressure sores (Castle & Anderson, 2011). Higher staffing levels and professional staff mix, along with lower turnover and use of agency staff, were found to be associated with higher quality on 15 out of 18 measures (Castle & Engberg, 2008). Using complex analytical models and/or longitudinal analyses, the strongest relationships have been found between higher staffing levels and fewer deficiencies (violations of regulations) in the USA (Kim, Harrington & Greene, 2009; Konetzka, Stearns & Park, 2008; Lin, 2014; Park & Stearns, 2009; Wagner, McDonald & Castle, 2013; Wan, Zhang & Unruh, 2006). At the same time, there is a minimum threshold of staffing that must be reached before staffing levels show higher quality (US CMS, 2001; Schnelle et al., 2004).

In nursing homes, research studies have found that higher staffing levels, especially RNs, result in improved quality and that conversely, low staffing levels have a negative impact. For example, higher staffing has been found to be related to improved physical functioning and a reduction in falls, less time in bed, fewer fractures, lower use of physical restraints and catheters, lower pressure ulcer rates, a lower risk of incontinence among long-stay residents, lower urinary tract infections, lower overall infection rates, and fewer adverse outcomes (Bostick et al., 2006; Castle, 2008; Dellefield et al., 2015; Jansen, 2010; Wagner & Rust, 2008). Higher staffing has been associated with less resident pain, better quality of life scores, and reduced malnutrition, weight loss, and dehydration (Bostick et al., 2006; Castle, 2008; Dellefield et al., 2015). For short-stay residents, higher RN ratios were related to high probability of stabilized medical conditions and discharge home, as well as a reduced risk of dying (Decker, 2006) and to lower overall morality (Tong, 2011). Many studies show higher RN staffing levels are associated with reduced hospitalizations by nursing homes (Decker, 2008; Grabowski et al., 2008; Konetzka, Spector & Limcangco et al., 2007; Thomas et al., 2014; Spector et al., 2013).

Higher Minimum Staffing Standards Increase Actual Staffing and Quality

Many US studies have identified the benefits of establishing minimum federal and state staffing standards. The proportion of residents with pressure ulcers, physical restraints, and urinary catheters decreased following the implementation of the Nursing Home Reform Act in 1987, with the 24-hour licensed nurse standard (Zhang & Grabowski, 2004). Higher state minimum RN and total staffing standards were positive predictors of total nursing hours per resident day, and higher standards had a stronger effect on staffing than higher Medicaid payment rates (Harrington, Swan & Carrillo, 2007). Higher state minimum staffing levels have positive effects on staffing levels and quality outcomes (Bowblis, 2011; Lin, 2014; Mukamel et al., 2012; Park & Stearns, 2009; Tong, 2011).

Staffing Levels Should Be Higher and Based on Acuity or Care Needs

Although studies of recommended nursing home staffing levels were not found outside the US and are needed, there have been many definitive studies in the US. A US Centers for Medicare and Medicaid Services (CMS) study established the importance of having a minimum of 0.75 registered nurse (RN) hours per resident day (hprd), 0.55 licensed nurse (LVN/LPN) hprd, and 2.8 (to 3.0) certified nursing assistant (CNA) hprd, for a total of 4.1 nursing hprd to meet federal quality standards (US CMS, 2001). As part of this study, a simulation model of direct care workers (CNAs) established the minimum number of staff necessary to provide five basic aspects of daily care in facilities with different levels of resident acuity or care needs. The results found that the minimum threshold for CNA staffing is 2.8 hprd to ensure consistent, timely care to residents (US CMS, 2001), which was later confirmed in an observational study (Schnelle et al., 2004).

A recent simulation study found that 2.8 CNA hprd is needed in nursing homes with low workloads in order to have less than 10% omissions in care and the level of 3.6 CNA hprd is needed in nursing homes with high workloads (Schnelle et al., 2016). A 3.6 CNA hprd staffing level translates to one CNA for every 5.5 residents on the day and evening shifts and one CNA to 11 residents on the night shift. By measuring the resident care needs based on the level of resident dependency for activities of daily living (i.e., incontinence care and toileting, repositioning, eating, dressing and hygiene, and exercise or range of motion), the specific nurse aide staffing levels can and should be objectively determined and used in every nursing home (Schnelle et al., 2016).

A number of organizations in the US have endorsed mandating a minimum level of 4.1 total hprd, at least 30% of total nursing care hours provided by licensed nurses, and RNs on duty 24 hours per day (Institute of Medicine, 2004; American Nurses' Association, 2014; Coalition of Geriatric Nursing Organizations, 2013). Some experts have recommended higher minimum staffing (a total of 4.55 hprd) to improve the quality of nursing home care, with adjustments for resident acuity (case-mix) (Harrington et al., 2000).

CMS's Medicare Nursing Home Compare five-star rating system developed a method to determine what nurse staffing levels are needed for each nursing home based on its resident acuity (US CMS, 2017). CMS calculates the "expected hours" of care based on the resident acuity (case-mix) obtained from the Resource Utilization Groups (RUGs) scores reported by each facility and CMS Staff Time Measurement Studies (US CMS, 2000). CMS's recent analysis of "expected" staffing levels, taking into account resident acuity, indicates that the average US nursing home should have 4.17 total nursing hprd, including 1.08 RN hprd (Harrington, Schnelle et al., 2016).

Staffing Levels and Standards Vary by Country and Are Lower than Recommended

Wide variations in staffing standards have been found across countries (Harrington, Choiniere et al., 2012). In the US, federal standards are minimal, requiring only an RN director of nursing during the day shift and a licensed nurse for evenings and nights, without taking into account facility size and resident acuity. Twenty states reported higher standards for licensed nurses and 34 states reported higher direct care staffing standards than the federal standards, with a wide range of standards across states (Harrington, Choiniere et al., 2012).

The direct care standards in Canada varied by province, and where specified, were generally lower than in the US (1.5–2.0 hprd) except in one province (Prince Edward Island) (Harrington et al., 2012). The Canadian standards for RNs were higher than in the US because most provinces (seven of nine provinces that reported information) required 24-hour RN staffing in facilities in 2011, although these standards generally did not vary by the size of the facility or the acuity of residents (Harrington et al., 2012). Daly and colleagues (2017) described the regulations for staffing and training in different provinces in Canada, Germany, and Norway. The paper pointed out that the variance in Canadian standards and staffing levels is related to the different provincial payment policies. Payment levels are higher (set for 3.6 hours per resident day) in Manitoba than in Ontario and British Columbia (Daly et al., 2017).

Germany has a staffing guidance that varies for five specific care grades (with grade 1 as the lowest and grade 5 the highest). It takes the number of residents into account but varies by region of the country (Daly et al., 2017; Harrington et al., 2012). For example, in North Rhine Westphalia, the gross resident-to-staff ratios are 1:8 for care grade 1; 1:4.66 for care grade 2; 1:3.05 for care grade 3; 1:2.24 for care grade 4; and 1:2 for care grade 5 (Tillmann & Sloane, 2017), but these numbers include vacations, sick days, and training, so the actual ratio of staff are lower (Hielscher et al., 2013). Germany requires 24-hour "elder carers or nurse staffing" (staff who have three years of vocational training) and 50% of the staff must be either an elder carer or a nurse (see Chapter 4 for more information on Germany).

In contrast, England, Norway, and Sweden did not have specific staffing standards for their facilities in 2011 (Harrington et al., 2012). England standards were reported as follows: "staffing numbers and skill mix of qualified and unqualified staff must be appropriate to the assessed needs of the service users, the size, layout, and purpose of the home at all times" (UK Care Quality Commission, 2010). In Norway, the unofficial standard of staffing was a ratio of 0.94 full-time workers for each resident, including all nurses, managers, and housekeeping staff. Norway also planned for nursing staffing (including RNs, LVNs, and NAs in total) that would provide 235 hours per week or a total of 4.2 total nursing hours per resident day (Harrington, Choiniere et al., 2012).

Sweden planned for a ratio of 0.95 full-time workers of all types for each resident or a total of 5.19 hours per resident per day (Harrington, Choiniere et al., 2012).

Staffing Levels Vary by Country and Are Low in Many Nursing Homes

Although facility-reported average US staffing levels have recently increased and the average home reports staffing close to the recommended minimums, many US nursing homes continue to have very low staffing. In 2015, the median nursing home in the US had 0.72 hprd of RN staffing, 0.81 LVN hprd, 2.40 CNA hprd, and 3.97 hprd of total staffing; these levels are below the recommended levels described earlier (Harrington et al., 2016). Twenty-five percent of the homes in the US reported CNA staffing below 2.08 hprd, which translates into ratios of about 10 to 11 residents to one CNA on the day and evening shifts when the most labor-intensive care (e.g., feeding assistance and incontinence care) is provided. The lowest quartile of nursing homes on staffing reported half or less than the expected RN staffing (Harrington et al., 2016).

In Canada, British Columbia reported that direct nursing care staffing (RNs, LPNs, and care aides) varied between 2.1 and 3.3 hprd in 2006 (McGregor et al., 2010). Ontario reported that paid hours of nursing and personal care ranged between 1.9 and 5.1 hprd in 2007 (Sharkey, 2008). Canada reported 4.7 total staff hprd, including all "direct care" and "general services," (i.e., administration and support staff) in 2007 (Harrington, Choiniere et al., 2012), but actual staffing information has been difficult to obtain from Canadian provinces.

Data on actual staffing levels were not available for England, Germany, or Norway. Sweden reported an average of 5.36 hprd on average in 2007, including nurses, managers, paramedical, and support staff (Harrington, Choiniere et al., 2012).

The wide variation in staffing standards and actual staffing levels both within and across countries is not surprising since each country has a unique system of long-term care financing, organization, ownership, and social-cultural traditions. For example, one comparative study of care aides and assistant nurses in residential care for older people in Canada and Sweden found that Canada has highly differential task-oriented work, while Sweden has an integrated care work model (Daly & Szebehely, 2011). Daly and colleagues (2017) pointed out that the prescriptiveness of each country's regulatory approach has a strong impact on nursing home organizations and standards. Prescriptive regulatory environments were a response to a higher concentration of for-profit providers.

The increasing acuity of nursing home residents has been reported to be a major concern because staffing should be adjusted for the needs and acuity levels of residents. British Columbia and Ontario both reported growing nursing home acuity (McGregor et al., 2010; Sharkey, 2008) as well as growing acuity in the US (MedPac 2017). Little evidence has been found that nursing homes adjust staffing to meet the acuity needs of residents in any country except Germany, which ties its standards directly to acuity.

Nursing Homes Spend a Small Proportion of Expenditures on Nursing Care

A study of nursing home expenditures in four locations found that even though nursing services are central to resident care in nursing homes, only a small proportion of funds are spend on direct care services (Harrington, Armstrong et al., 2015). In California, nursing homes spent about 35% of revenues on nursing and direct services in 2012, a level that had declined by 11% over the previous six years. Although actual financial data were not available in England, industry reports recommended that only 35% of total expenditures be allocated for all nursing care services in 2012; this was an 8% decline over a five-year period (Harrington, Armstrong et al., 2015).

Nursing homes in Ontario allocated 56% of expenditures for nursing and direct care services but this included equipment, supplies, and other charges not included in the California and England budgets. Canadian provinces determine the amount of staffing in part through their reimbursement system (Daly et al., 2017). In contrast, Norway allocated the majority – 60 % – of total expenditures to direct care workers (Harrington, Armstrong et al., 2015).

Staffing Levels Are Lower in For-Profit Nursing Homes

The growth in for-profit nursing homes is a particular concern, given the evidence from a recent systemic review and meta-analysis showing that for-profit nursing homes have poorer quality of care on average than not-for-profit homes (Comondore et al., 2009). For-profit homes have lower nursing staff levels than other types of homes in the US (Harrington et al., 2012). In British Columbia, the average total nursing hours were 3.3 hprd in health-region owned homes, 2.48 hprd in non-profit non-government, and 2.13 hprd in for-profit facilities in 2006, with a 0.56 RN hprd in health-region owned, 0.52 hprd in non-profit, and 0.43 hprd in for-profit nursing facilities (McGregor et al., 2010; McGregor & Ronald, 2011). In Ontario as well, for-profit facilities reported providing fewer hours of care than not-for-profits (Berta, Laporte & Valdmanis, 2005). Sweden also reported that private residential care facilities have an approximately 10% lower staffing ratio than public ones (Stolt, Blomqvist & Winblad, 2011). A new study in Sweden also found that public nursing homes have higher quality than privately operated homes because they have high staffing levels and better accommodations (Winblad, Blomqvist & Karlsson, 2017).

Labor costs in nursing homes are usually a mix of fixed costs (those that are relatively constant for caring for the average resident) and variable costs (such as overtime and temporary worker costs) related to changes in occupancy rates or acuity levels. Although there are variations in labor costs, many for-profit nursing homes attempt to maintain the lowest possible fixed costs and reduce or eliminate variable labor costs as a means of maximizing profits (Harrington, Olney, Carrillo & Kang, 2010; Harrington, Ross & Kang, 2015; Harrington et al. 2017).

One study of staffing expenditures in California nursing homes showed that non-profit nursing homes had significantly higher expenditures (47%) on nursing/direct care than for-profit chains at 34%, and for-profit non-chains, at 38% in 2011 (Harrington, Ross & Kang, 2015). For-profit nursing homes, except in Norway, often divert resources to administration, capital costs, and profits rather than ensure adequate nursing services and the results of such decisions are reflected in low staffing levels and quality problems (Harrington, Ross & Kang, 2015; Harrington, Stockton & Hoopers, 2014). Using a number of specific criteria, Ronald and colleagues (2016) show that there is sufficient evidence that for-profit nursing homes deliver inferior care to that of public or non-profit homes.

For-Profit Nursing Home Ownership Varies by Country but is the Dominant Model

In 2014, for-profit ownership of nursing homes was the highest in the UK (86%) and the US (70%) and substantially lower in Canada (37%), Sweden (18–19%), and Norway (6%) (Harrington et al., 2017). The proportion of for-profit ownership increased in all countries between 2005 and 2014 except in Canada (Harrington et al., 2017). In 2014, for-profit nursing home chains were the dominant providers in the UK (71%) and the US (56%), compared to 17% of homes in Sweden, 14.5% in Canada, and only 6% in Norway. The growth in chains occurred in all countries where data were available, with a large increase in the UK (from 44% to 64% of homes) and over double the percentage in Sweden and almost double in Norway since 2005 (Harrington et al., 2017). In Norway, the percentage of for-profit beds dropped from a high of 6.2% in 2015 to 6.0% in 2017, and the percentage of non-profit bed declined from 5.2 to 4.8%. Norway is therefore shifting back to public ownership/management of nursing homes (Statistics Norway, 2018).

For-Profit Nursing Home Chains Have an Overall Negative Impact on Nursing Home Quality

A recent study showed that the five largest US for-profit nursing home chains provided significantly fewer RN staff hours and total staffing than the level expected based on their resident acuity (Harrington et al., 2017). The findings of low nurse staffing levels, especially RN staffing levels, in the largest US for-profit chains were consistent with previous studies in other countries (Harrington, Olney et al., 2012; Hsu et al., 2016; McGregor et al., 2010). Unfortunately, data were not available on staffing and quality in Norway, Sweden, and the UK. Because nursing homes are labor-intensive, chains seeking high profit levels often reduce nurse staffing costs, especially RNs costs, and cut wages, benefits, and pensions to increase profits and shareholder values (Arfwidsson & Westerberg, 2012; Bos & Harrington, 2017; Harrington, Stockton & Hoopers, 2014). As chains have become major providers of nursing home care, researchers have concluded that countries need to focus greater attention on collecting and analyzing staffing data as well as quality of care data from nursing home chains.

Where data were available on quality, the large nursing home chains did not provide high-quality services. In Canada, for-profit homes had poorer quality of care than non-profits and municipal homes based on violations (deficiencies) judged by government inspections (although the difference was not significant) (Panos, 2016). Four of the largest US chains also had significantly more quality violations than the average nursing homes and they all had charges of fraudulent billing practices pending or settled (Harrington et al., 2017). The findings of higher deficiencies were consistent with previous studies of the poor quality of for-profit chains (Harrington, Olney et al., 2012; Banaszak-Holl et al., 2002; Harrington, Ross & Kang 2015; Grabowski et al., 2012; 2016; McGregor & Ronald, 2011).

In Germany, a study of ownership, quality, and prices found that for-profit nursing homes performed significantly worse than non-profit homes in six areas: nursing processes, documentation, outcomes, support services, quality management, and structures. For-profit nursing homes charged lower prices on average than non-profits and the prices charged were related to quality in four out of six quality areas (Geraedts et al., 2015).

A study of nursing home media scandals in five countries found scandals related to poor quality of care and financial problems in large for-profit chains. The scandals offered "disturbing examples of the conditions of work and care within some nursing homes" (Lloyd et al., 2014: 13). The media reports of scandals did result in some government actions and policy changes.

Nursing Home Staff and Caregiving Are Women's Issues

The vast majority of nursing home staff regardless of the type of job category are women. Of the total RNs working in US nursing homes, 90% are women and 77% are white, LPNs/LVNs are also 90% women but only 64% white, while nursing aides are 89% women and 56% white, and the remainder are black, Asian, or Hispanic and Latino (US BLS, 2018). For example, in the US, 1.6 million workers employed in nursing homes have very low wages ($38,520 annual wages) compared to the national average of $50,600 in 2017 (U.. 2017). Nursing assistants working in nursing homes had an annual wage o. $27,500, resulting in many nursing assistants living in poverty in the US in 2018.

At the same time, most nursing home residents are age 65 and older (85%) and 42% are age 85 and older while 70% are women (CDC, 2016). The higher percentage of women nursing home residents is, in part, related to the greater longevity of women and their loss of spousal care giving support as they age and become disabled.

Thus, low staffing levels and low wages in US nursing homes are inequities perpetrated by the industry and allowed to go unregulated by the government at least in part because workers are mostly women without equal bargaining power with men. The poor nursing home care provided to residents who are primarily older women is also an inequity not addressed by the larger society (Estes, 2001; Weitz & Estes, 2001).

Efforts to improve wages and benefits and working conditions for nursing home staff should focus on the inequities for women workers especially in the US. Government program policies that fund the majority of nursing home care should ensure that public and private nursing homes provide not only living wages and benefits to all workers but also adequate and safe working conditions.

The Nursing Home Industry Uses Political Power and Influence

Little attention has been given to the political pressures that may influence nursing home staffing and quality. Nursing home associations, like other health care industries, attempt to influence public policies through campaign contributions, association lobbying, and educational activities and have been forceful in preventing staffing regulations at the federal and state levels in the US. In 2013–2014, the American Health Care Association (representing nursing homes) was one of the top 16 health contributors to federal campaigns (Open Secrets, 2014). State political campaign contributions in the US have also involved the nursing home industry (Harrington et al., 2016). At the national level in the US, nursing home associations hire leading politicians and have large professional lobbying staff while consumer advocacy organizations and worker unions have few resources.

The nursing home industry in the US has been effective in blocking staffing regulations and effective enforcement of laws and regulations (Harrington et al., 2016). In 2017, the US nursing home industry was successful in its effort to reduce enforcement of federal nursing home standards, including postponing the requirements for nursing homes to determine staffing needs based on resident acuity (Rau, 2017; US CMS, 2017). The political policy influence of for-profit nursing homes varies across countries, and is likely related to the percentage of for-profits facilities in each country.

Political Actions Are Necessary to Increase Staffing Levels

The counterinfluence of professional associations, union organizations, and consumer groups varies by country and states/provinces. Some countries have a stronger professionalized and unionized workforce. In Ontario, Canada, the Canadian Union of Public Employees (CUPE, 2017) is a strong force for increasing staffing levels in nursing homes. The Service Employees International Union (2017) also advocates for increased nursing home staffing and the Canadian Federation of Nurses Unions (2018) is an active advocate.

In the US, an estimated 3.27 million direct care workers provide long-term care services (or 20% of the health workforce) (US GAO, 2016) but these workers generally have low wages and benefits and only a small proportion are unionized (SEIU, 2016). Since 1985, the proportion of nursing home workers covered by union contracts declined from 14.6% to 9.9% (Sojourner, Grabowski, Chen & Town, 2010). In addition, US nursing homes have high staff turnover rates, which saves money for nursing homeowners (Mukamel et al., 2009) and makes unionization difficult.

In addition, the American Nurses' Association (2014), with only a small RN membership from nursing homes, and the Coalition of Geriatric Nursing Organizations (CGNO, 2013) have advocated for higher nursing home staffing and stronger regulations. Unfortunately, these professional organizations have not had a strong voice representing nursing home staff in comparison to the powerful nursing home industry that currently dominates US nursing home policy debates.

In the US, the National Consumer Voice (2018) organization, the Medicare Advocacy program, the Long Term Care Consumer Coalition, and the California Advocates for Nursing Home Reform have been the most consistent and effective organizations in representing and advocating for nursing home ombudsman, residents and staff at the national and state levels. They have mounted effective campaigns at the national level to block the cutbacks in nursing home enforcement and staffing levels. The local and state nursing home ombudsman programs, established by US Older American Act, are valuable advocates that investigate nursing home complaints, conduct community and resident/family education, and monitor enforcement of laws and regulations (Hollister & Estes, 2013). Although strong advocates, these organizations have limited resources for advocating for 1.4 million nursing home residents in 15,600 nursing homes in the US. Moreover, as non-profit advocacy groups, they cannot participate in political campaigns, in contrast to the nursing home associations that make large contributions to local, state and national political campaigns.

One policy approach to improving staffing and care is for local, state and national governments, especially in the US, to facilitate equal input on policy issues by unions, professional associations, consumer organizations, and ombudsman programs compared to input by the nursing home associations. Since the advocacy organizations operate with few funds and rely heavily on volunteers, greater public funding for advocacy organizations would improve the protections for nursing home residents and support adequate staffing policies.

Nursing Home Unions Have Been Effective in Ensuring Staffing and Quality in Norway

Norway has a higher unionization rate in nursing homes than some other countries. About 50% of LPNs/LVNs are organized by the Fagforbundet union, and another 30% are organized by other unions. More than 80% of RNs are unionized and of those, 83% are represented by the Norwegian Nurses Association (NSF). Because the largest proportion of LPNs/LVNs are in one union (Fagforbundet) and RNs are in the NSF, these two organizations have strong bargaining power in the eldercare sector. With the majority of nurses unionized, the unions have been able to ensure adequate staffing and good working conditions in Norwegian nursing homes. Moreover, nursing and other nursing home staff are paid adequate wages and benefits in the majority of nursing homes in Norway (with the exception of some of the few for-profit nursing homes), which results in high worker satisfaction and low employee turnover rates.

Norwegian unions have also played an important role in improving the quality of nursing home care. In 2011, underpaid and overworked nursing home workers were found to be housed in primitive bomb shelters beneath a nursing home in Oslo run by Adecco, a for-profit actor operating nursing homes, hospitals, slaughterhouses, employment agencies and other ventures. Following the scandal, this Swiss-led multinational private equity company was ousted from the health and care sector in Norway (Lloyd et al., 2014). The scandal was a turning point with regard to the interest of unions and the media in nursing homes.

More recently, a nursing home resident with diabetes and painful leg wounds living in a Norlandia facility (a for-profit chain) in Moss, Norway, received insufficient and harmful wound care, and living maggots were found in his wounds. As the result of neglect, the resident later experienced serious health problems and died. The union Fagforbundet uncovered the scandal and alerted journalists (Winstad & Mortensen, 2017a). This scandal was followed by others at the same facility that were reported on by *Fagbladet*, the journal of the Norwegian Confederation of Trade Unions (LO), the largest union organization in Norway. In 2017, the Norwegian media investigated the case. The publicity encouraged relatives of Norlandia care home residents to come forward about other cases of neglect and deaths (Mortensen & Winstad, 2017). Reports found that the for-profit facility was understaffed and had inadequate and incompetent leadership, and that employees were afraid to speak out for fear of retribution from Norlandia (Winstad, 2017). In September 2017, the Moss municipality decided to end all contracts with Norlandia (Winstad & Mortensen, 2017b). This is an example of the important impact that nursing home unions have had on ensuring the quality of care in Norway.

Policy Approaches to Mitigate the Negative Impact of For-Profit Nursing Homes

Norway is the only country of the six that have been studied extensively to limit the use of for-profit nursing homes (see Chapter 2). Norway municipalities own and manage their own nursing home buildings and over 90% of the country's nursing homes are operated directly by municipalities (Harrington, Armstrong et al., 2015). Some municipalities contract with non-profit or for-profit companies to provide nursing home care. These contracts set rates and standards for the management and can be and have been cancelled when the care delivered does not meet standards (Harrington, Armstrong et al., 2015; Harrington et al., 2017; Lloyd et al., 2014). This seems to be an ideal model for maintaining adequate staffing and quality. Unfortunately, in most other countries, nursing home buildings are owned privately so it is very difficult for the government to cancel contracts or prevent the private purchases of nursing homes by for-profit companies, even when care is substandard (Harrington et al., 2017).

Other Recommended Policy Approaches

The best approach is to set strict nurse staffing standards so that nursing homes are required to meet minimum staffing levels and to adjust staffing to meet resident needs (Harrington, Schnelle et al., 2016). Nursing homes have actively lobbied against and prevented adequate standards from being put into place at the state and federal levels in the US (Rau, 2017). In the US, government has been complicit with this approach because of its extensive focus on cost controls rather than on quality. Nevertheless consumer and professional organizations and unions must continue to advocate for improvements in minimum staffing levels and for improvements in quality of care.

In the US, major policy efforts were made by consumer organizations to require increased transparency in reporting of actual staffing data by nursing homes. In 2010, the Affordable Care Act required each nursing home to report their staffing hours by type of staff (e.g. RNs, LVNs, nursing assistants, therapists, and other staff) based on actual payroll data (replacing self-reported nursing home data) (Wells & Harrington, 2013). The reporting was tested and reviewed in 2017 and put on the Centers for Medicare and Medicaid Services (CMS) national website that rates all nursing homes. These data are the first to report daily staffing hours, including weekends and holidays, on a quarterly basis. Starting in April 2018, the data are used as a part of the CMS 5-star nursing home rating system. CMS plans to give all nursing homes with inaccurate staffing reporting a one-star rating for staffing, which will drop the facility's composite rating (US CMS, 2018). Nursing homes that fail to meet the one RN on duty eight hours a day for seven days a week requirement will be given a one star on the rating system (five stars are highest). These new transparency requirements will improve accuracy in reporting, to give government agencies more oversight of staffing levels, and to inform the public. Transparency can be a first step toward improving staffing levels and should encourage political action to improve staffing standards.

Another approach is to regulate how government resources are used by private nursing homes to ensure that resources are used for nursing care and to prevent the diversion of funds away from care and into profits. With a few exceptions, the profits by the largest nursing home chains were high, ranging from 6% to 28% across the five countries, in spite of financial market fluctuations (Harrington, Armstrong et al., 2015; Harrington et al. 2017). A 2016 study found that government payers in five industrialized countries have not established financial limits on administration and profits and have not required public financial transparency of administrative costs and profits by individual nursing homes or their corporate owners (Harrington, Armstrong et al., 2015). Ontario payment rates are established separately for cost centers for nursing and personal care, program and support services, food, and other accommodations (Harrington, Armstrong et al., 2015). This approach, however, has not been entirely successful in Ontario because it limited the funds spent on nursing and personal care and allowed private nursing homes to increase charges for accommodations in order to increase profits and administrative costs.

Clearly limits on profits and administrative costs are needed to ensure that adequate resources are spent directly on care. Increasing the financial accountability of nursing homes can assure that government funds are used for care rather than to enhance shareholder and owner values (Harrington, Armstrong et al., 2015). When large nursing home chains can have such a major impact on the access, cost, and quality of nursing home residents, public accountability should be given a high priority by local, state, and country governments.

Summary and conclusions

The privatization of nursing home care has led to limitations in nursing services as a way to enhance shareholder and owner values and profits. This trend has occurred in the countries we have studied with the exception of Norway. The problems with low staffing and poor quality of nursing home care must be brought to the attention of the public and policy-makers so that quality becomes a primary focus.

The most successful approach has been in Norway where almost all nursing home building ownership and 92% of operations are controlled by municipalities. Once countries allow nursing homes to be privately owned and operated, it is difficult to return to public ownership (Harrington et al., 2017).

For countries with privatized ownership such as the US, we have discussed a number of policy approaches for ensuring adequate staffing and quality of care. These include: setting minimum staffing standards; setting minimum wages and benefits for workers; supporting the unionization and professionalization of workers; supporting consumer advocacy and ombudsman organizations; establishing greater financial transparency and accountability, and setting limits on profits and administrative expenses. Nursing home residents deserve far better quality of care than they receive in many nursing homes (Armstrong et al., 2009).

References

American Nurses' Association. (2014). Nursing staffing requirements to meet the demands of today's long term care consumer recommendations from the Coalition of Geriatric Nursing Organizations (CGNO). www.nursingworld.org

Arfwidsson, J. & Westerberg, J. (2012). *Profit seeking and the quality of eldercare*. Master's thesis. Stockholm: Sweden: Stockholm School of Economics.

Armstrong, P., Banerjee, A., Szebeheky, M., Armstrong, H., Daly T. & Lafrance S. (2009). *They deserve better: The long-term care experience in Canada and Scandinavia*. Ottawa: Canadian Centre for Policy Alternatives.

Banaszak-Holl, J., Berta, W. B., Bowman, D., Baum., J. A. C. & Mitchell, W. (2002). The rise of human service chains: Antecedents to acquisitions and their effects on the quality of care in US nursing homes, 1991–1997. *Managerial and Decision Economics*, 23(4–5), 261–282.

Berta, W., Laporte, A. & Valdmanis, V. (2005). Observations on institutional long-term care in Ontario: 1996–2002. *Canadian Journal on Aging*, 24(1), 71–84.

Bos, A. & Harrington C. (2017). What happens to a nursing home chain when private equity takes over? A longitudinal case study. *Inquiry*, 54, 1–10.

Bostick, J. E., Rantz, M. J., Flesner, M. K. & Riggs, C. J. (2006). Systematic review of studies of staffing and quality in nursing homes. *Journal of the American Medical Directors Association*, 7, 366–376.

Bowblis, J. R. (2011). Staffing ratios and quality: An analysis of minimum direct care staffing requirements for nursing homes. *Health Services Research*, 46(5), 1495–1516.

Canadian Federation of Nurses Unions (2017). *Staffing: More for less*. Report. October 19. https://nursesunions.ca/research/nurse-staffing-more-for-less/

Canadian Union of Public Employees (CUPE). (2017). Major step forward for Ontario seniors living in long-term care. https://cupe.ca/major-step-forward-ontario-seniors-living-long-term-care

Castle, N. G. (2008). Nursing home caregiver staffing levels and quality of care: A literature review. *Journal of Applied Gerontology*, 27, 375–405.

Castle, N. G. & Anderson, R. A. (2011). Caregiver staffing in nursing homes and their influence on quality of care. *Medical Care*, 49(6), 545–552.

Castle, N. G. & Engberg, J. (2008). Further examination of the influence of caregiver staffing levels on nursing home quality. *Gerontologist, 48*, 464–476.

Coalition of Geriatric Nursing Organizations (CGNO). (2013). Nursing staffing requirements to meet the demands of today's long-term care consumer recommendations. http://nadona.org/pdfs/CGNO%20Nurse%20Staffing%20Position%20Statement%201%20page%20summary.pdf

Comondore, V. R., Devereaux, P. J., Zhou, Q. & Stone, S. B. (2009). Quality of care in for-profit and not-for-profit nursing homes: Systematic review and meta-analysis. *British Medical Journal.* doi:10.1136/bmj.b2732

Daly, T. & Szebehely, M. (2011). *Unheard voices, unmapped terrain: Care work in long-term residential care for older people in Canada and Sweden.* Toronto, ON: York University; Stockholm, Sweden: Stockholm University.

Daly T., Struthers J., Muller B., Taylor D., Goldmann M., Doupe M. & Jacobsen, F. F. (2017). Prescriptive or interpretive regulation at the frontlines of care work in the three "worlds" of Canada, Germany and Norway. *Labour/Le Travail, 77*, 37–71.

Decker, F. H. (2006). Nursing staff and the outcomes of nursing stays. *Medical Care, 44*(9), 812–821.

Decker, F. H. (2008). The relationship of nursing staff to the hospitalization of nursing home residents, *Research, Nursing and Health, 31*(3), 238–251.

Dellefield, M. E., Castle, N. G., McGilton, K. S. & Spilsbury, K. (2015) The relationship between registered nurses and nursing home quality: An integrative review (2008–2014). *Nursing Economic$, 33*(2), 95–108; 116.

Estes, C.L. (2001). *Social policy and aging: A critical perspective.* Thousand Oaks, CA: Sage Publications.

Geraedts, M., Harrington, C., Schumacher, D. & Kraska, R. (2015). Trade-off between quality, price, and profit orientation in Germany's nursing homes. *Ageing International.* doi: 10.1007/212126-015-9227-1

Grabowski, D. C., Feng, A., Hirth, R., Rahman, M. & Mor, V. (2012). Effect of nursing home ownership on the quality of post-acute care: An instrumental variables approach. *Journal of Health Economics, 14, 32*(1), 12–21.

Grabowski, D. C., Hirth, R. A., Intrator, O., Li, Y., Richardson, J., Stevenson, D. G., Zheng, Q. & Banaszak-Holl, J. (2016). Low-quality nursing homes were more likely than other nursing homes to be bought or sold by chains in 1993–2010. *Health Affairs, 35*(5), 907–914.

Grabowski, D. C., Stewart, K. A., Broderick, S. M. & Coots, L. A. (2008). Predictors of nursing home hospitalization: A review of the literature. *Medical Care Research and Review, 65*(1), 339.

Harrington, C., Armstrong, H., Halladay, M., Havig, A., Jacobsen, F. F., MacDonald, M., Panos, J., Pearsall, K., Pollock, A. & Ross, L. (2015). Nursing home financial transparency and accountability in four locations. *Ageing International, 41*(1), 17–39. doi: 10.1007/s12126-015-9233-3

Harrington, C., Choiniere, J., Goldmann, M., Jacobsen, F. F., Lloyd, L., McGregor, M., Stamatopoulos, V. & Szebehely, M. (2012). Nursing home staffing standards and staffing levels in six countries. *Journal of Nursing Scholarship, 44*(1), 88–98.

Harrington, C., Jacobsen, F. F., Panos, J., Pollock, A., Sutaria, S. & Szebehely, M. (2017). Marketization in long-term care: A cross-country comparison of large for-profit nursing home chains. *Health Services Insights, 10*, 1–23.

Harrington, C., Kovner, C., Kayser-Jones, J., Berger, S., Mohler, M. & Burke, R. (2000). Experts recommend minimum nurse staffing standards for nursing facilities in the United States. *The Gerontologist, 40*(1), 1–12.

Harrington, C., Olney, B., Carrillo, H. & Kang, T. (2012). Nurse staffing and deficiencies in the largest for-profit chains and chains owned by private equity companies. *Health Services Research, 47*(1), Part I: 106–128.

Harrington, C., Ross, L. & Kang, T. (2015). Hidden owners, hidden profits and poor nursing home care: A case study. *International Journal of Health Services, 45*(4), 779–800.

Harrington, C., Schnelle, J. F., McGregor, M. & Simmons., S. F. (2016). The need for minimum staffing standards in nursing homes. *Health Services Insights, 9*, 13–19.

Harrington, C., Stockton, J. & Hoopers S. (2014). The effects of regulation and litigation on a large for-profit nursing home chain. *Journal of Health Politics, Policy and Law, 39*(4), 781–809.

Harrington, C., Swan, J. H. & Carrillo, H. (2007). Nurse staffing levels and Medicaid reimbursement rates in nursing facilities. *Health Services Research, 42*, 1105–1129.

Hielscher, V., Nock, L., Kirchen-Peters, S. & Blass, K. (2013). *Zwischen Kosten, Zeit und Anspruch: das alltägliche Dilemma sozialer Dienstleistungsarbeit.* Wiesbaden.

Hollister, B.A. & Estes, C.L. (2013). Local long-term care Ombudsman program effectiveness and the measures of program resources. *J. of Applied Gerontology, 32*(6), 708–728.

Hsu, A. T., Berta, W., Coyte, P. C. & Laporte, A. (2016). Staffing in Ontario's long-term care homes: Differences by profit status and chain ownership. *Canadian Journal of Aging, 35*(2), 175–189.

Institute of Medicine. (2004). *Keeping patients safe: Transforming the work environment of nurses.* Washington, DC: National Academy of Medicine.

Jansen, I. (2010). Residential long-term care: Public solutions to access and quality problems. Canadian Union of Public Employees. *HealthcarePapers, 10*(4), 1–22.

Kim, H., Harrington, C. & Greene, W. (2009). Registered nurse staffing mix and quality of care in nursing homes: A longitudinal analysis. *Gerontologist, 49*(1), 81–90.

Konetzka, R. T., Spector, W. & Limcangco, M. R. (2007). Reducing hospitalizations from long-term care settings. *Medical Care Research & Review, 65*, 40–66.

Konetzka, R. T., Stearns, S. C. & Park, J. (2008). The staffing outcomes relationship in nursing homes. *Health Services Research, 43*(3), 1025–1042. doi: 10.1111/j.1475-6773.2007.00803.x

Lin, H. (2014). Revisiting the relationship between nurse staffing and quality of care in nursing homes: An instrumental variables approach. *Journal of Health Economics, 37*, 13–24.

Lloyd, L., Banerjee, A., Harrington, C., Jacobsen, F. & Szebehely, M. (2014). "It is a scandal!" Comparing the causes and consequence of nursing home media scandals in five countries. *International Journal of Sociology & Social Policy, 34*(1/2), 2–18.

McGregor, M. J. & Ronald, L. A. (2011). *Residential long-term care for Canada's seniors.* Montreal: Institute for Research on Public Policy. www.irpp.org

McGregor, M. J., Tate, R. B., Ronald, L. A., McGrail, K. M., Cox, M. B., Berta, W. & Broemeling, A. (2010). Trends in long-term care staffing by facility ownership in British Columbia, 1996 to 2006. Statistics Canada. No. 82-003-XPE. *Health Reports, 21*(4), 1–7.

Medicare Payment Advisory Commission (MedPac). (2017). *Report to Congress: Medicare payment policy: skilled nursing facility services,* Chapter 8 (pp. 181–209). Washington, DC: MedPac.

Mortensen, Y. & Winstad, Ø. (2017). Nye avsløringer om Norlandia Skoggata bo-ogservicesenter (New disclosures on Norlandia Skoggata bo-og service center). *Fagbladet.* https://frifagbevegelse.no/nyheter/-mor-la-alene-pa-rommet-med-store-smerter-hun-ringte-etter-ansatte-men-ingen-kom-6.158.484378.fca0ed88cd

Mukamel, D. B., Spector, W. D., Limcangco, R., Wang, Y., Feng, Z. & Mor, V. (2009). The costs of turnover in nursing homes. *Medical Care, 47*(10), 1039–1045.

Mukamel, D. B., Weimer, D. L., Harrington, C., Spector, W. D., Ladd, H. & Li, Y. (2012). The effect of state regulatory stringency on nursing home quality. *Health Services Research, 47*(5), 1791–1813.

National Consumer Voice (2018). Better staffing: The key to better care. Consumer Voice's nursing home staffing campaign. http://theconsumervoice.org/betterstaffing

Open Secrets.org: Center for Responsive Politics. (2014). Health lobbying. Washington, DC. http://www.opensecrets.org/industries/indus.php?ind=H

Panos, J. (2016). Care for sale: Privatizing long-term care in Ontario. Presentation. London School of Economics, 4th International Conference on Evidence-based Policy in Long-Term Care. Invited Symposium Presentation. London, Sept. 5, 2016.

Park, J. & Stearns, S. C. (2009). Effects of state minimum staffing standards on nursing home staffing and quality of care. *Health Services Research, 44*(1), 56–78.

Rau, J. (2017). Trump administration eases nursing fines in a victory for the industry. *New York Times.* December 24. https://www.nytimes.com/2017/12/24/business/trump-administration-nursing-home-penalties.html

Ronald, L. A., McGregor, M. J., Harrington, C., Pollock, A. & Lexchin, J. 2016. Observational evidence of for-profit delivery and inferior nursing home care: When is there enough evidence for policy change? *PLOS Medicine.* doi:10.1371/journal.pmed.1001995

Schnelle, J. F., Schroyer, L. D., Saraf, A. A., & Simmons, S. F. (2016). Determining nurse aide staffing requirements to provide care based on resident workload: A discrete event simulation model. *Journal of the American Medical Directors Association, 17,* 970–977.

Schnelle, J. F., Simmons, S. F., Harrington, C., Cadogan, M., Garcia, E. & Bates-Jensen, B. (2004). Relationship of nursing home staffing to quality of care? *Health Services Research, 39*(2), 225–250.

Service Employees International (2017). Bill 148 to make a real difference for millions of workers across Ontario. Press release. http://www.seiuhealthcare.ca/bill_148_to_make_a_real_difference_for_millions_of_workers_across_ontario

Service Employees International (SEIU) (2016). Nursing home workers to join "Fight for $15" to raise wages, improve quality of care. April 12. http://www.seiu.org/2016/04/nursing-home-workers-to-join-fight-for-15-to-raise-wages-improve-quality-of-care

Sharkey, S. 2008. *People caring for people: Impacting the quality of life and care of residents of long-term care homes.* Toronto, ON: Ontario Ministry of Health and Long-Term Care.

Sojourner, A.J., Grabowski, D.C., Chen, M. & Town, R.J. (2010–2011). Trends in unionization of nursing homes. *Inquiry,* Winter; 47(4), 331–342

Spector, W. D., Limcangco, R., Williams, C., Rhodes, W. & Hurd, D. (2013). Potentially avoidable hospitalizations for elderly long-stay residents in nursing homes. *Medical Care, 51*(8), 673–681.

Statistics Norway. (2018). Statistics: Care Services, 2017. https://www.ssb.no/en/helse/statistikker/pleie/aar

Stolt, R., Blomqvist, P. & Winblad, U. (2011). Privatization of social services: Quality differences in Swedish elderly care. *Social Science & Medicine*, 72(4), 560–567.

Tillmann, R. and Sloane, K. (2017). Überleitung der Personalmenge Nordrhein-Westfalen: Personalschlüssel werden angepasst. *CAREkonkret*, 17.

Thomas, K. S., Rahman, M., Mor, V. & Intrator, O. (2014). Influence of hospital and nursing home quality on hospital readmissions. *American Journal of Management Care*, 20(11), 523–531.

Tong, P. K. (2011). The effects of California minimum nurse staffing laws on nurse labor and patient mortality in skilled nursing facilities. *Health Economics*, 20(7), 802–816.

UK Care Quality Commission. (2010). *Market profile, quality of provision and commissioning of adult social care services*. London, UK: Care Quality Commission.

US Bureau of Labor Statistics. (2017). May 2017 National industry-specific occupational employment and wage estimates. NAICS 6231000 – Nursing care facilities (skilled nursing facilities). Accessed 9/9/2018. https://www.bls.gov/oes/current/naics4_623100.htm

US Bureau of Labor Statistics. (2018). Labor force statistics from the current population survey. Table 11. Employed persons by detailed occupation, sex, race and Hispanic or Latino ethnicity. Accessed 9/9/2018. https://www.bls.gov/cps/cpsaat11.htm

US Centers for Disease Control and Prevention (CDC), National Center for Health Statistics, US Department of Health and Human Services (2016). Long-term care providers and services users in the United States: Data from the national study of long-term care providers, 2013–2014. *Vital and Health Statistics*. 3 (38). Hyattsville, M.D.

US Centers for Medicare and Medicaid Services (CMS). (2000). Nursing and therapy minutes used in calculating preliminary rates. Federal Register PPS Update. https://www.cms.gov/Medicare/Medicare-Fee-for-Service-Payment/SNFPPS/index.html

US Centers for Medicare and Medicaid Services (CMS). Prepared by Abt Associates Inc. (2001). Appropriateness of minimum nurse staffing ratios in nursing homes. Report to Congress: Phase II Final. Volumes I-III. Baltimore, MD: CMS.

US Centers for Medicare and Medicaid Services (CMS). (2017). Medicare nursing home compare. http://www.medicare.gov/NursingHomeCompare/search.aspx?bhcp=1

US Centers for Medicare and Medicaid Services (CMS). (2018). Transition to payroll-based journal (PBJ) staffing measures on the nursing home compare tool on Medicare.gov and the five star quality rating system. April 6. https://www.cms.gov/Medicare/Provider-Enrollment-and-Certification/SurveyCertificationGenInfo/Downloads/QSO18-17-NH.pdf

US Government Accountability Office (US GAO) (2016). Long-term care workforce. GAO-16-718. August. Washington, DC.

Wagner, L. M., McDonald, S. M. & Castle, N. G. (2013). Nursing home deficiency citations for physical restraints and restrictive side rails. *Western Journal of Nursing Research*, 35(5), 546–565.

Wagner, L. M. & Rust, T. B. (2008). *Safety in long-term care settings: Broadening the patient safety agenda*. Edmonton, AB: Canadian Patient Safety Institute.

Wan, T.T.H., Zhang, N.J., & Unruh, L. (2006). Predictors of resident outcome improvement in nursing homes. *Western Journal of Nursing Research* 28(8), 974–993.

Wells, J., & Harrington, C. (2013). *Implementation of Affordable Care Act provisions to improve nursing home transparency and quality*. Washington, DC: Kaiser Commission on Medicaid and the Uninsured.

Winblad, U., Blomqvist, P. & Karlsson, A. (2017). Do public nursing home care providers deliver higher quality than private providers? Evidence from Sweden. *BMC Health Serv Res.*, July 14, *17*(1), 487–499.

Weitz, T. and Estes, C.L. (2001) Adding aging and gender to the women's health agenda. *J. of Women & Aging*, 13(2), 3–20.

Winstad, Ø. (2017). Ansatte i Norlandia er redde for å kontakte fagforeningen sin (Norlandia employees are afraid to contact their union). *Fagbladet* 08.09.17. https://frifagbevegelse.no/nyheter/-ansatte-i-norlandia-er-redde-for-a-kontakte-fagforeningen-6.158.485944.fa612fcdbc

Winstad, Ø. & Mortensen, Y. (2017a). Åge hadde levende fluelarver i sårene før han døde (Åge had live maggots in his wounds before dying). *Fagbladet* 24.08.17. https://fagbladet.no/nyheter/age-hadde-levende-fluelarver-i-sarene-for-han-dode-6.91.483228.c783dcb97b

Winstad, Ø. & Mortensen, Y. (2017b). Moss kommune kaster ut privat omsorgsselskap etter avsløringene (Moss municipality have ousted a private care company after disclosures). *Fagbladet.* Retrieved February 14 2018 from https://fagbladet.no/nyheter/moss-kommune-kaster-ut-privat-omsorgsselskap-etter-avsloringene-6.91.488810.84e39584f6

Zhang, Z. X. & Grabowski, D. C. (2004). Nursing home staffing and quality under the Nursing Home Reform Act. *Gerontologist, 44*, 13–23.

Chapter 11

Devalued Later Life
Older Residents' Experiences of Risk in a Market System of Residential and Nursing Homes

Liz Lloyd

Variations in the extent and nature of privatization as well as in the historical antecedents of a market in care services have generated different organizational and cultural contexts that affect perceptions of vulnerability, risk, and protection in later life. Older people in residential long-term care might be perceived as vulnerable *per se* because of their age and health problems, but they are also vulnerable to the ways in which their needs are interpreted and their care organized. The organization of care home services for older people reflects social norms and values and thus shapes residents' experiences of vulnerability. The position of older residents reflects the low social status of those who require care – also experienced by those who provide it – and their physical separation from the public sphere adds an important dimension to their precarious state. Moreover, social inequalities across the life course persist into old age, so that those who rely on the state for help are in a more precarious position than those with their own resources, especially at a time of welfare state retrenchment.

Vulnerability, Risk, and Long-Term Residential Care

The definition of individuals and groups as vulnerable has long been a feature of welfare systems, necessary to ensure that resources are targeted at those who qualify, having satisfied eligibility criteria. Butler (2009), Grenier, Lloyd, & Phillipson (2017) and feminist ethicists such as Barnes (2012) and Tronto (1993) have challenged the idea that vulnerability is a property of particular groups, arguing instead that it is a characteristic of human life, which is inherently precarious. This perspective challenges the characterization of mainstream society as populated by autonomous and independent individuals who are separate from and superior to those groups identified as "the vulnerable." From this perspective, it is better to understand vulnerability as susceptibility to identifiable hazards and capacity to cope with these hazards. Thus, the focus is no longer solely on the individual or on particular individual characteristics that constitute vulnerability but on the hazards that people face. This is not to argue that all lives are equally precarious at all times but that certain lives are, at times, more precarious than others, with greater susceptibility to hazards and a greater need for care. This is a pertinent point in relation to old age because people of all ages have a stake in how the hazards of old age are managed, especially given increased life expectancy.

Particularly important for this discussion is an understanding of the *structural* factors that make a life more or less precarious in old age. These include not only the availability of health care and social services but also civic amenities and infrastructures that support social networks. As Butler (2009) argues, the separation, or "othering," of groups regarded as vulnerable reflects social, political, and cultural norms concerning what a life is worth. And while recognition of vulnerability might evoke a caring response it is also likely to evoke an abusive response that reflects public distaste for or hatred of a group so labelled. This analysis applies to groups such as disabled people and refugees as well as to older people who need care. As argued by Grenier and colleagues (2017), recognition of vulnerability as both existential (shared) *and* structured (experienced unequally) points to the need for purposeful courses of action to combat the exclusion of people who need care in old age and to find ways to ensure their lives are valued.

The privatization of care homes, part of a wider process of change in welfare systems, has had a significant impact on older residents' experiences of risk. At a wider level, according to Cordini and Ranci (2017), this process can be understood as a paradigm change, since it has altered the relationship between individual citizens, states, and the market for care. For example, reduced rights to social protections, changing rules on transactions between statutory bodies and private companies, practices of contracting and commissioning services, as well as encouraging individuals to purchase care services directly all reflect a shift in values about social welfare. Michael Sandel (2012: 9) observed that markets do not only allocate goods but "express and promote certain attitudes towards the goods being exchanged."

In the context of care homes for older people, this is a highly pertinent observation. In a market system, in contrast to the ideal of care as a public responsibility, care becomes a commodity to be bought and sold. It is important to emphasize that neither markets nor welfare systems have adequately grasped the complexity of care. The low status of older residents has a history that long predates the introduction of markets (Means, Morbey & Smith, 2002). Townsend (1986: 32) commented that residential homes "symbolise the dependence of the elderly and legitimate their lack of access to equality of status." Nevertheless, the introduction of markets in long-term residential care has been part of a process of reshaping public expectations and attitudes about the responsibility of states to older people. The "cradle to grave" certainties that the current cohort of older residents have lived with have given way to more precarious and contingent experiences of later life.

Both Butler (2009) and Standing (2010) use the concept of precarity to refer to the risks associated with contemporary conditions of globalization, neoliberal politics, and the loss of social protections. Standing's observations about precarity are evident in the conditions of employment for staff in care homes, where high levels of staff turnover contribute to diminished quality in staff-resident relationships and where staffing levels are reduced. Staffing levels are a structural prerequisite for good care (Stolt, Blomqvist & Windblad, 2011) and lower staffing levels, characteristic of private, for-profit organizations, undermine the quality of care (Baines & Armstrong, 2016).

Tensions between Protection and Risk

Their precarious position calls for the protection of older residents from harm but at the same time, questions need to be addressed concerning older residents' ability to control their lives, to take risks, and to make decisions that others may disapprove of or that cause inconvenience (Armstrong & Daly, 2017). There is a longstanding tension for older people in long-term care, between the promotion of personal autonomy and service-user control on the one hand, and service-provider responsibility for safety and accountability, on the other (Evans et al., 2018; Peace, Kellaher & Willcocks, 1997). This tension is an integral part of life in residential care and nursing homes and presents a daily challenge for care worker and managers. This is evident in the daily decisions made by frontline care workers, in the rules and regulations that govern daily practices of care, and in the guidance given to staff about how to avoid or manage risk. At a deeper level, the culture of every home shapes perceptions of protection and risk. Some organizational cultures are more risk averse than others and homes vary in their levels of compliance with national regulations and service standards. Although this tension is longstanding it is manifested in different ways, as identified in international research as well as by reference to historical developments in welfare (Baines & Stikuts, 2016; Brennan et al., 2012). Privatization not only affects the already tense relationship between risk and protection, it introduces *new* forms of risk for residents and their families.

The Necessity of Protection

The perception of a life as valued inevitably involves concern about its protection. For many older people, the fact that they live in long-term residential care might be an indication that they or their families desire greater security and safety than they would have if the older people were living at home. The comparison between home and care home is not straightforward, however, because a resident might find they are safer in some respects but at greater risk in others. For example, as in all areas of public life, health and safety standards and procedures apply to care homes and are codified in a range of legal instruments and regulatory regimes. They are also a matter of human rights for residents, as argued by the European Network of National Human Rights Institutions (ENNHRI). Based on their analysis of the rights of older people in long-term care across Europe, ENNHRI drew attention to unsafe environments in care homes, which they argued are a breach of residents' right to life, and to poorly heated homes, dirty facilities, and insufficient food, which are a breach of their social right to an adequate standard of living (ENNHRI, 2017).

Resident safety and protection are fundamental to acceptable standards in a home and a high priority in inspection and regulation systems. In England, for example, the Care Quality Commission, which inspects and regulates services in care homes, requires inspectors to consider as their *first* question: Are they safe? (CQC, 2017). Yet, in 2017, the CQC reported that 23 percent of the homes they inspected were failing on safety standards, including those rated satisfactory otherwise. Failure to assess risks faced by individual residents was a "recurring theme" in their inspections, as was inadequate or unsafe equipment and inadequate documentation of medicines. A related recurring theme in this inspection report was staffing, including staff-resident ratios, as well as staff training and skill level, which were key to safe practice but rated unsatisfactory. There is a significant gap therefore between the rhetoric and the reality of safety, shown up in the civil and criminal actions taken by the CQC against proprietors of the unsafe homes. A similar gap exists in the US, where strict regulatory regimes fail to provide residents with protection because the regulations are poorly enforced (Harrington, Stockton & Hoopers, 2014).

The risk to residents of abuse by care workers can be similarly understood within a human rights framework, with verbal or physical aggression being a breach of residents' rights to freedom from torture, inhuman and degrading treatment (an unlimited right under the European Convention on Human Rights). Yet, despite the development internationally of legal instruments designed to protect older people, abuse remains a problem, largely because of under-reporting. The right to freedom of movement and restraint is also breached when residents are given tranquilizers to prevent challenging behavior, doors are locked, brakes are applied on wheelchairs, or trays are placed on armchairs. At the same time, staff in care homes (who at times also face abuse by residents) grapple with difficult decisions that result in restrictions on residents' freedom, especially when those restrictions might be in a person's best interests or when the wellbeing and safety of some residents would be enhanced by placing restrictions on others. The complexity of these decisions challenges the notion that care work is unskilled.

One reason put forward for the continued breach of residents' rights is care workers' low level of knowledge and understanding of different approaches to care and ways of negotiating the tensions between rights and protection. Mitchell, Baxter Glendinning (2012), for example, identified how care workers were more likely to impose restrictive practices when they lacked confidence in their practice with people with fluctuating conditions, including mental health and mental capacity. Manthorpe, Samsi and Rapaport (2013: 370) point out that "restraint and deprivation of liberty are permissible and indeed in a person's best interests in some circumstances." Where residents have impaired mental capacity, compliance with statutory guidance is all the more important. Qureshi (2009: 26) noted that "all demonstrably successful models" for reducing the use of restraints involve staff training *as well as* ongoing expert support and commitment by the organization as a whole. Ongoing organizational commitment is essential to bolstering care workers' confidence in dealing with the tensions between risk and protection in daily practice.

Supporters of a market system of care claim that it is capable of greater efficiency, offering a "more for less" model, which is entirely congruent with political aims to reduce public spending on welfare. Whether it achieves efficiency or merely cost-cutting, is a moot point. Either way, evidence from research suggests strongly that residents as well as care workers are paying a high price. It is precisely in these areas of tension that the fundamental importance and complexity of care is revealed and the inadequacies of a commodified model of care exposed. From a feminist perspective, these inadequacies can be understood as deriving from the assumption that the predominantly female care workforce requires little training since care is a 'natural' disposition.

The Necessity of Risk

The longstanding tensions between risk and protection also emerge when considering residents' rights to take risks (Armstrong 2017). Research by Chalfont and Rodiek (2005) indicates that relatives and residents value care home environments that encourage curiosity in everyday activities. The right to take risks, to explore and engage with the world is life-enhancing and confirms one's sense of identity and personal autonomy as well as being fundamental to human rights. Although accepted in principle, it is difficult to achieve in practice, particularly if frontline care workers feel they are at risk of disciplinary action. Counteracting a tendency towards over-protection of residents and the prioritization of organizational demands requires *shared recognition* throughout provider organizations of the potential of risk-taking and a shared commitment by managers, staff, volunteers, and relatives to maximize opportunities to promote residents' ability to take risks. Moreover, if recognition and commitment within organizations are to be realized in practice, there needs to be a conducive legal, policy, and regulatory context.

A common anxiety in residential care concerns the risk that residents will fall. Baines and Armstrong (2016) give the example of a home in British Columbia that routinely placed residents in wheelchairs rather than run the risk that they would fall while walking. Consequently, residents lost the ability to walk as well as the ability to make decisions about where and when they wished to move around. They became dependent on others to assist them in making a move and were obliged to move when others thought they should. Research by Hawkins and colleagues (2017) focused on the movement of residents around homes and the encouragement of residents to be mobile at the same time as keeping them safe. It emphasized the necessity of shared commitment at all levels of a long-term residential care home in order to overcome the dangers of over-protective regimes of care. The management team's ability to translate abstract values of care into tangible care practices that are acceptable to care workers and empowering to residents was crucially important. Senior staff had to accept that the additional staff time their practices took was a price worth paying for the benefits to residents of maintaining and maximizing their mobility. However, a promising practice such as encouraging residents' mobility is likely to be undermined where there is a high turnover of staff and fewer training opportunities. A high turnover works against the development of an organizational culture of promoting positive risk-taking.

As argued by Baines and Armstrong (2016), the highly variable practices in relation to risk-taking in care homes affect older people's ability to do what they want to do. For example, in Ontario, caffeinated coffee was not permitted for residents in case they became agitated, while in a home in England residents drank caffeinated coffee routinely and had free access to alcohol. In a home in Germany, residents – including those with dementia – used sharp knives to help prepare vegetables. In a Norwegian home, according to an occupational therapist, exercise routines for residents "pushed them to their limits" and this was regarded as important to promote residents' strength and reduce the risk of falls as well as the risk of boredom. There is growing evidence of the benefits of exercise (and of related social benefits) to residents' physical and mental health, but as Lorenz and colleagues (2012) note, resource constraints and a lack of trained staff limit opportunities to realize these benefits. The chance to try out new things can also be fun, as a physiotherapist in an English care home explained. There, residents found the new experience of bouncing on a trampette to be exciting and enjoyable, in addition to being good for their health.

These are important points to consider in the context of care homes. One of the claims for markets in care is that they counteract the tendency towards institutionalization, long associated with state-run care homes. Markets in social care have developed hand-in-hand with a policy emphasis on individual choice and control, giving people greater agency. The consumer in a market for care should therefore expect greater variety and more individualized attention, in contrast to being the passive recipient of a bureaucratized, standardized welfare system. Looked at from this perspective, it might be assumed that privatization would be good for the promotion of positive risk-taking in care homes, but the evidence points to the contrary. An emphasis on efficiency and cost control promotes a different set of organizational priorities and care workers are more likely to be under time pressures (Harrington, 2013; Harrington et al., 2014). Risk avoidance is more likely to become the priority over other factors, with major consequences for residents' human rights and quality of life as well as for the satisfaction of care workers. The ability to form relationships with residents and develop a sense of community within a care home is highly valued by care workers (Baines & Armstrong 2016; Daly & Szehebely 2012) but in the pressured environment of a care home more likely to be a form of free emotional labor than an integral part of a job description. This is to the detriment of residents who look to care workers for emotional support as well as bodily care.

The Risks of a Market System

This section focuses on the risks to residents as consumers of services, rather than as citizens with rights to public services. The difference between these is evident in the context of a decision to move to a care home. As a consumer, an older person has rights but the principle of "buyer beware" applies, which creates particular problems. For example, when older people make a decision to move to a care home they are often vulnerable because of illness or bereavement. They make the decision as a matter of urgency because previous care arrangements have collapsed, because they have to leave hospital, or because their needs have changed significantly and suddenly (e.g., following a stroke). Frequently, their families also feel these pressures and the assumption that they are able to act as informed consumers is misplaced. Following serious concerns about the behavior of some providers and the collapse of the Southern Cross company in 2011, the Competitions and Markets Authority conducted a major review of care homes in the UK. It concluded that "those requiring care need greater support in choosing a care home and greater protections when they are residents" (CMA, 2017: 6).

The report produced by the CMA (2017) identified many areas of poor practice, including the failure of providers to comply with their legal obligations under consumer law. For example, there was a serious lack of information to assist older people and their families in making decisions. They pointed out that given the complexity and fragmentation of a privatized care system this is a particularly grievous failing. They also found residents faced unexplained demands for deposits and upfront payments as well as lack of clarity about what their payments covered. In addition, they identified several areas of malpractice, including demands for top-up payments, which families of residents often agreed to out of anxiety for their relative's comfort. Of course, providers of residential and nursing homes are not obliged to provide information to assist people: on the contrary, the onus is on potential residents to become informed consumers. With an insufficient supply in the care home market, as is the case in the UK, consumers are in a weaker position and more likely to accept disadvantageous terms.

Consumers also have the right to complain but the CMA found that residents and their families were reluctant to report shortcomings in services and worried that if they complained, their relative might face adverse consequences. The right to exit a service with which they are they are dissatisfied is also a basic principle of consumerism (Scourfield, 2007) but again, the privatized system of care homes exposes the limitations of this principle. It is hard for residents to exercise their choice to leave a home, because such a move could be stressful and damaging to their health or because there are limited alternatives. In their analysis of marketization in Nordic countries, Szehebely and Meagher (2013: 273) argue that these difficulties critically limit "the effectiveness of market mechanisms in ensuring care quality." Worse still, for residents in the UK, current contractual arrangements between care home providers and residents give providers wide discretion to evict residents, including at short notice, irrespective of the effect on residents' health. The CMA found that residents and their families find it difficult to challenge an eviction because of a lack of transparency in the decision. These underlying structural arrangements highlight the loss of social protections for older people in need of care and the extremely precarious position they are in as residents, particularly where they have dementia or other conditions that make it harder to challenge the provider's account of a problem.

The CMA also highlighted the practice of continuing to charge residents' families fees for up to four weeks after the residents' deaths – a practice that the British press has reported upon widely. Providers refute the claim that such charges are callous, arguing that care homes are businesses that need to plan their expenditure. A death is an unplanned event and an unoccupied room is a cost that they are unwilling or unable to bear (Ruddick, 2017a). Subsequent to their report, the CMA launched a consultation on law advice on the charging of fees after a resident's death, taking account of the needs of both providers and bereaved relatives.

In tackling these various problems within the UK's privatized system, the CMA is aiming for clarification of what constitutes "fair practice" under existing consumer law. In their view, consumer law (and action taken against providers that breach it) will be sufficient to guarantee residents' rights to fairness. They have also made recommendations on self-regulation and voluntary codes of practice, recognizing too the need for independent advocacy and support for residents to enable them to exercise their rights. Commenting on the CMA's research, however, the Relatives and Residents Association (RRA) point out that there is no evidence to support self-regulation. In fact, they argue, the evidence points to the contrary. Given residents' weak bargaining power (likely to be even weaker as demand rises for a shrinking number of places), it is even possible that self-regulation can lead to abuses of power (RRA, 2017). The involvement of large corporations in care markets has generated particular problems because it is unclear where residents should direct their complaints, particularly if the corporation is based overseas.

The greatest concern in the UK market for care homes currently, however, is the poor outlook for its future sustainability. This concern has been growing for several years, especially in the context of provider failure or near failure, and raises questions about the very nature of the market system currently in operation. In the UK, the care homes market is mixed, with around 41 percent of residents purchasing their place directly and 49 percent funded through local authorities, around a quarter of whom pay top-ups for particular services they want and can afford. Approximately 10 percent of residents have their care costs covered by the National Health Service. Local authorities have coped with years of austerity budgets, which have meant savage cuts to social services. This, in turn, has reduced the funds available for commissioning long-term residential care. On average, fees paid by self-funders at around £846 a week (about US$1,180), are 41 percent higher than the fees paid by local authorities (CMA, 2017), so self-funders are in effect subsidizing publicly funded residents. The effects of the market, as pointed out by Forder and Allan (2014), are not experienced equally but, on the contrary, reinforce inequalities between older people in long-term residential care.

Several recent developments have called into question the sustainability of this market. There has been a dramatic increase in the number of insolvencies (Ruddick, 2017b) as well as planned closures because providers choose to leave the market or are forced into a restructuring of their debt. The majority of insolvencies are among small operators (those with fewer than five care homes) who account for 55 percent of all places in homes and those with the highest proportion of publicly funded residents. Evidence suggests that providers are declining to engage in the market for publicly funded residents. Current investment is concentrated on homes for self-funders, which will reduce options for those who rely on public funding, while leaving self-funders open to the risk of eviction if their funds run out.

There have also been closures of larger companies. In late 2017, Four Seasons Health Care almost collapsed because it was unable to pay its debts, despite efforts to do so through the closure of over eighty homes in the previous two years. Its main creditor, a US hedge fund company, H/2 Capital Partners, agreed to defer the interest on the debt but the future of homes within this group is still precarious and disputes between Four Seasons and H/2 continue. The increase in care home closures has generated pressure on public bodies to exert financial oversight, to assist providers in carrying out closures in an organized way, and to take responsibility for the welfare of residents affected by closures (Holder & Jolley, 2012). The Four Seasons example highlights the precarity of the market model. According to Nick Hood, an insolvency specialist at Opus Restructuring

> What we have is the financialisation of the care home sector, where some of its biggest managers are operating on the private equity model and expecting returns of 12 or 14 per cent when the downward pressure on revenue and the upward pressure on costs means they can't possibly make that kind of money.
>
> (Plimmer, 2017)

The downward pressure on revenue arising from stagnation in local authority payments is a major bugbear for providers, not least because, for them, maintaining a satisfactory quality standard becomes increasingly difficult. The financial analysts, Company Watch, said that "residential care ... has become a commodity, and one for which its biggest customer (local government) is both unable and unwilling to pay an economic price" (Company Watch, 2016). The industry organization, Care England, points to the cost pressures arising from the introduction of higher statutory minimum wages for care workers, which has a significant impact in this sector where the salary bill represents a high proportion of the overall running costs. From this perspective, the market is failing because the state (in the form of local authorities) is starving it of income, while simultaneously raising its costs by improving the pay of care workers. At the same time, estate agents Knight Frank (2017: 11) commented in their Care Home Trading Performance Review that "the care home market has remained resilient and robust, particularly in direct comparison to other property types and the wider investment classes. Indeed, investor appetite for the sector is at its highest level for over 20 years." This is, indeed, a fragmented, differentiated, and unequal market.

Challenging the Low Value Placed on Residents in a Market System

The privatization of care has, as predicted by many commentators, failed to live up to the promise of higher-quality services in care homes, with enhanced choice, more individualized services, and greater autonomy and control for residents. The wellbeing of residents is compromised by poor practices and there are many weaknesses in the privatized system arising from low staffing levels, high staff turnover, inadequate staff training, and poor pay and conditions of work for care workers. In addition, markets have introduced new forms of risk for residents in long-term care, as evidenced in the British context. Taken together, the evidence points to the low value placed on the lives of care home residents in a market system. Residents in the *Reimagining Long Term Residential Care* study valued a sense of belonging and relationships with care staff that in many cases mirrored family relationships. These qualitative elements of life and work in a long-term care setting do not sit easily with the priorities of a market system that seeks to maximize revenues but are essential to a reimagined future.

As Michel Sandel (2012) argued, there is a need for a serious public debate about the role that markets and market reasoning should play in society. The market system has become so firmly entrenched that, despite its evident inherent instability and volatility, its suitability as a way of organizing care homes is seldom challenged. Instead, when companies that run care homes fail and the welfare of older residents is put at serious risk, the focus is on how statutory bodies should act to reduce the impact of the current failure and on how to prepare for future failure. Meanwhile, the market is able to continue to develop in the areas that generate the highest financial returns. In 2005, Netten, Williams and Darton pointed out that care home closures are implicit in the operation of competitive markets and will have short-term effects on the welfare of residents. They argued that at a societal level "the short-term welfare loss for a few is the price of the greater welfare gain for the many that we assume results from the operation of a market" (Netten et al., 2005: 320). The evidence of the operation of markets in long-term residential care in the subsequent 13 years raises serious questions about this assumption, not least in the capacity of a market to manage the tensions between risk and protection for residents, and to demonstrate that the lives of residents are valued.

References

Armstrong, P. (2017). Balancing the tensions in long-term residential care. *Aging International*, *43*(1), 74–90.
Armstrong, P. & Daly, T. (Eds.). (2017). *Exercising choice in long-term residential care*. Ottawa, ON: Canadian Centre for Policy Alternatives.
Baines, D. & Armstrong, P. (Eds.). (2016). *Promising practices in long term care: Ideas worth sharing*. Ottawa, ON: Canadian Centre for Policy Alternatives.
Baines, D. & Stikuts, C. (2016). Some hard facts on long term care. In D. Baines & P. Armstrong (Eds.), *Promising practices in long term care: Ideas worth sharing* (pp. 17–29). Ottawa, ON: Canadian Centre for Policy Alternatives.
Barnes, M. (2012). *Care in everyday life: An ethic of care in practice*. Bristol, UK: The Policy Press.
Brennan, D., Cass, B., Himmelweit, S. & Szehebely, M. (2012). The marketisation of care: Rationales and consequences in Nordic and liberal care regimes. *Journal of European Social Policy*, *22*(4), 377–391. doi: 10.1177/0958928712449772
Butler, J. (2009). *Frames of war: When is life grievable?* London, UK: Verso.
Care Quality Commission (CQC). (2017). *The state of adult social care services 2014 to 2017: Findings from CQC's initial programme of comprehensive inspections in adult social care*. http://www.cqc.org.uk/sites/default/files/20170703_ASC_end_of_programme_FINAL2.pdf
Chalfont, G. & Rodiek, S. (2005). Building edge: An ecological approach to research and design of environments for people with dementia. *Alzheimer's Care Quarterly*, *6*(4), 341–348.
Company Watch. (2016). *Squaring the unprofitability circle*. 30 June. https://www.companywatch.net/article/2016/06/squaring-unprofitability-circle
Competitions and Markets Authority (CMA). (2017). *Care homes market study: Final report*. https://assets.publishing.service.gov.uk/media/5a1fdf30e5274a750b82533a/care-homes-market-study-final-report.pdf
Cordini, M. & Ranci, C. (2017). Legitimising the care market: The social recognition of migrant care workers in Italy. *Journal of Social Policy*, *46*(1), 91–108. doi: 10.1017/S0047279416000398
Daly, T. & Szehebely, M. (2012). Unheard voices, unmapped terrain: care work in long-term residential care for older people in Canada and Sweden. *International Journal of Social Welfare*, *21*(2), 139–148. doi:10.1111/j.1468-2397.2011.00806.x
European Network of National Human Rights Institutions (ENNHRI). (2017). *"We have the same rights": The human rights of older persons in long-term care in Europe*. http://ennhri.org/IMG/pdf/ennhri_hr_op_web.pdf

Evans, E. A., Perkins, E., Clarke, P., Haines, A., Baldwin, A. & Whittington, R. (2018). Care home manager attitudes to balancing risk and autonomy for residents with dementia. *Aging & Mental Health, 22*(2), 261–269. doi:10.1080/13607863.2016.1244803

Forder, J. & Allan, S. (2014). The impact of competition on quality and prices in the English care home market. *Journal of Health Economics, 34*, 73–83. http://dx.doi.org/10.1016/j.jhealeco.2013.11.010

Grenier, A., Lloyd, L. & Phillipson, C. (2017). Precarity in late life: Rethinking dementia as a "frailed" old age. *Sociology of Health and Illness, 39*(2), 318–330. doi: 10.1111/1467-9566.12476

Harrington, C. (2013). Understanding the relationship of nursing home ownership and quality in the United States. In G. Meagher & M. Szebehely (Eds.), *Marketization in Nordic eldercare: A research report on legislation, oversight, extent and consequences* (pp. 229–240). Stockholm: Stockholm University.

Harrington, C., Stockton, J. & Hoopers, S. (2014). The effects of regulation and litigation on a large for-profit nursing home chain. *Journal of Health Politics, Policy and Law, 39*(4), 781–809. doi:10.1215/03616878-2743039

Hawkins, R., Prashar, A., Lusambili, A., Ellard, D. R. & Godfrey, M. (2017). "If they don't use it, they lose it": How organisational structures and practices shape residents' physical movement in care home settings. *Ageing & Society*. doi: 10.1017/So144686x 17000290

Holder, J. & Jolley, D. (2012). Forced relocation between nursing homes: Residents' health outcomes and potential moderators. *Reviews in Clinical Gerontology, 22*(4), 301–319. https://doi.org/10.1017/S0959259812000147

Knight Frank. (2017). *Care homes: Trading performance review.* London: Knight Frank. www.KnightFrank.com/Research

Lorenz, R. A., Gooneratne, N., Cole, C. S., Kleban, M. H., Kalra, G. K. & Richards, K. C. (2012). Exercise and social activity improve everyday function in long-term care residents. *American Journal of Geriatric Psychiatry, 20*(6), 468–476. doi: 10.1097/JGP.0b013e318246b807

Manthorpe, J. Samsi, K. & Rapaport, J. (2013). "Capacity is key": Investigating new legal provisions in England and Wales for adult safeguarding. *Journal of Elder Abuse and Neglect, 25*(4), 355–373. doi:10.1080/08946566.2013.770313

Means, R., Morbey, H. & Smith, R. (2002). *From community care to market care: The development of welfare services for older people.* Bristol, UK: The Policy Press.

Mitchell, W., Baxter, K. & Glendinning, C. (2012). *Risk, trust and relationships in an ageing society: Updated review of research on risk and adult social care in England.* York, UK: Joseph Rowntree Foundation.

Netten, A., Williams, J. & Darton, R. (2005). Care home closures in England: Causes and implications. *Ageing and Society, 25*(3), 319–338. doi:10.1017/S0144686X04002910

Peace, S., Kellaher, L. & Willcocks, D. (1997). *Re-evaluating residential care.* Buckingham, UK: Open University Press.

Plimmer, G. (2017). Care home crisis deepens under private equity owners: Battle between hedge fund and Four Seasons exposes risk of opaque structures. *Financial Times.* https://www.ft.com/content/330fde3c-e187-11e7-a8a4-0a1e63a52f9c

Qureshi, H. (2009). *Restraint in care homes for older people: A review of selected literature.* London, UK: Social Care Institute for Excellence. https://www.scie.org.uk/publications/reports/report26.pdf

Residents and Relative Association (RRA). (2017). *Response to CMA care home market study*. https://assets.publishing.service.gov.uk/media/5981ebf540f0b61e4b000054/the_relatives_and_residents_association_response_to_update_paper.pdf

Ruddick, G. (2017a). Care homes charging for rooms after residents die, watchdog finds. *Guardian*. https://www.theguardian.com/society/2017/apr/17/care-homes-charging-for-rooms-after-residents-die-watchdog-finds

Ruddick, G. (2017b). Record number of UK care homes declared insolvent. *Guardian*. https://www.theguardian.com/society/2017/may/05/social-care-crisis-record-number-of-uk-homes-declared-insolvent

Sandel, M. (2012). *What money can't buy: The moral limits of markets*. New York: Farrar, Straus & Giroux.

Scourfield, P. (2007). Are there reasons to be worried about the cartelization of care? *Critical Social Policy, 27*(2), 155–180. doi:10.1177/0261018306075707

Standing, G. (2010). *The precariat: The new dangerous class*. London, UK: Bloomsbury Press.

Stolt, R., Blomqvist, P. & Winblad, U. (2011). Privatization of social services: Quality differences in Swedish elderly care. *Social Science and Medicine, 72*, 560–567. doi: 10.1016/j.socscimed.2010.11.012

Szehebely, M. & Meagher, G. (2013). Four Nordic countries – four responses to the international trend of marketisation. In M. Szehebely & G. Meagher (Eds.), *Marketisation in Nordic eldercare: A research project on legislation, oversight, extent and consequences* (pp. 241–284). Stockholm: Stockholm University.

Townsend, P. (1986). Ageism and social policy. In C. Phillipson & A. Walker (Eds.), *Ageing and social policy: A critical assessment* (pp.15–44). Aldershot, UK: Gower.

Tronto, J. (1993). *Moral boundaries: A political argument for an ethic of care*. New York, NY: Routledge.

Chapter 12

Shifting Responsibilities for Care
The Experiences of Staff and Families in Long-Term Residential Care

Rachel Barken and Pat Armstrong

As the introductory chapter indicates, our team took a broad view of privatization. Practices that promote markets and emphasize consumer choice have given rise to a new term and a new concept: responsibilization. Instead of government regulation of markets and businesses for the public good, we get talk of corporate social responsibility free of government interference (Shamir, 2008). At the same time, the responsibility for health and safety at work is shifting from the employer to the individual, with employees blamed for violations of the standards that remain after deregulation (Gray, 2009). In the name of expanding patient choices, individuals are increasingly held responsible for their own health (Brown & Baker, 2012; Dent, 2006). When individuals are not able to look after themselves, it is mainly families and especially the women within them who are held responsible for care (Armstrong et al., 2002; Funk, 2013; Grant et al., 2004). In high-income countries, where welfare states had previously taken significant responsibility for public health and protection, this move to responsibilization is a form of privatization. Responsibilization is a gendered phenomenon in that women provide the bulk of paid and unpaid care across home and long-term care settings. Care work has traditionally been considered an intrinsic female capacity and is often disregarded as learned, skilled labor (Armstrong, 2013). When women perform care labor in the public sphere of paid work, its skilled nature is often obscured, and the job is poorly remunerated as a result of this and other forces that limit women's power (Palmer & Eveline, 2012). Caring labor is even less visible when the work is unpaid and undertaken within the private sphere of family relations, where women provide the majority of unpaid labor.

At the same time as individual employees and families are held responsible for more care, services are increasingly provided through non-governmental and often for-profit, corporate agencies. Based on the notion that governments should steer and not row (Osborne & Gaebler, 1993), states more often "govern at a distance" as they encourage the development of private and market-oriented organizations to deliver formerly public services. Accompanying this shift are accountability practices including budgets that are set centrally but managed locally, performance indicators, and evaluations such as auditing systems to monitor outcomes (Larbi, 1999; Rose, 2000). Strategies such as these are often purported to increase consumer choice and empowerment. They have been justified, in part, as an antidote to welfare forms of governance that were criticized for expanding social control while limiting individual autonomy (Henderson, 2005).

Neoliberal notions of individual responsibility and autonomy are particularly contradictory for women who do the bulk of paid and unpaid work in long-term residential care (LTRC) focused primarily on older adults. Pressures to reduce government spending, allow profit-taking in the system, and apply for-profit management practices – widespread trends across North America and Europe (Starke, 2006) – have resulted in funding cuts to operating budgets in the LTRC sector. Similar practices in the hospital sector, combined with the emphasis on aging in place – justified as everyone's first choice – mean that those who enter long-term care have much more complex care needs than in the past. That women with limited economic power also account for the overwhelming majority of residents contributes to the growing neglect of long-term residential care.

Pressure from families and media exposure of scandals in the wake of these strategies have revealed multiple concerns regarding the quality of care. Research from our team has shown that governments often respond with more and more regulation of the sector (Lloyd et al., 2014). In Canada and the United States, regulations tend to focus on the individuals directly engaged in care provision, rather than on ownership or on market strategies. Although there are certainly variations among the countries we visited, in many jurisdictions fewer staff are expected to care for a greater number of residents with increasingly complex health conditions. Most of these workers are women who are defined as low skilled and many are from racialized and/or immigrant communities (Colombo et al., 2011; Laxer et al., 2016). While managerial practices, working conditions, and regulations surrounding employees' scope of practice limit the extent to which they can exercise choice, they are nevertheless held responsible for not only the health and safety of residents but for themselves (Armstrong & Daly, 2017).

The auditing systems, most common in North America, simultaneously reinforce this responsibility and limit the capacity of workers to respond to individual needs. The focus on particular indicators, combined with low staffing levels, mean the non-medical aspects of care, or what is often called social care, receives less attention than required. Earlier research (Armstrong et al., 2009) reveals significant differences between Canada and Scandinavian countries in terms of time for social care, with the greater time devoted to social care coinciding with higher staffing levels and the more limited adoption of market approaches in Scandinavia.

With the neoliberal strategies that are particularly evident in North America, social care tends to be seen as the responsibility of unpaid carers rather than of publicly provided health services (Daly, Armstrong & Lowndes, 2015). Some of this family responsibility is made explicit and other kinds of responsibility result from gaps in care that also reflect for-profit strategies focused on particular kinds of efficiency. But even this approach has contradictions. Although families are expected to take responsibility for more aspects of care, within policies and practices they are regarded primarily as "visitors" rather than as care providers (Barken, Daly & Armstrong, 2017).

In many cases, 'family' stands as a euphemism for women's unpaid labor. Women are most likely to feel the impact of privatization because they do the majority of unpaid work in long-term care, often as daughters and as spouses. While there are certainly men who engage in caring labor, their work is more often celebrated and supported whereas women's is considered a duty (Calasanti, 2010). Women also typically do more hours of unpaid care work than men do, especially when it comes to personal care such as bathing and dressing (Cranswick & Dosman, 2008). Women also provide more of the care required on a daily basis (Duxbury, Higgins & Shroeder, 2009).

Drawing on our team research that is described in the Introduction, this chapter articulates the tensions that neo & liberal strategies and in particular responsibilization present for the work and autonomy of paid workers and unpaid family carers in LTRC. The team's analysis of administrative data and documents provides much of the background material used here while the ethnographic studies of publicly subsidized care homes serve to illustrate forms of privatization and their contradictions at work. Although our focus is on privatization in Canada and the United States, we use examples from the UK, Sweden, and Norway to show other strategies that allow for meaningful and autonomous care work.

Our analysis focuses on particular aspects of LTRC: food, laundry, staffing levels, and violence. In each of these areas, we witnessed tensions as policies and practices simultaneously held paid workers and family members responsible for care, and yet limited their capacity to act autonomously. As a contrast, we then illustrate some situations where individuals had the autonomy to engage in care work in desirable ways. In doing so, we not only highlight the contradictions that arise from market-oriented strategies, but we show how alternative approaches to the organization and delivery of LTRC can support meaningful work.

Staff

Neoliberal practices tend to simultaneously make staff more individually responsible and to create greater limits on their individual and collective autonomy, especially in terms of monitoring. This is particularly the case for the care aides who provide the overwhelming majority of care. Here we use the examples of staffing levels, performance measures, and action around violence to illustrate these patterns.

Reducing staff in the name of efficiency is just one aspect of neo-liberalism. Increasing numbers of residents require more intensive care, but with neo-liberal strategies this has not meant more staff to accommodate higher care needs. Only some jurisdictions have minimum staffing levels of hours per resident, and the levels that are set in North America are below the 4.2 hours of nursing care per resident that experts recommend (Harrington et al., 2012). According to a British Columbia (BC) registered nurse (RN) in our study, staffing shortages mean that care aides are often too rushed to even help residents use the washroom when they need to:

> Well, the only thing is that there's not enough working hands, right? I don't know if I'm right or not now because I know that how the government assigns the staff ratio is that they give only one and a half hours of care per resident per day. So basically that's not enough. That's not enough. And so I can see the care aides they are rushing all the time. And I think the bowel care that's the main problem. You can see some of them they are quite alert. They still know that they need to go to the washroom. They are sitting there, they are asking, but sometimes say they were sitting in the dining room, there's no call bell, they just yell. No one will go and help them.

It is mainly the care aide who is held responsible for helping residents to the bathroom and to eat, but over and over again in Canada we heard the "not enough hands" refrain from residents, families, and staff. The rush leaves the care aides with little autonomy and they are left with "no time to chat" or do the other things with residents that the care aides see as essential to care.

Regular staffing levels are too low, we were repeatedly told, and conditions are often made worse by the failure to replace staff on leave. A union representative in Manitoba we interviewed talked about how workers had few choices but to bend the rules to provide basic care. For example, because two people are required to use the Hoyer lift for transferring residents, workers developed alternative strategies when no other designated person was available:

> They end up being so short staffed. If somebody is a two person, you have to have two people to lift them or to Hoyer them, so what they do is they'll go get one of the housekeepers or one of the EMS [emergency medical services] guys because their building is attached to stand in the doorway so that they can do the lift. Even though they're doing it alone but a housekeeper or a laundry or a dietary or the EMS guy is standing there.

But such strategies to provide care while following the rules can lead to problems. Another union representative told us that "one of my co-workers was lifting, asked a housekeeper to come in while they were doing the transfer and that resident fell. So she was suspended." The worker was held responsible for the lack of staff.

In addition to keeping staffing levels as low as possible and not replacing staff on leave, neoliberal strategies also promote the hiring of part-time and casual staff. In this way employers can often avoid union and other protections while providing just enough and just-in-time staffing. Contracting out services can have a similar impact. For this BC cleaner, a switch in contractors not only meant lower pay but also working in different parts of the building, losing her valued contacts with residents and their families.

> I make jokes because actually for ten years I was working on the third floor. That was my area for ten years. Somehow when a new management, a new supervisor came they rotated us. Bad idea. Because now we're kind of like starting a new job. Since April I've been doing this stuff. Okay, I'm getting a bit to know.

Workers often complained to us that part-time and casual staff did not know the residents or the equipment, often causing more work for the regular employees who were responsible for ensuring care. Instability in staffing can also prohibit the development of functional team performance, and, in turn, the provision of high quality care (Havig, Skogstad, Veenstra & Romoren, 2013), something we saw in a number of homes.

We did see strategies designed to ensure that absent staff were replaced and that part-time workers knew the residents and the facility. A Manitoba home keeps their own list of staff to fill in for absences. As in the case of a Nova Scotia home, the part-time staff is regular and does not come through a for-profit agency that may send new workers each time there is a call. It is mainly women who fill in these gaps in staffing, in part because they are often doing domestic labor at home and are available to cover shifts on short notice.

At the same time as managerial practices hold staff responsible, they monitor them more closely in the name of ensuring quality care. In keeping with neoliberal managerial strategies, there is a move to standardize care and measure performance. This move is defended as a means of improving care but it "restricts the care plan to standardized interventions" (Kontos, Miller & Mitchell, 2010: 359) that limits the right of care aides to decide on the basis of their skills and knowledge about individual residents. It is structured through proprietary systems designed both to develop care plans and to monitor their application. And these monitoring systems take a lot of time away from care. As an Ontario care aide explained:

> Too much documentation. Too much ... you don't even have time to do certain things but you have to do documentation ... but what are you going to do? You have to do it ... You have to run from binder to binder ... You have a restraint ... You have what you're taking care of

> in the morning. You have to do that. You have the snack book. Like we give the dessert out we've got to put that in documentation, you know. It's a lot of writing.

It is not only time-consuming but useless monitoring in terms of ensuring quality care, according to one care aide:

> [W]e got the nutritional intake sheets to record that I find ridiculous ... We're all there feeding a patient. To me you report the ones who refuse to eat. It's paperwork that's putting us behind because you have to calculate that there ... you still have to record it in your binder so you're doing the same thing times two. Nobody looks at it.

While a nurse practitioner in BC recognized the extra workload created by these performance measures, she also saw them as fundamentally restricting nurses' autonomy and limiting their capacity to respond to differences among residents linked not only to diagnosis, but also, for example, to gender, race, and class:

> [I]t's weird. It almost is robotic mechanical. Yeah, that's really how I want to describe it. It's robotic mechanical nursing care. If this happens then you do this. If this happens then you do this. The computer is thinking for you and the humanity is lost in it ... [T]he thing is people are feeling incapacitated to make their own clinical judgments without having the "I don't know everything about it but the indicator came up." You shouldn't need to have the computer tell you what the problems are with your person. It just seems ridiculous to me because you're the one telling the computer so then the computer can then tell you.

These standardized processes "mediate the relationship between accountable service providers and the individuals whom they seek to help" (Woolford & Curran, 2011: 595), in the process holding staff responsible while limiting their autonomy.

Lack of time, lack of staff, more casual staff, and rising levels of dementia among residents contribute to the increasing number of violent incidents. In a survey of care home staff in Canada and Scandinavia, nearly 40 percent of Canadian direct care workers said they experienced violence more or less every day. Although the population in Scandinavian homes is similar to Canada's, Scandinavian direct care workers are much less likely to say they experience violence more or less every day. Only 7 percent of those in Norway and 6 percent in Sweden said this was the case (Armstrong et al., 2009: 29). Not incidentally, Scandinavia has resisted many neoliberal strategies, care homes have higher staffing levels, and workers typically have more autonomy, although as Chapter 2 on Norway and Sweden indicates there are moves in this direction.

A care aide in an Ontario home said, "And I mean we take abuse too, don't get me wrong, from them. Lots of abuse." They have been kicked, punched, spit at and bitten, not to mention being exposed to racist slurs. It was not uncommon for workers to explain away the abuse in medical terms: "But we know that it's the illness that's progressing. It's not who they were before." Other workers report they are told to "suck it up" if they mention the violence and racism they experience, with managers telling workers that it must be their fault because they did not handle the situation appropriately.

Knowledge of individual residents can help prevent violence, as can training. However, a reliance on part-time and casual staff makes it difficult to depend on such knowledge, as some Ontario care aides explained in a group interview:

> I find there's part-time people coming and they probably haven't even worked with Alzheimer's patients before.
> Yeah, they've worked in long-term care but ...
> Yeah, in different areas.
> It's not the same. It's not the same, like for them it's like "Whoa. I've never done this before." You know, and then when you're going somewhere different all the time and you've got different patients all the time, you get different behaviors.

Blaming the violence on illness or an individual's training though, ignores the structural factors that contribute to violence. Recall the RN quoted above who describes residents wanting to go to the toilet but unable to get attention except by yelling. And consider the quite different levels of violence in Scandinavia, where structural factors help limit the violence. In Scandinavia, staff not only have responsibility but autonomy. In a home we visited in Sweden, an assisting nurse explained that workers have the flexibility to decide and to respond to resident needs:

> Often I see the same situation like the family. This is our children. We are the parents and this is the apartment. What do you do in your home? You will clean, make food. But if we are a little late one day, maybe we eat one o'clock not twelve this is not a problem. So we are flexible here. They need medicine and food but if it's a little different time because something happened this is okay.

She went on to say they have autonomy to experiment with new approaches:

> I am not afraid to say something and they understand. Whatever you have idea we will not say "This is not good," no, no, no. Maybe I say 'I don't think it's so good but I want to try it." So I do not say no before I try. And the others say the same. We are open mind[ed] and we're friendly. We meet together after work.

It helps that this assisting nurse worked in a unit with only 15 residents, and enough staff to share the work and to creatively develop approaches that aligned with residents' needs.

A chef in a UK home also talked to us about the importance of being able to try things out. He observed that residents were overwhelmed by full plates delivered to their table, especially when some of them were not to their taste. In response, the chef experimented with different foods, based on an Internet search of the residents' history. He also produced food in appetizer size and allowed residents to choose which appetizers to eat. The result was that residents ate more and had more enjoyable meals. And the chef got satisfaction from exercising his skills and autonomy. This autonomy was only possible because the manager was committed to a philosophy of shared responsibility and decision-making, and was prepared to challenge the regulations that restricted such options.

Families

Families occupy ambiguous positions in LTRC. On the one hand, there are popular assumptions that families "abandon" older relatives in care homes, and the move to LTRC is often regarded as a failure on the part of families and individuals to provide enough care at home (Guberman, 2004). On the other hand, family involvement in long-term care is both encouraged and assumed. Models such as person-centered and family-centered care, which increasingly guide the organization and delivery of LTRC, emphasize partnerships with families and their active involvement in decision-making (Koren, 2010; Ward-Griffin et al., 2003). For example, resident and family handbooks – guiding documents that serve as touchstones for communication between LTRC facilities and families – typically encourage family members to visit and to spend time with residents (Barken, Daly & Armstrong, 2017). Families, residents, and staff alike often view family participation as a positive thing that can help to strengthen relationships among individuals involved in care (Bradshaw, Playford & Riazi, 2012; Ward-Griffin et al., 2003). At the same time, increased family responsibility for care is part of the invisible work, undertaken primarily by women, that results from funding cuts and the privatization of services. While families are held responsible for doing more of the work, they are left with little autonomy to decide if and how they want to participate.

Food work aptly illustrates some of the ways in which the privatization of services, even within publicly funded care homes, can increase family responsibility. At a BC care home, where food services were contracted out to a private company, residents and their family members often complained about the lack of meal choice and about the poor quality of the available options. Many residents were of Asian origin, and although families had successfully advocated for an alternative to the standard North American menu, the dietitian reported that soya sauce was not allowed because of the high salt content. Many family members and friends also stated that what was presented as Asian food did not resemble what many residents would have eaten at home. As a result, the women, in particular, often cooked or purchased additional food for the residents. The daughter of a Chinese resident, who supported her mother as well as a close male friend who lived in the facility, explained:

> Plus the food is not the greatest. I mean they do their best and I realize, you know, it's the budget and everything and they do their best but some of the dishes really aren't palatable ... I honestly don't have time to cook so I just go and buy food especially the Chinese food because they miss their Chinese food so I'll supplement with going out and buying Chinese food for them.

This daughter noted how much the residents enjoyed the meals she brought in. She felt a responsibility to continue bringing in food given a lack of other options:

I: Do you find that they have a better appetite when you bring things in?
A: Oh definitely, especially him. I mean it must be so hard for him because he was an excellent cook. Oh, everything he made was so good. So, you know, I mean when he first got here I was really afraid.

Given their limited capacity to make choices regarding the food served to residents, staff in this BC care home came to rely on families to provide residents with more interesting and varied meals. The dietitian explained how their solution to meeting residents' personal and cultural preferences was to ask families to bring in certain items:

I: What if they say "I like my food spicy"?
A: Then it's really difficult. Then I would suggest, um, we provide something, like we have a package of Mrs. Dash [spice seasoning] that we can provide on the tray to sprinkle and then I can encourage her family to bring in sauces or spices for them to sprinkle on. I don't think we have the resources to provide different spices for them. But the families have been pretty good actually. One of the ladies, a Vietnamese lady, she doesn't eat very well. The family bring all kinds of Vietnamese sauces and we have a fridge for the family so they can put it there if it needs to be refrigerated or leave in the room so they can bring it out with them when they want.

While privatization is often considered to increase consumer "choice," this autonomy does not always extend to the families of long-term care residents, who in some instances were relied upon to prepare and provide food when appropriate, quality meal options were lacking. At the same time, families often valued the opportunity to share meals with residents. This is unsurprising, given the social and cultural importance of sharing meals with family and friends. In other care homes, we observed some promising instances where available meals and snacks allowed families to feel welcome without rendering them responsible for food work. In a Nova Scotia care home, where all food was prepared in-house rather than contracted out, a daughter commented on the low cost of quality food: she could purchase a meal at the home for less than five dollars or bring in her own food if she chose to do so and enjoy dining with her relative. Similarly, in a UK care home, we observed families and other visitors sharing meals and snacks with residents:

> We went back to the dining room area and smelled cookies – it smelled so good, and we had one. There were about six residents in the lounge and two in the dining room. I chatted to a wife of a new resident who had only been here a month. She said it is "the best." Said they are so well cared for and families are welcome. She lives 15 minutes away and comes every day and stays for lunch.

The availability of food and snacks for families fostered a sense of community, but these relatives did not have the added responsibility of providing food for residents. They were therefore better positioned to make autonomous choices regarding their level of involvement.

Laundry services provide another example of the tensions between responsibility and autonomy in family care work. When workers must do laundry for many residents the result can be mismatched, ruined, or missing clothing. Residents and their families are instructed to bring clothing that can withstand hot dryers and/or to launder more delicate clothing at home. Families did much work to not only wash but to manage their relatives' clothing. Many LTRC facilities, especially in North America, outsource laundry services to reduce their spending, with clothing and linens sent elsewhere for cleaning (Armstrong & Day, 2017). Yet, the clear divisions of labor between laundry workers and other staff – a result of dividing up and outsourcing the work – made it difficult for families to communicate with staff to ensure their relative had clean clothing. A daughter at a BC care home described the struggles she faced in communicating with staff, and the costs that families incurred when clothing went missing:

> Today actually I came in and I had dropped four new undershirts for my mom to be labelled ... with a pink label because I do my mom's laundry at home versus have it done through laundry facilities. So I went up to the nursing station and asked to speak to the nurse that's looking after my mom's area and I said "I dropped off some shirts for my mom on Thursday." I said "I'm just following up to see where they are." "I can't help you. That's not our ..." How did she put it? I don't know

quote/unquote but we don't do the housekeeping or the laundry. And I said "I realize that. I'm just asking when I can expect my mom's clothes to be back" because some of her clothes have already gone missing. And clothes are expensive to replace. Ten minutes later the clothes were in the room so obviously a conversation took place.

An unintended consequence of privatization, and little integration among workers, was that families had to do more work to advocate on behalf of their relative and to communicate with staff about issues such as laundry.

Although many family members took responsibility for laundry, they did not all have the time, money, access to laundry facilities, or physical ability to wash clothing at home (Armstrong & Day, 2017). We observed an alternative in some care homes: laundry facilities for personal resident and family use. The availability of washers and dryers presented some contradictions regarding responsibility and autonomy. On the one hand, it allowed women especially to care more easily for their relative's clothing during their visits, and meant that those who could not transport laundry home and/or did not have a washer and dryer at home could still do their relatives' laundry. Families could then have greater autonomy regarding the care of their relative's clothing. As a support services manager at the same BC care home stated: "We have a machine here and some of them do bring down their own laundry, their things. It's better too. Otherwise you have a lot of headaches." On the other hand, washers and dryers for personal use can place an increased expectation on families to do laundry regularly. This invisible work is then written out of operating budgets and considerations for staffing, as administrators take for granted that families will take responsibility for laundry. Family members, for their part, are left with little autonomy to decide whether to do laundry: the alternative is that their relative may have dirty clothing. Furthermore, we observed that many residents do not have families who visit frequently and do tasks such as laundry. These residents may lack clothing that is clean and well-cared for.

The demands placed on families to manage their relatives' care is another area of concern. Many family members want to be involved in decision-making processes, and want staff to keep them informed of changes in their relative's health. But when families are held responsible for managing care, they often have a limited capacity to make choices regarding their level of engagement. At a Texas care home, we observed the extent to which workers and managers expected family members to organize themselves to keep informed about their relative's care. As a nurse stated:

Well it's a good thing to take care of their mom and their dad. You need to be involved. If you don't get involved you don't know what is going on with them. You don't know what medicine they are taking. You don't know why they are acting. Some of them are very forgetful. You say "Mom, remember in 1970 we used to do that?" Mom can't get it.

> She has forgotten. She doesn't get it. If you don't get involved you don't know why this medication was given because your mom is having poor memory. She can't remember. Or he is a dementia patient. He is getting this medicine because of dementia. If you are not involved you can't get it. But if you are involved you know every little bit of things.

In this care home, families were expected to keep informed and maintain a degree of responsibility for care. The medical director's comments make clear that families should be involved in ways that suit the needs of the facility and the physicians working within it, rather than the preferences of residents and their families:

> Having information that's not going to be given to you by a mental patient, a lot of the elderly don't always remember. It's a lot of information. Family involvement of course helps. When it gets to be a hindrance would be if multiple members come forward and want to be communicated with … Normally we say have a point to go to person, you know, that will get all the information from us who will give it to all your family members.

While such statements seemingly welcome family participation, families have little autonomy to decide how they want to be involved. Care practices like this also can also increase responsibility for an individual relative – most often a woman – rather than allowing multiple family members to be involved in ways that work for them.

By contrast, at a UK care home we observed that families felt welcome to participate, but did so autonomously because they found it to be enjoyable. They did not indicate a need to oversee care or to navigate relationships with workers. The female family members of one resident felt confident that their relative was well looked after, and could therefore relax and enjoy visits at times of their choosing:

> Granddaughter: Nan used to worry so if she couldn't get there for two days or something, you know, you had to go and make sure he was okay but here your mind is at rest.
> Wife: I don't worry now if I can't come. He don't know who I am. He don't know who I am but you've still got to look after them. But I don't worry now because I know he's being well looked after.
> I: And your mom, what does she think?
> Granddaughter: My mom is a lot happier now because she works full time as well so she can go working now knowing granddad is being well looked after and fed. It's peace of mind. That's the biggest thing isn't it? (…) She knows that you're okay, that grandpa is okay so she can go do her work and not worry basically. If there's any problems they phone up straight away and say "He's not too well. He's in bed today."

Supporting Autonomy for Paid and Unpaid Carers

The examples presented above illustrate instances where paid and unpaid carers experience contradictory forms of responsibilization. LTRC homes simultaneously depend on carers' labor and yet limit their autonomy. Neoliberal performance measures restrict workers' rights to decide based on their knowledge, while holding them responsible for care and reducing their time to care. Low staffing levels and the failure to replace absent workers further restrict workers' autonomy as they are pressured to focus on monitored tasks. The widespread assumption that illness is the cause of violence and racism, and that they can be handled through employee training renders individual workers responsible for violence while obscuring underlying structural factors. At the same time, the reliance on part-time and casual work means that it is harder to develop violence prevention strategies based on an individual worker's knowledge of the resident or even on their knowledge about dementia.

With the shifting responsibility that comes with neoliberal strategies, families also face contradictions concerning their involvement in care homes. Although many family members want to spend time with their relatives, as a result of various forms of privatization, they face pressures to fill in gaps in care and to ensure the well-being of their relative. This informal reliance on family, evident in various areas including food, laundry, and care management, can leave families with few choices but to do care work – work that women mostly do, and that seeps into family members' lives outside of the facility, such as preparing food in advance of visits or taking laundry home.

Despite the contradictions that emerge from responsibilization, our comparative research allowed us to witness some promising practices that support the autonomy of workers and families. In some care homes, especially in Scandinavia, staff have the opportunity to work in teams and to use their skills and knowledge to provide the kinds of care they perceive residents need. Moreover, in some care homes families are able to participate to the extent desired, but with supportive conditions they do not feel responsible for doing care work. As such, our research illustrates approaches that can be implemented to support meaningful autonomy for paid and unpaid carers in long-term residential care. These approaches value women's paid and unpaid caring labor, and seek to improve the conditions in which this work is undertaken.

References

Armstrong, P. (2013). Puzzling skills: Feminist political economy approaches. *Canadian Review of Sociology/Revue canadienne de sociologie, 50*(3), 256–83.
Armstrong, P., Amaratunga, C., Bernier, J., Grant, K., Pederson, A. & Willson, K. (Eds.) (2002). *Exposing privatization: Women and health care reform.* Aurora, ON: Garamond Press.

Armstrong, P., Banerjee, A., Szebehely, M., Armstrong, H., Daly, T. & Lafrance, S. (2009). *They deserve better: The long-term care experience in Canada and Scandinavia*. Ottawa, ON: Canadian Centre for Policy Alternatives.

Armstrong, P. & Daly, T. (Eds.). (2017). *Exercising choice in long-term residential care*. Ottawa, ON: Canadian Centre for Policy Alternatives.

Armstrong, P. & Day, S., (2017). *Wash, wear, and care: Clothing and laundry in long-termresidential care*. Montreal and Kingston, ON: McGill-Queen's University Press.

Barken, R., Daly, T. & Armstrong, P. (2017). Family matters: The work and skills of family members in long-term residential care. *Journal of Canadian Studies, 10*(50), 321–347.

Bradshaw, S. A., Playford, E. D. & Riazi, A. (2012). Living well in care homes: A systematic review of qualitative studies. *Age and Ageing, 41*(4), 429–440.

Brown, B. J. & Baker, S. (2012). *Responsible citizens: Individuals, health and policy under neoliberalism*. London: Anthem Press.

Calasanti, T. M. (2010). Gender relations and applied research on aging. *The Gerontologist, 50*(6), 720–34.

Colombo, F., Llena-Nozal, A., Mercier, J., & Tjadens, F. (2011). *Help wanted? Providing and paying for long-term care*. OECD Health Policy Studies. Paris: Organisation for Economic Cooperation and Development.

Cranswick, K. & Dosman, D. (2008). Eldercare: What we know today. *Canadian Social Trends, 86*, Catalogue no. 11-008. Ottawa: Statistics Canada. http://www.statcan.gc.ca/pub/11-008-x/2008002/article/10689-eng.htm.

Daly, T., Armstrong, P. & Lowndes, R. (2015) Liminality in Ontario's long-term care facilities: Private companions' care work in the space "betwixt and between". *Competition and Change, 19*(3), 246–263.

Dent, M. (2006). Patient choice and medicine in health care: responsibilization, governance and proto-professionalization. *Public Management Review, 8*(3), 449–462.

Duxbury, L., Higgins, C. & Shroeder, B. (2009). *Balancing paid work and caregiving responsibilities: A closer look at family caregivers in Canada*. Ottawa, ON: Human Resources and Skills Development Canada.

Funk, L. M. (2013). Home healthcare and family responsibility: A critical discourse analysis of talk and text. *Healthcare Policy, 9*, 87–97.

Guberman, N. (2004). Designing home and community care for the future: Who needs to care? In K.R. Grant., C. Amaratunga, P. Armstrong, M. Boscoe, A. Pederson, & K. Willson (Eds.), *Caring for/caring about: Women, home care, and unpaid caregiving* (pp. 75–90). Aurora, ON: Garamond.

Grant, K. R., Amaratunga, C., Armstrong, P., Boscoe, M., Pederson, A. & Willson, K. (Eds.) (2004). *Caring for/caring about: Women, home care, and unpaid caregiving*. Aurora, ON: Garamond.

Gray, G. C. (2009). The responsibilization strategy of health and safety: Neoliberalism and the reconfiguration of individual responsibility for risk. *British Journal of Criminology, 49*(3), 326–334.

Guberman, N. (2004). Designing home and community care for the Future: Who needs to care? In Grant et al. (Eds.), *Caring for/caring about (2004)* (pp. 75–90).

Harrington, C., Choiniere, J., Goldmann, M., Jacobsen, F., Lloyd, L., McGregor, M., Stamatopoulos, V., & Szebehely, M. (2012). Nursing home staffing standards and staffing levels in six countries. *Journal of Nursing Scholarship, 44*(1), 88–98.

Havig, A.K., Skogstad, A., Veenstra, M. & Romoren, T.I. (2013). Real teams and their effect on the quality of care in nursing homes. *BMC Health Services Research, 13*(499), 1–11.

Henderson, J. (2005). Neo-liberalism, community care, and Australian mental health policy. *Health Sociology Review, 14*(3), 242–254.

Kontos, P. C., Miller, K. L. & Mitchell, G. J. (2010). Neglecting the importance of the decision making and care regimes of personal support workers: A critique of standardization of care planning through the RAI/MDS. *The Gerontologist, 50*(3), 352–362.

Koren, M. J. (2010). Person-centered care for nursing home residents: The culture-change movement. *Health Affairs, 29,* 312–317.

Larbi, G. A. (1999). *The new public management approach and crisis states.* Geneva: United Nations Research Institute for Social Development.

Laxer, K., Jacobsen, F. F., Lloyd, L., Goldmann, M., Day, S., Choiniere, J. & Rosenau, P. V. (2016). Comparing nursing home assistive personnel in five countries. *Ageing International, 41*(1), 62–78.

Lloyd, L., Banerjee, A., Harrington, C., Jacobsen, F. F. & Szebehely, M. (2014). "It is a scandal!" Comparing the causes and consequences of nursing home media scandals in five countries. *International Journal of Sociology and Social Policy, 34*(1/2), 2–18.

Osborne, D. & Gaebler, T. (1993). *Reinventing government: How the entrepreneurial spirit is transforming the public sector.* New York: Plume.

Palmer, E. & Eveline, J. (2012). Sustaining low pay in aged care work. *Gender, Work and Organization, 19*(3), 254–275.

Rose, N. (2000). Government and control. *British Journal of Criminology, 40*(2), 321–339.

Shamir, R. (2008). The age of responsibilization: On market-embedded morality. *Economy and Society, 37*(1), 1–19.

Starke, P. (2006). The politics of welfare state retrenchment: A literature review. *Social Policy and Administration, 40*(1), 104–120.

Ward-Griffin, C., Bol, N., Hay, K. & Dashnay, I. (2003). Families and registered nurses in long-term-care facilities: A critical analysis. *Canadian Journal of Nursing Research, 35*(4), 150–174.

Woolford, A. & Curran, A. (2011). Neoliberal restructuring, limited autonomy, and relational distance in Manitoba's nonprofit field. *Critical Social Policy, 31*(4), 583–606.

Chapter 13

Promoting Public Care

Pat Armstrong[1]

To a large extent, the chapters in this book document a move towards privatization and the negative consequences of this development for those who live in, work in, manage, and visit nursing homes, as well as for the public more generally. The chapters grow out of our team project on reimagining long-term residential care and our search for conditions that not only treat those who work and live in nursing homes with dignity and respect, but allow them to flourish. In keeping with this purpose, we now turn to describing some promising practices for providing alternatives to for-profit ownership and approaches, as well as to some examples of successful resistance.

Creating Alternatives to Corporate Ownership

The first, and most promising alternative, is prevention and positive action to improve the conditions of work in the non-profit sector.

One way to prevent privatization is by offering public or non-profit options and by combining services in a way that can provide both new revenue and cross-subsidies. A municipality in the Canadian province of Ontario offers one example. Almost 70 years ago the provincial government put in place legislation that required every municipality of a certain size to have a home for the aged, later renamed long-term residential care (Struthers, 1997). Some of these public homes have been renovated over the years but recent regulations have left many of them out of date. At the same time, their resident populations have more complex care needs and require more equipment. The Association of Municipalities of Ontario (2011, p. 6) sets out seven options in response to these developments:

- Fulfill legislative requirements
- Change the requirements
- Outsource operations but keep public governance
- Maintain ownership but outsource operations and governance
- Sell the home and redirect contributions

- Transfer beds to non-profit and/or for profit ownership
- Create various forms of partnership

Instead of closing down, outsourcing, or turning to the for-profit sector, a municipality we studied decided to beat the for-profits at their own game. Cobbling together public money from multiple sources and public land that would otherwise be sold to private interests, it built a retirement community that included long-term care beds, assisted living units, affordable housing apartments, life-lease apartment suites, and homes with gardens. The life-lease options are designed for older adults, allowing them to gain equity under a market-value life-lease plan and receive continuity of care if their need for support increases. The housing complex is fully equipped with things like grab bars and bells to call for assistance. United in one location, all residents have access to programs and services, although many of these have some fees attached. The programs and services are provided primarily by employees of the facility or by the many certified volunteers.

Our fieldnotes describe:

> a large bright solarium filled to bursting with plants. This is the garden room, which is designed both for resident enjoyment and for them to care for the plants ... In the village centre itself, there was a big double sided fireplace, a grand piano, attractive dining areas with an open kitchen that served a wide range of food. We had our lunch here, and it was delicious, if served more "food court" than restaurant style. However, the comfortable upholstered seating – including some bar height tables (no wheelchairs there) and others, presented a relaxed and welcoming area. There was also a television over the fireplace with a news program on quietly. There was an artwork display on one wall that was installed by a local museum and changed regularly.

Another room has a shuffleboard, a popular item, we were told. There is also a lap pool, a well-equipped gym, and a pharmacy, in addition to a "number of quite flexible spaces, including a large gym-type room that was the central auditorium/ dance hall/ place of worship /movie theatre, complete with a giant screen that came down from the ceiling" (Fieldnote, Ontario).

There are obvious advantages to this prevention strategy. By combining various kinds of housing, the municipality is able to achieve some economies of scale while providing continuity in care services for aging residents at reasonable costs. At the same time, the revenue from some parts of the complex, outside of the services covered through government health care transfers, subsidizes other forms of support. Meanwhile, decision-making remains in public hands. Indeed, we saw examples of unions working with seniors' organizations and other community groups in other towns to ensure that municipalities took the public route, in the process contributing to democratic decision-making.

Our union partners drew on the team's research and on our individual team members to support their case. Aware of staff concerns about the new developments and as a result of union involvement, the municipality made sure staff knew their jobs would be transferred to the new development.

However, there is a risk that such public approaches will themselves end up adopting for-profit strategies. This can be particularly the case when it comes to organizing work. We saw multiple examples of strategies taken from the for-profit sector, with managerial control exerted from the top, lots of casual or part-time precarious work, especially for women, and a strict division of labor. We did, however, see examples of alternatives to these for-profit approaches and to improving the conditions of work.

One example comes from the Canadian province of Manitoba. The home was built by a religious organization that discovered, prior to the building's completion, that they did not have the money or other resources to meet their idea of care. They offered it to the local government, which decided to make it a public home. They appointed a director and gave her the power to select, train, and organize the workforce. In our meeting with that director, she explained their approach.

> The clear philosophy of [the home] is that "this is the resident's home. We don't really go to work. We go into the resident's home. The residents, over everything, come first." Explaining the origins of this philosophy, [the director] tells us that when the construction of [the home] was completed in 2007, she and the first executive director got together, in the empty building, to think through what should be the philosophy of the new home, which they decided should be "resident-first. We worked hard to get nurses to think through things to make it the best we could for the residents."
>
> (Fieldnote, Manitoba)

Working through a strategy to make this the residents' home meant involving the staff in reimagining care.

> The staff have a lot of input into the facility and into the changes they have made. "People want to work here because of our different philosophy. We were told by [the government agency] 'if you just follow the standards, you'll be fine.' Beyond that, we could do what we wanted." So, as an example, they developed their own system of charting "by the quarter" at the back of each resident's file. This is "integrated care" mapped on their chart, according to each quarter of the year. In this way, "everything is lumped together."
>
> (Fieldnote, Manitoba)

Although the home is required to use the proprietary MDS–RAI system, the staff basically work around it. According to the director,

they don't do resident charts by the day, unless something significant happens. "Medical charting requires a conclusion. Here we don't really have much of a conclusion. We chart around the social and environmental rather than the physical because there is not much we can do about that." MDS-RAI is an obligation but they mostly use it to scan for pain and pain relief and to get a second look at the care they are giving. As opposed to MDS-RAI, their staff prefer to do "free-texting."
(Fieldnote, Manitoba)

Asked for an example of staff decision-making, the director talked about being away from the home for three months.

While she was away, the home was "run by the nurses" and continued well without her. No temporary director was sent from the [government] to run it. "It has to be the staff. Without me." She noted that nurses all too often are not allowed to work up to their professional practice skills. "We wanted to give them that freedom. The philosophy is not 'my way.' It's the facility's way. They just continued to do that. It needs to be that way. Everyone needs to know what the facility's needs are and why. But you need to give them that power." She said "we don't have a name for the philosophy. It's just resident-focused care. What prevents people from giving good care is that they don't have the power to do what they need to do."
(Fieldnote, Manitoba)

This way of organizing work and ensuring accountability contrasted sharply with the hierarchical forms of work organization and decision-making based on business models and accountability systems that we saw in other places. In the approach of this CEO, the staff "really need the opportunity to think outside the box when they have to. If there's something that needs to be done, it can be done by anyone" (Fieldnote Manitoba).

In order to have the work done by anyone, you need to have everyone employed by the home. There was no outsourcing of services in this home, not even the food. As the director put it, "We prepare it all here. When you walk in and smell bacon, that's what it should be" (Fieldnote Manitoba). The majority of staff are full-time. Part-time staff are hired from the home's own roster in order to ensure both continuity in care and that all staff know each other and the residents. No staff agencies are used. That 60 percent of the staff have been there since the home opened in 2007 attests to the quality of the work environment and contrasts sharply with the high turnover rates common in the sector. The home provides additional education for staff focused on care relationships and empathy. For example, during orientation the staff experienced being swung in a lift and then bathed. A male care aide told us he had never felt so vulnerable, even though they let him wear a bathing suit. It changed the way he provided care.

The director explained that

> every staff person in the facility has to be out on the floor every day, to be with the residents at some point. It's written into their job description because the residents need to know who they are. Who's working here.
>
> (Fieldnote, Manitoba)

We saw the laundry worker put away clothes in residents' rooms while chatting with the resident. She knew not only who the clothes belonged to but how each person wanted their clothes folded and put away. The receptionist delivered the menus to each resident every day, giving her the opportunity to know every resident and often their families as well.

Although the director spoke about the pressures from budgets that do not keep up with changing demands and rising prices, she did not have to deal with investors requiring profits. Because everyone is an employee of the home, she does not have to deal with multiple contractors and everyone can be part of the team. Because she is responsible to a local authority, she can negotiate strategies to promote quality care.

In our site visits we saw examples of other creative strategies for addressing quality in the public system. In a German home, for instance, the management took advantage of a government apprenticeship program designed to prepare for a labor force shortage in this sector (Müller, Goldmann & Theobald, 2017). The 66 staff members were joined by 110 apprentices. These apprentices earn a monthly salary from the government and come to the home after completing a six-week care aide course. The presence of so many apprentices had an obvious impact on care. Our fieldnotes indicate there was a lively energy in the building and lots of variety for the residents. There was plenty of time for chatting and responding to individual residents, demonstrating that more staff means better care. However, the apprentices also mean more work for the regular staff, who are responsible for the education and supervision of those participating in the on-the-job training. Equally important, counting on new programs can be a precarious strategy because the program could easily disappear.

Union actions also have an impact on the quality of care in public homes and in this way can contribute to the prevention of privatization. They can also have an important impact on equity in a sector where low wages reflect the limited power of a population made of primarily of women, and of women who are often from immigrant groups and the assumption that this is low-skilled work any woman can do (Armstrong, 2013). One example of this prevention strategy is union efforts to ensure decent wages and benefits. As Kate Laxer (2014: Ch. 5) has shown, unionized workers in the nursing home sector in Canada are paid significantly more than their US non-unionized counterparts. As Chapter 6 indicates, the unions in the Canadian province of British Columbia were able to win some protections against contracting out as well as better wages and pensions for the female-dominated workforce. In Sweden, the unions have not only negotiated decent wages but also managed to remove the male/female wage gap common in other countries. These strategies have consequences for care. For example, earlier research by members of our team (Armstrong et al., 2009) has shown that compared to Canada levels of violence are lower in Nordic nursing homes, with better working conditions a factor. However, such strategies can be vulnerable to changes in government, as has been the case in BC. When the unions mounted a legal challenge to a government initiative supporting contracting out and eliminating many union protections, the Supreme Court of Canada's decision recognized the right to freedom of association and agreed that the prohibition of contracting out negotiated in a collective agreement should be protected. However, the court also recognized employers' right to contract out the work, even though they must consult with unions in order to do so, and refused to carry through on pay equity comparisons.

Union and community actions, combined with media reports of low quality care, have also led to other government action to expand services and improve the pay of workers in this sector. The Canadian province of Ontario provides one example. The Liberal Government responded to the outcries about care homes by expanding the number of beds and by raising the wages of personal support workers in all publicly funded ones, whether or not they had unions (Ontario, Ministry of Health and Long-Term Care, 2015). The result can be improved access and better quality in care and work.

In sum, preventing for-profit ownership and outsourcing can take the form of protecting working conditions within public and non-profit homes in order to support the quality of care as well as the quality of work. Unions have been important in these efforts but require more widespread support to combat the powerful forces pushing to gain ownership and to transform work practices. This in turn requires educating the public about the positive consequences of keeping profit and managerial strategies taken from the for-profit sector out of care. Amalgamating services can also help preserve non-profit care, as can strategies designed to increase the autonomy, teamwork and training of the workforce. As earlier chapters also suggest, there is a need for legislation that prevents the sale of public homes to for-profit organizations and that prevents the contracting out of services within them.

Reversing the Trends

Although the most promising practice is prevention, a great deal of privatization has already taken place. Although it takes a lot of collective work, it is possible to return homes and services to the non-profit sector.

As Linn Herning[2] explained to our team, the Norwegian example illustrates that it is possible to reverse the for-profit ownership of long-term residential care. An academic with a doctorate in history, Linn works full time on the

Campaign for the Welfare State. Initially formed in 1999 by national unions to oppose marketization and deregulation, this group has grown to involve a range of voluntary organizations, including users' groups.

In 2010, when Linn joined the organization, the Campaign decided to focus on the shift in ownership that was taking place in long-term care. As was the case in all countries in our study, private ownership increasingly meant ownership by large, for-profit companies rather than by small, voluntary or individually owned ones, but this distinction was blurred in public discussions and in the minds of the public. For-profit corporations and some politicians were promoting this shift in the name of contributing to what she translated as "the good forces in the welfare state" and of providing effective quality at a lower price. To oppose these claims, the Campaign began by doing three things, namely: getting the facts straight, analyzing the corporate and political arguments, and providing alternative arguments. All of these approaches became the basis for educating the public. This included education about the differences among forms of ownership, and especially the differences between small, individually-owned homes and those owned by corporations.

The Campaign first focused on educating union members and on participating in the local elections, learning in the process that the campaigners could not simply rely on common sense. Instead, they needed slogans and short messages as a way into the debate and as a way of educating the broader public. The Campaign gathered simple stories and simple arguments that provided concrete examples to show the consequences of this transformation in ownership. The purpose was to change the discourse and to create a new space by clearly distinguishing among forms of ownership.

The Campaign developed a new term, "welfare profiteers," which turned out to be an effective political slogan. Linn Herning (2015) wrote a book by that title, a book designed to be accessible to the public. She tested it out on a wide range of people to ensure that concepts such as equity investment were easily understood by a broad public. Although her academic friends wanted a different kind of book, the result was a popular and effective critique. Like the Campaign material, it focused on why we need public services. This defense of public services, Herning says, was really an update on "old arguments that need to be made again."

The Campaign's efforts were helped by nursing home scandals publicized in the media. They were also helped by people who had experienced the conditions leading to those scandals and who changed their position on for-profit ownership as a result. The organization spread its educational efforts to the national level and to political parties, coordinating the opposition and convincing some parties to support their position. And the Campaign has enjoyed some success in stopping or reversing privatization in this form.

The main shift happened in 2015, when the municipal governments of the four major cities (Oslo, Bergen, Tromsø and Trondheim) decided to end existing contracts with for-profits and to prohibit any new contracts. More recently, the medium-sized city of Moss did the same, after a series of scandals involving the Norlandia company. Although some other Norwegian municipalities still support for-profits in welfare services, the dominant trend right now seems to be in favor of public and non-profit ownership. In keeping with this shift and with federal legislation, some local governments give preferential treatment to non-profit homes by providing them with open-ended contracts in contrast to shorter contracts in the private sector that can be cancelled following changes in the market.

Clearly, the struggle to keep public services public is not over in Norway. However, the success of the Campaign in reversing corporate ownership demonstrates that the trend to corporate ownership of homes is not inevitable and that there are strategies that can change the public discourse. It is also important to note that this campaign was effective in transforming the discourse around care, making public service, public access and democratic control the language of the campaign and challenging the consumer labels.

In the Norwegian example, the entire home was returned to the public sector. But the issue of ownership is not restricted to the entire home and here too there is need for resistance. In terms of this form of privatization, we have seen examples of successful movements to end the outsourcing of services to corporations. One such example comes from the Canadian province of Ontario.

As is the case in a number of smaller urban centers, a municipality saved the public hospital and municipal nursing home by amalgamating them and by including the town's medical clinics in the building. The amalgamation also made it possible for the staff in these various services to belong to a single union. As a result the union for all the services bargained with a single employer and was able to create single wage rates across the complex, as opposed to the lower wages in nursing homes more common in the province. Although the union was initially not strong enough to prevent the outsourcing of their food services to one of Canada's largest for-profit meal providers, it was able to protect some jobs when the corporation started reducing the labor force. Seniority rules across the complex meant more than a few of the laid-off workers found other employment in the hospital or nursing home.

Along with the staff cutbacks and other "efficiencies" resulting from corporate ownership came cutbacks in the quality of food. Both the resident and family councils rebelled, as did the elected board responsible for the entire organization. They joined with the union to fight to get rid of the contracted company and to bring the food services back in-house. The turning point came when a new manager, whom the complex wanted to hire, refused to come unless they got rid of the corporate contract. Fortunately, the kitchen had remained in the premises during the outsourcing period and when the contract was cancelled, the staff previously laid off by the food service company returned to their kitchen. Everyone we interviewed was satisfied with the food now that the corporate contract had ended. As usual during our site studies, we tasted the food and agreed with their assessment. Indeed, the kitchen has just been recognized by a national organization for the health quality of its food.

In sum, reversing the move to for-profit, corporate ownership and delivery of services is possible with coalition support and collective strategies for change. Moreover, as earlier chapters point out, governments could buy back for-profit homes when they go bankrupt or close.

Regulating, Enforcing, and Transparency

Given the blurring of the boundaries between for-profit and not-for-profit nursing homes, it has become increasingly important to establish measures to support quality care, regardless of ownership and to ensure both that standards are met and that the public have the information they need on where their money goes, with what consequences.

One means is establishing minimum staffing levels.

As Chapter 8 in this volume makes clear, higher staffing standards can increase staffing levels and help promote better care. Collective efforts have led to such standards in the US (Harrington, 2001). Unions in Ontario have taken this research and worked with community organizations to have legislation introduced to require at least four hours of direct care per resident per day. Unfortunately, the legislation did not make it through the legislature before an election was called and a Conservative government came to office.

However, even if there are minimum staffing levels, monitoring them is difficult and minimums can be manipulated. One way is to include staff on leave in the calculations. In a Canadian facility we studied, a third of the staff was on leave for illness or injury but all those on leave would be counted as part of the staff under many reporting systems. Because minimum staffing regulations frequently refer only to nursing staff, another way companies can fill the requirements is to reduce those employed as laundry, dietary or housekeeping staff and require some of the nursing staff to do this extra work. As a result, the actual number on staff decreases while the requirements are fulfilled.

This strategy of playing the rules on minimums was addressed to some extent by the US Affordable Care Legislation in 2010 (Obamacare). The legislation requires each facility to report on the number of nurse and other professional staff in the home to Centers for Medicaid and Medicare Services (CMS). This reporting must be done online and on a quarterly basis, providing data for every single day. This allows the public to see the nurse staffing levels on weekends and holidays and the daily RN staffing levels, data the public has never had access to before. The reporting was tested and reviewed for the last three quarters of 2017. It was put up for the public to see on the CMS website. Starting in April 2018, the data will be used as a part of the CMS five-star nursing home rating system, replacing self-reported annual summary data. CMS (2018) reminds state agencies that conduct the surveys and enforcement that all nursing homes with inaccurate staffing reporting will receive a one-star rating for staffing that will drop the facility's composite rating. The federal law also requires a minimum of one RN on duty eight hours a day seven days a week. This new reporting allows the agency and the public to see which nursing homes are not meeting the standard. In addition, nursing homes that fail to meet the one RN seven-days-a-week requirement will be given one star on the rating system. Such transparency requirements can improve reporting accuracy and compliance with the regulations, providing both the oversight agencies and the public easier methods for monitoring staffing levels in individual homes. However, we still need stronger penalties for those failing to meet the quality standards, backed up by the means to close or take over homes that fail to meet the standards.

In addition, as Harrington and colleagues (2016) from our project demonstrate, the United States has gone farther than the other countries studied in requiring financial transparency from corporations owning nursing homes. This perhaps reflects the fact that, among the six countries in our research, the United States has the highest proportion of for-profit homes. While this reporting does provide for some accountability, the authors make it clear that there is still room for improvement. We also need better means to follow the public money. These means need to make it clear what organizations own and operate the homes, and who can be held responsible for care. Accountability can happen only if this information is made publicly and readily available, at no cost. In addition, these ownership data need to be correlated with other data such as those on staffing levels so that policymakers, unions and the public can track the impact of ownership on care.

Staffing levels are only one indicator of quality. As Chapter 7 explains, we need better measures of quality than the current primarily medical ones that focus on what can be readily counted. Injury and illness data, and especially on violence against workers, as well as time for baths and flexible eating schedules, are just a few examples of other factors than can be critical to care. Moreover, we need process measures that help capture what actually happens in nursing homes without requiring staff to spend hours recording data and without requiring data that has no impact on care. One such measure could be the extent to which work organizations allow staff the time and the autonomy to consult with each other. The reflection groups we saw in Sweden provide one example (Armstrong & Daly, 2017). These meetings were both scheduled and ad hoc, bringing together the entire range of staff and allowing them to brainstorm as well as problem-solve resident issues big and small. They could be required and required during paid work hours.

Which brings us to unpaid care. Staff are increasingly held responsible for care even when they face increasing workloads. We were told again and again that workers put in hours of unpaid overtime because they feel responsible and are held responsible for care quality. They go home exhausted and feeling guilty, even though they spend the extra time doing unpaid work. This is particularly the case for women, as Donna Baines (2004) as demonstrated, because women are assumed to be altruistic about care. We need to track this time and pay for it. At the same time, families and especially the women in them, are expected to do more of the unpaid work in the care home. This work too needs to be documented so that we can develop strategies to reduce the load. In Sweden we were told by nurses that it is their responsibility to take the load off families. Just one example of them doing this is shopping for clothes for residents, and doing so as part of their paid work time.

Finally, we need to record the growing financial costs of care. We need such public data so families can know what to expect. But we also need such data so that we can use it to pressure government to provide more support for the care of this vulnerable population. Such data should also indicate the extent to which residents have to give up all their assets in order to qualify for public funding.

In sum, we need different and better data. These data need to be publicly available to allow monitoring and to promote change. They need to be related to the regulations and support the enforcement of standards for quality care and work.

Drawing Conclusions

Our team did not start out to study privatization. However, as we conducted our analytical mapping and our ethnographic research, it became increasingly obvious that we needed to address privatization. Indeed, when we asked policy-makers, unions, and community groups what homes we should study to find ideas worth sharing, virtually all of them recommended not-for-profit or public homes. This view was reinforced by the public data available on quality indicators such as staffing levels.

The chapters in this book document moves towards privatization in the six countries in our study and identify many of their consequences. In this conclusion, we set out some ways we saw for combating these moves. The Norwegian Campaign for the Welfare State demonstrates that the steady increase in corporate ownership of nursing homes can be stopped. It requires research, as well as collaboration across constituencies, public education strategies and political action to challenge the ideas central to neoliberalism. In other words, it requires changing ideas as well as practices. One example from Ontario illustrates that the privatization of services within public homes can be reversed using similar strategies, while another example from Ontario shows how both expanding and amalgamating public services can provide alternatives to corporate ownership. The kinds of rules regarding transparency and reporting on staffing introduced in the United States can help provide the facts for such campaigns. All these strategies can help work to make homes more accountable at the same time as they support more democratic decision-making.

Strengthening the quality of the work environment can also prevent privatization by creating conditions that promote care. Unions, especially in Canada,

Norway, Sweden and Germany, have been major players in these strategies. By negotiating decent wages, benefits, and job security, unions contribute to the continuity in staffing that is central to maintaining care relationships as well as the health of the staff. Unions have also played a major role in community campaigns, especially around the funding and staffing that are critical to care. Strategies by individual managers, such as the one in Manitoba who rejected for-profit approaches to work organization, and the one in Germany who took advantage of government programs to dramatically increase staffing levels, demonstrate that public solutions are possible and that such solutions bring benefits to residents and families as well.

Together the chapters in this book expose the movement towards privatization in multiple forms while also demonstrating that such a movement has negative consequences for staff, residents, families, and managers. Privatization also limits democratic decision-making and changes not only our language but also the way we think about the right to care and to decent work. This final chapter provides examples that show this movement is not inevitable. Indeed it can be prevented through providing alternatives and reversed by collective strategies for change.

Notes

1 While all the chapters in this book represent collective work, this one relies especially on Susan Braedley, Charlene Harrington, Frode Jacobsen, and James Struthers.
2 This section on Norway is based primarily on a presentation that Linn Herning made to the research team.

References

Armstrong, P. (2013). Puzzling skills: Feminist political economy approaches. *Canadian Review of Sociology / Revue canadienne de sociologie, 50*(3), 256–283.

Armstrong, P., Banerjee, A., Szebehely, M., Armstrong, H., et al. (2009). *They deserve better: The long-term care experience in Canada and Scandinavia*. Ottawa: Canadian Centre for Policy Alternatives.

Armstrong, P. & Daly, T. (Eds.) (2017). *Exercising choice in long-term residential care*. Ottawa, ON: Canadian Centre for Policy Alternatives.

Association of Municipalities of Ontario (AMO). (2011). *Coming of age: The municipal role in caring for Ontario's seniors*. Toronto: Association of Municipalities of Ontario. https://www.amo.on.ca/AMO-Content/Reports/2011/Coming-of-Age-Municipal-Role-in-Long-Term-Care.aspx

Baines, D. (2004) Caring for nothing: Work organization and unwaged labour in social services. *Work, Employment and Society, 18*(2), 267–295.

Centers for Medicare and Medicaid Services (CMS). (2018). Transition to payroll-based journal (PBJ) staffing measures on the Nursing Home Compare tool on Medicare. gov and the five star quality rating system. https://www.cms.gov/Medicare/Provider-Enrollment-and-Certification/SurveyCertificationGenInfo/Downloads/QSO18-17-NH.pdf April 6, 2018

Harrington, C. (2001). Residential nursing facilities in the United States. *British Medical Journal, 323*, 507–510.

Harrington, C., Armstrong, H., Halladay, M., Havig, Anders K., Jacobsen, F., MacDonald, M., Panos, J., Pearsall, K., Pollock, A. & Ross, L. (2016). Comparison of nursing home financial transparency and accountability in four locations. *Ageing International, 41(1)*, 17–39.

Herning, L. (2015). *Velferdsprofitørene. Om penger, makt og propaganda i de norske velferdstjenestene*. Oslo, Norway: Tanum.

Laxer, K. (2014). *Mapping the division of labour in Long-term residential care across jurisdictions*. Dissertation submitted to the Faculty of Graduate Studies in Sociology. Toronto, ON: York University.

Müller, B., Goldmann, M. & Theobald, H. (2017). Apprentices: More hands are necessary but not sufficient. In P. Armstrong & T. Daly (Eds.), *Exercising choice in long-term residential care* (pp. 97–104). Ottawa, ON: Canadian Centre for Policy Alternatives.

Ontario, Ministry of Health and Long-Term Care (2015) *Health bulletin* health.gov.on.ca/en/news/bulletin/2015/hb_20150622.aspx

Struthers, J. (1997). Reluctant partners: State regulation of private nursing homes in Ontario, 1941–72. In R. Blake, P. Bryden & J. F. Strain (Eds.), *The welfare state in Canada: Past, present and future*. Concord, ON: Irwin Publishing.

Index

Note: Page numbers in **bold** type refer to **tables**
Page numbers in *italic* type refer to *figures*
Page numbers followed by 'n' refer to notes

access, health-based 96
accommodation, co-payments 166
accountability: and governance 6–7, 10; lack of (UK and USA) 59–61; non-profit homes 33; and private ownership 24; purchaser–provider split 141
accountability (Norway) 141–152; Adecco scandal 141, 146–148, 151; audits 144–145; dangerous incidents 147; deficiencies in care 146; "feminization" of the sector 145; for-profit ownership 142–144, 150; health care workers' pensions 151; history of social and health care services 142; home ownership structure 144, 148–150, *149*; interpretative regulation 144, 145, 152; large chain dominance 143; municipal autonomy 144–145; overview 141–142; prescriptive regulation 144; psychotropic drugs (excessive use) 151–152; quality indicators 145, 146, 150; regulatory environment 144–145; staff training 147; trade unions role 146, 147, 187–188; transparency 148–150; violation of workers' rights 146; voluntary organizations 142; what way and to whom? 150–152
acute care hospitals 88
Adecco scandal 141, 146–148, 151, 187
Affordable Care Act (2010) 59, 188
aging population 2, 156, 162

Ågotnes, G.: and Jacobsen, F. F. 24, 141–155; Jacobsen, F. and Szebehely, M. 38–50
Alberta Classification 128
Allan, S., and Forder, J. 204
almshouse system 54
Alzheimer's patients, staff training 215
Ambea 159
American Health Care Association (AHCA) 185
Ammerudlunden 146–147
analytical mapping 8
ancillary services, contracting out 22, 25, 75
Anttonen, A., and Meagher, G. 70
apprenticeship program, Germany 228, 235
Aramark 110
Arbeiderpartiet 45
Armstrong, P. 1–14, 224–236; and Armstrong, H. 17–37, 156; and Baines, D. 200; and Barken, R. 30, 209–223; Daly, T. and Choiniere, J. 130; *et al.* 87–101
assessment tools, standardized 7
assisted living, Manitoba 98
Association of Municipalities of Ontario 224–225
Attendo 161
Attendo Norway 151
auditing systems 210
audits 144–145
austerity, fiscal 103–105, 116–117

Index

Baines, D. 6, 8, 233–234; and Armstrong, P. 200
bankrupt chains, UK 26
Barken, R., and Armstrong, P. 30, 209–223
bathroom visits 212
Baum, J. 89
Baxter, K., Glendinning, C. and Mitchell, W. 199
BC Liberal Party 108, 110, 111
bed "blocking" 5
beds: acute care hospitals 88; lack of in publicly subsidized homes 27, 97; NHS long-stay 53; public beds in British Columbia 108, 115; rate per aged population USA 55; supply in Canada 88, 91, 97
Bercovitz, K. L. 19
Berg, B. 151
Berta, W., et al. 89
Biggs, S., Estes, C. L. and Phillipson, C. 17
Bismarck model 69
Bjerke, P., and Dahle, T. 151
bowel care 212
Branda, J. R. 90
Braverman, H. 3, 6
British Columbia 102–117; care aide starting wage 107–108, 113; collective bargaining 102, 103–104, 106, 108, 228–229; "contract flipping" 112, 113–114; contracting out services 107, 109–110, 111–112, 113; doctors' pay 110; downsizing public beds 108; firing of care aides 102, 109–110, 113–114; food services 216–217; government spending by sub-sector 104, *105*; HEABC membership termination 114–115; Labour Relations Code 109, 111; neo-liberalism and fiscal austerity 103–105, 116–117; "non-clinical" staff 108–109; non-profit homes 105, 113, 117; provisional government cutbacks 105, 112–113; public beds in 108, 115; publicly funded facilities 115, **116**; publicly funded LTRC system 102–103, 115; public–private partnerships 112, 114; Request for Proposals (REF) process 110–111, 115; rolling back of labor and care regime 108–116; Royal Commission on Health Care and Costs (1991) 106–107; sectoral bargaining model 106–107, 114, 115; social spending cuts 104; stable labor and care regime 106–108, 116–117; staffing levels 181; staffing shortages 212; stripping union rights 108–109, 111, 114, 117n1; third-party subcontractors 111–112; unionized care workers 117, 228–229
British United Province Association 56
Bruce, G. 111
BUPA 56
Burawoy, M. 4
bureaucracy, for-profit ownership 19, 24
Burns, T. 129
Butler, J. 196, 197

California Advocates for Nursing Home Reform 186
Campaign for the Welfare State 230–231, 234
campus model 98
Canada: bed supply 88, 91, 97; care standards 180; co-payments for accommodation 166; community care 88; contracting out services 93, 229, 231–232; Guaranteed Income Supplement 96; health cost-sharing (federal contribution) 104; health-based access 96; marketing LTRC facilities 157, 171; marketization overview 9–10; Old Age Security 96; public health care 18; spend on direct care of total expenditures 182; staffing levels 181; waiting lists 91, 162, 171, *see also* British Columbia; Manitoba; Nova Scotia; Ontario
Canada Health Act (1984) 87–88, 125
Canada (three provinces study) 87–98; assisted living 98; campus model 98; competitive tendering 90; Continuing Care Strategy 92–93, 95, 96; for-profit ownership 89, 95; government funding 96; home ownership patterns 93–94; lack of beds in subsidized homes 97; minimum staffing standards 95–96;

municipal and charity-based operators 90; municipal homes 93; non-profit homes 89; non-profit homes waiting lists 91; nursing home central locations 90; overview 87–89; per diem fees 88–89, 91–92, 97; privatization of costs 97–98; privatization and regulation 94–97; privatizing ownership and delivery 89–94; regulatory burden 95; Request for Proposals (REF) process 92–93; residential room costs of private sector homes 97–98; select adverse events 92; shared/private room rates 96
Canadian Federation of Nurses Unions (CFNU) 186
Canadian Gerontological Nursing Association (CGNA) 129
Canadian Institute of Health Information (CIHI) 133–134
Canadian Union of Public Employees (CUPE) 186
Capital Asset Management Framework 110
care, as a relationship 69, 106, 113–114, 117, 169–170
care aides: firing 102, 109–110, 113–114; starting wage 107–108, 113
care crisis, Germany 70
Care England 205
Care Home Trading Performance Review 205
care provision, de-universalization 43
care quality: for-profit ownership 89, 90, 116, 165, 183–184; indicators as proxies 137–138; measuring 127–130; promoting public care 232; and staff turnover 106; and staffing levels 116, 177–178; trade union role 187–188
Care Quality Commission (CQC) 59, 199
care tasks, lump sum payments 72, 73
care work: as commodity 43, 171–172, 197; countable tasks 31; de-qualification of 79–80; female workforce 5–6, 80, 184–185; gender roles 3, 5; household and informal network-based 142; intrinsic female capacity 209; organization of 5–6; part-time work 79; quality concept 7, 10; regulated professions 33; research overview 4–5; tasks for relatives in care homes 30; "third sector" 142; workload and staff turnover 6
care workers *see* health care workers
Carpenter, I., Hirdes, J. and Ikegami, N. 127–128
Centers for Medicare and Medicaid Services 179, 188–189, 232–233
Central Park Lodge 91
chains: bankrupt 26; dominance 143; nursing home share 183–184; UK large 56
Chalfont, G., and Rodiek, S. 200
Chartwell 159, 160, 161
Checklist Manifesto, The (Gawande) 137–138
Choiniere, J.: Armstrong, P. and Daly, T. 130; Erlandsson, S. and Lowndes, R. 32, 156–176
cleaning staff 25–26
clinical care, division of labor 77
co-payments, accommodation 166
collective bargaining 102, 103–104, 106, 108, 228–229
collective wage agreements, health care workers 75, 79
community care, Canada 88
Community Care Information Management (CCIM) 128
community-based supportive housing, Manitoba 98
Company Watch 205
Compass 110
Competitions and Markets Authority (CMA) 32, 202, 203
competitive markets, efficient allocation of resources 19, 33
competitive tendering 47, 90
comprehensive provision, Scandinavian countries 18
computer skills 129, 130, 131–132, 169
conceptual framework 3–4
Confederation of Norwegian Enterprise (NHO) 150, 152
congregate living alternatives 28
consumer law obligations, UK 32, 202, 203

Continuing Care Assistant (CCA) 95, 96
Continuing Care e-Health Program 128
Continuing Care Reporting System (CCRS) 131, 133
Continuing Care Strategy 92–93, 95, 96
"contract flipping" 112, 113–114
contracting out services: ancillary services 22, 25, 75; British Columbia 107, 109–110, 111–112, 113; Canada 93, 229, 231–232; food services 30, 94, 110, 231–232; Germany 75; housekeeping 110, 213; laundry services 29, 218–219; long-term care insurance (LTCI) 73, 74, 75; non-profit homes 93; overview 22, 25; returning to in-house 26; single nursing homes 39; unions legal challenge (Canada) 229
Cordini, M., and Ranci, C. 197
cost-containment policy, Germany 76–77, 80
costs: private-sector home rooms 97–98; privatization of 97–98
court cases, Human Rights Act (1998) 61, 64n1, 64n2, 64n3

Dahle, T., and Bjerke, P. 151
Daly, T. 24, 89, 125–140; Armstrong, P. and Choiniere, J. 130; et al. 144, 180, 181
Darton, R., Netten, A. and Williams, J. 205–206
data collection and reporting 125–138; algorithms 136; analysis process 133, 136; collection systems 135–137; consumer choices 137; data validity 133; infographics of LTRC indicators 133–134, *134*; measuring care quality 127–133; New Public Management 130, 131; Nursing Home Compare 134–135, *135*; Ontario cost and quality data trail 132, *132*; overview 125–126; "person-centred care" 126, 136; public health data reports 133–135, *134*, *135*; public reports 133–134, 137, 234; quality in discourse, policy, and practice 130–135; quality indicators 128, 131, 134, 137; quality as proxy 137–138; quality theory and quality politics 126–130; regulatory power and collection of big data 130–132; standardizing data collection 132–135, 136
de-qualification of care work 79–80
dementia patients: social care relationships 25; violence towards health care workers 214–215, 221
demographic data 2, 156, 162
dental care 30
doctors, pay 110
documenting care 213–214, 226–227
Donabedian, A. 126–127, 134, 137
Donabedian's framework 126
Doupe, M., et al. 87–101

economic boom, post-war 17
Enterprise Federation of Norway 150
Erlandsson, S.: Choiniere, J. and Lowndes, R. 32, 156–176; et al. 167
Esping-Andersen, G. 2
Estes, C. L. 3; Biggs, S. and Phillipson, C. 17
ethnographic fieldwork, Norwegian nursing homes 144
European Network of National Human Rights Institutions (ENNHRI) 198–199
Extendicare 22, 89–90, 91, 93–94; marketing website 158–159, 160, 161–162, 164, 167

Facilities Bargaining Association (FBA) 107
Fagforbundet 45, 146, 147, 148, 187
families: ambiguous positions 216; appointed go to person 220; autonomy to be involved or not 220; care home tasks 30; encouraged and assumed involvement 216; gap in care filled by 221; relatives' care decision-making process 219–220; unpaid care work 234
families' involvement, food services 216–217
Federal Housing Authority (USA), loan guarantee program 55
fees, per diem (Canada) 88–89, 91–92, 97
Feltenius, D. 48
female workforce, care work 5–6, 80, 184–185

feminist political economy 3, 17, 20, 126
financial transparency 59–61, 233
financing: and ownership 7–8; private capital 111
fiscal austerity 103–105, 116–117
food services: autonomy 216; contracting out services 30, 94, 110, 231–232; culturally specific preferences 216–217; dietary problems 30; families' involvement 216–217; marketing website analysis 164; price competition 78; reversing contracting out in Ontario 231–232
For the Welfare State 45
for-profit ownership: Canada 89, 95; dominance 183; lack on unionized health workers 75; lower care quality 89, 90, 116, 165, 183–184; lower staffing levels 182–183; Norway 142–144, 150, 188; quality indicators 150, *see also* Norway and Sweden (for-profit ownership)
Forder, J., and Allan, S. 204
Foucault, M. 130
Four Seasons 56, 61, 204
Free Democratic Party (FDP) 71, 76
funding: government 95; publicly funded 115, **116**; publicly-funded facilities 115, **116**; responsibility (UK) 53

Gaebler, T., and Osborne, D. 18
Gawande, A. 137–138
gendered construction, social relations 3, 5
Genesis HealthCare 57
Germany: apprenticeship program 228, 235; care crisis 70; "care dependency" definition 72, 73; care grades 180; care system historical background 69–71; commodification 73–76, 79; contracting out services 75; cost-containment policy 76–77, 80; family care focus 71; family-oriented focus 68; for-profit provision (increase) 75–76; gender-based division of labor 70; health care insurance 71, 81n1; insurance schemes 28; long-term care insurance (LTCI) 71–76; markethood education 79;

marketization 9, 68–81, **77**; marketization definition 69; outsourcing 75; social insurance 69, 71, 76, 81n4; study methods 68–69; Taylorization and standardization of care 76–79; welfare associations 70, 71, 72; working conditions 79–80
Glendinning, C., Baxter, K. and Mitchell, W. 199
Goldmeier, H. 31–32
governance, and accountability 6–7, 10
government: funding 95; information on UK nursing homes 60
government spending: block grants 40; British Columbia 104, *105*; health and social care 7; institutional care 28; USA 28
Grenier, A.: *et al.* 197; Lloyd, L. and Phillipson, C. 196
Guaranteed Income Supplement 96

Harrington, C. 137; *et al.* 6, 32, 89, 233; and Jacobsen, F. F. 89, 177–195; Pollock, A. M. and Sutaria, S. 23, 51–67
Harvey, D. 4
Havig, A. K. 143
Hawkins, R., *et al.* 200–201
health care workers: autonomy and reporting systems 95, 233; care aide starting wage (British Columbia) 107–108, 113; collective bargaining 103–104, 106, 108; collective wage agreements 75, 79; computer skills 129, 130, 131–132, 169; "contract flipping" 112, 113–114; data inputting time 136–137, 169; de-qualification of care work 79–80; documenting care 213–214, 226–227; home location and travel costs 90; illness and injury 6; information technology systems 129, 130, 131–132; low-paid staff 79–80; marketing website analysis 164–165; mass firing British Columbia 102, 109–110, 113–114; minimum staffing standards 95–96, 178, 179, 188, 212, 232; part-time work 79; problems

health care workers (*cont.*)
of privatization 25–27; psychological stress and emotional exhaustion 167; shifting responsibilities for care 211–212; shopping for residents 30; simulation studies 179; statutory minimum wage 205; stripping union rights 108–109, 111, 114, 117n1; task-oriented work 181; training and qualifications 77–80, 147, 151, 164–165, 199–200, 227; unionized 117, 228–229; unionized workers in Norway 146; unpaid care work 6, 10, 78, 233–234; violation of rights in Norway 146; violence towards 6, 214–215, 221, 229, 233; women 5–6, 80, 184–185

Health Employers Association of British Columbia (HEABC) 107, 108–109, 113, 114–115

Health Quality Ontario 134

health and safety at work 209

Health Sector Partnerships Agreement Act (Bill 94, BC, 2003) 111, 112, 114

health and social care, government spending 7

Health and Social Care Act (England, 2012) 54

Health and Social Services Delivery Improvement Act (Bill 29, BC, 2002) 108–109, 110, 114, 117n1

Health Systems Restructuring Commission 125

Herning, L. 229–230

Hirdes, J., Carpenter, I. and Ikegami, N. 127–128

Home and Community Care (Ontario) 162

homes: publicly subsidized 27; subsidized 97, *see also* non-profit homes; nurse staffing in nursing homes; nursing home ownership; nursing homes

Hood, N. 204

Hospital Employees' Union (HEU) 107

Hospital Services Restructuring Commission (HSRC) 128

hospitalization levels 23

hospitals, acute care 88

housekeeping staff 25–26; contracting out services 110, 213

human rights 18, 34n1

Human Rights Act (UK, 1998), court cases 61, 64n1, 64n2, 64n3

Ikegami, N., Hirdes, J. and Carpenter, I. 127–128

information technology systems: care workers' computer skills 129, 130, 131–132; care worker's time inputting data 136–137; clinical intervention "triggers" 136; data collection systems 135–137, 169; large-scale adoption 130, 131; staff surveillance 169; tablet-style devices 131–132

insurance, private 55, 71

insurance (Germany): schemes 28, *see also* long-term care insurance (LTCI)

interpretative regulation 144, 145, 152

Jacobsen, F. F.: and Ågotnes, G. 24, 141–155; Ågotnes, G. and Szebehely, M. 38–50; and Harrington, C. 89, 177–195

Johnson, J., Rolph, S. and Smith, R. 165

Journal of Canadian Studies 5

justice, general theory 4

Kayser-Jones, J. 165

Knight Frank 205

Kommunal 45

labor: costs of nursing homes 58, 183; gender-based division 70

labor movements, Norway and Sweden 45

Lar, R. 156

Larbi, G. 125

laundry services 29, 31; contracting out 29, 218–219; facilities to use at care home 219; family responsibility for 219; outsourcing 218–219; promoting public care 228

Laws of Medicine, The (Mukherjee) 138

Laxer, K. 228

Lessenich, S. 71

Life Care Centers of America (LCCA) 57

life-lease apartment suites 225

Index

Lloyd, L. 196–208; Grenier, A. and Phillipson, C. 196
local authority funded services, UK 53
Local Government Act (Sweden, 1991) 41
Local Government Act (UK, 1972) 52
Long Term Care Consumer Coalition 186
long-stay beds, NHS 53
Long-term Care Homes Common Assessment Project 128, 129
long-term care insurance (LTCI) 71–76, 81n1; "Bismarckian camouflage" 72; budgeting and standardization 72–73; "care dependency" definition 72, 73; commodification (regulated and forced) 74–75, 79, 80, 81n3; contract management 74, 81n3; for-profit companies 73–74; for-profit provision (increase) 75–76; individualization of costs 76, 81n4; "market-creating law" 73; outsourcing 73, 74, 75; overview 71–72; price competition 73, 74; quasi-markets 73–74; social care needs 72, 73, 81n2; social insurance 69, 71, 76, 81n4
Long-Term Residential Care: An International Study of Promising Practices 2
long-term residential care: medicalized approach 5; overview 1–2; publicly provided and funded 38; quality concept 7, 10
Longhurst, A., Ponder, S. and McGregor, M. 102–121
Lorenz, R. A., *et al.* 201
Lowndes, R., Choiniere, J. and Erlandsson, S. 32, 156–176

Macarov, D. 27
MacDonald, M. 28; *et al.* 87–101
McGregor, M., Longhurst, A. and Ponder, S. 102–121
Manitoba 91–92; community-based supportive housing 98; minimum staffing standards 96; part-time staff 213; per diem fees 97; residents first policy home 226–228, 235; Winnipeg 91, 98
Manthorpe, J., Samsi, K. and Rapaport, J. 199–200
market role and reasoning debate 205–206

marketing website analysis 156–172; Ambea 159; appeal to investors 162; Attendo 161; Canada 157; Chartwell 159, 160, 161; choice of phrases 160–161, 163; choice as theme 161–162, 170–171; cost of care 166; culturally specific accommodations 161; demographic data 156, 162; Extendicare 158–159, 160, 161–162, 164, 167; family engagement 170, 172n1; food services 164, 170; funding and quality measurement 159–160; growth as theme 162–163; large chain corporations 157–158; location choice/ information 161–162, 171; missing details 165–171; mission statements 163; overview 156–157; quality measurement tools 159–160, 168; quality as theme 158–160; representations of families 164; representations of residents 163–164; representations of staff 164–165; resident's out-of-pocket payments 166; revenue generation 158–159; Revera 159; senior care as a commodity 171–172; social care relationships 169–170; staff qualifications 164–165, 167; staff ratios and levels 166–170; staff surveillance 169; staff training 168; Sweden 156–157, 160, 172; target groups 157; testimonials by residents and families 161, 163, 164; themes 158; trust as theme 160–161; waiting lists 162, 171; website selection 157–158
marketization: definition 69; Germany 9, 68–81, **77**
markets, competitive 19, 33
Meagher, G.: and Anttonen, A. 70; and Szebehely, M. 203
media scandals 184, 187–188, 210
Medicaid 28; level and type of service 54–55; nursing home regulation violations 60
Medicare 28, 54, 60
Medicare Advocacy Program 186
minimum staffing standards: health care workers 95–96, 178, 179, 188, 212, 232; registered nurses (RNs) 59

Mitchell, W., Baxter, K. and Glendinning, C. 199
Mosebach, K. 80
Moss facility 147, 148
Muir, T. 28
Mukherjee, S. 138
Müller, B. 68–86
municipal homes, Canada 93

National Assistance Act (UK, 1948) 52
National Board of Health and Welfare (Sweden) 160
National Consumer Voice (US) 186
National Health Service and Community Care Act (UK, 1990) 51, 53
National Health Service (NHS, UK) 52; care costs covered by 204; long-stay beds 53
negative impacts of privatization *see* privatization (negative impacts of)
neo-liberal approach: Canada 88, 94, 103–105, 116–117; contradictions 19; deregulation 94; dominance 31–32; shifting responsibilities for care 210, 211, 213, 221; skepticism 19
neo-liberalism 103–105, 116–117
Netten, A., Williams, J. and Darton, R. 205–206
New Deal 17
New Democratic Party (NDP) 104–105, 106–107, 114
New Public Management 18–19, 42–43; Ontario 125, 126; regulatory power and collection of big data 130, 131; United Kingdom 51
NHO (Confederation of Norwegian Enterprise) 150, 152
"non-clinical" staff 108–109
non-profit homes: accountability 33; British Columbia 105, 113, 117; Canada 89, 91; contracting out services 93; democratic and accountable control 33; for-profit management 24, 34n2, 94; for-profit strategies 73; forced commodification 73, 79, 80; Ontario 224–225; religious organizations 40, 89, 142, 226; Request for Proposals (REF) process 111; voluntary organizations 142; waiting lists (Canada) 91
Nordic Welfare Model 48
Norlandia 147, 148; ownership structure 148–150, *149*; scandals 187–188, 231
North American Free Trade Agreement (NAFTA, 1994) 125
Norway: ending for-profit contracts 230–231; political parties' role 44, 45; regulatory environment 144–145, 188; staffing standards 180, 187–188; unions role in staffing standards 187–188, *see also* accountability (Norway)
Norway and Sweden (for-profit ownership) 38–48; competitive tendering 42, 47; culture of local democracy 48; de-universalization of care provision 43; differences between Norway and Sweden 42–43; different approaches by municipalities 46–48; and financial crisis 43; geographical contagion 47; historical development of privatization 40–42; lobbying against 46; municipal level responsibility 47; operation of homes not ownership of buildings 39–40; overview 38–39; political parties role 43–44; "privatization" 39–40; rate of increase 42; types of privatization 39; unions and interest groups 44–46
Norwegian Association of Local and Regional Authorities 145, 150
Norwegian Board of Health Supervision (NBHS) 144
Norwegian Confederation of Trade Unions 146, 187
Norwegian Nurses' Association (NSF) 146, 147, 187
Norwegian Union of Care Workers (Fagforbundet) 45, 146, 147, 148, 187
Norwegian Women's Public Health Association (NKS) 142
Nova Scotia 92–93; Auditor General's report 93; food services 94, 218; part-time staff 213; private sector operators 97–98; registered nurses 95; shared/private room rates 96
Nullmeier, F. 73

nurse staffing in nursing homes 177–190; mix of staff 178; acuity of residents 181–182; acuity/care needs 179; chains' growing share of market 183–184; for-profit ownership and care quality 183–184, 188; for-profit ownership model dominance 183; minimum staffing standards 178, 179, 188; nursing home labor costs 183; political power and influence of care industry 185; profit and administration cost limits 189; simulation studies 179; spend on direct care 182, 183; staff and caregiving as women's issues 184–185; staffing levels for-profit homes 182–183; staffing levels and political actions 186–187; staffing levels and quality of care 177–179; staffing levels and standards by country 180–182; staffing standards 188–189; task-oriented work 181; transparency of staffing data 188–189

nurses *see* registered nurses (RNs)

Nursing Home Compare 134–135, *135*

nursing home ownership: Canada 89, 93–94; complex structures 57; data 89, 93; for-profit ownership 21; large chains advantages 95; privatizing care 20–22; public-private partnerships 22; USA 55, 57

Nursing Home Reform Act (USA, 1987) 178

nursing homes: associations 185; labor costs 58, 183; media scandals 184, 187–188, 210, *see also* nurse staffing in nursing homes

Office of Seniors Advocate (BC) 116
Old Age Assistance Law (USA, 1915) 54
Old Age Security (Canada) 96
ombudsman programs 186
O'Neil, C. 135–136
Ontario 89–91; Alberta Classification 128; caffeinated coffee ban 201; food services 94, 231–232, 234; for-profit ownership 95; government 90; Liberal Government 229; municipal homes 93, 224–225; New Public Management 125, 126; payment rates 189; public health data reports 133–134; residential room costs 96, 97; spend on direct care of total expenditures 182; waiting lists 162, 171

Organization for Economic Cooperation and Development (OECD): lack of beds in publicly subsidized homes 27; skepticism of neo-liberal approach 19

Osborne, D., and Gaebler, T. 18

ownership: and financing 7–8; home 144, 148–150, *149*; private 24; privatizing 89–94, *see also* for-profit ownership; nursing home ownership

part-time staff/work 79, 213
partnerships, public–private 19, 22, 111, 112, 114
patient choices, responsibility for own health 209
pay, doctor's 110
pensions, health care workers' 151
per diem fees, Canada 88–89, 91–92, 97
performance-based indicators 7
"person-centered care" 126, 136
Phillipson, C.: Biggs, S. and Estes, C. L. 17; Grenier, A. and Lloyd, L. 196
political parties, Norway and Sweden 43–44, 45
Pollock, A. M.: Harrington, C. and Sutaria, S. 23, 51–67; Roderick, P. and Sutaria, S. 53
Ponder, S., Longhurst, A. and McGregor, M. 102–121
prescriptive regulation 144
price competition, Germany 73, 74
private capital financing 111
private equity firms 57
private insurance 71; long-term care 55
private ownership, and accountability 24
private sector homes, room costs 97–98
privatization (negative impacts of) 22–27, 58–62; control and standardization focus 26–27; excess profit-taking 62; failure to pay taxes 61–62; higher costs of services 61; housekeeping staff 25–26; impact on accountability 24; impact on costs 23–24; impact on quality 23; impact

privatization (negative impacts of) (*cont.*) on staff 25–27; lack of financial and regulatory accountability 60–61; lack of transparency 59–60; poor quality and low nurse staffing 58–59; staffing strategies 23

privatization by stealth 27–32; inadequate supply 27; shifting decision-making 32; shifting the dominant discourse 31–32; shifting payment 28–29; shifting work 29–31

privatizing ownership 89–94

Procurement Services Act (BC, 2003) 110

profit margins 3, 58

profit-taking excess 62

promoting public care 224–235; alternatives to corporate ownership 224–229; amalgamated services 229; conclusions 234–235; documenting care 226–227; German apprenticeship program 228; home ownership structure education 230; laundry services 228; minimum staffing standards 232; Norway as example 230–231; regulating, enforcing, and transparency 232–234; residents first policy home 226–228; retirement community complex 225; reversing the trends 229–232; training and qualifications 227, 228; union involvement 226, 228, 230, 234–235

property holding companies 56

provider failure and future sustainability 26, 203–206

psychotropic drugs, excessive use of 151–152, 199

public beds, British Columbia 108, 115

public care, promoting *see* promoting public care

public health care, Canada 18

public reports 133–134, 137, 234

publicly funded facilities 115, **116**

publicly subsidized homes, lack of beds 27

public–private partnerships 19; British Columbia 111, 112, 114; nursing home ownership 22

purchaser-provider model 41

qualifications, healthcare workers 77–80, 147, 151, 164–165, 199–200, 227

quality: concept 7, 10; measurement tools 159–160, *see also* care quality

quality indicators 128, 131, 134, 137; marketing website analysis 159–160, 168; Norway 145, 146, 150; staffing levels 233; Sweden 160

Qureshi, H. 200

Ranci, C., and Cordini, M. 197

Rapaport, J., Manthorpe, J. and Samsi, K. 199–200

real estate investment trusts (REITS) 21–22, 57

registered nurses (RNs): federal nursing home regulations 233; minimum staffing standards 59; Norway 187; staffing hours 58, 95–96, 143, 146, 167; staffing levels 178, 232

regulation: interpretative 144, 145, 152; prescriptive 144; and privatization 94–97

regulatory oversight, UK and USA 60–61, 63

Reimagining LTRC Project 158, 165, 167; nursing home staff 177; promising practices 168–169; relational care 205; social care relationships 169–170

relational care 69, 106, 113–114, 117, 169–170, 201–202, 205; auditing systems 210; continuity in staffing 235

relatives, care home tasks for 30

Relatives and Residents Association (RRA) 203

religious organizations, non-profit homes 40, 89, 142, 226

reporting *see* data collection and reporting

reputational rankings 23

Request for Proposals (REF) process 92–93, 110–111, 115

research, dialogue between theory and evidence 4

resident assessment instrument 7

Resident Assessment Instrument-Minimum Data Set (RAI-MDS) reporting system 95, 126, 127–133, 159, 169, 226–227

Resident Assessment Protocols (RAPS) 133

residential care, long-term 1–2, 5, 7, 10, 38
residents 196–206; abuse by care workers 199; as customers 31–32, 202; fall risk 200; fees charges after death 203; hazards of old age 197; increasing acuity 181–182; low social status 196, 205–206; majority of women 1, 185; market mechanism limits 203; mobility maintenance 201; necessity of protection 198–200; necessity of risk 200–202; over-protection of 200; positive risk-taking 201; precarity concept 197–198; publicly funded market 204; responsibility for payments 10, 88–89, 91–92, 166; restraint and deprivation of liberty 199–200; right to freedom of movement 199–200; rights to take risks 200; risk avoidance priority 201; self-funders 204; service shortcoming and choice to leave a home 202–203; service-provider responsibility 198; service-user control 198; tensions between protection and risk 198, 200, 206; tranquilizers 151–152, 199; vulnerability and risk 196–198; wellbeing of 205
Residents Long-Term Financial Data Tables (Statistics Canada) 93
resident–staff ratio 77–78, 81n6, 116, 151, 166–167, 212; quality of care 177–178
Resource Utilization Group-III (RUG-III) 133, 136, 179
responsibilities for care (shifting) 209–221; care aides 211; care work autonomy 221; consumer "choice" 216–217; decision-making process families involvement 219–220; documenting care 213–214; families autonomy 220; families involvement in care 216–220, 221; family (mainly women) unpaid labor 211; food services 216–218; laundry services 218–219; lift use rules 212–213; meals with family 218; minimum staffing standards 212; neo-liberal approach 210, 211, 213, 221; overview 209–211; staff 211–216; staff autonomy 215–216; staffing shortages 212–213, 221; standardized care and measuring performance 213–214; for your own health 209
responsibilization 19, 209, 221
retirement community complex 225
Retirement Homes Regulatory Authority (RHRA) 97
revenues, large chains in UK 56
Revera 159
right to freedom of movement 199–200
risk avoidance priority 201
Roderick, P., Pollock, A. M. and Sutaria, S. 53
Rodiek, S., and Chalfont, G. 200
Rolph, S., Johnson, J. and Smith, R. 165
Ronald, L. A. 183; et al. 58
Rothgang, H. 76
Royal Commission on Health Care and Costs (BC, 1991) 106–107

safety standards in care homes 199
Samsi, K., Manthorpe, J. and Rapaport, J. 199–200
Sandel, M. 197, 205
Scandinavian care workers, unpaid care work 31
Scandinavian countries: comprehensive provision 18; staff autonomy 215–216, 233; staffing levels 29, 214–215; welfare state 21, 38
sectoral bargaining model 106–107, 114, 115
self-funders, UK 204
Service Employees International Union 186
service universalism 38
services: and free market model 94, *see also* contracting out services; laundry services
Shannex 93
Sivesind, K. H. 48
skills, gendered construction 3, 7
Smith, A. 33
Smith, D. 6
Smith, R., Johnson, J. and Rolph, S. 165
social care: needs and long-term care insurance 72, 73, 81n2; unpaid work responsibility 210–211

social care relationships 106, 113–114, 117, 201–202, 205; auditing systems 210; continuity in staffing 235; dementia patients 25; gaps 29
Social Democratic Party 71
social insurance 69, 71, 76, 81n4
social relations, gendered construction 3
Social Security Act (USA, 1935) 54
social spending cuts 104
Sodexo 110
Solberg, E. 146–147
Southern Cross 26, 56, 59, 61, 202
spending *see* government spending
staff: cleaning 25–26; housekeeping 25–26, 110, 213; low-paid 79–80; "non-clinical" 108–109; surveillance 169; training 147, 215
staff turnover: and care quality 106, 201; lack of training staff 147; USA 186; and workload 6
staffing: minimum standards 95–96, *see also* nurse staffing in nursing homes
staffing levels: and care quality 116, 177–178; by country 180–182; for-profit ownership 182–183; minimum staffing standards 178, 188, 212, 232; political actions to increase 186–187; and quality of care 177–178; Scandinavian countries 29
staffing shortages: bending the rules 212–213; gaps filled by families 221
staffing strategies: mix of staff 75, 77, 78, 80, 81n6, 116, 178; low-paid staff 77, 79–80, 167, 184–185; resident–staff ratio 77–78, 81n6, 116, 151, 166–167, 177–178, 212
standards: care 180; minimum staffing 59, 95–96, 178, 179, 188, 212, 232
Standing, G. 197
Statistics Canada 93
Structure, Process, Outcomes Framework (Donabedian) 127
subcontractors, third-party 111–112
subsidized homes 97
supportive housing, community-based 98
sustainability, future 26, 203–206

Sutaria, S.: Harrington, C. and Pollock, A. M. 23, 51–67; Roderick, P. and Pollock, A. M. 53
Sweden: center-right political parties 44; co-payments for accommodation 166; demographic data 156–157; Local Government Act (1991) 41; marketing incentives 172; quality indicators 160; staff autonomy 215–216, 233; staffing standards 181, *see also* Norway and Sweden (for-profit ownership)
Swedish Social Democrats 45
Szebehely, M. 8; Ågotnes, G. and Jacobsen, F. F. 38–50; and Meagher, G. 203

tax havens 62
team ethnography 8–9
tendering, competitive 47, 90
Theobald, H. 79–80
"third sector" 142
third-party subcontractors 111–112
Thompson, E. P. 4
Thornton, P. 157
Thunes, K. 151
Townsend, P. 197
trade unions *see* unions
training: healthcare workers 77–80, 147, 151, 164–165, 199–200, 227; staff 147, 215
transparency: accountability in Norway 148–150; actual staffing data 188–189; home ownership structure 144, 233; lack of (UK and USA) 59–60; rules in USA 234
triple-net lease agreements 61
Tronto, J. 196

unions: increased staffing levels in homes 186; members in for-profit homes 75; Norway 146, 147, 187–188; Norway and Sweden 44–46; promoting public care 226, 228, 230, 234–235; role in care quality 187–188; stripping rights 108–109, 111, 114, 117n1, *see also* trade unions
United Kingdom (UK): bankrupt chains 26; bed availability 53; care home quality

concerns 59; consumer law obligations 32; financial crisis 53–54; food services 216, 218; home legal obligations in consumer law 202, 203; Human Rights Act (1998) 61, 64n1, 64n2, 64n3; large chain dominance 55–57; local authority funded services 53; negative impacts of privatization 52, 58–62; New Public Management 51; provider failure and future sustainability 203–206; reconsidering privatization 62–64; regulatory oversight 60–61, 63; safety standards in homes 199; self-funders 204; shift to private nursing homes 52–54; social care (call to renationalize) 63; spend on direct care 182; staffing standards 180; statutory minimum wage 205; universal health service 51; volunteers in care homes 30–31

United States of America (USA): Affordable Care Legislation (2010) 232; bed availability 55; chains' growing share of market 57, 183–184; failed homes 63; federal nursing home regulations 60, 185, 233; government funded institutional care 28; minimum staffing standards 178; negative impacts of privatization 52, 58–62; non-profit homes 183; Older American Act (1965) 186; private long-term care insurance 55; public health funding 51; reconsidering privatization 62–64; regulatory oversight 60–61, 63; safety standards in homes 199; spend on direct care 182, 183; stability of nursing home services 54–55; staff turnover 186; staffing levels 181; transparency rules 234; universal health care 18

universal risk 17

unpaid care work: documenting care 169; family and friends 28, 170, 172n1; family member obligations 5, 234; health care workers 6, 10, 78, 233–234; Scandinavian care workers 31; social care needs 210–211; women 70, 209, 211, 234

violence, health care workers 6, 214–215, 221, 229, 233
Voldnes, F. 148
voluntary organizations, non-profit homes 142
volunteers: Germany 80; UK car homes 30–31
vulnerable persons: care for 1; definition 196; "othering" of groups 197

wages: care aide starting 107–108, 113; collective agreements 75, 79
Wahl, A. 17
waiting lists, Canada 91, 162, 171
Warren, S. 136
Weil, D. 112
welfare associations, Germany 70, 71, 72
welfare regime typology 2
welfare services, users "freedom of choice" 46
welfare state 17, 18; Nordic Welfare Model 48; Scandinavian countries 21, 38, 142
Williams, J., Darton, R. and Netten, A. 205–206
Willingdon Park 113–114
Winnipeg, community-based supportive housing 98
Winnipeg Health Region 91
women: care providers 1, 184–185; health care workers 80, 184–185; majority of residents 1; social worth 5; unpaid care work 70, 209, 211, 234
workers see health care workers
workers' rights, violation 146
workforce, female 5–6, 80, 184–185
workload, care home 6
World Health Organization (WHO): care for the vulnerable 1; general theory of justice 4

Yalnizyan, A. 17